REEL SAN FRANCISCO STORIES

An Annotated Filmography of the Bay Area

Christopher Pollock

CONTENTS

Cover: the Golden Gate Bridge as seen from the U.S. Highway Route 101 vista point in the Marin Headlands, a high promontory where thousands of visitors descend via car, bus, bicycle, and even on foot to take in the magnificent view of the bridge. The iconic Golden Gate Bridge is the most often used image in locally filmed movies automatically setting the scene for a local story. Photo by the author.

First Edition

Publisher's Cataloging-in-Publication data

Pollock, Christopher.
Reel San Francisco stories : an annotated filmography of the Bay
Area / Christopher Pollock.
p. cm.
ISBN 978-0-578-13042-2
Includes bibliographical references.

1. Motion pictures—California—San Francisco Bay Area. 2. Motion
picture industry—California—San Francisco Bay Area—History. 3.
Motion picture locations—California—San Francisco Bay Area. I. Title.

PN1993.5.U718 .P65 2013
791.4309794/61—dc23
2013949743

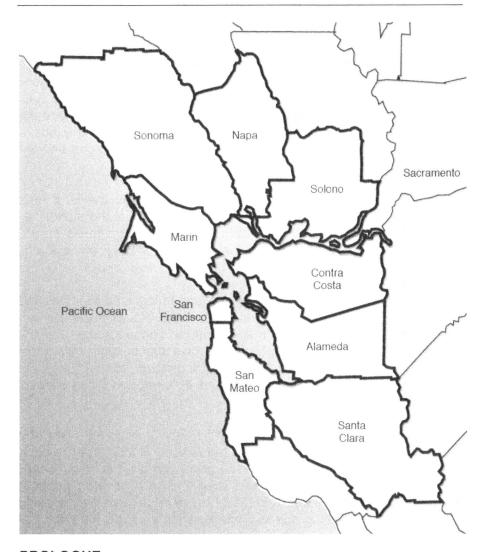

PROLOGUE

If you have ever wondered whether a movie you are watching was filmed in San Francisco or the Bay Area, this essential publication will satisfy your curiosity and identify locations. The focus of this filmography are the City and County of San Francisco and the eight other counties that surround San Francisco Bay and its northern extensions Richardson, San Pablo and Suisun Bays. These are San Mateo on the Peninsula and the South Bay county of Santa Clara; the East Bay counties of Alameda, Contra Costa and Solano; and the North Bay counties of Napa, Marin, and Sonoma. I have also included the "tail" of Sacramento County that stretches westward to the Delta which forms a natural geographical extension of the Bay Area.

Over time scripts filmed in the Bay Area have reflected every imaginable subject including sports, mysticism, alternative lifestyles, crime, politics, and the military. Some scripts have focused on futurism, music, animals, alcoholism, mobsters, teens, the devil and even angels. Films made in the Bay Area include a broad spectrum of genres such as comedy, tragedy, drama, horror, and film noir. Looking beyond the entertainment value of films, they are a snapshot of time and place, a record of visual history that documents changing landscapes and the ebb and flow of people and events.

Beyond the matter-of-fact location information about the Bay Area through the lens of the camera, this book tells some of the stories behind the films or about the sites used. It also highlights those actors, directors or technical staff who originated here or have come to call the Bay Area home.

San Francisco has many distinctive locations recognized by locals and visitors alike. Avid film fans are drawn to these places especially because they are associated with a favorite or famous scene and the perhaps memorable portrayal by actors of a particularly powerful or significant character or story. The most dedicated fans will seek out those places as if they were shrines and walk through those scenes, even speaking the dialogue.

My earliest brush with on-location movie making occurred when the Columbia Pictures comedy *It Happened to Jane* (1959) was filmed in Chester, Connecticut next door to the town where I grew up. There I saw a pair of temporary railroad tracks that were located far from where the train actually ran. A friend of my parents landed a speaking role in the town meeting scene. This experience made me aware of the on-location concept, and it lingered in my memory until I moved to San Francisco in the late 1970s. At that point I realized that I now lived in the area where *Harold and Maude* (1971) was made. The cult film has several special locations and includes more obscure but interesting locations on the San Francisco Peninsula.

That experience reawakened and nurtured the idea for this project after a friend gave me a copy of *The San Francisco Examiner Centennial* edition article, "The Definitive Films of Frisco," by Bob Grimes that came out on March 6, 1987. I found it to be an inspirational starting point, although the list was not as comprehensive as advertised. Now, decades later, this book represents a culmination of countless hours of tracking down and viewing hundreds of films in combination with researching their making.

After this introductory essay that explores the subject of Bay Area films in general, what follows is an annotated filmography that is laid out alphabetically by movie title. Interspersed are more than 150 boxes containing brief profiles about people related to movies shot in the Bay Area, who were born here, or who decided to make a commitment to live in the area. Other boxes give a brief history of a building or an event related to the movie.

A three-part appendix follows. The first part is a chronological list of the 600-plus movies shot in the Bay Area; the second lists those movies that are about the Bay Area but not shot there, and the last lists movies thought to have been shot in the Bay Area but I do not have corroborating information to support that information.

This is a work in progress as I have not been able to see every movie mentioned or find out where shooting of some films took place. Many older films are gone forever. Prior to the introduction of safety film in 1949, nitrate-based film stock was the standard—with unfortunate results. The highly unstable stock was brittle, prone to shrinkage and extremely flammable. It can also devolve into a white powder or a gooey substance in the worst cases.

The film preservation movement that has gained ground since the 1980s continues to discover increasing numbers of "lost" movies and restore them for public viewing. This holds out the hope for an abridged version of this publication in the future that will add to this list of films.

Finally—but importantly—when you visit film locations, please be respectful of the occupants of these properties.

Introduction
Since the early days of the medium the greater Bay Area has been host to so many on-location films that it has been known at times as Hollywood North. More than 600 movies, from blockbuster features to lesser-known "indies," have been set in San Francisco or the Bay Area since 1927, when "talkies" made their debut. Some were shot entirely in the Bay Area while others weave in far-off places or studio shots. The city's appearance on-screen has ranged from momentary cameos to full-blown on-location films. In addition the city has provided the setting for countless television commercials, made-for-television movies, and television series.

Early major studios formed in the favorable Mediterranean-like climate of Northern California, most notably Essanay Studios in Niles, San

Mateo's Pacific Studios and the California Motion Picture Corporation of San Rafael.

On November 3, 1927, San Francisco saw—and more importantly—heard the first true talkie that was shown in the Embassy Theater at 1125 Market Street. Warner Brothers' Vitaphone Talking Pictures was the medium of this breakthrough that used a phonograph disk synchronized with the film. The revolutionary addition of sound to what had been either written titles or explanatory mime provided a heightened realism to the movie theater experience. By 1930 the talking picture, first thought to be a fad by many, was in full flower. Even though local studios had closed by the dawn of the sound era the Bay Area continued to attract filmmakers at a breakneck pace.

Why San Francisco?
Many qualities combine to make the Bay Area a favorite setting for films. San Francisco has long been recognized as a film beauty with its diverse Districts, precipitous hills, unexpected perspectives, water-surrounded location with many bridges, and temperate climate—at times with dramatic fog banks—all qualities that draw moviemakers and tourists alike from around the globe. But the larger Bay Area presents many additional location sites including such diverse places as a former bayside fishing village, elegant sprawling country estates, small town main streets, tree-lined residential streets, the rolling hills of open countryside, and sleepy bayous.

It's not just San Francisco's pretty face that has drawn generations of filmmakers. Like many communities across the United States, San Francisco actively promotes itself as a setting for films with the knowledge that dollars can benefit the local economy by the multitude of services, including housing, extras, and food services required to support a film production. Movies that showcase the many attractions of the city can also stimulate tourism, the city's largest industry.

An all-out campaign to encourage the movie industry to come to the area occurred in November of 1920 when the *San Francisco Chronicle* newspaper announced its "Moving Picture Location Contest" that was intended to showcase any kind of scenic location found in San Francisco and Northern California for the newly burgeoning movie companies.

The following year a group of socially prominent San Francisco women, known as the Assistance League of Northern California, came up with a concept to benefit various local charities including the Children's Hospital and Girls' Recreation Club. The chapter's goal was to create a diverse directory of potential movie locations with the creation of their Motion Pictures Locations Bureau. The funds were paid by the motion picture companies to use sites such as the Peninsula's many photogenic private country estates. One film alone was cited to have netted $5000 for the charities. Some of the charity's women included Mrs. George T. Cameron, Mrs. C. Templeton Crocker, Mrs. Herbert Fleishhacker, and Mrs. Daniel Jackling whose grand estates were listed with the bureau.

Years later, in 1968, Mayor Joseph Alioto extolled the virtues of San Francisco by saying "I haven't tried any of [New York City] Mayor Lindsay's methods to lure movies here, but I find no objection to turning Hollywood into a suburb of San Francisco, the most photogenic city in the world." Alioto's successor Mayor George Moscone created what is now known as the Film and Video Arts Commission in the 1970s, and in the late '80s it was formally ratified as a full time agency under Mayor Art Agnos.

Virtually every county and large city in California has some sort of municipally sponsored mechanism, ranging from a single individual to an entire commission, whose charge is to entice on-location filming to their area. San Francisco's eleven-member commission, appointed by the mayor, and staff assist film companies by coordinating the permitting process with all city departments that may be involved and by finding and gaining access to locations. Its staff also handles neighborhood relations and issues like parking that impacts residents.

The number of movies shot in the Bay Area has risen and fallen over the decades. The high point was in the mid-1990s, but as of this writing it has slid to a new low as budgets tighten and some perceive that filming in San Francisco is just too expensive. In a twist of irony, on more than one occasion Vancouver, British Columbia, has stood in as San Francisco due to the associated costs.

In 2012 San Francisco Mayor Ed Lee signed legislation extending the "Scene in San Francisco Rebate Program," first implemented six years before, in an attempt to make filming in the city economically more attractive. Susannah Greason Robbins, executive director of the San Francisco Film Commission, noted "Gone are the days when production will shoot wherever the film is scripted. Instead, productions look to where they can get the biggest financial incentive for filming and will either re-write the script for that location, or fake the location and then shoot establishing scenes [also known as beauty shots] in the more expensive location." *The Guilt Trip* (2012) is a recent example where aerial shots of the San Francisco-Oakland Bay Bridge with downtown

San Francisco in the background give the illusion of being filmed there but when a string of Victorian-style residences come up on the screen—they are not in the Bay Area even though San Francisco is a pivotal point in the storyline.

Challenges of On-location
With all the potential benefits to the city—economic and otherwise—that can come with filming, they come also with a price that local residents may not wish to pay. Filming a movie requires controlling everything in the immediate environment. A typical on-location production entails a large quantity of trailers (some with noisy generators) containing costumes, electrical equipment, craft services, caterers, and dressing rooms. While residents may initially be thrilled by all the activity, thrill may turn to chill when problems appear. Displacing difficult to find street parking is the most common complaint, and it is important to get buy-in from area neighbors by addressing their concerns before filming starts. As just one example, in the filming of *Junior* (1994) at Alamo Square, home to the popular tourist attraction known as The Painted Ladies, the producers made a contractual agreement with the neighborhood to provide alternative parking for residents.

Each film crew that works in the streets of San Francisco may cause its own unique problems and there can be collateral damage. During the filming of *What's Up, Doc?* (1972), a car went hurtling down the south steps of Alta Plaza Park, chipping off some of the concrete stairs as it went. The city's film coordinator was unaware that this shot was to take place. Consequently all stunts, chase scenes, and special effects are now reviewed for approval by the film commission and police department coordinator.

In order to get the appropriate 1928-period ambiance, the movie crew for *Hammett* (1982) cut down stop signs, pulled out parking meters and painted over red zones. Needless to say this irritated the San Francisco's Public Works Department. Today the Department of Parking and Traffic is now also an integral member of the team that studios need to deal with as part of the permitting process.

Assistance of the police department takes the form of crowd control and removal of street obstructions. Motion picture detail is voluntary for officers, and film companies pay for police overtime. Local businesses in the path of the filming generally suffer lost profits to some degree since access to a business may be blocked. North Beach's Fior d'Italia restaurant took payment from Paramount because they were able to prove that the filming of *Jade* (1995) impacted their business receipts.

Images of glamorous celebrities in your midst can fade as inconveniences come into play. Filming in a residential District until an acceptable hour has caused problems on occasion. When director Phil Kaufman shot the remake of *Invasion of the Body Snatchers* (1978) he wanted to film well past 1 AM (10 PM is the standard maximum unless permission is asked), which is not desirable to sleeping residents.

Support facilities enhance the viability of creating an entire film in one place. Since the mid-1990s two converted former U.S. Navy hangars on Treasure Island have been designated as interior sound stage studios to augment location filming. The huge, high ceilinged and columnless spaces were used as a sound stage to film the lux home interiors for *Copycat* (1995). Other movies such as *Jade* (1995), *Metro* (1997), *Flubber* (1997), and *A Smile Like Yours* (1997) have used the facilities, too.

The effect of bringing movie companies to the Bay Area is not lost on government officials. The city receives a byproduct of free publicity to lure tourists and conventioneers. The bottom line is that filming in San Francisco brings in hotel, restaurant and retail revenue during the filming process. Despite the inconvenience to locals, these images will be captured for the long term and the place will become something special—even though some residents paid a small price for fame.

Directors' Choice
Directors know that filming on-location brings realism to audiences in a way that sound stages and back lots cannot provide. San Francisco's hills, especially, have provided some great tense moments including thrilling roller coaster-like rides in *Bullitt* (1968) and *Foul Play* (1978). I cannot imagine trying to duplicate these chase scenes in front of a rear projection or green screen. Getting the car to tilt, spin, and slam the pavement would not be convincing using these in-studio methods.

Today it is common to film outside of Hollywood, but that was not always so. Most early filming occurred in studios because of sound and camera equipment constraints. An early landmark example of on-location filmmaking was the silent feature *Greed* (1924). Director Erich von Stroheim, his cast and crew, spent eight months in San Francisco during 1923 filming at many sites around the Bay Area. With the advent of sound in the late 1920s it was back to the studio as the new technology was not yet suited to the challenges of the great outdoors.

Another benchmark was set when Alfred Hitchcock influenced the trend toward location shooting after the impact of his suspenseful

Shadow of a Doubt (1942). The movie was shot entirely around Santa Rosa, which Hitchcock selected as a typical idyllic small American hometown. His creativity was spawned by the federal government's World War II War Production Board that limited costs to $5,000 for sets. (He reportedly saved $2,000 by using real locations instead.) When *Life* magazine featured a six-page spread on the filming of *Shadow,* in January of 1943, it made shooting on-location fashionable —and provided highly desirable press for the movie. With the end of World War II on location moviemaking became commercially feasible as the equipment underwent a major improvement due to the needs of the war. This was combined with the beginning of the collapse of the major studios who held a monopoly on the equipment.

Hitchcock's *Vertigo,* released in 1958, is the epitome of a San Francisco on-location film. It was the first full-blown film in color to exploit the beautiful scenery of the Bay Area. *New Yorker* magazine writer David Denby cited the film as a "ravishingly beautiful hallucinatory nightmare" that used the setting for each scene to propel the story forward. Popular San Francisco spots brought life to the movie's scenes at genuine locations such as the historic Mission Dolores with its graveyard, the flower-filled Podesta Baldocchi shop on Grant Avenue, the stately California Palace of the Legion of Honor museum, the glowing International Orange of the Golden Gate Bridge, the eerie Conoly-Fortmann House where Madeleine mysteriously sits in the window, the Brocklebank Apartments atop Nob Hill where she lives, and many other locations.

Although places like the bookstore, dress boutique, and restaurant were adaptations created in the studio based on real San Francisco locations, they reflected the spirit of actual retailers in the city at that time. These places became an integral part of the story, authentically connecting the character and story. Alfred Hitchcock used the Bay Area in five of his 49 films. This was no accident as he resided in the Santa Cruz County town of Scotts Valley on weekends starting in 1942. Beyond *Vertigo* his locally shot films include *Shadow of a Doubt* (1943), *The Birds* (1963), a scene in *Marnie* (1964), and his last project *Family Plot* (1976), films very different from one another that show diverse facets of the region.

The Bridge
The Golden Gate Bridge, the most widely filmed landmark in the Bay Area, has been cast in scores of flicks, usually in cameo appearances, boosting the elegant span's fame as an icon the world over. In many films the bridge is shown in the establishing shot instantly setting the movie's overall location without the need for text or spoken lines. The

bridge has been recorded from every imaginable point of view: from a low vantage point at Fort Point in *Vertigo* (1958) and *Point Blank* (1967), among its supporting structure on the Marin County side in *Magnum Force* (1973), and at the apex of a suspension tower in *Ground Zero* (1973). However, when that script required that a dirigible try to plant a bomb, a model was used.

On the Beach (1959) showed the bridge with no traffic on it in a post-atomic wartime. Construction of the Golden Gate Bridge was shown in the 1935 movie *Stranded.* Although debuted in 1940, *If I Had My Way* with Bing Crosby also used historic footage of the Golden Gate Bridge's construction during the period 1933 through 1937. Crosby plays a construction worker on the bridge who helps raise a fellow worker's daughter, orphaned when her father dies in a construction accident.

Not all appearances of the bridge in film have been static. The bridge, or rather a model of the bridge, was wrecked in the Cold War paranoia flick *It Came from Beneath the Sea* (1955) by the flailing arms of a giant octopus, and blown to pieces in *The Core* (2003). Most recently the bridge was featured in *Rise of the Planet of the Apes* (2011) where the bridge is symbolically taken over by a large troop of super apes who use its exposed structure to swing and climb to heights unimagined. As the bridge is in use constantly, the film relied on an exterior set that was filmed and then combined with special effects backgrounds creating a very realistic viewer experience.

The west span of the San Francisco-Oakland Bay Bridge holds a similar distinction of being used often as it is close to downtown San Francisco and is shown to immediately establish a location. *Follow the Fleet* (1936) showed the eight-mile long Bay Bridge under construction. The bridge has appeared in scores of other films as well including the opening scene of the 1941 version of *The Maltese Falcon* where San Francisco was in the shot's background.

Scouting Locations
Icons like the Golden Gate Bridge or other favorite tourist spots like Fisherman's Wharf aren't the only locations that draw the attention of directors. The Georgian-style exterior entry court and ballroom scenes at the grand Filoli Estate in Woodside shown in *The Joy Luck Club* (1993) set a dignified, opulent tone. In *Maxie* (1985) the corner 1892 Victorian house across from Alamo Square is host to the return of Maxie Malone's spirit—long after her death. The broad waters of San Francisco, San Pablo, Richardson, and Suisun Bays were prominently seen in *Dumbarton Bridge* (1999), *Blood Alley* (1955), *The Lady from*

Shanghai (1948), and *Down Periscope* (1996). The large oil refineries of the East Bay shown in *Bedazzled* (2000) and *Desperate Measures* (1998) are unique settings with their industrial buildings and tall smokestacks flaring gaseous materials.

Sausalito's houseboats and arks have provided a distinctive and appealing setting in several films. Few people are not charmed by their cozy waterbound lifestyle. Bumbling cop Chevy Chase's character Tony Carlson lived on one in the comedy *Foul Play* (1978).

Outside the city many diverse landscapes provide a wide possibility of locations within a short distance of San Francisco. The Napa and Sonoma valleys, whose distinctive corduroy lines of grape vines define the dry landscape, have provided the background for movies like the drama *This Earth is Mine* (1959) with Rock Hudson. The Sacramento River Delta's sloughs and levees are similar to the South's lazily flowing bayous used in *The General's Daughter* (1999) where the film is set. The Victorian farmhouses of Marin and Sonoma counties evoke the rolling hills of rural settings in the Midwest and elsewhere seen in *The Farmer's Daughter* (1947), *Tucker: the Man and His Dream* (1988), and more recently *Cheaper by the Dozen* (2003).

The Bay Area's bygone era was captured in Robert Louis Stevenson's 1883 novel *Treasure Island* that was brought to the screen in 1934. The film captured the end of the wind-powered frigate age showing the docks and ships of the Alaska Fisheries fleet in Oakland. *Thieve's Highway* (1949) showed the bustling wholesale produce District that once was located where the Golden Gateway development in San Francisco now stands. In that movie the gritty, narrow and busy streets showed what the area looked like until redevelopment stepped in when the facility was moved south to Isalis Creek, in 1963, where it remains today.

Maritime transportation that once plied the waters of the Pacific show up in some movies before the popularity of jet travel. The China Clipper service, a flying boat, that was anchored in Alameda appeared in or inspired several films including its namesake *China Clipper* (1936). Civilian ships sailing from piers on the Embarcadero to Hawaii and beyond played a role in such films as *Road to Singapore* (1940), the first in a popular series of "Road to" movies by Paramount Studios.

At times directors have deliberately chosen to use well-known locations to set the scene and immediately establish a sense of place for stories. Introductory scenes and vistas either at San Francisco's street level or via aerial shots are shown in the openings of several movies like *Kiss Them for Me* (1957), and *Heart and Souls* (1993). Directors have presented a virtual armchair tour of the city in *The Lineup* (1958), *Vertigo* (1958), *Daddy's Gone A-Hunting* (1969), and *Getting Even with Dad* (1994).

Scripts about the Bay Area such as *Escape from Alcatraz* (1979), which comes from a book by former *San Francisco Chronicle* reporter Campbell Bruce, appeal to both residents and tourists. The true story dramatizes the only successful escape attempt from the island penitentiary. Screenwriter and director John Huston's *The Maltese Falcon* (1941) is a home-grown classic based on the 1930 fictional novel by local writer Dashiell Hammett using his experiences as a private detective. The writer Kathryn Forbes, a San Francisco native, created the book *Mama's Bank Account* on which the sentimental movie (and later the TV series) *I Remember Mama* (1948) was based. It portrayed a fictional account of the lives of Norwegian immigrants.

The left leaning liberal attitudes of the Bay Area have been a springboard for some storylines. Early in San Francisco's life it became a Mecca for the Bohemian life or alternate lifestyles. In the 1950s it was the Beats and in the 1960s the Hippies who blossomed. San Francisco has always been a spiritual center of changing mores. No film showed this with more impact than *Serial* (1980), a comedy about the self searching residents of Marin County dabbling with new age consciousness-raising. In contrast, the very serious *Guess Who's Coming to Dinner* (1967) dealt with the taboo of an integrated couple and used big name actors to convey the message that a racially mixed relationship was acceptable. Another off limits subject, alcoholism, was confronted in *Days of Wine and Roses* (1962) (where Alcoholics Anonymous first appeared on film) followed many years later by *When a Man Loves a Woman* (1994) with a similar subject. The Mitchell Brothers' *Behind the Green Door* (1972) was a big player in launching the sexual revolution with its sexual themes in plain sight.

These movies don't always show the most pleasant situations. Frank slices of the Tenderloin District's many facets are the basis for the storylines in *Harrison Montgomery* (2008), and *Tenderloin* (2009), the later even has its comic moments among the problems of a residence hotel's occupants.

The rise of the internet in what has become our digitally driven lives is also reflected in movies. Two stories choose to capitalize on the dark side of those seeking connection to the outside world. *The Net* and *Copycat,* both released in 1995, showed us early examples of what cyber terrorists could do through a computer. The location was no accident with the Bay Area a prime computer technology locus.

A few movies' story lines have tried to project what the future might bring. *Bicentennial Man* (1999) showed a world of the not so far off time where androids served mankind while becoming more human. During the course of the movie scenes of Nob Hill's Grace Cathedral surrounded with huge skyscrapers and the Golden Gate Bridge with two separate levels startle the imagination. In *Star Trek: The Motion Picture* (1979) a flying space pod soars near the Golden Gate Bridge, and at the south end of the bridge sits a gigantic structure, the Starfleet Skytram Station where the pods are launched. Other large round buildings are sited at the north end of the bridge—something that will never happen thanks to the creation of the Golden Gate National Recreation Area.

 In the opening sequence of *The* Towering Inferno, released in 1974, one aerial scene looking northeast along Market Street showed a pair of giant towers among the many low-rise buildings of the area. Little did the makers of the movie know that this would become a portent of things to come: construction of the 1,070-foot tall Transbay Tower, way taller than the 853-foot-tall Transamerica Pyramid, the record holder to date. Futuristic architecture such as famed architect Frank Lloyd Wright's unique Marin Civic Center was seen in George Lucas' *THX-1138* (1971) or U.C. Berkeley's Brutalist-style Lawrence Hall of Science in *Colossus: The Forbin Project* (1969) set a forward thinking visual tone to these movies evoking the 1927 masterpiece *Metropolis* that projected what the future might be like.

A number of films touted as filmed in the Bay Area were actually filmed on sound stages. These films used what is known as stock footage or still photographs to set the scene. *The Maltese Falcon* (1941) is unquestionably tied to San Francisco due to its storyline, however it was not shot on location. Rather, filmed scenes of the San Francisco-Oakland Bay Bridge and Ferry Building establish the location. Cinematic still views out the windows of the Spade and Archer office of an artificial lower Market Street cityscape and Bay Bridge give the impression of being in a typical Financial District office of the period.

Another technique of appearing to be on location is to film actors in front of a rear screen projection known as a process shot. The action scenes are shot on location as backgrounds and the actors are superimposed in front of a rear projection screen on a sound stage. This is a money saving technique while giving the impression of a location shoot – albeit with dubious results. Some movies, usually period pieces of bygone times set in the Bay Area, simply portray a time and place, some more technically accurate than others. *Flame of Barbary Coast* (1945) with John Wayne and Ann Dvorak gives the impression of the city's notorious Barbary Coast at the turn of the 19th to 20th century.

Film Noir
The French term film noir ("black film") describes a highly stylized genre of psychological thrillers that exploits paranoia, fear, greed and entrapment. Produced approximately between the early 1940s through the early 1950s, noir encompasses more than a script; it is an all-inclusive approach to filming in which the sets, costumes and cinematography all contribute to the goal of creating a work of art through craft and discipline.

Usually done in high contrast, black-and-white with stark shadows, a high percentage of noir films were made in the Bay Area due to its atmosphere. Many of them are landmarks of the genre. The city's dark side and moody character worked well with the shadowy tones of the stories. The area is blessed with sudden gray clouds of protective enveloping fog that help create the unique atmosphere augmented by the penetrating sound of far off fog horns. Noir at its finest, *Dark Passage* (1947) takes place, in part, at the hillside corner Art Deco style apartment building atop San Francisco's Telegraph Hill and around the Golden Gate Bridge. Enhanced by the use of black-and-white film the streamlined curves of the stylized apartment house on Montgomery Street complement the robust span of the same design era. The distinctive style of each is enhanced by the arty extreme upward and downward angled camera views used in some scenes.

The Bay Area has both the former federal penitentiary of Alcatraz and still operating San Quentin State Prison. They have figured in a number of films illustrating the cruelty of incarceration as well as the possibility of reform. Veering into the politically charged arena of the death penalty the 1958 movie *I Want to Live!* tells the real life story of "Bloody Babs" Barbara Graham, a woman gone astray, played by Susan Hayward. Alcatraz, the unique island-bound federal prison, is the stage for the symbolically caged Robert Stroud in *Birdman of Alcatraz* (1962), who shows a warm side in his affection for caged birds. Many other films were done there, several in the film noir vein.

Bay Area Innovators
As with any technology, there are baby steps in its creation, and some developments that contributed to the emergence of film beyond static

magic lantern projections occurred in the Bay Area. True to the creative spirit of the West, Bay Area inventors and dreamers have, and
continue to, create major technological steps in the film industry's evolution.

The public debut of the first commercial true moving image was given
by the brilliant and eccentric pioneering photographer Eadweard J.
Muybridge with the financial aid of railroad magnate and former California governor Leland Stanford. The pragmatic Stanford was interest-
ed in veterinary science and a passion of his was to analyze the mus-
cular system of horses. Muybridge, a man of vision, camera artist, and
technician teamed with Stanford to create the now famous first stop-
motion photographs. Muybridge conducted his research during 1878-
1879 at Stanford's Palo Alto Stock Farm.

Neither Muybridge nor Stanford realized that their work's end result
would be a significant step in the creation of the moving picture medium. This step occurred when Muybridge combined the photographs of
motion with the techniques of animation and projection. Using a device
originally called the Zoogyroscope, sequentially illuminated unposed
illustrations of a horse were projected having been taken with individual cameras at intervals. The first generation of images projected were
just silhouettes; tracings of photographs, discrete but closely-related
images one after the other, placed along the rim of a 16-inch diameter
circular glass disk. As the disk was spun on its axis it was combined
with a shutter that was a rotating opaque disk with radial slot that spun
in the opposite direction to the glass disk. This rapid succession of
projected illustrations gave the impression of motion to the viewer.

Many San Francisco citizens saw the result in May of 1880 at the San
Francisco Art Association. At that venue Muybridge demonstrated this
technique and although black-and-white, silent and of very short dura-
tion, the moving pictures were enthusiastically received by the public.
This was the first instrument to successfully project illustrations depicting continuous motion and with these elements, the basic visual com-
ponent of the film industry was born.

Another local innovator was Leon Forrest Douglass who patented
some fifty inventions during his lifetime including color film. Among his
list of other patents related to the film industry were special effect
techniques and the zoom lens. In 1906 Douglass moved from Philadelphia to San Rafael. He established the Douglass Natural Color Motion Picture Company that patented the first successful process for
color filming in 1916. His technique was called "natural color" as it was
achieved in the film processing rather than the time-consuming hand

tinting that was the method used at the time. With this advancement he produced what was one of the earliest American feature-length color films that was titled *Cupid Angling,* in 1918, starring Ruth Roland with superstars of their day Mary Pickford and Douglas Fairbanks in guest roles.

The Digital Age

Special and visual effects are unique to the realm of motion pictures, and the Bay Area is home to many different kinds of studios specializing in the digital and the three-dimensional crafts. Silicon Valley's digital revolution spawned several firms. Used from the inception of cinema, the tricks of the trade include several painting techniques, including painting on glass or on opaque surfaces, meant to simulate 3-D. Shooting on the same film twice is one in-camera technique that allows the merging of two different components. Scale models and animation play parts in the visual effects industry, too.

Today, many movies have special effects, some so subtle that there is no obvious trace (similar to retouching of photos) and others, quite dramatic. A cutting-edge special effects technology is computer generated digital imaging that has the ability to modify scenes convincingly. The computer, a powerful tool in film making, can enhance shots, create realistic environments including buildings and interiors; remove unwanted items like aerial flight cables, and insert objects into a scene which were not actually there. Special effect artists can remedy visual flaws found after a film has been shot, providing the best possible production.

Before there were digital special effects there were various analog techniques to modify a film's frames. A startling example appeared in *Pollyanna* (1960), the opening scene of which shows a towering four-story Victorian style residence. In fact the building is a two-story building on McDonald Avenue in Santa Rosa known as Mableton. The lens panned upward to reveal a huge yellow house, but in fact a matte painting was inserted to make the house much more impressive, conveying the message that this is the residence of the town's most important benefactor.

Those familiar with San Francisco will be confused by a special effect in *I Remember Mama* (1948). In one scene the family's home is located on the north side of Russian Hill with a view to Alcatraz Island. However, the street is lined with houses that are actually on the 500 block of Liberty Street located far across the city in the Eureka Valley District.

In the dark comedy *Bartleby* (2001) the opening scene is an office building perched on top of a steep hill. This scene, like most of the movie, was filmed in San Rafael, however the scene is so manipulated no one would ever guess the location. The building at One Thorndale Drive located just west of the Northgate Mall was used as the basic building in the scene. But through a matte painting technique over a still photo two additional stories were added to the 1970s Brutalist style building. In addition, footage of a car driving a curvy road in the Marin Headlands was inserted to provide some live action. Lastly a foreground consisting of several actual highways and viaducts was added to create a composite scenario. Two other office buildings located in San Rafael were used in other scenes of the movie compositing similar elements to create otherworldly scenes set to weird sounding music created on a Theremin synthesizer.

Period scripts, whether about the past or future, require representation of a place in time that must appear convincingly realistic. As originally shot in front of the Ferry Building on San Francisco Bay, the establishing scenes of *I Remember Mama* (1948) showed the San Francisco-Oakland Bay Bridge in the background. Because the story is set in a time before construction of the bridge, it was later manually erased by covering it with painted clouds to give the impression of turn-of-the-century San Francisco. *A Walk in the Clouds (1995)* created a moody, post-World War II San Francisco-like ambiance without using any of the actual place.

The action thriller *The Rock* (1996) featured several remarkable scenes that were a composite of real action visual effects and computer animation. One signature shot occurred at the climax of a destructive chase where an exploding cable car was blown 20 feet into the air in a fiery blast. The car was actually mechanically launched with hydraulic pistons, called rams, surrounded by some flames. After the filming, special effects artists digitally added more flames and erased the mechanical rigs, creating an enhanced illusion. The dizzying final scenes of the same movie featuring an aerial shot of Alcatraz Island being blown-up was a composite of several real and artificial elements. A shot of the island was taken from an altitude of 2,000 feet that was then combined with a realistically 3-dimentionally modeled computer generated F-18 fighter jet. The further addition of an actual explosion using gasoline bombs shot from an aerial crane 170 feet above a Los Angeles back lot enhanced the illusion.

They Call the Bay Area Home

Everybody is from somewhere, and the Bay Area is native or adopted turf to many actors, directors, producers, writers and technical professionals. A high percentage of film creators hail from the area. Director Wayne Wang *Eat a Bowl of Tea* (1989), *Chan is Missing* (1981), and *The Joy Luck Club* (1993) used his backyard on many occasions for movies focusing on life in Chinatown. Despite the high cost of production in Baghdad-By-the-Bay, Chris Columbus was so taken with the place that he based his production company, known as 1492, in San Francisco setting movies such as Mrs. *Doubtfire* (1993) and *Nine Months* (1995) there. Other independent producers like Francis Ford Coppola and George Lucas, who also have steered clear of Hollywood, have sought the Bay Area to set up their studios. Many industry-related support staff, including writers and special effects creators, like the wizards at Lucasfilm, reside here due to the independent, creative environment. This environment with its culture of innovation and tolerant attitudes stems from "the personality profile that began in 1849 (gold rush pioneers) of an independent-minded individualist [that] carries on in San Francisco today" according to author Geri Spieler in a *Huffington Post* article published in 2011. This special brew draws talent from around the globe to the Bay Area.

Besides recognition of place in on-location scenes, filmgoers will recognize local personalities or "celebrities" who have, usually, cameo or walk-on roles in many locally made movies. Television news anchor staff, portraying themselves and what they do, figure in dozens of appearances in the movies. They are already members of the national actors union, the Screen Actors Guild, and are well known to local residents that lend authenticity to a film. The first such role was by David McEllhatton in Hitchcock's *Vertigo* (1958). Although originally deleted during the editing process, the scene now appears in the DVD version. Anchor Elaine Corral Kendall has logged the most locally shot movies to date with appearances in six different movies, sometimes along side another local news personality. Other local anchors who have appeared include Leslie Griffith, Julie Haener, Dennis Richmond, and Frank Sommerville.

A host of non-actor city notables have performed in movie cameo roles for a variety of reasons. Former Mayor and Speaker of the California Assembly Willie Brown played roles in Disney's *George of the Jungle* (1997), *Just One Night* (2000) and *The Princess Diaries* (2001). Another politico is openly gay Tom Ammiano, who appeared as himself in the biopic *Milk* (2008).

Longtime newspaper wit Herb Caen appeared as one of his occupation in *Nora Prentiss* (1947), global renaissance woman Maya Angelou appeared as Aunt Jane in *Poetic Justice* (1993). Ernie's Restaurant owners Roland and Victor Gotti played bit parts as the maître d' and a bartender in *Vertigo* (1958). The classic San Francisco French restaurant, now gone, was a favorite of director Hitchcock's.

Flamboyant San Francisco "King of Torts" lawyer Melvin Belli appeared in two locally filmed movies between 1973 and 1978. Another personality was Cyril Magnin who was informally dubbed "Mr. San Francisco," the city's Chief of Protocol and unofficial city ambassador. When the producers of *Foul Play* (1978) asked Magnin, a Jew, to play Pope Pius XIII who is about to be murdered, he expressed concern about offending his Catholic friends. He shared the script with two friends, a Catholic priest and the Archbishop of San Francisco, who felt the idea was fine. When the film opened in San Francisco's Regency Theater on July 14, 1978, the theater's marquee boldly proclaimed "Goldie Hawn, Chevy Chase and Cyril Magnin." He also appeared in *Maxie* (1985) as Mr. San Francisco.

Smartly dressed local icons, identical twins Vivian and Marion Brown, have a brief walk-on in the opening sequences of the movie *9 to 5* (1980), which set the scene of a busy urban sidewalk in an unspecified city. The place was Market Street, and the sequence included the historic landmark Albert S. Samuels Clock, constructed in 1915, that resides in front of 856 Market Street.

Biographical movies, or at least using someone's life as the basis for a film, have memorialized a number of notable Bay Area residents, some natives while others were transplants. A few were remarkable individuals while others were just part of a sensational story. Movies, being mostly entertainment, portray the famous—and sometimes infamous. Acerbic comedian Lenny Bruce was the subject of *Lenny* (1974), played by Dustin Hoffman, which was nominated for six Oscars and several other prestigious awards. In 1944 some of the revolutionary ideas of shipbuilding industrialist Henry J. Kaiser were shown in *Man From Frisco*. Another person on a very different mission was San Francisco madam Sally Stanford, portrayed in *Lady of the House* (1978), who then moved north across the bay to the sleepy town of Sausalito, setting herself up in the restaurant business and where she ultimately became mayor.

Newspaper heiress Patricia Campbell Hearst Shaw is vividly recalled in *Patty Hearst* (1988) where portrayal of her 1974 political kidnapping argues for a case of brainwashing by her captors, who were members of the Symbionese Liberation Army. In one case a documentary spawned a full-blown movie years later. The initial portrayal of an activist was in the documentary *The Times of Harvey Milk* (1984), winner of an Academy Award and other prestigious awards. With time passing and with more perspective, a movie treatment ending with the assassination of San Francisco's Mayor Moscone and the first openly gay city supervisor simply titled *Milk* was released in 2008 with superstar Sean Penn playing the lead.

San Francisco as a Stand-in
For all its visual distinction, sometimes the Bay Area masquerades as another place entirely. Much of Philip Kaufman's *The Right Stuff* (1983) is notable for portraying the region as other places. The now defunct Hamilton Air Force Base in Marin County pretended to be Patrick Air Force Base located in Florida. The Cow Palace, the large exhibition hall south of downtown San Francisco, was draped with bunting and became the Houston Coliseum, while NASA's Ames Research Center in Mountain View played the part of Langley Air Force Base in Virginia. As only celluloid reality could show, a fourth floor corridor of San Francisco's City Hall was a Washington power center, and four blocks of the Financial District's Sansome Street stood in for New York, providing the stage for the astronaut heroes' ticker tape parade.

In another example, the 1946 comedy *The Show-Off* starring Red Skelton, San Francisco stands in for Philadelphia. For a scene driving down one of that city's main thoroughfares MGM used stock footage of San Francisco's lower Turk Street continuing on a stretch of Market Street to about Montgomery Street with the historic Flood Building and other notable buildings in full view.

San Francisco's Brutalist-designed Embarcadero Center represents the oil boom town of Houston, Texas, in *Telefon* (1977). Francis Ford Coppola, teamed with Lucasfilm/Universal, used the Beaux Arts classical-style City Hall as the interior and exterior settings for a Chicago courthouse in *Tucker: The Man and His Dream* (1988). *Howard the Duck* (1986) was set in Cleveland, but actually used the Academy of Sciences in Golden Gate Park and sites around Marin County.

A Japanese story set in pre-World War II and during the war was the subject of *Memoirs of a Geisha* (2005). Some of the scenes that convincingly portrayed Japan were shot in numerous places in the Bay Area from Marin to the South Bay using tightly focused scenes that appear bona fide to the viewer. These pieces were cleverly intercut to create a stunning visual, evoking the time and place. Another more recent example is the 2012 HBO movie *Hemingway and Gellhorn,* which used many parts of the Bay Area to stand in for Shanghai, Finland, Spain, Cuba, Key West and Idaho. None of the film's story actually takes place anywhere in the Bay Area.

Many landscapes in the Bay Area have made short but impactful appearances in movies otherwise set and shot elsewhere. Sometimes the Bay Area has just what is required for a particular director's vision of what the film calls for cinematically. In *The Witches of Eastwick* (1987), the story took place on the East Coast. But the precipitously hilly landscape of the Marin Headlands and the roiling waters of the Golden Gate below are in a short scene where the menacing Van Horne mansion is set. This was a special effects scene that dropped the mansion into the otherwise barren cliffs.

The chilling movie *The Boston Strangler* (1968) was filmed primarily in Boston, but when a pick-up scene was required after filming wrapped there, San Francisco's Victorian-era Jackson Square area stood in for the required addition. During a sequence about two-thirds of the way through the movie, DeSalvo (Tony Curtis) is being chased by Boston Police through alleys of brick buildings and emerges onto Jackson Street continuing east to Montgomery Street, and then turning south where he is hit by a car. San Francisco has few Victorian brick buildings to match those of Boston's Beacon Hill but the historic Jackson Square area was a perfect match and the untrained eye would never notice the seamless editing. This completes the director's vision by adding a missing link to tie the story together.

Counter to the idea of showing a recognizable place, some films avoided mentioning where the story takes place, as is the case in *Every Girl Should Be Married* (1948) and *Take the Money and Run* (1969). Each uses parts of San Francisco but never mentions the place. Why they bothered is a mystery.

Even when a project's original story might have been set elsewhere, directors like Alfred Hitchcock reworked narratives just so they could be filmed here. Hitchcock usually preferred working within the constraints of a sound stage where all the elements could be controlled. But as a part-time resident of Scotts Valley, south of San Francisco, he knew the area well. *The Birds* (1963) takes place in the remote hamlet of Bodega Bay, north of San Francisco, although the setting for the original story, part of a Daphne du Maurier novelette published in 1952, is post-World War II England. *Vertigo* comes from a French novel *D'entre les Morts* by Pierre Boileau set in Paris.

Longtime Bay Area resident director Philip Kaufman's *Invasion of the Body Snatchers* (1978) was an updated version of the classic Cold War-era 1956 production with its story transplanted from a small California town to urban San Francisco. Harry Callahan of *Dirty Harry* (1971) fame was originally to be a member of the New York Police

Department, but a last-minute script change put him in San Francisco, and four other spin-offs followed over a 16-year period. Eastwood made the change to San Francisco a stipulation of his accepting the role. Likewise the chase movie *Bullitt* (1968) was originally set in Seattle, but the Bay Area's hills won out when casting the film's location—through the insistence of its star Steve McQueen. Director Garry Marshall moved the story of *The Princess Diaries* (2001), originally known as *The Princess of Tribeca,* from New York City to San Francisco. Likewise the translation of the 1940 Rodgers and Hart musical *Pal Joey* to the loosely adapted 1957 film moved the story from Chicago to San Francisco.

The substitution of one place for another real one is a common occurrence in the movies. This may be due to a variety of constraints including cost or availability. The sequence of shots around the San Francisco Civic Center in the romantic comedy *Foul Play* (1978) shows the exterior and purported lobby of the War Memorial Opera House. The interior lobby shots actually took place in the grander City Hall rotunda across the street. Since both buildings were designed, in part, by Arthur Brown Jr., in the Classic French Renaissance Revival style, there appears to be no discontinuity. Along similar lines *Milk* (2008) was filmed in 50 United Nations Plaza, which stood in for nearby City Hall. Again the architectural design was by Brown, and the overall ambiance of the then-vacant building filled the bill—right down to the toilet rooms.

Editing is crucial to the outcome of a movie. Location trivia enthusiasts get a kick out of some movies that are not quite what they seem. *Dogfight,* released in 1991 by Warner Brothers, is set in San Francisco, but the scenes actually flip back and forth between Seattle and San Francisco during the movie. The editing was crafted to make the transitions seamless to most people—and use only the necessary footage of the more expensive to film in San Francisco scenes. Alfred Hitchcock was fabled for his editing of seemingly continuous places that are nowhere near each other in many movies shot here and elsewhere during his long career. Several driving scenes in *Vertigo* are, as Jeff Kraft and Aaron Leventhal's book about Hitchcock in San Francisco *Footsteps in the Fog* relates, a "geographically discontinuous series of locations." These look good in the editing room but are sometimes across town from each other—or maybe in another state or country.

Not all effects are digital or in the film. In a sleight of hand, fake cable car tracks were painted on the pavement of Nob Hill's Jones Street from California Street to Colin Alley for scenes using motorized cable cars in *Metro* (1997). This way scenes are not limited to the existing cable car lines that are in demand for public transportation. Producer Irwin Allen edited together scenes from different places that appeared as one in *The Towering Inferno* (1974) where he mated the Bank of America tower's exterior base with lobby interiors from the Hyatt Regency Hotel, located several blocks away.

Capturing the Changing Cityscape
A fortunate unintended benefit of the cinema is that it has recorded vanished times and places for posterity. In some cases these are the only preserved images and give a more three-dimensional appearing view than that of a static photograph.

Regrettably, the 1882 San Francisco Victorian rooming house that Kim Novak's enigmatic character haunted in *Vertigo,* at Eddy and Gough Streets, was demolished in 1959. Known as the Conoly-Fortmann House, it was located at the current site of a sports field for Sacred Heart School. Diagonally across the street was St. Paulus Church, also shown in *Vertigo,* which burned in November of 1995.

There is no trace of the Varni's Roaring Twenties Club at 807 Montgomery Street, which is shown in both *Experiment in Terror* (1962) and *Machine Gun McCain* (1968). The fern bar club featured girls on swings and lots of Victorian stained glass windows. The Palace of Fine Arts, shown in *Vertigo,* was built as a temporary structure for the 1915 Panama-Pacific International Exhibition. It no longer exists as originally built, but happily it was exactly reproduced in longer lasting concrete and has recently received structural reinforcing so it may continue to delight all who visit its romantic setting.

One of the places lost to the evolution of San Francisco's Financial District was Lick Place, an alley where the Crocker Galleria stands today but shown in *Experiment in Terror,* which debuted in 1962. Don't try to find the funky cottage on the Greenwich Steps shown in *The Wild Parrots of Telegraph Hill* (2003). It was renovated into a very different structure as part of the ending of film.

It's no accident that some buildings that play a part in movies were demolished during the process of filming or soon afterward. Vacant buildings are desirable to filmmakers as they are a blank canvas to fill in whatever the script requires without interference from occupants. In *The Candidate* (1972) a row of cottages on a hillside was shown burning. The National Park Service had planned removal of these cottages, designed by renowned architect Julia Morgan, anyway. Today the foundations remain as part of the cultural resource's Immigration Center on Angel Island in San Francisco Bay. The funeral home shown in *Swing* (2003) was vacant at the time and was demolished soon after filming; today residential condominiums occupy the site. The elegant Art Deco office building in *My Name is Kahn* (2010) was the long-vacant Pacific Telephone and Telegraph Building in the South of Market District, which as of this writing is undergoing renovation.

An inadvertent by-product of on-location filming is glimpses of structures under construction. In the 1961 production of *Susan Slade* a view from Pacific Heights to Nob Hill reveals the steel skeleton of The Comstock skyscraper apartments at 1333 Jones Street rising at the hill's summit. The Russian Hill residential skyscraper at 10 Miller Place appears prominently in the opening scene's foreground of 1964's *Where Love Has Gone.* An icon of architecture was recorded when the 52-story signature Bank Of America building's structural frame was seen in *Daddy's Gone A-Hunting* in 1969. The next year the reconstruction of the city's main artery Market Street was shown in MGM's *The Strawberry Statement* (1970). The construction was to accommodate the underground Muni and BART tunnel system and showed the chaos that locals and tourists alike had to contend with during the several year cut-and-cover tunneling period. With Sidney Poitier at Lt. Virgil Tibbs, *The Organization* showed similar scenes in its 1971 release.

Embarcadero Center Two, the second of five structures comprising the original Embarcadero Center, appeared in *The Laughing Policeman* that came out in 1973. The in-process building of 505 Sansome Street played a part in *Die Laughing* (1980) when the main character, Pinsky (played by Robby Benson), was escaping from a thug who was after what he was carrying. Later in the same film, two Victorian houses (1986 and 1984 Ellis Street) are shown set on wood cribbing after being moved. These shots record the redevelopment of the Western Addition after an ill-conceived tear down of much of the area that started in the late 1950s; these were but a few of the token houses saved and relocated after an outcry about removal of the Victorian housing stock.

The special effects demolition of a warehouse building that sat at the northwest corner of the intersection of Drumm Street and Sacramento Street was graphically shown in the opening scenes of *The Killer Elite* (1975) that would later become the site of Embarcadero Center Three. *Basic Instinct,* released in 1991, captured a place in time during the very long gestation of the gigantic South of Market redevelopment project, Yerba Buena Center, first approved by the Board of Supervisors in 1966—and not yet complete.

Homage to Previous On Location Movies

Avid fans viewing Bay-Area-filmed movies will pick up the passing vis-ual references to older locally made films seen in newer films. These wink of the eye references also help to set the scene. One is the com-edy *Dream for an Insomniac* (1998) where a poster from the movie *Pal Joey* (1957) appears as well as a record album cover of composer Henry Mancini's sound track from *Days of Wine and Roses* (1962). Another is the poster advertising Hitchcock's *Vertigo* that appeared in the video store of 1999's *Ed TV*. A lobby poster advertising *Dirty Harry* (1971) appeared in the 2007 movie *Zodiac* recalling the earlier period when the film is set. During a trip to the movies in *Under the Tuscan Sun* (2003) an homage to another filmed-in-San Francisco movie is shown: *George of the Jungle* (1997). A backward glance was shown in *Tenderloin* (2009) where the child Robby was watching scenes from *It Came from Beneath the Sea* (1955) on the television. These small scenes make a locally shot film a little more fun to watch.

A film reflects the combined efforts of many business people, artists, craftspeople and technicians. Each one celebrates the skill and imagi-nation of the gifted directors, art directors, production designers, and cinematographers who selected and photographed these locations. The frequent use of the Bay Area by filmmakers reflects everybody's love of the place—including its eccentricities and anything-goes liberal atmosphere. Few places mix such a cocktail of picture postcard scen-ery, mild weather and human diversity. Be ready to fall in love with San Francisco and the Bay Area for the first time—or all over again!

FADE OUT

ANNOTATED FILMOGRAPHY

Each entry lists the movie's name in alphabetical order, the release date (versus the copyright date), distributor, and a brief synopsis. If another title was also used that is also listed. If the movie was based on a work such as a novel or story, the author and title of the original work is cited. If no title is cited that means that the name of the work was not changed when made into a film. This is followed by just a few of the creative staff who were critical to the direction, story and look of the film, as well as some of the cast. The location listings give the name of the site with its street address. A note about reading the entries: unless otherwise noted every place identified in this filmography is in the City of San Francisco.

About Cherry

2012, IFC Films

A young woman gets involved in pornography and aligns herself with a cocaine-addicted lawyer.

Director: Stephen Elliott
Screenwriters: Stephen Elliott, Lorelei Lee
Cinematographer: Darren Genet
Partial Cast: Ashley Hinshaw, Lili Taylor, Dev Patel, Diane Farr, Jonny Weston, James Franco

• Great Highway, Outer Sunset District
• Intersection of Castro Street and Market Street, Eureka Valley District
• San Francisco Armory, 1800 Mission Street, Mission District
• Dolores Park, Mission District
• Veteran's Memorial Building, 401 Van Ness Avenue, Civic Center

SAN FRANCISCO ARMORY

Pivotal to this movie is the use of the long abandoned military armory, at the intersection of 14th Street and Mission Street, as the movie shows its current use. The fortress-like castellated design building is faced in clinker brick with details of limestone and was designed by architects Woollett and Woollett of Albany, New York. The 200,000 square-foot building was completed in 1914 at a cost of $500,000. Its original use was as a U.S. National Guard facility until 1976 when it fell to disuse. In the meantime the space was used as a sound stage by Lucasfilm to film parts of the initial *Star Wars* movie. In 2006 the building was purchased by kink.com for use as studios to produce pornography for the Internet, but the former cavernous drill court portion is being leased out as various community center uses. The building was placed on the National Register of Historic Places in 1978.

The Abyss

1989, Twentieth Century Fox

The crew of an oil platform search for a nuclear powered submarine.

Director: James Cameron
Screenwriter: James Cameron
Production Designer: Leslie Dilley
Art Directors: Russell Christian, Joseph C. Nemec III
Cinematographer: Mikael Salomon
Partial Cast: Ed Harris, Mary Elizabeth Mastrantonio, Michael Biehn, Leo Burmester, Todd Graff, John Bedford Lloyd

• Golden Gate Bridge
• South of Market District

Adventure

1945, Metro Goldwyn Mayer

A roughneck sailor marries a librarian, but only settles down when their child is born.

Director: Victor Fleming
Screenwriters: Frederick Hazlitt Brennan, Vincent Lawrence
Author: Clyde Brion Davis (novel)
Art Directors: Cedric Gibbons, Urie McCleary
Cinematographer: Joseph Ruttenberg

Partial Cast: Clark Gable, Greer Garson, Joan Blondell

• Broadway, Russian Hill District
• Golden Gate Bridge
• San Francisco-Oakland Bay Bridge

The Adventurers
1995, China Star Entertainment
AKA: *Da Mao Xian Jia*
After the murder of his parents and only sister at the hands of a villainous gun-running billionaire, the crack jet pilot vows revenge.

Director: Ringo Lam
Screenwriters: Ringo Lam, Sandy Shaw, Kwong-Yam Yip
Art Director: Luk Tze Fung
Cinematographers: Ardy Lam, Arthur Wong
Partial Cast: Andy Lau, Rosamund Kwan, Chien-lien Wu, Ron Yuan

• Golden Gate Bridge
• Fisherman's Wharf District
• Mitchell Brothers O'Farrell Theatre, 895 O'Farrell Street, Tenderloin-mural of whales
• 807 Montgomery Street, Jackson Square District-office
• Portsmouth Square, Chinatown District-lion dancers
• South Beach Billiards, 270 Brannan Street, South of Market District-shootout with police
• Bunker Road, Marin Headlands, Golden Gate National Recreation Area
• Building 960, Marin Headlands, Golden Gate National Recreation Area
• Conzelman Road, Marin Headlands, Golden Gate National Recreation Area-lighting strikes

After the Thin Man
1936, Metro Goldwyn Mayer
A couple solve another murder with their dog in tow.

Director: W. S. Van Dyke II
Screenwriters: Frances Goodrich, Albert Hackett
Author: Dashiell Hammett (story)
Art Director: Cedric Gibbons
Cinematographer: Oliver T. Marsh
Partial Cast: William Powell, Myrna Loy, James Stewart, Elissa Landi, Joseph Calleia, Jessie Ralph, Alan Marshal, Sam Levene

• Market Street scene with Hayes Street Streetcar
• Coit Tower, Pioneer Park, 1 Telegraph Hill Boulevard, Telegraph Hill District
• de Young Residence, 1919 California Street, Pacific Heights District

VANISHED SITES CAPTURED

An unintended benefit derived from on-location movies is the record of places that have been lost due to demolition, or fire, or have otherwise disappeared. As a historical reference of a time and place, the cinema has captured the way it was but no longer is. Such was the case with the flamboyant three-story Victorian residence of socially prominent Mr. and Mrs. Michael H. de Young designed by B. MacDougall and Son. De Young was co-founder of the *San Francisco Chronicle* newspaper and later benefactor of the first city-sanctioned museum. Built in 1878, the 42-room mansion was purchased by de Young in 1881. The de Youngs' lavish social gatherings included receiving Theodore Roosevelt. The mansion was demolished in 1942 and the site is currently occupied by a modern multi-story apartment building. The only surviving remnant of the property is a granite retaining wall stanchion with a pediment and carved ornamentation that abuts the sidewalk. That stanchion is now part of 1969 California Street built on the adjacent lot for de Young's daughter Constance and husband Joseph Tobin.

Air Force
1943, Warner Brothers
A B-17 and her Air Force crew arrive in Pearl Harbor just after a devastating surprise attack by the Japanese.

Director: Howard Hawks
Screenwriters: William Faulkner, Leah Baird, Dudley Nichols
Art Director: John Hughes
Cinematographers: Elmer Dyer, James Wong Howe, Charles A. Marshall
Partial Cast: John Garfield, Harry Carey, George Tobias, Gig Young, Arthur Kennedy, James Brown, John Ridgely

• Hamilton Air Force Base, Novato
• Aerial view of San Francisco Peninsula

Al Capone

1959, Allied Artists
Biography of gang lord Al Capone that follows his rise and fall in Chicago during the Prohibition era.

Director: Richard Wilson
Screenwriters: Malvin Wald, Henry F. Greenberg
Production Designer: Hilyard M. Brown
Cinematographer: Lucien Ballard
Partial Cast: Rod Steiger, Martin Balsam, Fay Spain

• Alcatraz Federal Prison, Alcatraz Island, Golden Gate National Recreation Area

Alcatraz Island

1937, Warner Brothers
The U.S. Federal Government decides to construct a top security prison on an island.

Director: William C. McGann
Screenwriter: Crane Wilbur
Art Director: Esdras Hartley
Cinematographer: L. William O'Connell
Partial Cast: John Litel, Ann Sheridan, Mary Maguire, Gordon Oliver, Dick Purcell

• San Francisco
• San Quentin State Prison, San Quentin

Alexander's Ragtime Band

1938, 20th Century Fox
AKA: *Irving Berlin's Alexander's Ragtime Band*
Two songwriters vie for the affections of a rising musical comedy star.

Director: Henry King
Screenwriters: Irving Berlin, Richard Sherman, Kathryn Scola, Lamar Trotti
Art Directors: Bernard Herzbrun, Boris Leven
Cinematographer: J. Peverell Marley
Partial Cast: Tyrone Power, Alice Faye, Don Ameche, Ethel Merman, Jack Haley, Jean Hersholt, Helen Westley, John Carradine

• Cliff House, 1090 Point Lobos Avenue, Golden Gate National Recreation Area

Alien Hunter

2003, Columbia TriStar
A black box is found at the South Pole where a government agency is conducting botanical experiments.

Director: Ron Krauss
Screenwriters: J. S. Cardone, Boaz Davidson
Production Designer: William Ladd Skinner
Art Director: Valentina Mladenova
Cinematographer: Darko Suvak
Partial Cast: James Spader, Janine Eser, John Lynch

• Sather Gate, University of California Campus, Berkeley
• Valley Life Sciences Building, University of California Campus, Berkeley
• Sather Tower, University of California Campus, Berkeley

All About Eve

1950, 20th Century Fox
AKA: *Best Performance*
An aging Broadway actress suffers from the actions of a ruthless and ambitious young actress.

Director: Joseph L. Mankiewicz
Screenwriters: Joseph L. Mankiewicz, Erich Kastner, Mary Orr
Art Directors: George W. Davis, Lyle Wheeler
Cinematographer: Milton Krastner
Partial Cast: Bette Davis, George Sanders, Anne Baxter, Celeste Holm, Thelma Ritter, Gary Merrill, Hugh Marlowe, Gregory Ratoff, Marilyn Monroe

• Curran Theater, 445 Geary Boulevard, Union Square District

COLBERT NOT AT THE CURRAN

Claudette Colbert was originally cast to play the part of Margo Channing in *All About Eve*. But just two weeks before shooting was to begin she ruptured a disk while filming a rough scene in another movie. In true Hollywood fashion the show went on—but with Bette Davis in Colbert's place.

The interior theater shots took place in Market Street's Curran Theater, which had been leased for a two-week period and filming started on April 11, 1950. The story takes place in a large New York-type theater, but no theater in Los Angeles filled the bill. Since New York was too far away and consequently expensive, the decorative Curran got the role. Bette Davis arrived by train while some of the other principal cast members were flown in from Los Angeles on production chief Darryl Zanuck's seaplane. A total of

55 members of the cast and crew took over the theater and most stayed at the Fairmont Hotel on Nob Hill. It was fitting that when *Applause*, the stage musical version of the story, later went on a national tour with Lauren Bacall and Penny Fuller, it played at the Curran Theater.

All About You
2001, Urbanworks
AKA: *Love the Way*
Two people run from the pain of their broken past and when they discover each other, they find themselves at a crossroad where the only thing that stands between them and a second chance is each other.

Director: Christine Swanson
Screenwriter: Christine Swanson
Production Designer: Nanci Noblett
Cinematographers: Wolf Baschung, David Scardina
Partial Cast: Renee Goldsberry, Terron Brooks, Debbie Allen, Lisa Raye, Lou Meyers, Vanessa Bell Calloway

• Golden Gate Bridge
• City College of San Francisco, 50 Phelan Avenue, Sunnyside District
• 80 Gold Street, Jackson Square District-site of Toomies Restaurant
• 555-557 14th Avenue, Outer Richmond District
• Dolores Park, Eureka Valley District
• Intersection of 24th Street and Noe Street, Noe Valley District
• Domaine Carneros Winery, 1240 Duhig Road, Napa

The All-American Boy
1973, Warner Brothers
A young boxer rises to the top too fast and is depressed by the future.

Director: Charles Eastman
Screenwriter: Charles Eastman
Art Director: Cary Odell
Cinematographer: Philip H. Lathrop
Partial Cast: Jon Voight, Ned Glass, Anne Archer, Art Metrano, Bob Hastings, E. J. Peaker

• Vacaville

All My Sons
1948, Universal International
A young man establishes that his

father knowingly sold defective airplanes during World War II.

Director: Irving Reis
Screenwriter: Chester Erskine
Author: Arthur Miller (play)
Art Directors: Hilyard M. Brown, Bernard Herzbrun
Cinematographer: Russell Metty
Partial Cast: Edward G. Robinson, Burt Lancaster, Mady Christians, Howard Duff

• Grace Residence, 815 McDonald Avenue, Santa Rosa

All the King's Men
1949, Columbia
An ambitious man starts out as a model politician but is corrupted by the very system he tries to reform—becoming a ruthless big shot.

Director: Robert Rossen
Screenwriter: Robert Rossen
Author: Robert Penn Warren (novel)
Art Director: Sturges Carne
Cinematographer: Burnett Guffey
Partial Cast: Broderick Crawford, John Ireland, Mercedes McCambridge, Joanne Dru, John Derek, Anne Seymour, Shepperd Strudwick, Paul Ford

• Sacramento River, Rio Vista
• Carquinez Bridge, between Crockett and Vallejo

Alone Across the Pacific
1963, Ishihara International
AKA: *Alone on the Pacific; My Enemy, the Sea*
A Japanese man crosses the Pacific Ocean to the United States in a small sailboat.

Director: Kon Ichikawa
Screenwriters: Kenichi Horie, Natto Wada
Art Director: So Matsuyama
Cinematographer: Yoshihiro Yamazaki
Partial Cast: Yujiro Ishihara, Masayuki Mori, Kinuyo Tanaka

• Golden Gate Bridge
• San Francisco Marina Yacht Harbor, Marina District

American Graffiti
1973, Universal and Lucasfilm
Teens in 1962 California look at their futures.

Director: George Lucas
Screenwriters: George Lucas, Gloria Katz,
Willard Huyck
Art Director: Dennis Lynton Clark
Cinematographers: Jan D'Alquen, Ron Eveslage
Partial Cast: Richard Dreyfuss, Ronny Howard,
Paul le Mat, Charlie Martin Smith, Cindy
Williams, Candy Clark, Mackenzie Phillips,
Suzanne Somers

• Mel's Drive-In, 140 South Van Ness Avenue,
South of Market District
• Fourth Street, San Rafael-street scene with cars
• Tamalpais High School, 700 Miller Avenue, Mill
Valley-gym
• Petaluma Boulevard North, Petaluma
• D Street, Petaluma
• Washington Street, Petaluma
• Old Opera House, 149 Kentucky Street,
Petaluma
• McNear Building, 15-23 Petaluma Boulevard,
Petaluma
• Old Adobe Road, Petaluma

GEORGE LUCAS

George Lucas is the Walt Disney of
his time. His visionary and ground-
breaking work in several arenas of the
film industry have moved the medium
forward at a breakneck pace. The
development of the Pixar Image Computer, the first completely computer-
generated movie sequence, the technique of morphing, and THX sound
are all products that were created
under his direction. His trademark
approach of mythic storytelling is the
byword of his work. Today the company is fully integrated with motion
picture and TV studios, visual effects,
and sound and video games that have
made Lucas one of the most successful movie executives in the industry.
His company has earned numerous
Oscars and other awards for technical
achievements.

George Walton Lucas Jr. was born on
May 14, 1944 to Dorothy (Bomberger)
and George Sr. who was the owner of
a stationery store. The family of six
lived on a walnut ranch in the Central
Valley town of Modesto. Just after
graduating from Downey High School
Lucas hoped to be a drag car racer
but he was severely wounded in an
accident the day before graduation,
and shifted his view about his life's
direction. His next step was to attend
Modesto Junior College and then on
to film school at the University of
Southern California's School of Cinematic Arts where he attained a Bachelor of Arts and Sciences degree in
1969. The independent spirit returned
north afterward to his roots. He spent
one term at San Francisco State University in the art department. With his
degree in hand Lucas teamed with
Francis Ford Coppola in 1969 to create American Zoetrope Films in a
rented South of Market District warehouse loft. They wanted to take a personal approach to the movie-making
business; this was purposefully away
from Hollywood and the rules of the
big studios. He founded Lucasfilm in
1971 with the release of the futuristic
movie *THX-1138*. His low budget production *American Graffiti*, released in
1973 with Lucas as the director and
co-writer, struck a chord with audiences. With the wild success of *Star Wars*
in 1977 Lucas was able to purchase
what would become Skywalker Ranch
in the secluded Marin town of Nicasio;
the facility opened in 1985. The early
1980s were prolific for Lucasfilm with
the release of a series of blockbusters
including *Star Wars: Episode V The
Empire Strikes Back* (1980), *Raiders
of the Lost Ark* (1982), *Star Wars:
Episode VI-Return of the Jedi* (1983),
and *Indiana Jones and the Temple of
Doom* (1984). In the meantime the
studio developed THX sound that
brought a dimension to movies that
had been lacking. He won the prestigious Irving G. Thalberg Memorial
Award from the Academy of Motion
Picture Arts and Sciences in 1992.
The award is periodically given to creative producers, whose bodies of work
reflect a consistently high quality of
motion picture production. Skywalker
Ranch was enlarged to a total of
6,100 acres with the addition of Big
Rock Ranch, which was completed in
2002. A high-profile ground breaking
for Lucas' visionary 17-acre Letterman
Digital Arts Center, located in San
Francisco's Presidio, took place on
February 8, 2003 with Mayor Willie
Brown and Senate Representative

Nancy Pelosi who turned spades of earth to commemorate the launch of work, which was completed in 2005. With an eye for the next part of his career Lucas hired Kathleen Kennedy, a longtime collaborator, as eventual president of Lucasfilm. In 2012 he sold Lucasfilm Ltd. to Disney for a reported $4.05 billion. He intends to focus on his educational philanthropy and making personal films.

American Wedding
2003, Universal
AKA: *American Pie 3*, *American Pie 3: The Wedding*
Friends come together for a wedding in this sequel to the *American Pie* series.

Director: Jesse Dylan
Screenwriter: Adam Herz
Production Designer: Clayton Hartley
Art Director: Gregory A. Weimerskirch
Cinematographer: Lloyd Ahern II
Partial Cast: Jason Biggs, Seann William Scott, Alyson Hannigan, Eddie Kaye Thomas, Thomas Ian Nicholas, January Jones, Eugene Levy

• Ritz-Carlton Hotel, 1 Miramontes Point Road, Half Moon Bay

American Yearbook
2004, All Planet Studios
A story about high school bullying in a post-Columbine world.

Director: Brian Ging
Screenwriter: Brian Ging
Art Director: Julie Tancill
Cinematographer: Dan Coplan
Partial Cast: Nick Tagas, Jon Carlo Alvarez, Giovannie Espiritu

• Fairfield
• Acalanes High School, 1200 Pleasant Hill Road, Lafayette
• Moraga
• Oakland
• Various spots along Market Street, Financial District
• Yerba Buena Gardens, South of Market District
• The Embarcadero
• Vacaville

The Andromeda Strain
1971, Universal

A group of scientists trace a new lethal virus that is alien to the planet.

Director: Robert Wise
Screenwriters: Michael Crichton, Nelson Gidding
Production Designer: Boris Leven
Art Director: William H. Tuntke
Cinematographer: Richard H. Kline
Partial Cast: Arthur Hill, Kate Reid, Paula Kelly, David Wayne, James Olson

• San Francisco International Airport

And the Band Played On
1993, HBO Pictures
Doctors investigate a disease apparently affecting only homosexual men but find out it has much larger implications than was thought.

Director: Roger Spottiswoode
Screenwriter: Arnold Schulman
Author: Randy Shilts (book)
Production Designer: Victoria Paul
Art Director: Lee Mayman
Cinematographer: Paul Elliott
Partial Cast: Matthew Modine, Alan Alda, Richard Gere, Bud Cort, Anjelica Huston, Steve Martin, Lily Tomlin, B. D. Wong

• 300 block of Broadway, Telegraph Hill District
• View to Coit Tower along Filbert Street from Russian Hill
• Market Street-march

B. D. WONG

Native San Franciscan Bradley Darryl Wong was born on October 24, 1960, the son of Roberta (Leong) and William D. Wong. Bradley attended Abraham Lincoln High School in the Sunset District, graduating in 1978. He continued his education at San Francisco State University. His first film acting job was in *The Karate Kid, Part II* (1986) when he appeared as a boy on the street. His prolific career has spanned TV, film and the stage. He garnered a Tony Award for his role as Song Liling in the Broadway production of *M. Butterfly* in 1988 playing opposite John Lithgow. In 1993 he appeared in Steven Spielberg's *Jurassic Park* as Henry Wu. He is best known for his TV role in the long-running series *Law and Order: Special*

Victims Unit as Dr. George Huang; he appeared in that series from 2001 to 2012 spanning 227 episodes. He has a child, Boaz Dov Wong, born in 2000 with former partner Richie Jackson; they were together between 1988 and 2004.

...And Justice for All

1979, Columbia

A defense lawyer disgusted with rampant legal corruption is asked to defend a judge he despises in a rape trial.

Director: Norman Jewison
Screenwriters: Valerie Curtin, Barry Levinson
Production Designer: Richard MacDonald
Art Director: Peter Samish
Cinematographer: Victor J. Kemper
Partial Cast: Al Pacino, Jack Warden, John Forsythe, Lee Strasberg, Christine Lahti, Sam Levene, Jeffrey Tambor

• San Francisco City Hall, 1 Carlton B. Goodlett Place, Civic Center District-as rotunda and corridors in Baltimore

JEFFREY TAMBOR

Born in San Francisco, Jeffrey Michael Tambor also appeared in the partly locally shot movies *Doctor Dolittle* (1998), and *Under the Tuscan Sun* (2003). His parents were Eileen (Salzberg), a stay-at-home mother, and Michael Tambor who laid linoleum for flooring contractor Peterson-Cobby. The family resided at 1863 31st Avenue in the Sunset District when their son was born on July 8, 1944. He later studied acting at San Francisco State University where he received his BA. For graduate studies he went onto Wayne State in Detroit, Michigan to receive his Masters. After some repertory theater experience he made his Broadway debut in the 1976 comedy *Sly Fox*. His career has included numerous guest appearances on a variety of different TV shows and during most of the 1980s he appeared in 22 episodes as Judge Alan Wachtel in the well received *Hill Street Blues*. He appeared in the locally shot movie

No Small Affair (1984) as the mother's boyfriend. Part of his career has also included voice work for several films including his role as the Mayor of Whoville in Ron Howard's *How the Grinch Stole Christmas* (2000). With several Emmy nominations under his belt, he is best known for his bent, off-the-wall characterizations that utilize his expressive looks.

And Then Came Lola

2009, Fast Girl Films

A talented, but distracted photographer, on the verge of success in both love and work, could lose it all if she doesn't arrive in time for a crucial meeting on time.

Directors: Ellen Seidler, Megan Siler
Screenwriters: Ellen Seidler, Megan Siler
Production Designer: Meghan Hade
Cinematographer: Jennifer Derbin
Partial Cast: Ashleigh Sumner, Jill Bennett, Cathy DeBuono, Jessica Graham

• Ulloa Street, West Portal District
• Intersection of Cole Street and Carmel Street, Cole Valley District-tire booting
• Market Street at 23rd Street, Upper Market District-spiral ramp walkway
• Dolores Park, Mission District
• Haight Street Gate, Golden Gate Park
• The Embarcadero
• California Street Cable Car, Nob Hill District
• Chinatown District
• Liberty Street Steps, Noe Valley District
• Painted Ladies, 700 block of Steiner Street, Western Addition District
• Muni station, Carl Street near Cole Street, Cole Valley
• Berwick Place, South of Market District-murals
• Harvey Milk Plaza, Eureka Valley District
• Air Bar, 492 9th Street, Oakland
• Thirsty Bear Bar and Restaurant, 661 Howard Street, South of Market Street-rear entry

Angels in the Outfield

1994, Buena Vista

AKA: *Angels*

A bad tempered manager of an unsuccessful team gets help from an angel.

Director: William Dear
Screenwriters: Dorothy Kingsley, George Wells, Holly Goldberg Sloan, Richard Conlin
Production Designer: J. Dennis Washington
Art Directors: Carlos Arguello, Tom Targownik
Cinematographer: Matthew F. Leonetti

Partial Cast: Danny Glover, Brenda Fricker,
Tony Danza, Christopher Lloyd,
Matthew McConaughey, Ben Johnson

• Oakland/Alameda County Coliseum,
700 Coliseum Way, Oakland
• 500 Hale Avenue, Oakland-as foster home

The Animal
2001, Columbia
AKA: *Animal* and *Zoo Boy*
After receiving organ transplants from
various animals, a man finds himself
taking on their traits.

Director: Luke Greenfield
Screenwriters: Tom Brady, Rob Schneider
Production Designer: Alan Au
Art Director: Domenic Silvestri
Cinematographer: Peter Lyons Collister
Partial Cast: Rob Schneider, Colleen Haskell, Ed
Asner, John C. McGinley, Michael Caton

• Sonoma City Hall/Veterans Memorial Building,
Sonoma-as police station
• Sonoma Plaza, Sonoma

ROB SCHNEIDER

Born in San Francisco on October 31,
1963, Robert Michael Schneider was
the youngest of five children. His parents are Pilar (Monroe), a former kin-
dergarten teacher, and Marvin, a real
estate broker. He grew up in the seaside Pedro Point area of Pacifica and
graduated in 1982 from that town's
Terra Nova High School. He developed his comedy act in San Francisco
clubs such as the Holy City Zoo and
The Other Café after graduating from
high school. For higher education he
attended San Francisco State University. His major network television debut occurred in 1987 on *The David
Letterman Show*. In 1990 Lorne
Michaels saw Schneider's appearance
on HBO's *13th Annual Young Come-
dians Special* and hired him to be a
regular on *Saturday Night Live*. During
his four seasons at SNL, Schneider
was nominated for three Emmys and
a Peabody Award. His first appearance in film was in *Martians Go Home*
(1989) as a Martian voyeur. He has
been married three times; he and his
current partner Patricia Arce have one
child together. Besides the dual role of

screenwriter and actor in *Animal*,
Schneider also appeared in the Bay
Area filmed *The Beverly Hillbillies*
(1993), *Down Periscope* (1996), and
50 First Dates (2004). He currently
starts in the TV comedy *Rob* that centers on his marrying into a large Mexi-
can-American family.

Another 48 Hours
1990, Paramount Pictures
This sequel starts at the end of a
seven-year lockup when the prisoner
gets a visit from his old friend who
needs the ex-con's help to catch a
drug kingpin and clear his name.

Director: Walter Hill
Screenwriters: Roger Spottiswoode, Walter Hill,
Larry Gross, Steven E. de Sousa, Eddie Murphy,
John Fasano, Jeb Stuart
Production Designer: Joseph C. Nemec III
Art Director: Gary Wissner
Cinematographer: Matthew F. Leonetti
Partial Cast: Eddie Murphy, Nick Nolte, Brion
James, Kevin Tighe, Ed O'Ross

• Connecticut Street, Potrero Hill District
• San Francisco-Oakland Bay Bridge
• Intersection of Broadway and Columbus
Avenue, Telegraph Hill District

Around the Fire
1999, A-Pix Entertainment
A student learns a whole new life of
late nights, illegal drugs, and loud
music. He follows a hippie girl on a
band tour and ends up in rehab—only
to face his real problems head on.

Director: John Jacobsen
Screenwriters: John Comerford, Tommy Rosen
Production Designer: David Lubin
Art Director: Tracey Gallacher
Cinematographer: Eliot Rockett
Partial Cast: Devon Sawa, Bill Smitrovich, Tara
Reid, Eric Mabius, Coleman Domingo, Charlayne
Woodard

• Samuel P. Taylor State Park, 8889 Sir Francis
Drake Boulevard, Lagunitas
• Stafford Lake Park, 3549 Novato Boulevard,
Novato
• Cypress Hill Memorial Park, 430 Magnolia
Avenue, Petaluma
• San Rafael
• San Francisco Theological Seminary,
105 Seminary Road, San Anselmo
• Henry J. Kaiser Convention Center,
10 Tenth Street, Oakland

The Assassination of Richard Nixon

2004, Think Film Inc.

An antisocial, unstable salesman plots a warped version of the American dream.

Director: Niels Mueller
Screenwriters: Kevin Kennedy, Niels Mueller
Production Designer: Lester Cohen
Cinematographer: Emmanuel Lubezki
Partial Cast: Sean Penn, Naomi Watts, Don Cheadle, Mykelti Williamson, Jack Thompson, Brad William Henke

• Kahn and Keville, 500 Turk Street, Western Addition-as tire shop
• 50 United Nations Plaza, Civic Center
• The Lucerne, 766 Sutter Street, Nob Hill District
• Tosca Café, 242 Columbus Avenue, Jackson Square District
• Rockridge District, Oakland
• Broadway, Oakland
• West Oakland
• Oakland International Airport, 1 Airport Drive, Oakland
• Alameda Point, Alameda

August Rush

2007, Warner Brothers

The child of two musicians is raised by an opportunistic stranger who nurtures the child's musical talent. The prodigy uses that talent to draw his absent parents to him.

Director: Kirsten Sheridan
Screenwriters: Nick Castle, James V. Hart
Authors: Paul Castro, Nick Castle (story)
Production Designer: Michael Shaw
Art Director: Mario Ventenilla
Cinematographer: John Mathieson
Partial Cast: Freddie Highmore, Keri Russell, Jonathan Rhys Meyers, Terrence Howard, Robin Williams

• Intersection of California Street and Front Street, Financial District

The Bachelor

1999, New Line Cinema

A commitment-phobic man goes in search of a bride in order to take possession of his grandfather's $100 million inheritance.

Director: Gary Sinyor
Screenwriters: Steve Cohen
Author: Roi Copper Megrue *Seven Chances* (play)

Production Designer: Craig Stearns
Art Director: Randy Moore
Cinematographer: Simon Archer
Partial Cast: Chris O'Donnell, Renée Zellweger, Artie Lange, Ed Asner, Hal Holbrook, Peter Ustinov, Brooke Shields, Mariah Carey

• Palace of Fine Arts, 3601 Lyon Street, Marina District
• Crissy Field, Presidio, Golden Gate National Recreation Area
• Pacific Stock Exchange, 301 Pine Street, Financial District
• 2500 Filbert Street, Pacific Heights District
• Sutter-Stockton Garage, 444 Stockton Street, Union Square District
• California Academy of Sciences, Steinhart Aquarium, 55 Music Concourse Drive, Golden Gate Park
• Saints Peter and Paul Church, 666 Filbert Street, Washington Square, North Beach District
• Grant Avenue, Telegraph Hill District
• Columbus Avenue, North Beach District
• Danilo Bakery, 516 Green Street, Telegraph Hill District
• Transbay Terminal, 425 Mission Street, South of Market District
• 52 Second Street, South of Market District

Bandits

2001, Metro Goldwyn Mayer
AKA: *Outlaws*

Two bank robbers fall in love with the girl they have kidnapped.

Director: Barry Levinson
Screenwriter: Harley Peyton
Production Designer: Victor Kempster
Art Director: Dan Webster
Cinematographer: Dante Spinotti
Partial Cast: Bruce Willis, Cate Blanchett, Billy Bob Thornton, Troy Garity

• Pt. Montara Lighthouse, State Highway Route 1, Montara
• Flamingo Resort Hotel and Conference Center, 2777 Fourth Street, Santa Rosa
• Nick's Cove Restaurant, 23240 State Highway Route 1, Marshall
• Mare Island, Vallejo
• Not-A-Bank, 26975 Shoreline Highway, State Highway Route 1, Tomales
• Fireside Inn, 115 Shoreline Highway, Mill Valley

PT. MONTARA FOG SIGNAL AND LIGHT STATION

Pt. Montara Fog Signal and Light Station stands where a light station was first established in 1875 to guide ships along the rocky Pacific Ocean coastline. Now the active lighthouse site is doing double duty as a hostel run by Hostelling International American

Youth Hostels and California State Parks created in cooperation with the U.S. Coast Guard. The existing 30-foot-high steel structure was built in 1928.

Bartleby
2001, Parker Film Company
AKA: *Bartleby at the Office*
A clueless boss has no idea what to do with his mundane office worker whose refusal of duties only gets worse with every passing minute.

Director: Jonathan Parker
Screenwriters: Jonathan Parker, Catherine DiNapoli
Author: Herman Melville "Bartleby the Scrivener" (short story)
Production Designer: Rosario Provenza
Art Director: Deborah Parker
Cinematographer: Wah Ho Chan
Partial Cast: David Payner, Crispin Glover, Glenne Headly, Maury Chaykin, Joe Piscopo, Dick Martin, Seymour Cassel, Carrie Snodgress

• One Thorndale Drive, San Rafael-office building
• Pedestrian overpass, intersection of Belle Avenue and U.S. Highway Route 101, Redwood Highway, San Rafael
• Sutter Terra Linda Health Plaza, 4000 Civic Center Drive, San Rafael-as new office building
• House of Bagels/Central Deli, 640 Fourth Street, San Rafael-as Free Dining Room
• Tamalpais Avenue, between Fourth Street and Fifth Street, San Rafael-as railroad tracks
• Luther Burbank Savings Building, 1050 Fourth Street, San Rafael-office building

Basic Instinct
1992, Tri Star Pictures
AKA: *Ice Cold Desire*
A woman who is a brilliant killer entices a cop to her.

Director: Paul Verhoeven
Screenwriter: Joe Eszterhas
Production Designer: Terence Marsh
Art Directors: Mark Billerman, William Cruse
Cinematographer: Jan de Bont
Partial Cast: Michael Douglas, Sharon Stone, George Dzundzu, Jeanne Tripplehorn

• 2102 Broadway, Pacific Heights District
• 2930 Vallejo Street, Pacific Heights District
• Conzelman Road, Marin Headlands, Golden Gate National Recreation Area
• Tosca Café, 242 Columbus Avenue, Jackson Square District
• State Highway Route 1, Muir Beach
• 35 Liberty Street, Petaluma

• Hall of Justice, 850 Bryant Street, South of Market District
• Intersection of Columbus Avenue and Gibb Alley, Chinatown District
• 1158-70 Montgomery Street, Telegraph Hill District
• Rawhide II Bar, 280 Seventh Street, South of Market District-as The Stetson
• Below San Francisco-Oakland Bay Bridge approaches, South of Market District
• 2201 Broadway, Oakland
• Yerba Buena Gardens, South of Market District-car crash
• Pier 7, Embarcadero

Beaches
1988, Touchstone Pictures
AKA: *Forever Friends*
Two women from very different backgrounds share a lifetime of trials and tribulations.

Director: Garry Marshall
Screenwriters: Iris Ranier Dart, Mary Agnes Donohue
Production Designer: Albert Brenner
Art Directors: Bill Barclay, Frank Richwood
Cinematographer: Dante Spinotti
Partial Cast: Bette Midler, Barbara Hershey, John Heard, Spalding Gray, Lainie Kazan

• San Francisco General Hospital, 1001 Potrero Avenue, Mission District

Bedazzled
2000, 20th Century Fox
A man sells his soul for seven wishes in hopes of landing his dream girl.

Director: Harold Ramis
Screenwriters: Larry Gelbert, Harold Ramis, Peter Tolan
Authors: Peter Cook, Dudley Moore (story)
Production Designer: Rick Heinrichs
Art Director: John Dexter
Cinematographers: Phil Mehuex, Bill Pope
Partial Cast: Brenden Fraser, Elizabeth Hurley

• McKesson Building, 600 Market Street, Financial District
• San Francisco-Oakland Bay Bridge
• Club DV8, 11 Folsom Street, Rincon Hill District
• Washington Square, North Beach District
• North Beach District
• Justin Herman Plaza, The Embarcadero
• Saints Peter and Paul Church, 666 Filbert Street, Washington Square, North Beach District
• San Francisco City Hall, 1 Carlton B. Goodlett Place, Civic Center District-rotunda
• 1155 Filbert Street, Russian Hill District

Bee Season
2005, 20th Century Fox

A wife and mother begins a downward emotional spiral, as her husband avoids their collapsing marriage by immersing himself in his daughter's quest to become a spelling bee champion.

Directors: Scott McGhee, David Siegel
Screenwriters: Myla Goldberg, Naomi Foner
Production Designer: Kelly McGehee
Art Director: Michael E. Goldman
Cinematographer: Giles Nuttgens
Partial Cast: Juliette Binoche, Richard Gere, Flora Cross, Max Minghella, Kate Bosworth

• Masonic Auditorium, 1111 California Street, Nob Hill District
• 1075 Mariposa, Avenue, Berkeley-bungalow residence
• Golden Gate Bridge
• San Francisco-Oakland Bay Bridge
• Port of Oakland shipping terminal
• Doe Library, University of California Campus, Berkeley
• Valley Life Sciences Building, University of California Campus, Berkeley
• Albany High School, 603 Key Route Boulevard, Albany
• Kwik Hamburgers, 6215 International Boulevard, Oakland
• Lake Merritt, Oakland
• Church, near Lake Merritt
• Berkeley Marina
• Altenheim, Inc., 1720 MacArthur Boulevard, Fruitvale District, Oakland
• Malcolm X Arts and Academics Magnet School, 1731 Prince Street, Berkeley
• Toy Safari, 1410 Park Street, Alameda
• Piedmont District, Oakland

STUDYING THEIR PARTS

To get a more authentic feeling for his part as Saul, Richard Gere audited a class of the University of California, Berkeley philosophy professor John Searle. Gere was looking for techniques in his film role as a religious-studies professor. Co-star Julia Binoche did the same at Children's Hospital Oakland Research Institute where she spent time with scientist and oncologist Julie Saba gleaning tips on her part as Miriam, a cellular biologist.

Behind That Curtain
1929, Fox

Murder follows when an irresponsible man aspires to marry an heiress.

Director: Irving Cummings
Screenwriters: Sonya Levin, George Middleton, Wilbur Morse Jr., Clarke Silvernail
Author: Earl Derr Biggers (novel)
Cinematographers: Conrad Wells, Vincent J. Farrar, Dave Ragin
Partial Cast: Warner Baxter, Lois Moran, Gilbert Emery, Claude King, Philip Strange, Boris Karloff

• Panorama of waterfront from San Francisco Bay
• Intersection of Pine Street and Grant Avenue, Chinatown District
• Market Street

THE FABULOUS FOX

Hollywood tycoon William Fox dubbed his San Francisco creation a "Monument to the Muses." The Fox Theatre held its gala opening on June 28, 1929 with the presence of Hollywood glamour-by-the-dozen including the likes of Douglas Fairbanks Jr., Buster Keaton, Mary Pickford, Norma Shearer, Joan Crawford, Will Rogers, Wallace Beery, Louis B. Mayer, and Irving Thalberg. That evening Earl Derr Biggers' feature film story *Behind That Curtain* was premiered to the world with a full house filling all 4,651 seats. Facing Market Street, the lavish theater built at the height of the motion picture palace era, was designed by Thomas W. Lamb in a grand French style. Requiring a staff of 300 including doormen and usherettes, the venue boasted a mighty Wurlitzer organ. Sadly the Fox's venue, opened on the cusp of the Great Depression, had a checkered and short career. Operating in the red much of the time, it closed in 1963. The wrecking ball swung shortly thereafter and today's windswept Archstone Fox Plaza and 29-story tower occupy the site.

Behind the Green Door
1973, Mitchell Brothers
A girl is kidnapped and willingly allows herself to have sex with a variety of partners in front of an audience.

Directors: Artie J. Mitchell, James J. Mitchell
Screenwriters: Artie J. Mitchell, James J. Mitchell
Art Director: Don Sidle
Cinematographer: Jon T. Fontana
Partial Cast: Marilyn Chambers, George S. McDonald, Johnnie Keye, Lisa Grant, Yank Levine

• State Highway Route 1, Stinson Beach
• Alta Mira Hotel and Restaurant, 125 Buckley Avenue, Sausalito

THE MITCHELL BROTHERS

Produced by small town brothers Jim and Artie Mitchell from Antioch this X-rated movie was a cultural benchmark. Its presentation launched soft porn films as socially acceptable helping create an era of sexual freedom. The Mitchell Brothers opened their 200-seat O'Farrell Theater on July 4, 1969 in San Francisco's Tenderloin District. The police department raided the theater on many occasions. Ironically, and a boon to the success of *Behind the Green Door*, Marilyn Chambers' career was launched at the same time; she was the wholesome blonde Ivory Snow girl pictured on the front of every box of the company's washing detergent. Sadly the Mitchell Brothers, who legally made a fortune from the movie, had other problems to iron out—Jim mortally shot Artie on February 27, 1991 in Artie's Corte Madera home. Jim was incarcerated in nearby San Quentin Prison for only three years despite evidence that reeked of manslaughter. The surviving brother died in 2007.

Being Human
1993, Warner Brothers
A man learns the meaning of courage across four lifetimes spread centuries apart.
Director: Bill Forsyth
Screenwriter: Bill Forsyth
Production Designer: Norman Garwood
Cinematographer: Michael Coulter
Partial Cast: Robin Williams, John Turturro, Anna Galiena, Vincent D'Onofrio, Hector Elizondo, Lorraine Bracco, Lindsay Crouse

• Stinson Beach, Golden Gate National Recreation Area

The Beloved Bachelor
1931, Paramount
A man falls for his adopted daughter.

Director: Lloyd Corrigan
Screenwriters: Sidney Buchman, Raymond Griffith, Agnes Brand Leahy
Author: Ed Peple *The Prince Chap* (play)
Cinematographer: Charles Rosher
Partial Cast: Paul Lukas, Dorothy Jordan, Betty Van Allen, Charles Ruggles, Vivienne Osborne

• Aquatic Park, San Francisco Maritime National Historic Park, Golden Gate National Recreation Area

Berkeley
2005, Rivercoast Films
An eighteen-year-old boy attends U.C. Berkeley in 1968 to study accounting and avoid the draft.

Director: Bobby Roth
Screenwriters: Bobby Roth
Production Designer: Henry G. Sanders
Art Director: Andrew Steinberg
Cinematographer: Steve Burns
Partial Cast: Nick Roth, Laura Jordan, Henry Winkler

• Shakespeare and Co., 2499 Telegraph Avenue, Berkeley
• Berkeley Marina, Berkeley
• Wheeler Hall, University of California Campus, Berkeley
• Sather Gate, University of California Campus, Berkeley

Berkeley in the 60s
1990, P.O.V. Theatrical Films
Documentary about militant student political activity at the University of California, Berkeley during the 1960s.

Director: Mark Kitchell
Screenwriters: Susan Griffin, Mark Kitchell, Stephen Most
Cinematographer: Stephen Lighthill
Partial Cast: Jackie Goldberg, Jack Weinberg, John Gage, Max Rafferty, Michael Rossman, Mario Savio, Jentri Anders, John Searle, Francis E. Walter, Frank Bardacke, Ruth Rosen, Suzy Nelson, David Hilliard, James Rector, Hardy Frye, Phil Ochs, Barry Melton, Mike Miller, John de Bonis

• San Francisco City Hall, 1 Carlton B. Goodlett Place, Civic Center District-exterior, rotunda and Board of Supervisors Chamber
• Sproul Plaza, University of California Campus, Berkeley
• Union Square, 333 Post Street

• Sheraton Palace Hotel, 2 New Montgomery Street, South of Market District
• Greek Theatre, University of California Campus, Berkeley
• Various streets, Oakland
• Haight Street, Haight-Ashbury District
• Market Street
• People's Park, Haste Street at Bowditch Street, Berkeley

The Beverly Hillbillies
1993, 20th Century Fox
A hillbilly family strikes oil and move to the West Coast to live in a Beverly Hills mansion.

Director: Penelope Spheeris
Screenwriters: Laurence Konner, Mark Rosenthal, Jim Fisher, Jim Staahl
Author: Paul Henning (TV series)
Production Designer: Peter Jamison
Cinematographer: Robert Brinkman
Partial Cast: Diedrich Bader, Dabney Coleman, Erika Eleniak, Cloris Leachman, Rob Schneider, Lea Thompson, Lily Tomlin, Jim Varney, Buddy Ebsen, Zsa Zsa Gabor, Dolly Parton

• Fort Ross Road, Jenner
• Jenner-opening scenes with forested hills and cabin

Beverly Hills Cop III
1994, Paramount Pictures
While investigating a car theft ring a cop comes across something much bigger.

Director: John Landis
Screenwriters: Danilo Bach, Daniel Petri Jr., Steven E. de Souza
Production Designer: Michael Seymour
Cinematographer: Mac Ahlberg
Partial Cast: Eddie Murphy, Jon Tenney, Joey Travolta, Eugene Collier

• Paramount's Great America Amusement Park, 4701 Great America Parkway, Santa Clara

Beyond the Door
1974, Film Ventures International
A young woman is pregnant with the Devil's baby.

Directors: Ovidio G. Assontis, Robert Barrett
Screenwriters: Ovidio G. Assontis, Antonio Troiso, Robert Barrett, Giorgio Marini, Aldo Crudo, Alex Rebar, Christopher Cruise
Art Directors: Piero Filippone, Franco Velchi
Cinematographer: Roberto D'Ettorre Piazzoli

Partial Cast: Juliet Mills, Gabriele Lavia, Richard Johnson

• Golden Gate Bridge
• Marina Boulevard, Marina District
• Crookedest Street in the World, 1000 block of Lombard Street, Russian Hill District
• Golden Gateway Center, The Embarcadero
• Houlihan's Restaurant, 660 Bridgeway, Sausalito
• Ghirardelli Square, Waterfront-cafe
• Pt. Lobos Avenue, Outer Richmond District
• Marina Green, Marina District
• Alcoa Building, One Maritime Plaza, 300 Clay Street, Golden Gateway-doctor's office
• F.A.O. Schwarz, 180 Post Street, Union Square District
• Bank of America Plaza, 555 California Street, Financial District
• Jefferson Square, Western Addition District
• Union Square
• Houseboats, Sausalito
• San Francisco-Oakland Bay Bridge
• Friedel Klussmann Memorial Cable Car Turnaround, Aquatic Park, San Francisco Maritime National Historic Park, Golden Gate National Recreation Area

Bicentennial Man
1999, Touchstone and Columbia
A robot's artificial intelligence grows until it becomes human.

Director: Chris Columbus
Screenwriter: Nicholas Kazan
Author: Isaac Asimov "The Bicentennial Man" (short story), *The Positronic Man* (novel) with Robert Silverberg
Production Designer: Norman Reynolds
Art Directors: Bill Hinley, Bruton Jones, Mark W. Mansbridge
Cinematographer: Phil Meheux
Partial Cast: Robin Williams, Sam Neill, Embeth Davitz

• Fleishhacker Family Estate, "Green Gables," 329 Albion Avenue, Woodside-rear and steps to pool used as Martin Family Residence
• Baker Beach, Presidio, Golden Gate National Recreation Area
• Oracle Campus, 500 Oracle Parkway, Redwood Shores-as robot maker's offices
• San Francisco skyline from Telegraph Hill-view outside lawyer's window
• Grace Cathedral, 1100 California Street, Nob Hill District-interior and exterior
• James J. Nealon Baseball Diamond, Big Rec, Golden Gate Park
• Fort Point National Historic Site, Marine Drive, Golden Gate National Recreation Area
• Jones Beach, State Highway Route 1, Half Moon Bay-beach
• Golden Gate Bridge-with two levels
• Old St. Mary's Church, Nicasio Valley Road, Nicasio

- Mission Clay Pipe Company, Niles Canyon Road, Niles-brick kilns
- Painted Ladies, 700 block of Steiner Street, Western Addition District-park with chess tables
- San Francisco City Hall, 1 Carlton B. Goodlett Place, Civic Center District-rotunda
- Palace of Fine Arts, 3601 Lyon Street, Marina District

GREEN GABLES

Built as a summer home for Bella and Mortimer Fleishhacker Sr., a banker and paper magnate, the 29-room structure was designed by architect Charles Sumner Greene of the iconic Greene and Greene Brothers of Pasadena. The Greene Brothers were purveyors of the casual California bungalow style but this structure was a departure from their style that could be seen in the Pasadena area. The house is sited on a scenic promontory within the wooded 75 acres, the largest parcel the Greenes had ever designed on. The picturesque composition evoked an English-style country house with a thatched roof and exterior walls of sprayed-on concrete in an earthen color—all of which speaks to the unpretentious and informal nature of the design that its owner requested. Additionally the undulating roof imitates the lines of straw thatch but used steam-bent redwood shingles, which would last longer than thatch. Greene continued to finish the project over a 22-year period. Formal gardens, a lily pond, and a water garden that features a sculptural colonnade recalling the ancient Italian one located at Hadrian's Villa in Italy are surrounded by massive green lawns. The compound includes three later-built family homes (one by architect William Wurster of the Second Bay Area Tradition) not visible from the main house. The entire complex is maintained and occupied by descendants of its original owner.

The Bigamist

1953, Englewood Entertaiment and The Filmmakers, Inc.

A traveling salesman has two wives, each in different cities.

Director: Ida Lupino
Screenwriters: Larry Marcus, Lou Schor, Collier Young
Art Director: James W. Sullivan
Cinematographer: George E. Diskant
Partial Cast: Joan Fontaine, Edmund Gwenn, Ida Lupino, Edmond O'Brien, Kenneth Tobey, Jane Darwell

- San Francisco-Oakland Bay Bridge

JOAN FONTAINE

The younger sister of actress Olivia de Havilland, Joan de Beauvoir de Havilland was born on October 22, 1917 to English émigré parents Lillian A. (Ruse) and Walter A. de Havilland, a patent attorney, who were residing in Tokyo, Japan. In 1919 Lillian and her two daughters left Asia for the United States to live in the Bay Area. The couple divorced in 1925 and mother and daughters settled in San Jose when Lillian then married Danny Fontaine, an investment counselor. The girls' stepfather turned out to be brutal, and both teenage girls left their home to escape his harsh treatment. Joan initially attended Los Gatos High School but the 15-year-old contacted her father in Japan and she returned to Japan and graduated from the American School in 1935. Shortly thereafter, at age 18, she became an RKO contract player. Her film debut was in No More Ladies (1935) where she was billed as Joan Burfield. She was nominated three times for Best Actress for the Academy Awards from 1940 through 1943 and won in 1941 for her role as the shy Lina opposite Cary Grant's character Johnnie in director Hitchcock's Suspicion. As luck would have it her involvement with The Bigamist was purely accidental: her husband of the time, independent producer Collier Young (whom she married in 1952) initially cast actress Jane Greer, but shortly before production began, Greer withdrew from the production. The producer's company could not afford a long delay in production so wife Joan stepped in, at a much-reduced salary, and played the part. Joan went on to appear in movies virtually every year of her career, and sometimes more than once a year, until 1962. Another highlight was in 1940, again in a Hitchcock vehicle *Rebecca*, with co-star Laurence Olivier. Her last theatrical film appearance was in *The Witches* in 1966. Following a waning film career she appeared in many stage productions, among them Noel Coward's *Private Lives*, and *The Lion in Winter*. She acted in a few made-for-TV films starting in the late 1970s through the early 1990s. She penned the book *No Bed of Roses*, which was published in 1978, telling the details of her life to that point. She married four times and had one child, Deborah with William Dozier. Today she resides, not far in distance from her early days, in the seaside town of Carmel-by-the-Sea on the Monterey Peninsula.

Big Trouble in Little China
1986, 20th Century Fox
A philosophizing truck driver finds himself combating an ancient, evil Chinese magician.

Director: John Carpenter
Screenwriters: Gary Goldman, David Z. Weinstein
Production Designer: John J. Lloyd
Art Director: Les Gobruegge
Cinematographer: Dean Cundey
Partial Cast: Kurt Russell, Kim Cattrall, Dennis Dun, James Hong, Victor Wong, Kate Burton

• Golden Gate Bridge
• Interstate Highway Route 280, John F. Foran Freeway, Potrero Hill District
• Dragon Gateway to Chinatown, intersection of Grant Avenue and Bush Street, Chinatown District
• Commercial Street, between Kearny Street and Grant Avenue, Chinatown District

Bird
1988, Warner Brothers
The life of musician Charlie Parker who excelled on the alto saxophone.

Director: Clint Eastwood

Screenwriter: Joel Oliansky
Production Designer: Edward C. Carfagno
Cinematographer: Jack N. Green
Partial Cast: Forest Whitaker, Diane Venora, Michael Zelniker

• Birds Landing, Sacramento River Delta
• Locke, Sacramento River Delta

Birdemic: Shock and Terror
2008, Moviehead Pictures
Packs of birds attack the residents of a small town.

Director: James Nguyen
Screenwriter: James Nguyen
Cinematographer: Daniel Mai
Partial Cast: Alan Bagh, Whitney Moore, Tippi Hedren, Rick Camp, Patsy van Ettiger

• Cameron's Restaurant and Inn, 1410 Cabrillo Highway South, State Highway Route 1, Half Moon Bay
• Sea Horse Ranch, 1828 Cabrillo Highway North, State Highway Route 1, Half Moon Bay

"No matter what happens to me, no matter where I am, if I ever get a chance to punish you further, I'll do it."

The Birdman of Alcatraz
1962, United Artists
The biography of Robert Stroud whose 60 years of imprisonment is lightened by his passion for birds.

Director: John Frankenheimer
Screenwriter: Guy Trosper
Author: Thomas E. Gaddis (book)
Art Director: Fernando Carrere
Cinematographer: Burnett Guffey
Partial Cast: Burt Lancaster, Karl Malden, Thelma Ritter, Betty Field, Edmond O'Brien, Telly Savalas

• Pier 43, Fisherman's Wharf District

The Birds
1963, Universal Pictures

A wealthy socialite pursues a man to a small Northern California town that slowly takes a turn for the bizarre when black birds suddenly attack the residents.

Director: Alfred Hitchcock
Screenwriter: Evan Hunter
Author: Daphne du Maurier (story)
Production Designer: Robert F. Boyle
Cinematographer: Robert Burks
Partial Cast: Rod Taylor, Tippi Hedren, Suzanne Pleshette, Jessica Tandy, Angela Cartwright

• Robison's Pet Store, 135 Maiden Lane, Union Square District-exterior of bird shop
• Union Square, 333 Post Street
• Potter School, Bodega Lane, Bodega
• Tides Restaurant and dock, 835 Shoreline Highway, State Highway Route 1, Bodega Bay
• Church of the Assumption, 26825 Shoreline Highway, State Highway Route 1, Tomales
• Bodega Bay

SIR ALFRED HITCHCOCK

Alfred Joseph Hitchcock was born on August 13, 1899 in the East End of London to parents Emma J. (Whee-lan) and William Hitchcock, a green-grocer and poultry merchant. Alfred was the second son and the youngest of three children. He attended Salesi-an College and St. Ignatius College, but he left to get further technical training at the London County Council School of Engineering and Navigation in 1913. In 1915 he was hired by the Henley Telegraph and Cable Compa-ny as a draftsman and advertising designer. He entered the film industry in 1920, designing title cards for silent films at the Famous Players-Lasky Company. In 1925 he directed his first film but as luck would have it neither this or his other films that followed would see the screen until 1927, when his first thriller *The Lodger: A Story of the London Fog* was released to criti-cal acclaim. (He would later refilm the story as *Frenzy* in 1972.) Several oth-er films followed, reflecting his distinc-tive directorial style and unique brand of storytelling. He and Alma Reville, his assistant director, were married in 1926 and they had one child, Patricia. Alma would figure heavily in many different facets of Hitchcock's work as his closest collaborator for the re-mainder of his career. The suspense-ful *The 39 Steps* (1935) would be his first use of the famous "McGuffin," a plot device. With World War II in the making, Hitchcock moved his family to California when David O. Selznick signed him to a seven-year contract in 1939. His first Hollywood film was *Rebecca* (1940), which won the Best Picture Oscar. In late 1940 he and Alma purchased the secluded 200-acre Cornwall Ranch located near Scotts Valley in the Santa Cruz Moun-tains. This was their weekend resi-dence for the next 30 years; they maintained their primary residence in the tony Bel Aire section of Los Ange-les as well. Hitchcock made more than 50 films; and it's no accident then that four of his films were primarily filmed, and another one had scenes shot, in the Bay Area. Sixteen of his films re-ceived Oscar nominations. He won the prestigious Irving G. Thalberg Memorial Award from the Academy of Motion Picture Arts and Sciences in 1968. He also hosted the TV show, *Alfred Hitchcock Presents*, and he was known as "The Master of Sus-pense." He died on April 29, 1980 having been knighted the year before by his native country for his extraordi-nary influence on the medium of film.

Birdy
1984, Tri-Star Pictures
A war veteran thinks he is able to fly like a bird.

Director: Alan Parker
Screenwriters: Sandy Kroopf, Jack Behr
Author: William Wharton (novel)
Production Designer: Geoffrey Kirkland
Art Directors: W. Stewart Campbell, Armin Ganz
Cinematographer: Michael Seresin
Partial Cast: Matthew Modine, Nicolas Cage, John Harkins, Sandy Baron

• Agnews Developmental Center West, Montague Expressway at Lafayette Street, Santa Clara

Black August
2007, Warner Home Video

Biopic of a Black Panther who was one of the most infamous prisoner-activists of the civil rights movement.

Director: Samm Styles
Author: George Jackson
Production Designer: Douglas Freeman
Cinematographer: Kevin Robertson
Partial Cast: Gary Dourdan, Darren Bridgett, Ezra Stanley, Vonetta McGee, LeRoy Mobley

• Dunsmuir House and Gardens, 2960 Peralta Oaks Court, Oakland
• Alcatraz Island, Golden Gate National Recreation Area
• San Francisco-Oakland Bay Bridge
• Golden Gate Bridge
• San Quentin State Prison, San Quentin
• Marin Civic Center, San Rafael-shootout site
• Oakland Tribune Tower, 410 13th Street, Oakland
• St. Andrew's Missionary Baptist Church, 2624 West Street, Oakland
• 1200 Lakeshore Drive, Lake Merritt, Oakland

SAMM STYLES

Also known as Samm Wallace, the Oakland native graduated from San Francisco State University's film school. He started out his film career directing music videos: *Black August* was his directorial debut in a big budget film. He was on the advisory board for the Oakland International Film Festival for 2009. As part of one of the few African American-based film companies he has co-produced *Milk Money* (2011), which tells the story of an Oakland native with bad luck. He acted as the cinematographer for the made-for-TV movie *A Cross to Bear* (2012), a story about a young girl's long road to redemption. He is currently working on the in-process filming of *The Legend of Billy Do*, based on Oakland's oldest urban legend.

The Black Bird
1975, Columbia
Sam Spade's offspring deals with crooks who are after the Maltese falcon.

Director: David Giler
Screenwriters: Gordon Cotler, Gordon Giler, Don Mankiewicz

Author: Dashiell Hammett (characters)
Production Designer: Harry Horner
Cinematographer: Philip H. Lathrop
Partial Cast: George Segal, Stéphane Audran, Lee Patrick, Elisha Cook Jr.

• California Palace of the Legion of Honor, Lincoln Park, Outer Richmond District

Black Eyed Dog
1999, Vanguard Cinema
A musician dreams of making it big with his band but his sordid past keeps biting him on the heels.

Director: Richard O'Connell
Screenwriter: Richard O'Connell
Cinematographer: Brian Tramontana
Partial Cast: Paul Barnett, Kevin P. Kearns, Kevin Barry Artt

• Civic Center Plaza, Civic Center District
• Bethlehem Shipyard, 900 Illinois Street, Potrero Hill District
• Golden Gate Bridge
• The Last Day Saloon, 406 Clement Street, Inner Richmond District
• St. Paul's Church, 1660 Church Street, Noe Valley District
• Johnny Foley's Irish Pub and Restaurant, 243 O'Farrell Street, Union Square District
• Intersection of 20th Street and Wisconsin Street, Potrero Hill District
• Alamo Square, Western Addition District
• Great American Music Hall, 859 O'Farrell Street, Tenderloin District
• Playground and tunnel between 9th and 10th Avenues at Fulton Street, Golden Gate Park

Black Rain
1989, Paramount
Two New York cops escort a vicious killer back to his native Japan and land in the middle of a gangland battle.

Director: Ridley Scott
Screenwriters: Craig Bolotin, Warren Lewis
Production Designer: Norris Spencer
Art Directors: John Jay Moore, Herman F. Zimmerman
Cinematographer: Jan de Bont
Partial Cast: Michael Douglas, Andy Garcia, Ken Takakwa, Kate Capshaw

• Silverado Country Club, 1600 Atlas Peak Road, Napa-motorcycle chase

The Black Stallion Returns
1983, Metro Goldwyn Mayer and United Artists

A teen's horse is stolen and he experiences several adventures in the Sahara Desert before seeing the steed again.

Director: Robert Dalva
Screenwriters: Richard Kletter, Jerome Kass
Author: Walter Farley (novel)
Art Director: Aurelio Crugnola
Cinematographer: Carlo Di Palma
Partial Cast: Kelly Reno, Vincent Spano, Allan Garfield

• Pier 3, Fort Mason Center, Golden Gate National Recreation Area-as embarkation pier

Blonde Ambition
2007, Millennium Films
A bumpkin strikes out on her own in New York and encounters some nasty people.

Director: Scott Marshall
Screenwriters: David McHugh, Mathew Flanagan
Authors: John Cohen, David McHugh, Matthew Flanagan (story)
Production Designer: Bob Ziembicki
Art Director: Richard Fojo
Cinematographer: Mark Irwin
Partial Cast: Jessica Simpson, Luke Wilson, Rachel Leigh Cook, Andy Dick, Penelope Ann Miller, Willie Nelson, Larry Miller

• Embarcadero One, Embarcadero Center, Financial District-skyscraper exterior with window washing rig

Blood Alley
1955, Warner Brothers
AKA: William A. Wellman 's Blood Alley
An American sailor is assisted by locals to escape from a Chinese jail and in return he helps them to get to Hong Kong.

Director: William A. Wellman
Screenwriter: Albert Sidney Fleishman
Author: Albert Sidney Fleishman (novel)
Production Designer: Alfred Ybarra
Cinematographer: William H. Clothier
Partial Cast: John Wayne, Lauren Bacall, Anita Ekberg, Victor Sen Yung

• China Camp State Park, North San Pedro Road, San Rafael

CHINA CAMP STATE PARK

China Camp State Park, a state historic landmark, sits on the shores of San Pablo Bay. In operation by 1870 as a Japanese-occupied village whose income came from the bay, China Camp was one of the earliest and productive fishing villages in the state. The tiny island seen in the film is Rat Island, just north of the village. The feudal-looking building on the bluff above the beach was built for the movie and several of the junk sailing vessels were built at a shipyard in San Francisco's India Basin. The frozen in-time beach front has also appeared in the movies Smooth Talk (1985) and Hemingway and Gellhorn (2012).

Blood In, Blood Out
1993, Hollywood Pictures
AKA: Bound by Honor
True-life story about members of an East Los Angeles gang and how a violent crime and the influence of narcotics alter their lives.

Director: Thomas Hackford
Screenwriters: Jimmy Santiago Baca, Jeremy Iacone, Floyd Mutrux
Author: Ross Thomas (story)
Art Direction: Marek Dobrowolski
Production Designer: Bruno Rubeo
Cinematographer: Gabriel Beristain
Partial Cast: Damian Chapa, Jesse Borrego, Benjamin Bratt

• San Quentin State Prison, San Quentin

Blue Jasmine
2013, Paramount
After everything in her life falls to pieces, including her marriage to a wealthy businessman, an elegant New York socialite moves into her sister's modest apartment to try to pull herself together.

Director: Woody Allen
Screenwriter: Woody Allen
Production Designer: Santo Loquasto
Art Directors: Michael E. Goldman, Doug Huszti
Cinematographer: Javier Aguirresarobe
Partial Cast: Cate Blanchett, Alec Baldwin, Sally Hawkins, Michael Emerson, Peter Sarsgaard
Local Cast: Diva Val Diamond

• San Francisco International Airport
• 301-307 South Van Ness Avenue, Mission District

- Inner Sunset District
- Grant Avenue, Chinatown District
- The Ramp Restaurant, 855 Terry Francois Street, Mission Bay District
- Ocean Beach, Golden Gate National Recreation Area
- Marin Headlands, Golden Gate National Recreation Area
- Intersection of 20th Street and Lexington Street, Mission District
- Motel Capri, 2015 Greenwich Street, Cow Hollow District
- Aub Zam Zam Bar, 1633 Haight Street, Haight-Ashbury District
- Intersection of Ulloa Street and Claremont Boulevard, West Portal District
- Shreve & Co., 200 Post Street, Union Square District
- Marina Green, Marina District
- Gaspare's Pizza House and Italian Restaurant, 5546 Geary Boulevard, Outer Richmond District
- Larkspur
- 8 Britton Avenue, Belvedere Island
- South Park, South of Market District

Bombardier
1943, RKO Radio Pictures
Cadet bombardiers learn the realities of war while performing bombing raids on Japan.

Directors: Richard Wallace, Lambert Hillyer
Screenwriters: John Twist, Martin Rackin
Art Directors: Albert S. D'Agnostino, Alfred Herman
Cinematographers: Nicholas Musuraca, Joseph F. Biroc
Partial Cast: Pat O'Brien, Randolph Scott, Anne Shirley, Eddie Albert

- Ferry Building and waterfront, The Embarcadero

Born to Be Bad
1950, RKO Radio Pictures
A cunning woman plots to get everything she wants.

Director: Nicholas Ray
Screenwriters: Edith Sommer, Charles Schnee
Author: Anne Parrish *All Kneeling* (novel)
Art Directors: Albert D'Agostino, Jack Okey
Cinematographer: Nicholas Musuraca
Partial Cast: Joan Fontaine, Robert Ryan, Zachary Scott, Joan Leslie, Mel Ferrer

- General establishing views of San Francisco

Born to Be Wild
1995, Warner Brothers
AKA: *Katie*

A juvenile delinquent keeps getting into trouble.

Director: John Gray
Screenwriters: Paul Young, John Bunzel
Production Designer: Roy Forge Smith
Art Director: Gilbert Wong
Cinematographer: Donald M. Morgan
Partial Cast: Wil Horneff, Jean Marie Barnwell, Helen Shaver, John C. McGinley, Marvin J. McIntyre, Peter Boyle

- Sonoma Coast State Beach, Goat Rock, State Highway Route 1, Jenner

"If we're going to carry on a conversation, it'd help for you to talk."

Born to Kill
1947, RKO Radio Pictures
AKA: *Deadlier than the Male*, *Lady of Deceit*
A psychotic involves his bride in his acts of crime.

Director: Robert Wise
Screenwriters: Eve Greene, Richard Macaulay
Author: James Gunn *Deadlier Than the Male* (novel)
Art Directors: Albert S. D'Agostino, Walter E. Keller
Cinematographer: Robert De Grasse
Partial Cast: Lawrence Tierney, Claire Trevor, Walter Slezak

- San Francisco-Oakland Bay Bridge
- Ferry Building, The Embarcadero

The Boston Strangler
1968, 20th Century Fox
Account of the sex maniac and killer who terrified Boston in the 1960s.

Director: Richard Fleisher
Screenwriter: Edward Anhalt
Author: Gerold Frank (book)
Art Directors: Richard Day, Jack Martin Smith
Cinematographer: Richard H. Kline
Partial Cast: Tony Curtis, Henry Fonda, George Kennedy, Mike Kellin, Hurd Hatfield, Sally Kellerman

- Jackson Street between Sansome Street and Montgomery Street, Jackson Square District-pick-up shots of chase scene

Bottle Shock
2008, Freestyle Releasing
The story of the early days of modern California wine making featuring the now infamous, blind Paris wine tasting of 1976 that has come to be known as the "Judgment of Paris."

Director: Randall Miller
Screenwriters: Jody Slavin, Randall Miller, Ross Schwartz
Production Designer: Craig Stearns
Cinematographer: Mike Ozier
Partial Cast: Chris Pine, Alan Rickman, Bill Pullman

• Buena Vista Vineyards, 18000 Old Winery Road, Sonoma
• Chateau Montelena Vineyard, 1429 Tubbs Lane, Calistoga
• Knude Estate and Vineyards, 10155 Sonoma Highway, Kenwood
• Lincoln Street, Calistoga
• Sonoma Plaza, Sonoma
• Hotel Toscano, 20 East Spain Street, Sonoma

Boys and Girls
2000, Dimension Films
AKA: *Boys, Girls and a Kiss*
A friendship is put to the ultimate test when two best friends wind up in bed together.

Director: Robert Iscove
Screenwriters: Andrew Lowery, Andrew Miller (The Drews)
Production Designer: Marcia Hinds-Johnson
Art Director: Bo Johnson
Cinematographer: Ralf Bode
Partial Cast: Freddie Printz Jr., Claire Forlani, Jason Biggs, Amanda Detmer, Alyson Hannigan

• Doe Library, University of California Campus, Berkeley
• Valley Life Sciences Building, University of California Campus, Berkeley
• Marin Headlands, Golden Gate National Recreation Area
• Golden Gate Bridge
• Crookedest Street in the World, 1000 block of Lombard Street, Russian Hill District
• Sproul Plaza/Sather Gate, University of California Campus, Berkeley
• Kearny Street, between Vallejo Street and Broadway, Telegraph Hill District
• San Francisco-Oakland Bay Bridge
• Fisherman's Wharf District
• Ferry Building, The Embarcadero
• San Francisco City Hall, 1 Carlton B. Goodlett Place, Civic Center District
• Aquatic Park, San Francisco Maritime National Historic Park, Golden Gate National Recreation Area

• 628 Cole Street, Cole Valley District
• Brainwash, 1122 Folsom Street, South of Market District
• The Cypress Club Restaurant, 500 Jackson Street, Jackson Square District
• Various fraternity houses, University of California Campus, Berkeley
• Palace of Fine Arts, 3601 Lyon Street, Marina District
• Haight Street, Haight-Ashbury District

Brainwaves
1983, Motion Picture Marketing
The victim of a traffic accident undergoes an experimental treatment to regain her consciousness—with the result of living another person's trauma.

Director: Ulli Lommel
Screenwriters: Ulli Lommel, Buz Alexander, Suzanna Love
Art Director: Stephen E. Graff
Cinematographer: Jon Kranhouse, Ulli Lommel
Partial Cast: Keir Dullea, Suzanna Love, Vera Miles, Ryan Seitz, Percy Rodrigues, Paul Willson, Tony Curtis

• Golden Gate Bridge
• 700 Steiner Street, Western Addition District-Leila's apartment
• 1940 Webster Street, Pacific Heights District
• Mutual Food Shop, 1098 Jackson Street, Nob Hill District
• O'Farrell, Jones and Hyde Street Cable Car, intersection of Washington Street and Taylor Street-accident site
• Coit Tower, Pioneer Park, 1 Telegraph Hill Boulevard, Telegraph Hill District
• Pier 39, Waterfront
• Marin Headlands, Golden Gate National Recreation Area-fall site
• Toll both, Golden Gate Bridge

Breathless
1983, Orion Pictures
A small time Las Vegas hood captivates a French girl.

Director: Jim McBride
Screenwriters: L. M. Kit Carson, Jim McBride
Authors: Jean-Luc Godard, François Truffaut "À bout de souffle" (story)
Production Designer: Richard Sylbert
Cinematographer: Richard H. Kline
Partial Cast: Richard Gere, Valérie Kaprisky, Art Metrano

• University of California Campus, Berkeley

Broadway Bill
1934, Columbia

A horse trainer finds he has a winner on his hands.

Director: Frank Capra
Screenwriters: Mark Hellinger, Robert Riskin, Sidney Buchman
Cinematographer: Joseph Walker
Partial Cast: Myrna Loy, Warner Baxter, Walter Connolly, Helen Vinson, Margaret Hamilton, Jason Robards Sr., Lucille Ball, Ward Bond, Alan Hale

• Tanforan Racetrack, El Camino Real, San Bruno

BROADWAY BILL: SOCIETY SWELLS

Filming for *Broadway Bill* started at the Tanforan Racetrack on June 17, 1934. Local banker William H. Crocker gathered many of his society friends from San Francisco and the Peninsula. Additionally, 1,000 paid extras used in the film donated their salaries to benefit Children's Hospital. During filming on July 4, 1934, the track was opened free (it had been closed during filming) to the public to watch filming. The movie premièred on December 20,1934 at The Orpheum Theatre in San Francisco. Tanforan, opened in 1899, was a project of Prince Andre Poniatowski, a self-proclaimed heir to the Polish throne, with fiscal assistance from banker William H. Crocker. The racecourse's lush landscaping was on par with European equals, unusual in America in the prince's eyes. In 1942 the facility became known as the Tanforan Assembly Center, housing more than 8,000 persons of Japanese descent after the attack on Pearl Harbor. The track structures burned in 1964; the mall sited there today opened in 1971.

Burnt Offerings
1976, Metro Goldwyn Mayer and United Artists
The morbid story of a living house that nourishes itself on its tenants.

Director: Dan Curtis
Screenwriters: William F. Nolan, Dan Curtis

Production Designer: Eugène Lourié
Cinematographer: Jacques Marquette
Partial Cast: Karen Black, Oliver Reed, Burgess Meredith, Eileen Heckart, Bette Davis

• Dunsmuir House and Gardens, 2960 Peralta Oaks Court, Oakland

Bullitt
1968, Warner Brothers
A policeman is determined to find out who killed a witness under his protection.

Director: Peter Yates
Screenwriter: Alan Trustman, Harry Kleiner
Author: Robert L. Fish *Mute Witness* (novel)
Art Director: Albert Brenner
Cinematographer: William A. Fraker
Partial Cast: Steve McQueen, Jacqueline Bisset, Robert Vaughn, Don Gordon, Robert Duvall, Simon Oakland

• 1153-1157 Taylor Street-as Bullitt's apartment
• Mark Hopkins Hotel, 999 California Street, Nob Hill District-driveway
• Coffee Cantata, 2030 Union Street, Cow Hollow District
• Grace Cathedral, 1100 California Street, Nob Hill District
• 2700 Vallejo, Pacific Heights District
• Bimbo's 365 Club, 1025 Columbus Avenue, Russian Hill District
• Kezar Stadium, Golden Gate Park
• Embarcadero Freeway, Waterfront
• Army and Navy YMCA, 166 The Embarcadero
• Enrico's Sidewalk Cafe, 504 Broadway, Telegraph Hill District
• Fillmore Street, between Broadway and Vallejo, Pacific Heights District
• San Francisco General Hospital, 1001 Potrero Avenue, Mission District
• Guadalupe Canyon Parkway, San Bruno Mountain, Brisbane and Daly City-car chase
• Thunderbolt Hotel, 401 East Millbrae Avenue, Millbrae

Burglar
1987, Warner Brothers
A retired burglar goes straight by running a bookstore but is forced out of retirement to clear her name.

Director: Hugh Wilson
Screenwriters: Joseph Loeb III, Matthew Weisman, Hugh Wilson
Author: Lawrence Block (novels)
Production Designer: Todd Hallowell
Art Director: Michael Cornenblith
Cinematographer: William A. Fraker
Partial Cast: Whoppi Goldberg, Bob Goldthwait, G. W. Bailey, Lesley Ann Warren
Local Cast: TV anchor Elaine Corral, TV anchor Dennis Richmond

• 845 California Street, Nob Hill District-Deco apartment building
• 298 Missouri Street, Potrero Hill District-Bernice's home
• California Academy of Sciences, Steinhart Aquarium, 55 Music Concourse Drive, Golden Gate Park
• Green Valley Restaurant, 510 Green Street, Telegraph Hill District
• Stern Grove, 19th Avenue at Sloat Boulevard, Parkside District

Butterflies Are Free
1972, Columbia Pictures
A blind man wants a place of his own but his mother interferes, much to the consternation of his kooky girlfriend.

Director: Milton Katselas
Screenwriter: Leonard Gershe
Production Designer: Robert Clatsworthy
Cinematographer: Charles B. Lang
Partial Cast: Goldie Hawn, Edward Albert, Eileen Heckart

• 1355-1359 Kearny Street, Telegraph Hill District
• Perry's Bar, 1944 Union Street, Cow Hollow District
• City Lights Bookstore, 261 Columbus Street, Jackson Square District

CITY LIGHTS BOOKSELLERS AND PUBLISHERS

City Lights is "a lighthouse of international literature and radical thought," according to National Public Radio reporter Cy Musiker. An icon, City Lights Booksellers & Publishers resides in a three-story triangular plan brick building constructed in 1907. It was designated a city landmark in 2001 due to its cultural importance. Initially an Italian bookstore A. Cavalli & Co., Beat poet Lawrence Ferlinghetti and Peter D. Martin founded the current incarnation based on selling only paperbacks in June 1953 with the initial imprint Pocket Poet Series. The independent firm specializes in world literature, the arts, and progressive politics.

The Caddy
1953, Paramount
A gifted golfer acts as coach and caddy for a friend.

Director: Norman Taurog
Screenwriters: Danny Arnold, Edmund L. Hartman, Ken England
Art Directors: Franz Bachelin, Hal Pereira
Cinematographer: Daniel F. Fapp
Partial Cast: Dean Martin, Jerry Lewis, Donna Reed

• Miscellaneous views of San Francisco from a Telegraph Hill District rooftop

The Caine Mutiny
1954, Columbia
A U.S. Naval Captain displays signs of instability and he faces court martial for mutiny.

Director: Edward Dmytryk
Screenwriters: Stanley Roberts, Michael Blankfort
Author: Herman Wouk (novel)
Production Designer: Rudolph Sternad
Art Director: Cary Odell
Cinematographer: Franz Planer
Partial Cast: Humphrey Bogart, José Ferrer, Van Johnson, Fred MacMurray, Tom Tully, E. G. Marshall, Lee Marvin, Claude Akins, Jerry Paris

• Pier 1, The Embarcadero, San Francisco
• San Francisco-Oakland Bay Bridge
• Golden Gate Bridge
• Building 1, conference room, second floor, Treasure Island-as court room set

FRED MACMURRAY

Frederick Martin MacMurray Jr. was born to parents Maleta (Martin) and Frederick MacMurray in 1908. He was born in Kankakee, Illinois, but his family moved to Beaver Dam, Wisconsin, where he graduated from the local high school in 1926. His father was a concert violinist, so it was no accident that Fred was musically inclined and played several instruments including the saxophone. He attended Carroll College in Waukesha, Wisconsin planning to become a musician. In 1930 he appeared on Broadway and in 1934 Paramount tapped him for a seven-year players contract—despite his never having had an acting lesson. He married Lillian Lamont in 1936 and they adopted two children. She died in 1953, and the next year he wed actress June Haver. (They also adopted two children.) His performance in The Caine Mutiny showed that he could play against type as a cynical and spineless military man. He appeared in numerous movies but a standout was the Oscar-winning *The Apartment* (1960) with Shirley MacLaine and Jack Lemmon. In 1960 he starred in the popular television series *My Three Sons* that ran for 12 seasons. During that period he also appeared in two Walt Disney comedies *The Absent Minded Professor* (1961) and *Son of Flubber* (1963). He retired from the entertainment business to his Sonoma County ranch in 1978 and died in 1991. MacMurray's connection to the Bay Area was a long one. He purchased a 1,500-acre tract of land on Westside Road in Healdsburg adjacent to the Russian River in 1941. It was called Twin Valley Ranch and there he raised cattle. Today the ranch is home to daughter Kate MacMurray and now operates under the Gallo label as the MacMurray Ranch winery.

The Californians
2005, Fabrication Films
Satire about a real estate mogul and his environmentalist sister who launches a campaign to stop him.

Director: Jonathan Parker
Screenwriters: Jonathan Parker, Catherine DiNapoli
Author: Henry James *The Bostonians* (book)
Production Designer: Thomas Carnegie
Art Director: Lisa Clark
Cinematographer: Steven Fierberg
Partial Cast: Noah Wyle, Illeana Douglas, Kate Mara, Cloris Leachman, Valerie Perrine

• State Highway Route 1
• Woodlands Market, 735 College Avenue, Kentfield
• Stone Tree Golf Course, 9 Stone Tree Lane, Novato
• Baker Beach, Presidio, Golden Gate National Recreation Area
• Crissy Field, Presidio, Golden Gate National Recreation Area
• Golden Gate Bridge
• Intersection of Second Street and Folsom Street, South of Market District
• Roy's Redwoods Preserve, Nicasio Valley Road, San Geronimo-woods
• Old St. Hillary's Open Space Preserve, Tiburon-development site
• Jose Patio, Stinson Beach-beach house

MARINCELLO

Although the storyline of *The Californians* is based on Henry James' novel *The Bostonians*, there is another true local story that was woven into the script. A vast tract of 2,100 pristine acres was sold by the U.S. military to a private developer in the 1960s. The hilly area, now known as the Marin Headlands, Golden Gate National Recreation Area in southern Marin County overlooking the Golden Gate, was to be the site of a planned community called Marincello to house some 30,000 people in 50 apartment towers, hundreds of homes and townhouses. Additionally there was to be retail and light manufacturing on the site. As a series of legal situations played out against the developer, the land was sold to the Nature Conservancy in 1970 and transferred to the GGNRA for all people to share and enjoy.

The Candidate
1972, Warner Brothers
A candidate for U.S. Senate from California has little hope of winning the seat so he challenges the establishment.

Director: Michael Ritchie
Screenwriter: Jeremy Larner
Production Designer: Gene Callahan
Cinematographers: Victor J. Kemper, John Korty
Partial Cast: Robert Redford, Peter Boyle, Don Porter, Allen Garfield, Karen Carlson, Quinn Redeker, Morgan Upton, Melvyn Douglas, Natalie Wood

• San Francisco City Hall, 1 Carlton B. Goodlett Place, Civic Center District-front steps
• KBHK TV 44 Studios Building, 420 Taylor Street, Union Square District-sidewalk shot and lobby
• St. Francis Hotel, 335 Powell Street, Union Square District
• Montgomery Street, from Market Street to California Street, Financial District-parade
• Eastridge Mall, 2200 Eastridge Loop, San Jose
• Corbit's Garage, 3880 Gravenstein Highway South, Sebastopol
• Sande Schlumberger Gallery, Santa Rosa

- Immigration Center, Angel Island, Golden Gate National Recreation Area-burning of several residences
- Howarth Park, Summerfield Road, Santa Rosa-rally
- Marin Art and Garden Center, 30 Sir Francis Drake Boulevard, Ross
- Sather Gate, University of California Campus, Berkeley
- Fisherman's Wharf District
- Paramount Theater of the Arts, 2025 Broadway, Oakland-exterior marquee and interior lobby as campaign headquarters

ART DECO PARAMOUNT THEATER

Now known as Paramount Theater of the Arts this elaborate example of Depression-era Art Deco movie palace, completed in 1931, was the creation of the architectural firm of Miller and Pflueger. An exuberant exterior tile mural hints at the monumentally scaled soaring lobby that features a luminous glass sculpture depicting cascading water. But it is the 3,000-seat auditorium that is the true sanctuary to the Deco style where elaborately carved wall panels soar to the ceiling in glistening metallic colors. The building has garnered State Historic Landmark number 884.

Can't Stop the Music
1980, Associated Film Distributors
A pseudo autobiography of disco's singing group The Village People.

Director: Nancy Walker
Screenwriters: Allan Carr, Bronte Woodard
Art Director: Harold Michelson
Cinematographer: Bill Butler
Partial Cast: Alex Briley, David Hodo, Glenn Hughes

- Golden Gate Bridge
- Galleria, 101 Henry Adams Street, Potrero Hill District

Cardiac Arrest
1980, Film Ventures International
A murderer is terrorizing San Francisco as he tracks down victims and removes their hearts.

Director: Murray Mintz
Screenwriter: Murray Mintz
Cinematographer: Jon Else
Partial Cast: Garry Goodrow, Michael Paul Chan, Max Gail
Local Cast: TV anchor Dave McElhatton

- The Rapahel Hotel, 386 Geary Street, Union Square District
- 240 Santa Clara Avenue St. Francis Wood District
- Hall of Justice, 850 Bryant Street, South of Market District
- Portsmouth Square, Chinatown District
- Ralph K. Davies Hospital, 45 Castro Street, Duboce Triangle District
- Grace Cathedral, 1100 California Street, Nob Hill District-exterior
- Intersection of Broadway and Columbus Avenue, Telegraph Hill District
- Schumate's Pharmacy, 2390 Sutter Street, Pacific Heights District
- 875 Vermont Street, Potrero Hill District
- Rustic Bridge, Stow Lake, Golden Gate Park
- The Embarcadero
- Gramercy Towers, 1177 California Street, Nob Hill District
- California Academy of Sciences, 55 Music Concourse Drive, Golden Gate Park
- Music Concourse, Golden Gate Park
- Malm Luggage, 222 Grant Avenue, Union Square District
- Safeway, 2300 16th Street, Potrero Hill District
- Muni bus storage yard, Mission Bay District

Case of the Curious Bride
1935, Warner Brothers
This Perry Mason mystery solves how a widow is being blackmailed by her dead husband.

Director: Michael Curtiz
Screenwriters: Erle Stanley Gardner, Tom Reed, Brown Holmes
Art Director: Carl J. Weyl
Cinematographer: David Abel
Partial Cast: Warren William, Margaret Lindsay, Donald Woods, Calire Dodd, Errol Flynn

- Fisherman's Wharf District
- The Earl Warren State Office Building, 350 McAllister Street, Civic Center
- Lotta's Fountain, intersection of Kearny Street and Market Street, Financial District
- Van Ness Avenue
- Intersection of Laguna Street and Washington Street, Pacific Heights District

Casualties of War
1989, Columbia and Tri-Star
Inspired by a true incident during the Vietnam War, this story tells of a

soldier shocked by his comrades who kidnap and rape a village girl.

Director: Brian De Palma
Screenwriter: David Rabe
Author: Daniel Lang (book)
Production Designer: Wolf Kroeger
Art Director: Bernard Hides
Cinematographer: Stephen H. Burum
Partial Cast: Michael J. Fox, Sean Penn, Don Harvey

• Muni Metro N Line, Duboce Park, Duboce Triangle District
• Muni Metro J Line, Dolores Park, Mission District

Catch the Heat
1987, M'Amsel Tea Entertainment
A one-woman strike force heats up the war on drug trafficking.

Director: Joel Silberg
Screenwriter: Sterling Silliphant
Production Designer: Jorge Marchegiani
Cinematographer: Nissim Nitcho
Partial Cast: David Dukes, Tiana Alexandra, Rod Steiger

• Golden Gate Bridge
• Merchant Road, Presidio, Golden Gate National Recreation Area
• 2300 block of Hyde Street with Powell/Hyde Cable Car, Russian Hill District
• 900 block of Grant Avenue, Chinatown District
• Terminal 1, San Francisco International Airport

Cats and Dogs: The Revenge of Kitty Galore
2010, Warner Brothers
The ongoing war between the canine and feline species is put on hold when they join forces to thwart a rogue cat spy with her own sinister plans.

Director: Brad Peyton
Screenwriters: Ron J. Friedman, Steve Bencich, John Requa, Glenn Ficarra
Production Designer: Rusty Smith
Art Director: Sandra Tanaka
Cinematographer: Steven Poster
Partial Voice Cast: Bette Midler, Chris O'Donnell, Jack McBrayer

• San Francisco-Oakland Bay Bridge
• Coit Tower, Pioneer Park, 1 Telegraph Hill Boulevard, Telegraph Hill District
• Alcatraz Federal Prison, Alcatraz Island, Golden Gate National Recreation Area

Cell 2455, Death Row
1955, Columbia
AKA: *Cell Block*
Convicted for a real life rape and murder, Caryl Chessman uses the court appeal process to his advantage for 10 years before succumbing to his execution.

Director: Fred F. Sears
Screenwriters: Caryl Chessman, Jack DeWitt
Author: Caryl Chessman (book)
Art Director: Robert Peterson
Cinematographer: Fred Jackman Jr.
Partial Cast: William Campbell, Robert Campbell, Kathryn Grant, Vince Edwards

• San Quentin State Prison, San Quentin

Chalk
1996, Tenderloin Action Group
Two sons of a pool hustler work a Richmond pool hall and one takes on a bet that could ruin his family.

Director: Rob Nilsson
Screenwriter: Don Bajema
Production Designer: Lee Putzer
Art Director: Stacie Krajchir
Cinematographer: Mickey Freeman
Partial Cast: Don Bajema, Tim Alexander, Denise Concetta Caveliene, Destiny Costa

• Tenderloin District

ROB NILSSON

Independent director, actor, writer and producer Nilsson is of Norwegian descent who was born in 1939, in Rhinelander, Wisconsin. He moved to California in 1953 and currently resides in San Francisco. He is known as the creator of a reality film style called "direct action" that seeks emotional depth and authenticity. His Bay Area works as a director include *Chalk*, where between 1992 and 2005, Nilsson worked with his San Francisco Tenderloin YGroup (formerly known as Tenderloin Action Group), conducting workshop acting classes and making feature films with the homeless, inner city residents, local actors and all comers. From a technical standpoint he was a pioneer in the techniques of video to film transfer that led to today's digital world. His other locally filmed works include *Signal 7* (1983), the first small format video feature to be enlarged to film format; *On the Edge* (1985) with Bruce Dern and *Heat and Sunlight* (1987) that won the Grand Jury Prize at the Sundance Film Festival. He also appeared in *Copycat* (1995) as the SWAT Commander. In 2005 the Pacific Film Archive hosted the World Premiere of his film *Security*, a direct action feature film produced during his residency at the University of California, Berkeley.

The Changeling
2008, Universal
The mother of a missing boy takes on the LAPD when it stubbornly tries to pass off an obvious impostor as her missing child.

Director: Clint Eastwood
Screenwriter: J. Michael Straczynski
Production Designer: James J. Murakami
Art Director: Patrick M. Sullivan Jr.
Cinematographer: Tom Steern
Partial Cast: Angelina Jolie, Colm Feore, Amy Ryan

• San Quentin State Prison, San Quentin

Chan is Missing
1982, New Yorker
Two cabbies search for a mysterious character who has disappeared with their money. They go on a journey that tells of the many problems experienced by Chinese-Americans trying to assimilate into contemporary American society.

Director: Wayne Wang
Screenwriters: Isaac Cronin, Wayne Wang
Cinematographer: Michael G. Chin
Partial Cast: Wood Moy, Marc Hayashi, Laureen Chew, Peter Wang

• Ross Alley, Chinatown District

WAYNE WANG

Hong Kong-born director Wang (born 1949) grew up in a high-rise apartment in Kowloon, the most congested part of Hon Kong. His parents were refugees from Jinan, a rail hub in northern China's Shandong Province. Over time his father tried several businesses and finally prospered with an import/export company. Wang graduated high school from the Sister of the Immaculate Conception, a Catholic private boys school run by Irish Jesuits. He emigrated to the United States in 1967 at age 17 to attend Foothill College in the Peninsula's Los Altos Hills. He had thoughts of medical school but went into studying painting, filmmaking and television at the California College of Arts and Crafts in Oakland. He briefly returned to Hong Kong but went back to San Francisco with *Chan is Missing* as his first film project (with an all Asian-American cast producer and director) that became an art house favorite with its funny and quirky look at San Francisco's Chinatown. This was followed by the subtle *Dim Sum* in 1985 and *Eat a Bowl of Tea*, set in New York's Post World War II Chinatown, which was released in 1989. The next year he released *Life is Cheap...but the toilet paper is expensive* (1990) and in 1993 the locally shot *The Joy Luck Club* from Amy Tan's novel about four Chinese-American mothers and their difficulties in bringing up their American-born daughters. At this time he and his wife Cora Miao, a Hong Kong-born actress (and former Miss Hong Kong), have bi-coastal residences in New York and San Francisco.

Charlie Chan and the Curse of the Dragon Queen
1981, United Artists
The villainous Dragon Queen puts a curse on Chan and his descendants.

Director: Clive Donner
Screenwriters: David Axelrod, Stan Burns
Author: Earl Derr Biggers (characters)
Cinematographer: Paul Lohmann

Partial Cast: Peter Ustinov, Lee Grant, Brian Keith, Angie Dickinson, Roddy McDowall, Michelle Pfeiffer

• Financial District
• Golden Gate Bridge
• Stanford Court Hotel, 905 California Street, Nob Hill District
• Golden Gate Park Riding Academy, Golden Gate Park
• Ocean Beach, Golden Gate National Recreation Area
• Fort Baker, Marin Headlands, Golden Gate National Recreation Area

Charlie Chan at Treasure Island
1939, 20th Century Fox
Charlie investigates a phony psychic during the 1939 Golden Gate International Exposition on San Francisco's Treasure Island that leads him to expose a suicide as a murder.

Director: Norman Foster
Screenwriter: John Larkin
Author: Earl Derr Biggers (characters)
Cinematographer: Virgil Miller
Partial Cast: Sidney Toler, Victor Sen Yung, Cesar Romero

• 1939 Golden Gate International Exposition, Treasure Island

Charlie Chan's Secret
1936, 20th Century Fox
The heir to a fortune, who was thought to be drowned, appears and is then murdered.

Director: Gordon Wiles
Screenwriters: Robert Ellis, Helen Logan, Joseph Hoffman
Author: Earl Derr Biggers
Art Directors: Duncan Cramer, Albert Hogsett
Cinematographer: Rudolph Mate'
Partial Cast: Warner Oland, Rosina Lawrence, Charles Quigley, Henrietta Crosman

• China Clipper flies over San Francisco

Cheaper by the Dozen
2003, 20th Century Fox
With his wife away on a book tour, a father of 12 must handle a new job and his unstable brood.

Director: Shawn Levy

Screenwriters: Sam Harper, Joel Cohen, Alec Sokolow
Authors: Frank B. Gilbreth Jr., Ernestine Gilbreth Carey (novel)
Production Designer: Nina Ruscio
Art Director: Scott Meehan
Cinematographer: Jonathan Brown
Partial Cast: Steve Martin, Bonnie Hunt, Hilary Duff

• Two Rock Ranch, 1051 Walker Road, Petaluma
• Railroad Square, Fourth Street, Santa Rosa

Cherish
2002, Fine Line Features
After a martini-induced rampage, a fantasy-prone young woman is placed under house arrest.

Director: Finn Taylor
Screenwriter: Finn Taylor
Production Designer: Don Day
Art Director: Guy Harrington
Cinematographer: Barry Stone
Partial Cast: Robin Tunney, Tim Blake Nelson, Brad Hunt

• Berkeley
• Oakland
• Intersection of 20th Street and Illinois Street, Potrero Hill District

China Clipper
1936, Warner Brothers
An aviator neglects his wife while building up a trans-Pacific aviation link business.

Director: Ray Enright
Screenwriters: Frank Wead, Norman Reilly Raine
Art Director: Max Parker
Cinematographer: Arthur Edeson
Partial Cast: Pat O'Brien, Humphrey Bogart

• Aerial panorama of Ferry Building and waterfront
• Aerial panorama of San Francisco-Oakland Bay Bridge
• Aerial panorama of Golden Gate Bridge

CHINA CLIPPER

The first flying boat craft was launched in 1935 as Pan American World Airways' *China Clipper*, a moniker harkening back to the fast transoceanic sailing ships that plied the oceans of the past. The inaugural flight journeyed from Alameda's Naval Marina (now a state historic landmark) and eventually to Manila several days later, having made four stops along the way to distribute and pick up airmail. The ships were incredibly expensive to build and the fare was only available to the super rich like the Concorde of the latter 20th century. Treasure Island's Clipper Cove was originally opened in 1939 with the idea of using San Francisco Bay as a commercial landing strip for planes, including airships, but that did not play out. The cove was used by the Clippers during the Golden Gate International Exposition of 1939-1940 and is a marina today. One of the few surviving examples can be seen at the Oakland Aviation Museum at the Oakland International Airport. Similar craft were also seen in the Bay Area filmed movies *Charlie Chan's Secret* (1936), *China Clipper* (1936), *Too Hot to Handle* (1938), *Raiders of the Lost Ark* (1981), and *Indiana Jones and the Temple of Doom* (1984).

The Chinatown Kid
1977, World Northal Pictures
Struggling to survive murderous gang wars, a young martial arts street fighter successfully takes on all challengers.

Screenwriters: Cheh Chang, Kuang Ni
Art Director: Johnny Tsao
Cinematographer: Mu-To Kung
Partial Cast: Sheng Fu, Chien Sun, Jenny Tseng, Lung Wei Wang, Philip Kwok, Shirley Yu, Meng Lo, Yin-Yin Shaw

• Dragon Gateway to Chinatown, intersection of Grant Avenue and Bush Street, Chinatown District

Chinatown at Midnight
1949, Columbia Pictures
When a thief is caught in the act of stealing antique vases, and murders two Chinese men, a manhunt is set off in Chinatown.

Director: Seymour Friedman
Screenwriters: Robert Libott, Frank Burt
Art Director: Paul Palmentola
Cinematographer: Henry Freulich
Partial Cast: Hurd Hatfield, Jean Willes, Tom Powers

• Chinatown Telephone Exchange Building, 743 Washington Street, Chinatown District

A Christmas Without Snow
1980, Columbia Broadcasting System
A recently divorced mother looks for a new life and joins a church choir where she experiences several life lessons.

Director: John Korty
Screenwriters: John Korty, Richard Beban, Judith Anne Nielsen
Author: John Korty (story)
Art Director: Don De Fina
Cinematographer: Mike Fash
Partial Cast: Michael Learned, John Houseman

• 1100 block of Kearny Street, Telegraph Hill District
• BART entrance, Market Street
• San Francisco Public Schools Administration, 135 Van Ness Avenue, Civic Center District
• 595 Market Street, South of Market District-office building lobby
• 23-33 Linda Street, Mission District-Zoe's residence
• The ship *Ellen*, Sailing Ship Restaurant, Pier 42, The Embarcadero
• Trinity Lutheran Church, 722 South Van Ness Avenue, Mission District
• Tourist Club, 30 Ridge Avenue, Mt. Tamalpais Park, Mill Valley-hiking club
• Houseboats, Sausalito
• Union Square, 333 Post Street
• Huntington Park, California Street, Nob Hill District

Chu Chu and the Philly Flash
1981, 20th Century Fox
A female street entertainer and a homeless man vie for a lost briefcase.

Director: David Lowell Rich
Screenwriters: Henry Barrow, Barbara Dana
Production Designer: Daniel A. Lomino
Cinematographer: Victor J. Kemper
Partial Cast: Alan Arkin, Carol Burnett, Jack Worden, Danny Aiello, Danny Glover, Ruth Buzzi, Lou Jacobi
Local Cast: Artist and puppeteer Ralph Chessé

• Oakland-downtown razed urban buildings
• Oakland Central Train Station, intersection of 16th Street and Wood Street, Oakland-as bus depot
• Intersection of Second Street and Harrison Street, South of Market District-street brawl

• Sailors' Union of the Pacific Building, 450 Harrison Street, South of Market District
• 832 Carolina Street, Potrero Hill District-Chu Chu's residence
• Intersection of 22nd Street and Carolina Street, Potrero Hill District
• Ferry Building, The Embarcadero-briefcase drops to pavement
• Fairmont Hotel, 950 Mason Street, Nob Hill District
• Cable car on California Street, Nob Hill, Chinatown and Financial Districts
• Mission Creek, Mission Bay District-houseboat
• 340 Division Street, South of Market District-diner
• BART/Muni entrance, intersection of Market Street and Fourth Street, South of Market District
• Alta Plaza Park, Pacific Heights District-carnival venue
• Flood Mansion, 2222 Broadway, Pacific Heights-as Russian Consulate
• Embarcadero Freeway, The Embarcadero-driving to Oakland

DANNY GLOVER

Outspoken political activist, actor, director and producer Danny LeBern Glover was born in San Francisco on July 22, 1946. His postal worker parents, Carrie (Hunley) and James Glover, were both involved in union organizing and the NAACP. He attended George Washington High School in the Outer Richmond District, graduating in 1964, and then San Francisco State University majoring in economics. While there he participated in forcing the creation of a Department of Black Studies, the first such in the United States. An alumnus of the Black Actors' Workshop at the American Conservatory Theater, Glover initially started his theater career as a stage actor. He debuted in film appearing as an inmate in *Escape from Alcatraz* (1979). Many appearances followed including *Out* (1982), and in Alice Walker's *The Color Purple* (1985) as Celie's husband, played by Whoppi Goldberg. In 1990 he garnered his first top-billing role in *Predator 2* as Lt. Mike Harrigan. As sometimes happens Francis Ford Coppola did not credit him for his appearance as Judge Tyrone Kipler in *The Rainmaker* (1997). He appeared in scenes of *How Stella Got Her Groove Back* (1998) but as it happened they ended up on the cutting room floor. He was married to former jazz singer Asake Bomani, from 1975 through 1999.

City of Angels
1998, Warner Brothers
An angel is spotted by a doctor in an operating room.

Director: Brad Silberling
Screenwriters: Wim Wenders, Peter Handke, Richard Reitlinger, Dana Stevens
Author: Wim Wenders *Wings of Desire* (screenplay)
Production Designer: Lilly Kilvert
Art Director: John Warnke
Cinematographer: John Seale
Partial Cast: Nicolas Cage, Meg Ryan, Andre Braugher, Dennis Franz, Colin Feore, Robin Bartlett

• San Francisco Public Library, 100 Larkin Street, Civic Center

Class Action
1991, 20th Century Fox
Estranged father and daughter lawyers find themselves at odds when they face each other in court.

Director: Michael Apted
Screenwriters: Carolyn Shelby, Christopher Ames, Samantha Shad
Production Designer: Todd Hallowell
Art Director: Mark Billerman
Cinematographer: Conrad L. Hall
Partial Cast: Gene Hackman, Mary Elizabeth Mastrantonio, Colin Friels, Lawrence Fishburne, Joanna Merlin, Donald Moffat
Local Cast: Politicians Mayor Art Agnos, Angela Alioto, Harry Britt

• San Francisco City Hall, 1 Carlton B. Goodlett Place, Civic Center District-exterior
• 80 Hawthorne Street, South of Market District-as law firm
• 101 California Street, Financial District-entry to office building
• 2700 Scott Street, Pacific Heights District-Maggie's residence
• Beach Chalet, 1000 Great Highway, Golden Gate Park-as dance hall
• Vesuvio Cafe, 255 Columbus, Jackson Square District-as Ward law firm
• San Francisco City Hall, Board of Supervisors Chamber, 1 Carlton B. Goodlett Place, Civic Center District-as courtroom
• 24th Street and York Street Mini Park, Mission District
• Old Mission Dolores, 320 Dolores Street, Mission District-funeral
• Bix Restaurant, 56 Gold Street, Telegraph Hill District

• 11100 Petaluma-Pt. Reyes Road, Nicasio-farm
• Tech Mart, Great America Parkway, Santa Clara-as Argo Motors
• San Francisco Art Institute, 800 Chestnut Street, Russian Hill District

SAN FRANCISCO CITY HALL

The civic epicenter of government was the focus of a flap when the makers of *Bicentennial Man* wanted to rent the newly renovated building's Board of Supervisors Chambers. The building underwent a $300 million makeover that took many years after incurring damage from the 1989 Loma Prieta Earthquake. These anxieties came true on June 17, 1999 when filming was taking place in the in the rotunda. Very hot lights set off two sprinklers flooding corridors and making the grand marble staircase into a water cascade. Ten years earlier there was a precursor to this concern when 20th Century Fox was initially denied use of the ornate Board of Supervisors Chamber for filming courtroom scenes for *Class Action*; use of the stately wood paneled Legislative Chamber for filming was historically denied. This stemmed from the general feeling that film companies did not treat spaces with respect. But, as a push to the city being used for more on location filming, the question was put to a vote by the supervisors and the film company prevailed. With an insurance policy in hand, and the threat of Hollywood not using San Francisco in the future, 20th Century Fox got its way.

Clifford
1994, Columbia
AKA: *Jurassic Boy*
A ten-year-old troublemaker puts his family, and others, through hell.
Director: Paul Flaherty
Screenwriters: Jay Dee Rock, Bobby von Hayes
Production Designer: Russell Christian
Art Director: Bernie Cutler
Cinematographer: John A. Alonzo
Partial Cast: Martin Short, Charles Grodin, Mary Steenburgen, Dabney Coleman

• City Lights Bookstore, 261 Columbus Street, Jackson Square District

Close to My Heart
1951, Warner Brothers
A couple tries to adopt a baby but the husband runs afoul of the birth line.

Director: William Keighley
Screenwriters: William Keighley, James R. Webb
Author: James R. Webb *A Baby for Midge* (novel)
Art Director: Leo K. Kuter
Cinematographer: Robert Burks
Partial Cast: Ray Milland, Gene Tierney

• San Quentin State Prison, San Quentin

Cloud Atlas
2012, Warner Brothers
Multiple plotlines set across six different eras explore how the actions and consequences of individuals impact one another.

Directors: Tom Tykwer, Andy Wachowski, Lana Wachowski
Screenwriters: Tom Tykwer, Andy Wachowski, Lana Wachowski
Author: David Mitchell (novel)
Cinematographer:
Partial Cast: Tom Hanks, Halle Berry, Jim Broadbent

• Panorama of Financial District with Transamerica Pyramid-as circa 1973

Coach Carter
2005, Paramount
AKA: *All Day Long*
Controversy surrounds high school basketball coach Ken Carter after he benches his entire team for breaking their academic contract with him.

Director: Thomas Carter
Screenwriters: Mark Schwahn, John Gutins
Production Designer: Carlos Barbosa
Art Director: Tim Beach
Cinematographer: Sharon Meir
Partial Cast: Samuel L. Jackson
Local Cast: TV Reporter Mark Jones

• Golden Gate Bridge

The Cock-Eyed World
1929, Fox
AKA: *The Cockeyed World*
Two Marines are sent to a South Sea island where they vie for a local girl.

Director: Raoul Walsh

Screenwriters: Maxwell Anderson, Tom Barry, William Mizner, Laurence Stallings, Raoul Walsh, William K. Wells
Cinematographer: Arthur Edeson
Partial Cast: Victor McLaglen, Edmund Lowe, Lili Damita

• Mare Island, Vallejo
• USS *Henderson* in San Francisco Bay

Colma: the Musical
2006, Lionsgate
Best pals fresh out of high school explore a new world of part-time mall jobs and crashing college parties. As revelations and romances challenge their relationships with one another and their parents, they must assess how to best follow their dreams.

Director: Richard Wong
Screenwriters: H. P. Mendoza, Richard Wong
Cinematographer: Richard Wong
Art Direction: Vedo Florez
Partial Cast: Jake Moreno, H. P. Mendoza, L. A. Rengen, Sigrid Sutter, Brian Raffi, Larry Soriano, Gigi Guizado, Jim Wierzba, Kat Kneisel

• Miscellaneous San Francisco locations leading out of the city to the south
• Target, 5001 Junipero Serra Boulevard, Colma
• Lincoln Park Market, 2955 Clement Street, Outer Richmond District
• Java on Ocean Coffee House, 1700 Ocean Avenue, Ingleside District
• BART Station, 365 D Street, Colma
• Italian Cemetery, 540 F Street, Colma
• Mission Street, Colma
• Malloy's Tavern, 1655 Mission Road, Colma-bar

Colossus: The Forbin Project
1969, Universal Pictures
AKA: *Colossus 1980*, *The Day the World Changed Hands* and *The Forbin Project*
An artificially intelligent computer is created and reveals its sinister agenda.

Director: Joseph Sargent
Screenwriter: James Bridges
Author: Dennis F. Jones *Colossus* (novel)
Art Directors: Alexander Golitzen, John J. Lloyd
Cinematographer: Gene Polito
Partial Cast: Eric Braeden, Susan Clark, Gordon Pinsent, William Schallert

• Lawrence Hall of Science, 1 Centennial Drive, University of California Campus, Berkeley

The Competition
1980, Columbia
Competing pianists are torn between love and ambition.

Director: Joel Oliansky
Screenwriters: Joel Oliansky, William Sackman
Production Designer: Dale Hennesy
Cinematographer: Richard H. Kline
Partial Cast: Richard Dryfuss, Amy Irving, Lee Remick

• Golden Gate Bridge
• Hotel Del Sol, 3100 Webster Street, Marina District-motel
• Koshland Mansion, 3800 Washington Street, Presidio Heights District
• California Academy of Sciences, 55 Music Concourse Drive, Golden Gate Park
• Mark Hopkins Hotel, 999 California Street, Nob Hill District-exterior and lobby
• Steps at intersection of Taylor Street and Vallejo Street, Russian Hill District
• Union Street, Cow Hollow District-defection site
• Lovers Lane, Presidio
• Wharf Wax Life Museum, 145 Jefferson Street, Fisherman's Wharf District

AMY IRVING

Amy Davis Irving was born on September 10, 1953 in Palo Alto. Her father was a professor in the San Francisco State College drama department who, with his wife Pricilla (Pointer), co-founded the prestigious San Francisco Actor's Workshop in 1952. The youngest of three children, she grew up in San Francisco in the Golden Gate Heights section of the Sunset District initially, and later in the nearby Forest Hill District. It would have been difficult not to have some sort of career in the theater as she was constantly exposed to the medium through her parents work. Her first stage appearance was at age two in a play that her father directed. She was sent to the Professional Children's School in New York City in preparation for higher learning. She received training at San Francisco's American Conservatory Theater appearing in several productions followed by further work at the London Academy of Music and Dramatic Arts where she graduated in the mid-1970s. Shortly thereafter she was cast as Sue Snell in the hit film *Carrie* (1976) by horror master Stephen King. Her brush with the Oscars occurred when she was nominated for Best Supporting Actress as the character Hadass in the Barbra Streisand directed/written vehicle *Yentyl* in 1983. Her career has threaded in and out of the stage, TV and film over time. She was married to high profile director and producer Steven Spielberg between 1985 and 1989 and has been married twice since, more recently to director Kenneth Bowser. For *The Competition* she went through rigorous work to make her keyboard performance appear authentic. Although she had played piano in her childhood, she practiced six hours a day on a dead piano keyboard. Another Bay Area filmed movie she was in was *Causalities of War* (1989), but don't look for her face, it was her uncredited voice of a girl riding on a train.

KOSHLAND MANSION

Originally built as the residence of Marcus and Corinne Koshland (of the Levi Strauss family) in 1904, "Le Petit Trianon" is a takeoff on Madame de Pompadour's residence funded by Louis XV that is located at Versailles, France. The architect for this version was Frank S. Van Trees who designed many other residences in the Bay Area. The three-story mansion consists of some 21,000 square feet and is sited on one-half acre in the prestigious Presidio Heights District with views to San Francisco Bay. Many of its 22 rooms focus on a Roman-inspired sky-lit center atrium. There are eight bedrooms, and a ballroom that can accommodate 100 guests. The sandstone-faced building withstood the 1906 Earthquake but some of the façade fell to the ground. With many relatives and friends displaced from their homes due to the event, the Koshland's home became a temporary home to some 60 people.

The highly formal building was designated as San Francisco Landmark 95. It was also seen in the made-for-television movie *Lady of the House* (1978).

Contagion
2011, Warner Brothers
A deadly disease poses a threat and an international team of doctors contracted by the U.S. Centers for Disease Control and Prevention deal with the outbreak.

Director: Steven Soderbergh
Screenwriter: Scott Z. Burns
Production Designer: Howard Cummings
Art Directors: Abdellah Baadil, Simon Dobbin, David Lazan
Cinematographer: Steven Soderbergh
Partial Cast: Matt Damon, Marion Cotillard, Kate Winslet, Gwyneth Paltrow, Jude Law, Laurence Fishburne, Elliott Gould

• Music Concourse, Hagiwara Tea Garden Way, Golden Gate Park
• 800 block of De Haro Street, Potrero Hill District
• Potrero Hill District
• Earl Warren State Office Building, 455 Golden Gate Avenue, Civic Center
• Civic Center Plaza, Civic Center District
• Bill Graham Civic Auditorium, 99 Grove Street, Civic Center-as vaccination center
• San Francisco Chronicle Building, 901 Mission Street, South of Market District
• Candlestick Park, 602 Jamestown Avenue, Bayview District-as vaccination center

The Conversation
1974, Paramount Pictures
A paranoid surveillance expert has a crisis of confidence when he suspects his work will lead to murder.

Director: Francis Ford Coppola
Screenwriter: Francis Ford Coppola
Production Designer: Dean Tavoularis
Cinematographer: Bill Butler
Partial Cast: Gene Hackman, John Cazale, Allen Garfield, Frederic Forrest, Cindy Williams, Terry Garr, Harrison Ford, Robert Duvall

• Union Square, 333 Post Street
• City of Paris, 199 Geary Street, Union Square
• Alta Plaza Park, Pacific Heights District
• Embarcadero Center
• Alcoa Building, One Maritime Plaza, 300 Clay Street, Golden Gateway
• Jack Tar Hotel, 1101 Van Ness Avenue, Cathedral Hill District

Copycat

1995, Warner Brothers
An agoraphobic psychologist and a female detective work together to take down a serial killer who copies serial killers from the past.

Director: Jon Amiel
Screenwriters: Ann Biderman, David Madsen
Production Designer: Jim Clay
Art Director: Chris Seagers
Cinematographer: László Kovács
Partial Cast: Sigourney Weaver, Holly Hunter, Dermot Mulroney, Harry Connick Jr.
Local Cast: TV anchor Dennis Richmond

• College of San Mateo, 1700 West Hillsdale Boulevard, Library/KCSM Building 9, San Mateo-campus
• Fort Mason Center, Pier 1, Golden Gate National Recreation Area-exterior of doctor's apartment
• Great Lawn, Fort Mason Center, Golden Gate National Recreation Area-San Francisco Blues Festival
• Police Department Shooting Range, 700 John Muir Drive, Lake Shore District
• 194 Connecticut Street, Potrero Hill District-murder scene
• Alta Plaza Park, Pacific Heights District
• South Peak, Twin Peaks-murder scene

• Sound Factory dance club, 525 Harrison Street, Rincon Hill District
• Java House, Pier 40, The Embarcadero
• South Park Shell service station, 551 Third Street, South Park District
• Building 1101-1103, Kober Street, Fort Baker, Marin Headlands, Golden Gate National Recreation Area-fire

The Core

2003, Paramount
AKA: *Core*
The Earth is saved from catastrophe when scientists drill down to its core and set it spinning again.

Director: Jon Amiel
Screenwriters: Cooper Layne, John Rogers
Production Designer: Philip Harrison
Art Directors: Andrew Neskoromny, Sandi Tanaka
Cinematographers: John Lindley, Phil Meheux
Partial Cast: Aaron Eckhart, Nicole Leroux, Hilary Swank, Alfre Woodard

• Golden Gate Bridge

Counselor at Crime

1973, Joseph Green
The godson of a crime lord wants to leave the business.

Director: Alberto De Martino
Screenwriters: Adriano Bolzoni, Alberto De Martino, Vincenzo Flamini, Leonardo Martin
Cinematographers: Joe D'Amato, Rafael Pacheco
Partial Cast: Martin Balsam, Tomas Milian, Francisco Rabal

• Golden Gate Bridge
• Piers, The Embarcadero
• Tenderloin District

Crackers

1984, Universal Pictures
A gang plans the burglary of a pawnshop.

Director: Louis Malle
Screenwriter: Jeffrey Alan Fiskin
Production Designer: John J. Lloyd
Cinematographer: László Kovács
Partial Cast: Donald Sutherland, Jack Warden, Sean Penn

• 2918-2920 24th Street, Mission District-pawn shop
• 3333-3343 24th Street, Mission District-Weslake's apartment building
• 1025-1027 Treat Street, Mission District-house behind pawn shop

• 3135 24th Street, Mission District-auto painting shop

The Crazy-Quilt
1966, The Walter Reade Organization, Inc.
Two oddly matched lovers search for an elusive happiness.

Director: John Korty
Screenwriter: John Korty
Author: Allen Wheelis "The Illusionless Man and the Visionary Maid" (story)
Cinematographer: John Korty
Partial Cast: Tom Rosqui, Ina Mela, Ellen Frye, Burgess Meredith (narrator)

• Stow Lake, Golden Gate Park
• Colonial Historic Trees Meadow, Golden Gate Park
• Lloyd Lake, Golden Gate Park
• Music Concourse, Hagiwara Tea Garden Way, Golden Gate Park-statues
• Rustic Bridge, Stow Lake, Golden Gate Park
• Doggie Diner, 601 Van Ness Avenue, Civic Center
• California Palace of the Legion of Honor, Lincoln Park
• Stinson Beach, Golden Gate National Recreation Area

JOHN KORTY

John Korty was born on July 22, 1936 in the Midwest town of Lafayette, Indiana. While in his mid-teens he began the exploration of making films. He attended Antioch College in Yellow Springs, Ohio where he graduated in 1959; during his higher education he worked as an animator for television commercials. With a move to California he was living and working in an old Stinson Beach barn in 1963. Building his repertoire his 1964 short *Breaking the Habit* was nominated for an Academy Award. *The Crazy-Quilt* was his first indie feature film and he spent just $40,000 to film the comic fable with only three professionals and 12 non-professionals. Korty served as writer-director and cameraman for this and the two films that followed; *Funnyman* in 1967, an epic improvisational work, and *Riverrun* (1970) portraying the implications of a couple who escape urban living. Continuing to steer clear of Hollywood Korty shared quarters in the South of Mar-

ket's Folsom Street for a period with the like-minded Francis Ford Coppola and his American Zoetrope studio at one point. Korty became well-known to the public in 1974 with his *The Autobiography of Miss Jane Pittman* that aired on TV to millions garnering him a Best Director Emmy. He worked out of a Mill Valley studio on Miller Avenue starting in the mid-1970s. For *The Candidate* (1972) and George Lucas' *The Ewock Adventure* (1984) he worked as cinematographer. Another film, *Who Are the DeBolts? And Where Did They Get Nineteen Kids?* (1977), was a three-year exploration of a family who adopted handicapped children; this brought him an additional Academy Award in the documentary category. More recently he explored the detailed restoration of a 1927 Steinway piano in *Miracle in a Box* (2009). Now located in Pt. Reyes Station, Korty Films LLC continues with a socially conscious agenda in the mostly made-for-TV vein.

Crazy in Alabama
1999, Columbia Pictures and Sony Pictures Entertainment
An eccentric woman is on her way to Hollywood to pursue her dreams of TV stardom–with the head of her abusive husband stored safely in a hatbox.

Director: Antonio Banderas
Screenwriter: Mark Childress
Author: Mark Childress (novel)
Production Designer: Cecilia Montiel
Art Director: Michael Atwell
Cinematographer: Julio Macat
Partial Cast: Melanie Griffith, David Morse, Lucas Black, Cathy Moriarty, Meat Loaf, Rod Steiger

• Golden Gate Bridge

Creator
1985, Universal
AKA: *The Big Picture*
An eccentric scientist looks for a way to clone his deceased wife.

Director: Ivan Passer
Screenwriter: Jeremy Leven
Art Director: Josan F. Russo

Cinematographer: Robbie Greenberg
Partial Cast: Peter O'Toole, Mariel Hemingway, Vincent Spano, Virginia Madsen, David Ogden Stiers, John Dehner

• Alexian Brothers Hospital, 225 North Jackson Avenue, San Jose-as hospital

The Creature Walks Among Us
1956, Universal International
A creature is converted from a gill-breather to lung-breather and mayhem ensues because of its unhappiness over the conversion.

Director: John Sherwood
Screenwriter: Arthur A. Ross
Art Directors: Alexander Golitzen, Robert A. Gausman
Cinematographer: Maury Gertsman
Partial Cast: Jeff Morrow, Rex Reason, Leigh Snowden, Gregg Palmer, Maurice Manson

• Panorama of San Francisco

Crime of Passion
1957, United Artists
A smart newspaper columnist funnels her energy into helping her unambitious husband rise through the ranks of the police department.

Director: Gerd Oswald
Screenwriter: Jo Eisinger
Art Director: A. Leslie Thomas
Cinematographer: Joseph LaShelle
Partial Cast: Barbara Stanwyck, Sterling Hayden, Raymond Burr, Fay Wray, Virginia Grey, Stuart Whitman

• California Street Cable Car, Chinatown District

Cross Country Romance
1940, RKO Radio Pictures
An heiress follows a doctor on a transcontinental adventure.

Director: Frank Woodruff
Screenwriters: Jerry Cady, Bert Granet
Author: Eleanore Browne *Highway to Romance* (novel)
Art Director: Van Nest Polglase
Cinematographer: J. Roy Hunt
Partial Cast: Gene Raymond, Wendy Barrie, Hedda Hopper

• Golden Gate Bridge

Cry Vengeance
1954, Allied Artists
A violent ex-cop goes to Alaska seeking to revenge an old enemy.

Director: Mark Stevens
Screenwriters: Warren Douglas, George Bricker
Art Director: Dave Milton
Cinematographer: William A. Sickner
Partial Cast: Mark Stevens, Martha Hyer, Skip Homeier

• Hotel Henry, 106 6th Street, South of Market District-as pawn shop
• Intersection of Washington Street and Jackson Street, Presidio Heights-cable car line
• San Francisco Airport, central passenger terminal

Cujo
1983, Lionsgate
A rabies-infected St. Bernard dog becomes a wild killer.

Director: Lewis Teague
Screenwriters: Don Carlos Dunaway, Lauren Currier
Author: Stephen King (novel)
Production Designer: Guy Comtois
Cinematographer: Jan de Bont
Partial Cast: Dee Wallace, Daniel Hugh-Kelly, Christopher Stone, Ed Lauter, Danny Pintauro

• Scott Ranch, Corona Road, Petaluma
• Intersection of Bodega Avenue and Baker Street, Petaluma
• 600 block of Baker Street, Petaluma
• Thompson Ranch, 7301 Sonoma Mountain Road, Glen Ellen

Curse of Alcatraz
2007, Lionsgate Films
A mummified corpse is discovered on Alcatraz Island and the investigating forensic team becomes infected by a deadly curse.

Director: Daniel Zirilli
Screenwriters: D. Glase Lomond, Doyle Sigerson, Daniel Zirilli
Production Designer: Laura Monteleone
Cinematographer: Jason Dittmer
Partial Cast: Alex A. Quinn, Jessie Camacho, Candise Lakota, José Solano

• Golden Gate Bridge
• Alcatraz Federal Prison, Alcatraz Island, Golden Gate National Recreation Area-various exterior and interior shots
• Panorama of San Francisco from San Francisco Bay

• Blue and Gold Fleet ferry, San Francisco Bay
• Alta Bates Summit Medical Center, 2450 Ashby Street, Berkeley
• Oakland Police Department-interiors

Daddy's Gone A-Hunting

1969, Warner Brothers

An English émigré girl befriends a psychotic man who plunges her into a nightmare.

Director: Mark Robson
Screenwriters: Larry Cohen, Lorenzo Semple Jr.
Art Directors: Stan Johnson, James W. Sullivan
Cinematographer: Ernest Laszlo
Partial Cast: Carol White, Paul Burke, Mala Powers

• International Terminal, San Francisco International Airport
• Bayshore Boulevard, Brisbane
• Embarcadero Freeway, Embarcadero
• Airlines Terminal, 375 O'Farrell Street, Union Square District
• Bernstein's Fish Grotto, 123 Powell Street, Union Square District
• Golden State Hotel, 114 Powell Street, Union Square District
• Mark Hopkins Hotel, 999 California Street, Nob Hill District-porte cochere, lobby, Top of the Mark Nightclub, and roof
• One Maritime Plaza, 300 Clay Street, Golden Gateway
• Garden Court Restaurant, Sheraton Palace Hotel, 2 New Montgomery Street, South of Market District
• Grace Cathedral, 1100 California Street, Nob Hill District
• City of Paris, 199 Geary Street, Union Square District
• Cal Train Rail Station, 599 El Camino Real, San Carlos
• Crocker-Citizens Bank, One Post Street, Financial District
• KBHK TV 44, San Mateo
• Curran Theater, 445 Geary Boulevard, Union Square District
• Cable Car 502
• Intersection of Powell Street and California Street, Nob Hill District-cable car control house
• Golden Gateway Apartments, 460 Davis Street, Golden Gateway
• San Francisco-Oakland Bay Bridge
• Bank of America, 555 California Street, Financial District-under construction

Dangerous Minds

1995, Buena Vista

AKA: *My Posse Don't Do Homework*
An ex-marine and teacher gain the confidence of her urban misfit but

intelligent senior students, helping them to learn.

Director: John N. Smith
Screenwriter: Ronald Bass
Author: LouAnne Johnson *My Posse Don't Do Homework* (book)
Production Designer: Donald Graham Burt
Art Director: Nancy Patton
Cinematographer: Pierre Letarte
Partial Cast: Michelle Pfeiffer, George Dzundza, Courtney B. Vance, Robin Bartlett, Beatrice Winde, Renoly Santiago, Lorraine Toussaint

• San Mateo High School, 506 North Delaware Street, San Mateo-library
• Burlingame High School, 400 Carolan Avenue, Burlingame-exteriors
• Carlmont High School, 1400 Alameda De Las Pulgas, Belmont

LOUANNE JOHNSON

Johnson grew up in Youngsville, Pennsylvania and after graduating from high school enrolled at Indiana University of Pennsylvania, but soon dropped out. She enlisted in the Navy in 1971 and served nine years active duty and then transferred to the U.S. Marine Corps. While in the military she earned the Navy Commendation Medal and Air Force Achievement Award for her work as a journalist/radio-TV broadcaster. After receiving a B.S. in Psychology from Southern California's University of La Verne she then obtained a master degree in teaching English from Notre Dame de Namur in Belmont. With schooling behind her she went on to teach at Carlmont High School in Belmont as an intern in 1989. The following year she taught English and reading to non-English speaking students. In 1991 she was appointed department chair of a special program for at-risk teens—one of ten pilot programs scattered around the country. She is the author of eight books, her first was *Making Waves: A Woman in This Man's Navy* that was published in 1986; it told of her experiences in the military. Her 1992 book *My Posse Don't Do Homework* was the basis for the movie *Dangerous Minds*. The movie *Becoming Edwardo* (2009) is another story of an at-risk teenage

Dark Passage

1947, Warner Brothers
A man convicted of murdering his wife
escapes from prison and works with a
woman to prove his innocence.

Director: Delmer Daves
Screenwriter: Delmer Daves
Author: David Goodis (novel)
Art Director: Charles H. Clarke
Cinematographer: Sidney Hickox
Partial Cast: Lauren Bacall, Humphrey Bogart,
Agnes Moorehead, Bruce Bennett

• San Quentin State Prison, San Quentin
• Paradise Drive, Tiburon
• U.S. Highway Route 101, Waldo Grade Tunnel,
Sausalito
• Golden Gate Bridge
• Lincoln Boulevard, Presidio, Golden Gate
National Recreation Area
• 1360 Montgomery Street, Telegraph Hill
District-exteriors of Irene's apartment
• Market Street
• Bluff above Fort Point National Historic Site,
Marine Drive, Golden Gate National Recreation
Area
• Intersection of McDowell Avenue and Crissy
Boulevard, Presidio, Golden Gate National
Recreation Area
• The Tamalpais Apartments, 1201 Greenwich
Street, Russian Hill District-exterior of Madge's
residence
• Powell/Hyde Cable Car, Hyde Street, Russian
Hill District
• Union Square, 333 Post Street
• 228 Filbert Street Steps, Telegraph Hill District
• Hallidie Plaza, Market Street at Powell Street-
cable car turnaround

The Darwin Awards

2006, Metro-Goldwyn-Mayer
An unlikely pair search for those who
improve the human species by
accidentally removing themselves
from it.

Director: Finn Taylor
Screenwriter: Finn Taylor
Production Designer: Peter Jamison
Art Director: Don Day
Cinematographer: Hiro Narita
Partial Cast: David Arquette, Ty Burrell, Josh
Charles, Kevin Dunn, Nora Dunn, Joseph
Fiennes, Winona Ryder, Josh Kornbluth,
Jeanette Etheredge
Local Cast: Literary luminary Lawrence
Ferlinghetti, Diva Val Diamond, TV Anchor Mike
Sugarman

• Dair's Speed Wash, 607 Ellis Street, Tenderloin
District
• City Lights Bookstore, 261 Columbus Street,
Jackson Square District
• Oakland City Hall, One Frank H. Ogawa Plaza,
Oakland
• Creekside Village, La Honda Road, La Honda
• Downtown Crockett
• Old Carquinez Bridge
• Tillie's Diner, 1500 Webster Street, Alameda
• Original Kaspers, 4521 Telegraph Avenue,
Oakland
• Holiday Bowl, 29827 Mission Boulevard,
Hayward
• Tosca Café, 242 Columbus Avenue, Jackson
Square District
• Vesuvio Cafe, 255 Columbus, Jackson Square
District
• Lincoln's Address Bar, 1304 Lincoln Avenue,
Alameda

and her father specializes in scholarly work about drug history and literature. The family briefly lived in Colombia with Chilean revolutionaries during the mid-1970s and returned to the U.S. in 1974 eventually landing in a remotely located Northern California commune called Rainbow located on 300 acres near Elk. When Winona was ten years old the family moved south to Petaluma, California. Soon after she enrolled as an acting student at the American Conservatory Theater in San Francisco. She made her film debut in the teen romance film *Lucas* (1986) playing Rina who is a friend of the lead character. Her breakthrough movie, this while still a teenager, was her appearance in *Beetlejuice* (1988) where she played a Goth teenager—a dark offbeat role that would pigeonhole her in future parts. She graduated from Petaluma High School in 1989 and the following year she appeared in Tim Burton's *Edward Scissorhands* along side her then boyfriend Johnny Depp. This was followed with a dual role in Francis Ford Coppola's chilling *Bram Stoker's Dracula* (1992) where she played Dracula's love interest and past lover. The third major remake of *Little Women* won her a Best Actress Oscar nomination in the 1994 production. In the early 2000s she was arrested for shoplifting that sidelined her for a few years only to finally have the major charges reduced to misdemeanors.

Days of Wine and Roses

1962, Warner Brothers
A couple is pulled into, but his wife doesn't recover from her addiction.

Director: Blake Edwards
Screenwriter: J. P. Miller
Art Director: Joseph C. Wright
Cinematographer: Philip H. Lathrop
Partial Cast: Jack Lemmon, Lee Remick, Charles Bickford, Jack Klugman

• Marina Yacht Harbor, Marina District
• Pacific Gas and Electric Building, 77 Beale Street, South of Market District-lobby and exterior

• Place Pigalle, 3721 Buchanan Street, Marina District-bar
• 200 block of Union Street, Telegraph Hill District-residence
• 1800 Pacific Avenue, Pacific Heights District-Clay residence
• 100 block of Maiden Lane, Union Square
• Sharon Playground, Golden Gate Park-carousel

Dead & Breakfast

2004, Anchor Bay Entertainment
AKA: *Dead and Breakfast*
Six friends stay at a bed-and-breakfast only to find the townspeople are possessed by an evil spirit.

Director: Matthew Leutwyler
Screenwriters: Matthew Leutwyler, Jun Tan, Billy Burke
Production Designer: Don Day
Art Director: Guy Harrington
Cinematographer: David Scardina
Partial Cast: Billy Burke, Ever Carradine, Bianca Lawson, Jeffery Dean Morgan, David Carradine

• Concannon Winery, 4590 Tesla Road, Livermore-as Lavaná B&B
• Pleasanton

Dead Pit

1989, Skouras Pictures
A newly arrived mental hospital patient accidentally reawakens the spirit of a long-ago murdered doctor who performed sinister experiments on his patients.

Director: Brett Leonard
Screenwriters: Gimel Everett, Brett Leonard
Cinematographer: Marty Collins
Partial Cast: Jeremy Slate, Cheryl Lawson

• Agnews Developmental Center West, Montague Expressway at Lafayette Street, Santa Clara

The Dead Pool

1988, Warner Brothers
AKA: *Dirty Harry in the Dead Pool*
Inspector Harry Callahan investigates a murder involving a game where bets are placed on certain personalities dying within a specific timeframe.

Director: Buddy Van Horn
Screenwriters: Harry Julian Fink, Rita M. Fink, Steve Sharon, Durk Pearson, Sandy Shaw
Production Designer: Edward C. Carfagno
Cinematographer: Jack N. Green

Partial Cast: Clint Eastwood, Patricia Clarkson, Liam Neeson, Evan C. Kim, David Hunt, Jim Carrey

• 1954 Mason Street, North Beach District
• 710 Steiner Street, Western Addition District
• San Francisco City Hall, 1 Carlton B. Goodlett Place, Civic Center District
• Saints Peter and Paul Church, 666 Filbert Street, Washington Square, North Beach District
• San Francisco-Oakland Bay Bridge
• KGO/ABC newsroom offices, 900 Front Street, The Embarcadero
• Potrero Hill District
• Alamo Square, Western Addition District
• The Embarcadero
• Hall of Justice, 850 Bryant Street, South of Market District
• San Francisco National Cemetery, 1 Lincoln Boulevard, Presidio, Golden Gate National Recreation Area
• The Cannery, 2801 Leavenworth, Street, Fisherman's Wharf District
• Potrero Hill District
• 550 El Camino Del Mar, Seacliff District
• Eber Electronics, 2355 Market Street, Eureka Valley District
• 1301 Illinois Street, Potrero Hill District
• San Quentin State Prison, Main Street, San Quentin-main gate
• Pier 3, The Embarcadero
• Portsmouth Square, Chinatown District
• Bethlehem Shipyard, 900 Illinois Street, Potrero Hill District
• San Francisco General Hospital, 1001 Potrero Avenue, Mission District
• Silver Restaurant, 737 Washington Street, Chinatown District

Dear Brigitte
1965, Twentieth Century Fox
AKA: *Erasmus With Freckles*
A precocious boy wants to meet the bombshell French actress Bridget Bardot.

Director: Henry Koster
Screenwriters: Nunnally Johnson, Hal Kanter
Author: John Hasse *Erasmus With Freckles* (book)
Art Directors: Malcolm Brown, Jack Martin Smith
Cinematographer: Lucien Ballard
Partial Cast: James Stewart, Fabian, Glynis Johns, Cindy Carol, Billy Mumy, Jessie White, Bridget Bardot, Ed Wynn

• Panorama of San Francisco
• Golden Gate Bridge
• Gate 6, Sausalito boat harbor-houseboats

Death in the Red Jaguar
1968, Constantin Film

An FBI agent tackles an organization of assassins who kill to order.

Director: Harald Reinl
Screenwriter: Herbert Reinecker
Production Designer: Ernst H. Albrecht
Cinematographer: Franz Xaver Lederle
Partial Cast: George Nader, Heinz Weiss, Daniela Surina

• San Francisco International Airport
• Golden Gate Bridge

The Deep End
2001, 20th Century Fox
A woman spirals out of control while trying to keep her son from being found culpable in a murder investigation.

Directors: Scott MGehee, David Siegel
Screenwriters: Scott MGehee, David Siegel
Author: Elisabeth Sanxay Holding *The Blank Wall* (novel)
Production Designers: Kelly McGehee, Christopher Tandon
Cinematographer: Giles Nuttgens
Partial Cast: Tilda Swinton, Goran Visnjic, Jonathan Tucker

• Backflip Bar, Phoenix Hotel, 601 Eddy Street, Tenderloin District

Desperate Measures
1998, Sony Pictures Entertainment and Tri-Star
A police officer frantically searches for a compatible bone marrow donor for his terminally ill young son.

Director: Barbet Schroeder
Screenwriter: David Klass
Production Designer: Geoffrey Kirkland
Art Director: Sandy Getzler
Cinematographer: Luciano Tovoli
Partial Cast: Michael Keaton, Andy Garcia, Brian Cox, Marcia Gay Harden

• San Francisco-Oakland Bay Bridge
• Hall of Justice, 850 Bryant Street, South of Market District
• Potrero Hill
• Rincon Hill

Destination Tokyo
1943, Warner Brothers
In order to provide information for the first air raid over Tokyo, a U.S. submarine sneaks into Tokyo Bay and places a spy team ashore.

Director: Delmer Daves
Screenwriters: Delmer Daves, Albert Maltz
Author: Steve Fisher (story)
Art Director: Leo K. Kuter
Cinematographer: Bert Glennon
Partial Cast: Cary Grant, John Garfield, Alan
Hale, John Ridgely, Dane Clark, John Forsythe

• Drydock, Mare Island, Vallejo

DELMER DAVES

Actor, director and producer "Del" Lawrence Daves (1904-1977) hailed from San Francisco. His parents were Arthur L., an accountant, and Nannie P. Daves; they eventually had an additional three children. By 1910 his family moved to the La Ballona Township section of what is now Los Angeles where he graduated from Polytechnic High School. He then attended Stanford University and to pay for expenses he worked as a draftsman for the City of Palo Alto. While there he studied engineering and law but only secured a law degree that he never exercised—a career path that was derailed when he became a prop boy for the silent movie *The Covered Wagon* (1923). Studying at the Pasadena Playhouse he started acting in late silent pictures and early talkies and then turned his talent to writing screenplays and original stories. He married Mary Lawrence (born Mary Lou Lender), an actress, in 1938 and they went on to have three children. *Destination Tokyo* was his directorial debut but he also worked on the script. Later he also wrote and directed the popular film noir movie *Dark Passage* (1947) and the teen romance *Susan Slade* (1961). Credits in other Bay Area shot pieces include the screenplay for *Stranded* (1935) and *The Go-Getter* (1937).

Devil Ship
1947, Columbia
A boat used to ferry prisoners from the mainland to Alcatraz becomes the vehicle for other events.

Director: Lew Landers

Screenwriter: Lawrence Taylor
Art Director: Robert Peterson
Cinematographer: Allen G. Siegler
Partial Cast: Richard Lane, Louise Campbell,
William Bishop, Damian O'Flynn, Myrna Liles

• Alcatraz Federal Prison, Alcatraz Island, Golden
Gate National Recreation Area

Die Hard II
1990, Fox
AKA: *Die Hard II: Die Harder*
A man is forced to battle mercenaries who seize control of an airport's communications and threaten to cause plane crashes if their demands are not met.

Director: Renny Hurlin
Screenwriters: Steven E. de Sousa, Doug Richardson
Author: Walter Wager *58 Minutes* (novel)
Production Designer: John Vallone
Art Director: Christiaan Wagener
Cinematographer: Oliver Wood
Partial Cast: Bruce Willis, Bonnie Bedelia,
William Atherton, Reginald Vel Johnson, Franco
Nero, William Sadler, John Amos, Dennis Franz,
Arthur Evans, Fred Dalton Thompson

• Santa Rosa Air Center, Finley Avenue, Santa
Rosa

Die Laughing
1980, Orion and Warner Brothers
A young cab driver wants to be a rock musician, but when he becomes implicated in the murder of a nuclear physicist, his main pursuit is to stay alive.

Director: Jeff Werner
Screenwriters: Scott Parker, Jerry Segal
Author: Scott Parker (story)
Production Designer: James H. Spencer
Partial Cast: Robby Benson, Charles Durning,
Elsa Lanchester, Bud Cort, Peter Coyote

• University of California Campus, Berkeley
• Intersection of California Street and Sansome Street, Financial District
• Embarcadero BART station, Market Street
• 505 Sansome Street, Financial District-building under construction
• 1984 and 1986 Ellis Street, Western Addition-houses being moved
• Intersection of Willard Street and Belmont Avenue, Upper Haight District-jumping across roofs
• 721 Filbert Street, Russian Hill District-taxi cab garage

• Congregation Sherith Israel Synagogue, 2266 California Street, Pacific Heights District
• 1049 Irving Street, Inner Sunset District-as Masquerade Costume Shop
• California Pacific Medical Center Health Sciences Library, 2395 Sacramento Street, Pacific Heights District-audition venue
• 145 Laurel Street, Presidio Heights District-apartment building
• Spring Street, Chinatown District
• Fort Point National Historic Site, Marine Drive, Golden Gate National Recreation Area
• Carquinez Bridges-viewed from Morrow Cove, Carquinez Strait

Dim Sum: A Little Bit of Heart

1984, Orion Classics

A Chinese-American family tries to maintain a link to their cultural heritage while confronted by the changing world.

Director: Wayne Wang
Screenwriter: Terrel Selzer
Art Director: Danny Yung
Cinematographer: Michael Chin
Partial Cast: Laureen Chew, Kim Chew, Victor Wong, Ida F. O. Chung

• Outer Richmond District
• San Francisco-Oakland Bay Bridge
• Li Po Cocktail Lounge, 916 Grant Avenue, Chinatown District
• Portsmouth Square, Chinatown District
• San Francisco International Airport
• Great Eastern Restaurant, 649 Jackson Street, Chinatown District
• Cemetery, Colma
• Chinese Hospital, 845 Jackson Street, Chinatown District
• Saks Fifth Avenue, 384 Post Street, Union Square
• Golden Gate Park
• Nob Hill District

Dirty Harry

1971, Warner Brothers

A cop uses unorthodox methods to capture a sniper.

Director: Don Siegel
Screenwriters: Harry Julian Fink, Rita M. Fink, Dean Riesner, John Milius, Jo Heims
Art Director: Dale Hennessey
Cinematographer: Bruce Surtees
Partial Cast: Clint Eastwood, Andrew Robinson, John Vernon, Reni Santoni, Harry Guardino

• 750 Kearny Street, Chinatown District-pool on roof
• Bank of America Building, 555 California Street, Financial District-rooftop

• Pacific Gas and Electric Building, 245 Market Street, South of Market District
• 1520 Stockton Street, Chinatown District-shootout on rooftop
• Intersection of Sierra Street and Texas Street, Potrero Hill District
• Portsmouth Square, Chinatown District
• Hall of Justice, 850 Bryant Street, South of Market District
• Marina Yacht Harbor, Marina District
• Bison Paddock, JFK Drive, Golden Gate Park
• California Hall, 625 Polk Street, Civic Center
• Saints Peter and Paul Church, 666 Filbert Street, North Beach District
• Mt. Davidson Cross, Miraloma Park District
• Forest Hill Muni station, Dewey Boulevard at Laguna Honda Boulevard, Forest Hill District
• Civic Center
• San Francisco City Hall, 1 Carlton B. Goodlett Place, Civic Center District-rotunda and Mayor's office on second floor
• San Francisco General Hospital, 1001 Potrero Avenue, Mission District
• Beltline Railroad tunnel under Fort Mason Center, Golden Gate National Recreation Area
• Park Emergency Hospital, 811 Stanyan Street, Golden Gate Park
• Kezar Stadium and Pavilion, Golden Gate Park
• Battery Spencer, Conzelman Road, Golden Gate National Recreation Area
• Conservatory of Flowers, 100 JFK Drive, Golden Gate Park
• Grandview Park, 15th Avenue and Noriega Street, Golden Gate Heights District
• Golden Gate Bridge
• Train trestle over Sir Francis Drake Boulevard, intersection of State Highway Route 101, Larkspur-jump onto bus roof
• Brick Kiln Development, 125 East Sir Francis Drake Boulevard, Larkspur-quarry

DIRTY HARRY: THE SERIES

Dirty Harry was the first of what became a popular crime thriller series featuring the fictional character of Police Inspector Harry Callahan. The film was followed by four sequels: *Magnum Force* (1973), *The Enforcer* (1976), *Sudden Impact* (1983), and finally *The Dead Pool* (1988). Callahan became a new kind of movie cop who does not hesitate to cross professional and ethical lines in the pursuit of his own vision of justice, especially when the law is poorly served by an inept city bureaucracy. In 2012 *Dirty Harry* was selected for preservation in the National Film Registry by the Library of Congress for being "culturally, historically, and aesthetically significant."

> "I want to report a murder."
> "Sit down. Where was this murder committed?"
> "San Francisco, last night."
> "Who was murdered?"
> "I was."

D.O.A.
1950, United Artists
A man who is slowly poisoned tracks his own killer.

Director: Rudolph Maté
Screenwriters: Russell Rouse, Clarence Greene
Art Director: Duncan Cramer
Cinematographer: Ernest Laszlo
Partial Cast: Edmund O'Brien, Pamela Britton, Luther Adler, Beverly Garland

• San Francisco Bay
• St. Francis Hotel, 335 Powell Street, Union Square District
• Hyde/Powell Cable Car, intersection of Powell Street and California Street, Nob Hill District
• Chambord Apartments, 1298 Sacramento Street, Nob Hill District-as medical building
• Southern Pacific Railroad Hospital, 1400 Fell Street, North of Panhandle District
• Market Street-running scene
• View to Ferry Building and San Francisco-Oakland Bay Bridge with The Fisherman Bar, The Embarcadero

The Doctor
1991, Touchstone
A surgeon becomes a patient in his own hospital and finds atonement.

Director: Randa Haines
Screenwriter: Robert Caswell
Author: Ed Rosenbaum *A Taste of My Own Medicine* (book)
Production Designer: Ken Adam
Art Director: William J. Durrell Jr.
Cinematographer: John Seale
Partial Cast: William Hurt, Christine Lahti, Mandy Patinken, Elizabeth Perkins, Bill Macy

• Twin Peaks Boulevard, Clarendon Heights District
• Rincon Towers, 88 Howard Street, South of Market District-as hospital
• 75 Howard Street, South of Market District-as parking garage

• Intersection of California Street and Mason Street, Nob Hill District
• Intersection of Montgomery Street and Green Street, Telegraph Hill District
• 325 Mississippi Street, Potrero Hill District

Doctor Dolittle
1998, 20th Century Fox
A doctor finds out that he can understand what animals are saying, and the animals find out that he understands them.

Director: Betty Thomas
Screenwriter: Nat Mauldin, Larry Levin
Author: Hugh Lofting (stories)
Production Designer: William A. Elliott
Art Director: K. C. Fox
Cinematographer: Russell Boyd
Partial Cast: Eddie Murphy, Ossie Davis, Peter Boyle

• 1101 Leavenworth Street, Russian Hill District-Deco apartment building
• Panorama of Ghirardelli Square and Alcatraz Island, Golden Gate National Recreation Area
• Sinbad's Pier II Restaurant, Pier 2, The Embarcadero
• San Francisco-Oakland Bay Bridge
• Ghirardelli Square/Aquatic Park, Waterfront
• Coit Tower, Pioneer Park, 1 Telegraph Hill Boulevard, Telegraph Hill District

Dr. Dolittle 2
2001, 20th Century Fox
AKA: *DR2*
Woodland creatures ask for help to save their habitat.

Director: Steve Carr
Screenwriter: Larry Levin
Author: Hugh Lofting *Dr. Dolittle* series (books)
Production Designer: William Sandell
Art Directors: Bruce Crone, Brad Ricker
Cinematographer: Daryn Okada
Partial Cast: Eddie Murphy, Kristen Wilson, Kevin Pollak

• Golden Gate Bridge
• Pt. Reyes National Seashore

KEVIN POLLAK

Actor and stand-up comedian Kevin Elliot Pollak was born in San Francisco in 1957. His family then moved to San Jose, a place of orchards, when he was two. (His Russian immigrant grandfather once ran Tommy's Joynt restaurant, the popular tourist restaurant on Van Ness Avenue.) He learned stand-up at age 10 by lip-synching to Bill Cosby routines. But a paid one-nighter position in the South Bay's town of Campbell, his first, launched his professional debut. In 1982 he won second place in the San Francisco International Comedy Competition and one year later he moved to Los Angeles to appear in clubs including the famed springboard club The Improv. In Los Angeles he evolved a broad style from comic to dramatic into a well-respected supporting character actor in both TV and on the silver screen. He landed his first film role in the Ron Howard directed *Willow* in 1988. He also appeared in the locally filmed *The Wedding Planner* (2001).

Doctor Dracula
1978, Independent International Pictures
AKA: *Lucifer's Women* and *Svengali*
An evil hypnotist puts a beautiful woman under his spell.

Directors: Al Adamson, Paul Aratow
Screenwriters: Paul Aratow, Cecil Brown, Gary Reathman, Samuel M. Sherman
Cinematographers: Gary Graver, Robbie Greenberg
Partial Cast: John Carradine, Don "Red" Barry

• 500 block of Broadway, Telegraph Hill District

Doctor Goldfoot and the Bikini Machine
1965, American International Pictures
A doctor has invented an army of bikini-clad robots who are programmed to seek out wealthy men and charm them into signing over their assets.

Director: Norman Taurog
Screenwriters: Robert Kaufman, James H. Nicholson, Elwood Ullman
Art Director: Daniel Haller
Cinematographer: Sam Leavitt
Partial Cast: Vincent Price, Frankie Avalon, Dwayne Hickman, Annette Funicello, Tommy Kirk

• San Francisco International Airport

Doctor Goldfoot and the Girl Bombs
1966, American International Pictures
The doctor plots to take over the world using his female robots as bombs to blow up high-ranking generals of NATO.

Director: Mario Bava
Screenwriters: Giuseppe Moccia, Franco Castellano, Franco Dal Cer, Louis Heyward, Robert Kaufman, Fulvio Lucisano, James Nicholson
Art Director: Gastone Carsetti
Cinematographer: Antonio Rinaldi
Partial Cast: Vincent Price, Fabian

• Marina Green, Marina District
• L Taraval Muni line portal, West Portal District

Dogfight
1991, Warner Brothers
A group of friends have a party on the night before being shipped out to fight in the Vietnam War and make a wager on the opposite sex.

Director: Nancy Savoca
Screenwriter: Bob Comfort
Production Designer: Lester Cohen
Art Director: Daniel Talpers
Cinematographer: Bobby Bukowski
Partial Cast: River Phoenix, Lili Taylor, Richard Panebianco

• San Francisco-Oakland Bay Bridge
• Powell/Hyde Cable Car, intersection of Powell Street and Geary Street, Union Square
• Stockton Street Tunnel, south portal, Nob Hill District
• City Lights Bookstore, 261 Columbus Street, Jackson Square District
• Broadway, Telegraph Hill District

The Domino Principle
1977, Associated General Films
A murderer is offered his freedom in exchange for assassinating a national figure.

Director: Stanley Kramer
Screenwriter: Adam Kennedy
Author: Adam Kennedy (book)
Production Designer: William J. Creber
Art Director: Ron Hobbs
Cinematographers: Fred J. Koenekamp, Ernest Laszlo

Partial Cast: Gene Hackman, Candice Bergen, Eli Wallach, Richard Widmark, Mickey Rooney, Edward Albert

• San Quentin State Prison, San Quentin
• Golden Gate Bridge
• Hyatt Regency Hotel, 5 Embarcadero Center-exterior and Room 1705
• Fisherman's Wharf District
• BART train

The Doors
1991, Carolco
AKA: *Lizard King*
The fast life and turbulent times of rock music star Jim Morrison.

Director: Oliver Stone
Screenwriters: Randall Jahnson, Oliver Stone
Production Designer: Barbara Ling
Art Director: Larry Fulton
Cinematographer: Robert Richardson
Partial Cast: Val Kilmer, Meg Ryan, Kyle MacLachman

• Haight-Ashbury District
• The Panhandle, Golden Gate Park

Dopamine
2003, Sundance Channel
A computer programmer falls for a teacher and they work out whether love is chemical or chemistry.

Director: Mark Decena
Screenwriters: Timothy Breitbach, Mark Decena
Production Designer: S. Quinn
Art Director: Joe Schlick
Cinematographer: Robert Humphreys
Partial Cast: John Livingston, Sabrina Lloyd, Bruno Campos

• Forest, Presidio, Golden Gate National Recreation Area
• South Park, South Park Avenue, South of Market District
• Live Oak School, 1555 Mariposa Street, Potrero Hill District-as classroom
• Golden Gate Bridge
• Jay 'N Bee Club, 2736 20th Street, Mission District-corner bar
• Fort Point National Historic Site, Marine Drive, Golden Gate National Recreation Area
• 101 South Park Avenue, South of Market District-side of building on Center Street
• Bam Buddha Lounge, Phoenix Hotel, 601 Eddy Street, Tenderloin District
• 540 Hayes Street, Hayes Valley District-as art gallery
• Just north of fishing pier, Terry A. Francois Avenue, Mission Bay District
• Caffe Centro, 102 South Park Avenue, South of Market District
• San Francisco-Oakland Bay Bridge

• Intersection of Steuart Street and Market Street-as Critical Mass bicycle gathering point
• 1302 Kobbe Avenue, Presidio, Golden Gate National Recreation Area
• Crissy Field Avenue, Presidio, Golden Gate National Recreation Area
• 140-144A Linda Street, Mission District

Double Harness
1933, RKO Radio Pictures
AKA: *The Faintheart, Mr. Faintheart*
A woman tricks a playboy into marrying her and then tries to make him legitimately fall in love with her.

Director: John Cromwell
Screenwriter: Jane Murfin
Author: Edward Poor Montgomery (play)
Cinematographer: J. Roy Hunt
Partial Cast: Ann Harding, William Powell, Lucille Browne, Henry Stephenson, Reginald Owen

• Union Square, 333 Post Street
• California Street, Nob Hill District-driving
• Fisherman's Wharf District
• Podesta Baldocchi, 224 Grant Street, Financial District-florist

Down Periscope
1996, Twentieth Century Fox
A lieutenant commander is assigned to head a rust bucket submarine for maneuvers with a crew of misfits.

Director: David S. Ward
Screenwriters: Hugh Wilson, Andrew Kurtzman, Eliot Wald
Production Designer: Michael Corenblith
Art Director: Dan Webster
Cinematographer: Victor Hammer
Partial Cast: Kelsey Grammer, Lauren Holly, Rob Schneider, Harry Dean Stanton, Bruce Dern, William H. Macy

• Various spots around San Francisco Bay using historic submarine USS *Pampanito*-as USS *Stingray*
• Fort Mason Center, Golden Gate National Recreation Area
• Rafted World War II Liberty ships, Suisun Bay
• Naval Air Station Alameda, Alameda Island

USS *PAMPANITO*

The USS *Pampanito* (SS-383), a Balao-class submarine, was constructed at the Portsmouth Navy Yard in Kittery, Maine during World War II and launched in 1943. During its short service life the undersea man-of-war sailed six combat commissions before being decommissioned in 1945. Later she served as a Naval Reserve Training ship from 1960 through 1971 at Mare Island, Vallejo. Today it sits on San Francisco's waterfront as a floating museum and is part of the San Francisco Maritime National Park Association; the sub was designated a National Historic Landmark in 1986.

Down to You

2000, Miramax Films

A young man wins, and then loses, the first serious love of his life.

Director: Kris Isacsson
Screenwriter: Kris Isacsson
Production Designer: Kevin Thompson
Art Director: Marc Dabe
Cinematographer: Robert D. Yeoman
Partial Cast: Freddie Prinze Jr., Julia Stiles, Selma Blair

• Painted Ladies, 700 block of Steiner Street, Western Addition District

Dragon: the Bruce Lee Story

1993, Universal Pictures

A lionized account of the life of the martial arts superstar.

Director: Rob Cohen
Screenwriters: Edward Khmara, John Raffo, Rob Cohen
Authors: Robert Clouse Bruce Lee: The Biography (book), Linda Lee Cadwell Bruce Lee: The Man Only I Knew (book)
Production Designer: Bob Ziembicki
Art Director: Ted Berner
Cinematographer: David Eggby
Partial Cast: Jason Scott Lee, Lauren Holly, Robert Wagner, Nancy Kwan

• Golden Gate Bridge
• View of Coit Tower from intersection of Lombard Street and Hyde Street, Russian Hill District

BRUCE LEE

Lee Jun Fan was born on November 27, 1940 in San Francisco at Chinatown's Jackson Street Chinese Hospital to parents Lee Hoi Chuen and Grace Ho. His father was a Cantonese-born opera and film actor and his

mother a Chinese American who came from an affluent Hong Kong family. The couple had four other children, two boys and two girls. Lee made his first film appearance, as a baby, in the 1941 locally filmed Golden Gate Girl. His family returned to live in the Kowloon area of Hong Kong when Lee was three months old where he remained until he was 18. In 1959 he traveled back to the United States where he stayed in San Francisco for three months before moving on to Seattle to attend Edison Technical School, graduating in 1960. The next year he enrolled at the University of Washington, majoring in drama, but in 1964 he dropped out and returned to the Bay Area to share living quarters in Oakland with James Yimm Lee, a well-known Chinese martial artist. Lee began to train students in Chinese Ging Fu and during this period married Linda Emery and they went on to have two children, Brandon and Shannon. He developed his own version of martial arts that he called Jeet Kune Do in schools in Oakland and Los Angeles teaching celebrities such as actor Steve McQueen. His appearance in the Green Hornet TV show and later exposure made him famous. He died prematurely in Hong Kong at age 37, on July 20, 1973, of an excess accumulation of water in the brain–although other theories exist for his untimely death.

Dragon Fight

1989, Grand March Movie Production Company

Two Chinese martial arts friends show off their talents, but one wants to defect to the United States.

Director: Hin Sing Tang
Screenwriters: Sally Nichols, James Yuen
Art Director: Hoosen Abdul Ganni
Partial Cast: Jet Li, Dick Wei, Nina Li Chi

• San Francisco-Oakland Bay Bridge
• Golden Gate Bridge
• Various aerial views of San Francisco
• International Terminal, San Francisco International Airport

• 350 Broadway, Telegraph Hill District-as Police Station
• Oasis Bar, 1500 Folsom Street, South of Market District-rooftop bar
• The Embarcadero-driving
• 300 block of Townsend Street, South of Market District-accident site
• Third Street Bridge, China Basin
• The Baldwin Apartments, 1036 Polk Street, Polk Gulch District
• 85 Cedar Street, Tenderloin District-fight
• Finochhio Club, 506 Broadway, Telegraph Hill District-neon sign on roof
• Yerba Buena Island-above Bay Bridge
• Dunsmuir House and Gardens, 2960 Peralta Oaks Court, Oakland-meeting site
• Powell and Mason Cable Car, Nob Hill District
• Prescott Court, Telegraph Hill District-mugging
• Marina Green, Marina District
• Fisherman's Wharf District
• 681 Sutter Street, Nob Hill District-store
• St. Francis Hotel, 335 Powell Street, Union Square District-restaurant
• Crissy Field, Presidio, Golden Gate National Recreation Area
• Intersection of Sutter Street and Taylor Street, Nob Hill District-shootout with police
• Sutro Baths ruins, 1000 Pt. Lobos Avenue, Golden Gate National Recreation Area

Dream for an Insomniac

1998, Columbia TriStar
A waitress is on the lookout for Mister Right.

Director: Tiffanie DeBartolo
Screenwriter: Tiffanie DeBartolo
Production Designer: Gary T. New
Art Director: John P. Jockinsen
Cinematographer: Guillermo Navarro
Partial Cast: Ione Skye, Jennifer Aniston, Mackenzie Astin, Michael Landes

• San Francisco-Oakland Bay Bridge
• 1040 Pine Street, Russian Hill District-bar
• Wash House Blues, 775 Haight Street, Lower Haight District-laundromat
• Baker Beach, Presidio, Golden Gate National Recreation Area
• Cable Car
• Emeryville

Dream With the Fishes

1997, Sony Pictures Classics
A suicidal man is saved by another man who is terminally ill and they are drawn together by their closeness to death.

Director: Finn Taylor
Screenwriters: Finn Taylor, Jeffrey D. Brown
Production Designer: Justin McCartney
Art Director: Christopher Frank

Cinematographer: Barry Stone
Partial Cast: David Arquette, Brad Hunt

• San Francisco-Oakland Bay Bridge
• Pier 39, Waterfront
• Sea Bowl, 4625 Coast Highway, State Highway Route 1, Pacifica
• Half Moon Bay-bank robbery
• First Congregational Church of Pescadero, Stage Road at North Street, Pescadero
• Mt. Hope/St. Anthony's Cemetery, Stage Road, Pescadero
• Windsor Bowl, 8801 Conde Lane, Windsor

FINN TAYLOR

Writer and director Finn William Taylor was born in Oakland on July 4, 1958. During his childhood years he lived in Norway for a time. He attended the University of Montana and then San Francisco State University where he studied poetry and playwriting. In the late 1980s he was literary director for the San Francisco Intersection for the Arts. His first feature film as writer was *Pontiac Moon* with Ted Dansen and Mary Steenburgen. Debuted at the Sundance Film Festival *Dream With the Fishes* was his first directorial project. He also wrote and directed two other filmed in the Bay Area films, *Cherish* (2002) and *The Darwin Awards* (2006).

Duffy of San Quentin

1954, Warner Brothers
A true story of how the prison's warden fought for and received respect even from the hardest inmates.

Director: Walter Doniger
Screenwriters: Walter Doniger, Berman Swarttz
Authors: Clinton T. Duffy, Dean Jennings *The San Quentin Story* (book)
Cinematographer: John Alton
Partial Cast: Louis Hayward, Joanne Dru, Maureen O'Sullivan

• San Quentin Sate Prison, San Quentin

CLINTON DUFFY

Warden Clinton Truman Duffy (1898-1982) had his life's training on the grounds of San Quentin. His father

William was a guard and justice of the peace there and "Clint" was born and raised within the prison's property. He attended San Quentin's town grammar school and graduated from San Rafael High School. In 1921 he married his school sweetheart Gladys Carpenter who was the daughter of a prison officer. After a stint with the United States Marines in World War I he returned to the prison to become administrative assistant to Warden Holohan. Moving upward he became the secretary and historian to the Board of Prison Directors and one of the secretaries to the Parole Board for five years. With a void in the Wardenship, Duffy assumed the role of Acting Warden and soon after he was appointed to a four-year term as Warden. Taking over from a previously Draconian administrative regime, Duffy became known as a humanitarian whose decent, good intentioned philosophy recast the role of warden by instigating educational, recreational and a variety of rehabilitation programs. He also fired brutal guards, abolished corporal punishment, eliminated the dungeon and use of whips. He was the first to introduce Alcoholics Anonymous to a reform setting. The Duffy family occupied an 11-bedroom house that was staffed by trusted prisoners. After his 11 1/2-year tenure, wife Gladys and he moved to nearby Kentfield—the first time Duffy lived off of Quentin Point. In 1950 he authored *The San Quentin Story* on which the film was based. If the film and its sequel *The Steel Cage* (1954) seem episodic in nature that's because they were both created from episodes of a never-telecast television series based on Duffy's career.

Dumbarton Bridge
1999, Vanguard Cinema
A mixed-race couple's life is thrown out of balance when his half-Vietnamese daughter shows up and father and daughter search for belonging and identity.

Director: Charles Koppelman
Screenwriter: Charles Koppelman
Production Designer: Pamela B. Warner
Cinematographer: Barry Stone
Partial Cast: Esperanza Catubig, Art Desuyo, Daphne Ashbrook, Leo Burmester, Kelvin Han Yee, Tom Wright

• Dumbarton Bridge, State Highway Route 84
• Don Edwards San Francisco Bay National Wildlife Refuge, 9500 Thornton Avenue, Newark
• Coyote Hills Regional Preserve, Newark
• The Garden, 1960 University Avenue, East Palo Alto
• Stanford Shopping Center, 1 Stanford Shopping Center, Palo Alto
• New Park Mall, 2086 New Park Mall, Newark
• Sun Microsystems, 4000 Network Circle, Redwood City
• Fort Point National Historic Site, Marine Drive, Golden Gate National Recreation Area
• Edward's Grinding, 6756 Central Avenue, Newark
• Cargill Salt Company, 295 Seaport Boulevard, Redwood City
• International Terminal, San Francisco International Airport
• San Francisco Bay salt evaporator ponds

Dying Young
1991, 20th Century Fox
A terminally ill man falls in love with his nurse.

Director: Joel Schumacher
Screenwriter: Richard Friedenberg
Art Directors: Guy J. Comtois, Richard L. Johnson
Cinematographer: Juan Ruiz Anchia
Principal Cast: Julia Roberts, Campbell Scott, Vincent D'Orofrio, Colleen Dewhurst, Ellen Bursten

• Lyon Street steps, Pacific Heights District
• Haas Lilienthal House, 2007 Franklin Street, Pacific Heights District
• Golden Gate Bridge
• South San Francisco
• Filoli Estate and Gardens, 86 Cañada Road, Woodside
• Stag's Leap Ranch, 6150 Silverado Trail, Napa

Eat a Bowl of Tea
1989, Columbia Pictures
A Chinese-American man brings his Chinese-born bride to post World War II New York, but pressure by his relatives interferes with his sexual performance.

Director: Wayne Wang
Screenwriter: Judith Rascoe
Author: Louis Chu (novel)
Production Designer: Bob Ziembicki

Art Director: Timmy Yip
Cinematographer: Amir M. Mokri
Partial Cast: Cora Miao, Russell Wong, Victor Wong, Siu-Ming Lau

• Golden Gate Bridge

Ed TV
1999, Universal
A man with little ambition is put on television day and night, and his life becomes a lot more interesting.

Director: Ron Howard
Screenwriters: Émile Gaudreault, Sylvie Bouchard, Lowell Ganz, Babaloo Mandel
Production Designer: Michael Corenblith
Art Director: Dan Webster
Cinematographer: John Schwartzman
Partial Cast: Mathew McConaughey, Jenna Elfman, Ellen DeGeneres, Woody Harrelson, Martin Landau, Sally Kirkland, Rob Reiner, Elizabeth Hurley, Dennis Hopper, Clint Howard

• Sutro Tower, Mt. Sutro District
• 1398 Grant Avenue, Telegraph Hill District-video store
• Nob Hill District
• Castro Theatre, 429 Castro Street, Eureka Valley District-chase
• Market Street at Second Street
• 3665 Scott Street, Marina District-Deco apartment building
• Marina Green, Marina District-football scenes
• 34 Sixth Street, South of Market District-SRO hotel
• San Jose Arena, 525 West Santa Clara Street, San Jose

Electric Dreams
1984, Metro Goldwyn Mayer and United Artists
An artificially intelligent PC and its human owner find themselves in a romantic rivalry over a woman.

Director: Steve Barron
Screenwriter: Rusty Lemorande
Production Designer: Richard MacDonald
Art Director: Richard Dawking
Cinematographer: Alex Thomson
Partial Cast: Lenny von Dohlen, Virginia Madsen, Maxwell Caulfield, Bud Cort
Local Cast: TV anchor Elaine Corral

• Transamerica Pyramid, 600 Montgomery Street, Financial District
• 1111-1113 Mason Street, Nob Hill District-apartment house
• Alcatraz Federal Prison, Alcatraz Island, Golden Gate National Recreation Area
• Pier 39, Waterfront
• ACT Geary Theater, 405 Geary Street, Union Square District

• Davies Symphony Hall, 201 Van Ness Avenue, Civic Center
• Golden Gate Bridge

"What we got here is a well organized group of militants with enough explosives to blow up San Francisco."

The Enforcer
1976, Warner Brothers
AKA: *Moving Target*
Police Inspector Harry Callahan is teamed with a new, and unwelcome, female partner and they hunt down blackmailing terrorists.

Director: James Fargo
Screenwriters: Harry Julian Fink, Rita M. Fink, Gail Morgan Hickman, S. W. Schurr, Stirling Silliphant, Dean Riesner
Art Director: Allen E. Smith
Cinematographer: Charles W. Short
Partial Cast: Clint Eastwood, Tyne Daly, Harry Guardini, Bradford Dillman

• State Highway Route 1, Muir Beach
• Panoramic aerial view of waterfront
• Enrico's Sidewalk Cafe, 504 Broadway, Telegraph Hill District
• Hall of Justice, 850 Bryant Street, South of Market District
• 1967 Sutter Street, Western Addition District-barber shop
• 139 Second Street, South of Market District-liquor store
• St. Francis of Assisi Church, 610 Vallejo Street, North Beach District-church interior
• San Francisco City Hall, 1 Carlton B. Goodlett Place, Civic Center District-rotunda
• Coit Tower, Pioneer Park, 1 Telegraph Hill Boulevard, Telegraph Hill District-park
• Aquatic Park, San Francisco Maritime National Historic Park, Golden Gate National Recreation Area-fishing pier
• Candlestick Park, 602 Jamestown Avenue, Bayview District
• Third Street Bridge, China Basin, South of Market District
• Alcatraz Island, Golden Gate National Recreation Area
• Fort Baker, Marin Headlands, Golden Gate National Recreation Area
• Pier 50, The Embarcadero

Enough

2002, Sony Pictures Entertainment

Tired of an abusive husband, a young mother realizes she is capable of fighting back.

Director: Michael Apted
Screenwriter: Nicholas Kazan
Production Designer: Doug Kramer
Art Director: Andrew Menzes
Cinematographer: Rogier Stoffers
Partial Cast: Jennifer Lopez, Bill Campbell, Tessa Allen, Juliette Lewis

• Intersection of Montgomery Street and Broadway, Telegraph Hill District

Escape from Alcatraz

1979, Paramount

A convict plots to escape from the notorious Alcatraz Island prison.

Director: Don Siegel
Screenwriter: Richard Tuggle
Author: J. Campbell Bruce (book)
Production Designer: Allen E. Smith
Cinematographer: Bruce Surtees
Partial Cast: Clint Eastwood, Patrick McGoohan, Robert Blossom, Jack Thibeau, Larry Hankin

• Alcatraz Federal Prison, Alcatraz Island, Golden Gate National Recreation Area
• Angel Island, Golden Gate National Recreation Area

Escape to Witch Mountain

1974, Buena Vista

Two orphaned siblings have special powers.

Director: John Hough
Screenwriter: Robert M. Young
Author: Alexander H. Key (novel)
Art Directors: John B. Mansbridge, Al Roelofs
Cinematographer: Frank V. Phillips
Partial Cast: Eddie Albert, Ray Milland, Donald Pleasence, Kim Richards, Ike Eisenmann, Rita Shaw, Denver Pyle

• Coleman Mansion, Peninsula Way and Berkeley Avenue, Menlo Park-as Pine Woods Orphanage

meant for the both of them. The structure sat vacant until 1906 when it was purchased by the Catholic Archdiocese of San Francisco for use as a boy's school. Between 1906 and 1909 residents of the nearby earthquake-damaged St. Patrick's Seminary were occupants. In 1925 it was acquired by the Peninsula School and is a private school now known as the Peninsula School for Creative Education. Architect Augustus Laver, who also designed San Francisco's first purpose-built City Hall, designed the richly detailed structure. "The Big Building," its moniker within the school, became a celebrity when boarding school scenes for the Disney movie were filmed there for a week in 1974. Every child who wished to participate was used as an extra, and they pooled their earnings to use half the money for a paid position for P.E. teacher Karol Jones, who had been interning at the school; the other half was used to buy gym equipment.

Eve of Destruction
1991, Orion
A robot, modeled on its creator, with killing instincts becomes a danger to mankind.

Director: Duncan Gibbins
Screenwriters: Duncan Gibbins, Yale Udoff
Production Designer: Peter Lamont
Cinematographer: Alan Hume
Partial Cast: Gregory Hines, Renée Soutendijk, Michael Greene

• 341 California Street, Financial District-shootout
• Golden Gate Bridge
• General views of Napa

Ever Since Eve
1937, Warner Brothers
A beautiful secretary transforms herself into a plain-jane secretary to keep her boss on deadline.

Director: Lloyd Bacon
Screenwriters: Lawrence Riley, Earl Baldwin, Lillie Hayward
Authors: Margaret Lee, Gene Baker (story)
Art Director: Robert M. Haas
Cinematographer: George Barnes

Partial Cast: Marion Davies, Robert Montgomery

• Various views of San Francisco

Ever Since the World Ended
2001, Epidemic Films
Pseudo documentary about San Francisco 12 years after a holocaust.

Directors: Calum Grant, Joshua Atesh Litle
Screenwriter: Caulm Grant
Cinematographer: Joshua Atesh Litle
Partial Cast: James Curry, Linda Noveroske, Dan Plumlee

• Muni station, Market Street
• Commercial Street, Financial District
• Montgomery Street, Financial District
• Golden Gate Bridge
• Baker Beach, Presidio, Golden Gate National Recreation Area
• Marin Headlands, Golden Gate National Recreation Area
• Corona Heights Park, Corona Heights District
• Nicasio Reservoir, Nicasio Valley Road, Nicasio
• Pacific Coast Stock Exchange Building, 301 Pine Street, Financial District
• Castro Theatre, 429 Castro Street, Eureka Valley District

Every Girl Should Be Married
1948, RKO Radio Pictures
A girl is determined to find just the right husband.

Director: Don Hartman
Screenwriters: Stephen Morehouse Avery, Eleanor Harris, Don Hartman
Art Directors: Carroll Clark, Albert S. D'Agostino
Cinematographer: George E. Diskant
Partial Cast: Cary Grant, Franchot Tone, Diana Lynn, Betsy Drake

• Union Square, 333 Post Street
• I. Magnin and Co., 233 Geary Street, Union Square-as Roger Sanford & Company

Experiment Alcatraz
1950, RKO Radio Pictures
A doctor tests his theory that blood diseases can be cured by atomic radiation by using prison inmates as experiments.

Director: Edward L. Cahn
Screenwriters: George W. George, Orville H. Hampton, George F. Slavin
Art Director: Boris Leven

Cinematographer: Jackson J. Rose
Partial Cast: John Howard, Joan Dixon, Walter Kingsford

• Alcatraz Federal Prison, Alcatraz Island, Golden Gate National Recreation Area

Experiment in Terror
1962, Columbia
A robber who intends to force a bank teller to be his accomplice stalks the bank teller and her younger sister.

Director: Blake Edwards
Screenwriters: The Gordons (Gordon Gordon, Mildred Gordon)
Art Director: Robert Peterson
Cinematographer: Philip Lathrop
Partial Cast: Glenn Ford, Lee Remick, Stefanie Powers, Ross Martin
Local Cast: San Francisco Giants baseball Team members Willie Mays, "Stretch" Willie McCovey, Mike McCormick

• San Francisco-Oakland Bay Bridge
• 100 St. Germain Street, Twin Peaks District-as Sherwood Residence
• 206 Palo Alto Street, Twin Peaks District
• George Washington High School, 600 32nd Avenue, Richmond District
• Crocker Anglo National Bank, 1 Post Street, Financial District-banking hall
• 2632 Larkin Street, Russian Hill District
• Lick Place, Financial District
• Varni's Roaring Twenties Club, 807 Montgomery Street, Telegraph Hill District
• Top of Crookedest Street in the World, 1000 block of Lombard Street, Russian Hill District
• St. Francis of Assisi Church, 610 Vallejo Street, North Beach District
• Kaiser Foundation Hospital, 2425 Geary Boulevard, Anza Vista District
• The Wizard Restaurant, 6100 Geary Boulevard, Outer Richmond District-as The Hangout
• Fisherman's Wharf, intersection of Taylor Street and Jefferson Street, Fisherman's Wharf District
• Orange Grove Fruit Bowl, 57 Lick Place, Financial District-restaurant
• Candlestick Park, 602 Jamestown Avenue, Bayview District
• Marin Town and Country Club, Pastori Avenue at Lansdale Street, Fairfax

Explorers
1985, Paramount
An alien-obsessed boy dreams of a circuit board and he and his misfit friends discover they have been given the basis for a starship that they launch to another galaxy.

Director: Joe Dante
Screenwriter: Eric Luke
Production Designer: Robert F. Boyle

Art Director: Frank Richwood
Cinematographer: John Hora
Partial Cast: Ethan Hawke, River Phoenix, Bobby Fite, Jason Presson, Amanda Peterson

• West Petaluma Creek, Petaluma
• La Cresta Drive, Petaluma
• Petaluma River, Petaluma
• 920 D Street, Petaluma-Victorian house

An Eye for an Eye
1981, Avco and Embassy
A policeman is forced to resign his post in the narcotics division when his partner is murdered.

Director: Steve Carver
Screenwriters: James Bruner, William Gray
Production Designer: Sandy Veneziano
Art Director: Vance Lorenzini
Cinematographer: Roger Shearman
Partial Cast: Chuck Norris, Christopher Lee, Richard Roundtree, Matt Clark, Mako

• 2415/17 Franklin Street, Pacific Heights District
• Golden Gate Bridge
• St. Mary's Cathedral, 1111 Gough Street, Cathedral Hill District
• Bank of America, 555 California Street, Financial District-lobby and roof

BANK OF AMERICA BUILDING

The iconic 52-story Bank of America Building at 555 California Street was designed by architects Wurster, Bernardi and Emmons; Skidmore Owings and Merrill with design consultant Pietro Belluschi, which was completed in 1969.

Formerly this site was the location of the public debut of the first commercial true moving picture. In the spring of 1880 photographer Eadweard Muybridge (underwritten by magnate Leland Stanford) used a projector called Zoogyroscope to present projected sequential unposed photographs of life-motion to a large audience in the exhibition hall of the San Francisco Art Association at 430 Pine Street. The event, where Muybridge described how the illusion of motion was created, was recorded in an article titled "Moving Shadows" that was published in the *San Francisco Chronicle* on May 5, 1880 as "presenting a sight as

Eye of the Beholder
1999, Destination Films
A private eye shadows a woman for more than a decade, without her ever knowing and he occasionally acts as her guardian angel.

Director: Stephan Elliott
Screenwriter: Stephan Elliott
Author: Marc Behm (novel)
Production Designer: Jean-Baptiste Tard
Art Director: Réal Proulx
Cinematographer: Guy Dufaux
Partial Cast: Ashley Judd, Ewan McGregor, Patrick Bergin

• Golden Gate Bridge
• Palace of Fine Arts, 3601 Lyon Street, Marina District
• Cable Car
• Mark Hopkins Hotel, 999 California Street, Nob Hill District
• Presidio Gate, intersection of Lombard Street and Lyon Street, Presidio, Golden Gate National Recreation Area

Eye of the Cat
1969, Universal
AKA: *Wylie*
A young man who is afraid of cats stays with a crippled aunt who has a house full of felines.

Director: David Lowell Rich
Screenwriter: Joseph Stefano
Art Directors: William D. DeCinces, Alexander Golitzen
Cinematographers: Ellsworth Fredericks, Russell Metty
Partial Cast: Michael Sarrazin, Gayle Hunnicutt, Eleanor Parker

• Golden Gate Bridge
• Lafayette Park, Pacific Heights District
• 2200 block of Octavia Street, Pacific Heights District
• Spreckels Mansion, 2080 Washington Street, Pacific Heights District

The Facts of Life
1960, United Artists
A view of suburban life where two middle-aged marrieds attempt to have an affair.

Director: Melvin Frank

Screenwriters: Melvin Frank, Norman Panama
Art Directors: J. McMillan Johnson, Kenneth A. Reid
Cinematographer: Charles Lang Jr.
Partial Cast: Lucille Ball, Bob Hope, Ruth Hussey, Don DeFore, Louis Nye

• San Francisco International Airport

The Falcon in San Francisco
1945, RKO Radio Pictures
A couple gets involved with what appears to be a silk smuggling ring.

Director: Joseph H. Lewis
Screenwriters: Robert E. Kent, Ben Markson
Art Directors: Albert S. D'Agostino, Charles F. Pyke
Cinematographers: Virgil Miller, William A. Sickner
Partial Cast: Tom Conway, Rita Corday, Edward Brophy

• Ferry Building, The Embarcadero
• Intersection of Sea Cliff Avenue and El Camino Del Mar, Sea Cliff District

Falling Uphill
2012, Blue Creek Pictures
Two roommates fall for each other but one has to return home to his parents. With only three days until the flight, he struggles to admit his true feelings toward her.

Director: Richard J. Bosner
Screenwriter: Richard J. Bosner
Production Designer: Schuyler Robertson
Cinematographer: Jesse Dana
Partial Cast: Ari Kanamori, Jessiqa Pace, Jenna Hunt, Jack McGee

• 560 Scott Street, Western Addition District-Leo's apartment
• Adobe Bookshop, 3166 16th Street, Mission District
• Alamo Square, Western Addition District
• Cole Hardware, 956 Cole Street, Cole Valley District
• 620 Cabrillo Street, Inner Richmond District
• Moscone Park, Marina District
• Washington Square, North Beach District
• Mojo Bicycle Café, 639 Divisadero Street, Western Addition
• Wasteland, 1660 Haight Street, Haight-Ashbury District
• Excelsior Lane Steps, intersection of Bridgeway, Sausalito
• Ferry Terminal, intersection of El Portal Street and Tracy Way, Sausalito
• San Wang Restaurant, 1680 Post Street, Japantown District

- Angelino Restaurant, 621 Bridgeway, Sausalito
- Muni Metro stop, intersection of Church Street and Duboce Street, Duboce Triangle District
- Duboce Park, Duboce Triangle District
- BART-train to airport

Family Plot
1976, Universal Studios
A phony psychic/con artist and her taxi driver/private-investigator boyfriend encounter a pair of kidnappers.

Director: Alfred Hitchcock
Screenwriter: Ernest Lehman
Author: Victor Canning *The Rainbird Pattern* (novel)
Production Designer: Henry Bumstead
Cinematographer: Leonard J. South
Partial Cast: Karen Black, Bruce Dern, Barbara Harris

- Grace Cathedral, 1100 California Street, Nob Hill District-steps and interior
- 2230 Sacramento Street, Pacific Heights District-house
- Fairmont Hotel, 950 Mason Street, Nob Hill District-porte cochere

The Fan
1996, TriStar and Mandalay Entertainment
An all star baseball player becomes the unhealthy focus of a down-on-his luck salesman.

Director: Tony Scott
Screenwriter: Phoef Sutton
Author: Peter Abrahams (book)
Production Designer: Ida Random
Art Directors: Mayne Berke, Adam Lustig
Cinematographer: Dariusz Wolski
Partial Cast: Robert De Niro, Wesley Snipes, Ellen Barkin, John Leguizamo, Benicio Del Toro

- San Francisco-Oakland Bay Bridge
- Chinatown District
- Ritz-Carlton Hotel, 600 Stockton Street, Nob Hill District
- Candlestick Park, 602 Jamestown Avenue, Bayview District

CANDLESTICK PARK

Affectionately known as "The Stick," the striking Brutalist-style reinforced concrete structure enclosing Candlestick Park opened on April 12, 1960 with Vice President Richard Nixon throwing out the first pitch. As the new home of major league baseball's San Francisco Giants team, the 69,000 seat venue almost doubled the seating capacity beyond their former home of Seals Stadium. But the new stadium, designed by the architectural firm of John S. Bolles only started a love/hate relationship with players and spectators alike as winds and fog could make the new stadium uncomfortably chilly. In 1972 an extension of the upper deck to fully surround the outfield by the same architect helped —but only somewhat. The stadium became an international cultural landmark when The Beatles played their last live commercial concert there on August 29, 1966. In 1971 the San Francisco 49ers NFL team moved into the park from Kezar Stadium, a strategy that used the facility virtually all year long. Another prime event was to host Pope Paul II who celebrated mass there in 1987. In recent decades the park has suffered a case of multiple personalities. The short-lived name of 3-Com Park came about when the financially strapped City of San Francisco auctioned off the ballpark's naming right to Silicon Valley's 3Com Corporation in 1994. When that commitment ended it officially became the San Francisco Stadium at Candlestick Point, and then Monster Park. Since 2008, the name has reverted to the original. Although efforts to build a better ballpark started just ten years after Candlestick's opening, it was not until 1999 that the warmer and cozier Pacific Bell Park, now known as AT&T Park, drew baseball fans back to downtown San Francisco. With the 49ers move to Santa Clara County, Candlestick will be demolished in favor of new construction consisting of housing and retail.

Farmer and Chase
1997, Arrow Releasing
A career criminal's son continues in his father's footsteps and the FBI is on to him.

Director: Michael Seitzman

Screenwriter: Michael Seitzman
Production Designer: Douglas Freeman
Cinematographer: Michael Maley
Partial Cast: Todd Field, Ben Gazzara, Lara Flynn Boyle

• San Francisco
• Sonoma
• Intersection of First Street and G Street, Petaluma
• San Rafael
• Fairfax
• San Anselmo

The Farmer's Daughter
1947, Selznick
AKA: *Katie for Congress*
A Congressman's maid rises to be a political force.

Director: H. C. Potter
Screenwriters: Hella Wuolijoki, Allen Rivkin, Laura Kerr
Author: Hella Wuolijoki *Hulda, Daughter of Parliament* (play)
Art Directors: Albert S. D'Agostino, Field M. Gray
Cinematographer: Milton Krasner
Partial Cast: Loretta Young, Joseph Cotten, Ethel Barrymore, Charles Bickford

• Scott Ranch, Adobe Road, Penngrove

SCOTT RANCH

The two-story Victorian house was the locus of the Scott Ranch, which had various outbuildings and a silo as seen in the movie's opening and closing scenes. An off-camera shot during the movie shoot revealed that the barn with mural on its side was built as a set piece. An opening scene shows the sign painter painting a mural on the fake barn. The entire ranch was demolished sometime after the movie was made and no trace of it exists today except for the rolling landscape it sat within.

The Fatal Hour
1940, Monogram Picture Corporation
A detective uncovers a smuggling ring on the waterfront and unmasks a Killer in the process.

Director: William Nigh
Screenwriters: Scott Darling, George Waggner, Hugh Wiley
Cinematographer: Harry Neumann
Partial Cast: Boris Karloff, Marjorie Reynolds, Grant Withers

• Coit Tower, Pioneer Park, 1 Telegraph Hill Boulevard, Telegraph Hill District
• Panorama of Financial District from Telegraph Hill
• Old Hall of Justice, 750 Kearny Street, Financial District
• Intersection of Grant Avenue and California Street, Chinatown District
• Intersection of Market Street and Kearny Street, Financial District

Fathers' Day
1997, Warner Brothers
A woman cons two old boyfriends into searching for her runaway son by convincing both that they are the boy's father.

Director: Ivan Reitman
Screenwriters: Lowell Ganz, Babaloo Mandel
Author: Francis Veber *Les Compères* (film)
Production Designer: Thomas E. Sanders
Art Director: Daniel T. Dorrance
Cinematographer: Stephen H. Burum
Partial Cast: Robin Williams, Billy Crystal, Julia Louis-Dryfus, Nastassja Kinski

• Zuni Café, 1658 Market Street
• Emporio Armani Boutique, 1 Grant Avenue
• 530 Folsom, South of Market District-as Tip Top Towing
• San Francisco-Oakland Bay Bridge
• Clipper Cove, Treasure Island-as Tiburon dock
• Mark Hopkins Hotel, 999 California Street, Nob Hill District-porte cochere
• Nicasio Reservoir, Nicasio Valley Road, Nicasio

Fat Man and Little Boy
1989, Paramount
AKA: *Shadow Makers*
The U.S. Army and scientists clash when developing the first atom bomb.

Director: Roland Joffé
Screenwriters: Bruce Robinson, Roland Joffé
Production Designer: Gregg Fonseca
Art Directors: Larry Fulton, Peter Lansdown Smith
Cinematographer: Vilmos Zsigmond
Partial Cast: Paul Newman, John Cusak, Laura Dern

• Painted Ladies, 700 block of Steiner Street, Western Addition District

Fearless
1993, Warner Brothers
A man's personality is irrevocably changed when he becomes a jet crash victim.

Director: Peter Weir
Screenwriter: Rafael Yglesias
Author: Rafael Yglesias (novel)
Production Designer: John Stoddart
Cinematographer: Allen Daviau
Partial Cast: Jeff Bridges, Isabella Rossellini, Rosie Perez

• Market Street
• 147-149 Varennes Street, Telegraph Hill District-as Klein Residence
• Embarcadero Freeway-closed freeway ramp
• Ferry Building, The Embarcadero
• San Francisco-Oakland Bay Bridge
• 1011-A Shotwell Street, Mission District-as Rodrigo Residence
• Kohl Building, 400 Montgomery Street, Financial District-rooftop
• Oakland Tribune Building, 410 13th Street, Oakland
• The Women's Building, 3543 18th Street, Mission District-mural
• Paramount Theater of the Arts, 2025 Broadway, Oakland-mural
• Fox Theater and office building, 1815 Telegraph Avenue, Oakland
• San Francisco General Hospital, 1001 Potrero Avenue, Mission District-entry and roof terrace

The Fighting Sullivans
1944, Twentieth Century Fox
Five sons of one family give their lives in World War II combat.

Director: Lloyd Bacon
Screenwriters: Edward Doherty, Mary C. McCall Jr., Jules Schermer
Art Directors: James Basevi, Leland Fuller
Cinematographer: Lucien N. Androit
Partial Cast: Anne Baxter, Thomas Mitchell, Selena Royale, Edward Ryan, Ward Bond

• 8 Morgan Street, Santa Rosa-as Waterloo, Iowa
• Old Railroad Depot, 9 Fourth Street, Santa Rosa Northwestern Pacific Depot, Railroad Square, Santa Rosa
• Russian River-boat scenes
• Ranch, Hill Road, Petaluma-quarry used as motorcycle race site

50 First Dates
2004, Columbia and Sony Pictures
AKA: *Fifty First Kisses, 50 First Kisses*

A man falls in love with a woman who has memory problems.

Director: Peter Segal
Screenwriter: George Wing
Production Designer: Alan Au
Art Directors: John Hockridge, Domenic Silvestri
Cinematographer: Jack N. Green
Partial Cast: Adam Sandler, Drew Barrymore, Sean Astin, Rob Schneider, Blake Clark

• Six Flags Marine World, 1001 Fairgrounds Drive, Vallejo
• Rainforest Café, 145 Jefferson Street, Fisherman's Wharf District

Final Analysis
1992, Warner Brothers
A psychiatrist has an affair with a patient's sister and falls into a diabolical plot.

Director: Phil Joanau
Screenwriters: Robert Berger, Wesley Strick
Production Designer: Dean Tavoularis
Art Director: Angelo P. Graham
Cinematographer: Jordan Cronenweth
Partial Cast: Richard Gere, Kim Basinger, Uma Thurman

• Bix Restaurant, 56 Gold Street, Telegraph Hill District
• Hotaling Alley, Jackson Square District-outdoor restaurant
• San Francisco City Hall, 1 Carlton B. Goodlett Place, Civic Center District-side driveway and interior rotunda
• Golden Gate Bridge
• Presidio Yacht Club, Horseshoe Cove, Fort Baker, Marin Headlands, Golden Gate National Recreation Area-marina
• Crookedest Street in the World, 1000 block of Lombard Street, Russian Hill District
• Powell and Market Cable Car, Hyde Street, Russian Hill District
• House of Shields Bar, 39 New Montgomery Street, South of Market District
• Highland General Hospital, 1411 East 31st Street, Oakland
• Pigeon Point Light Station State Historical Park, 210 Pigeon Point Road, State Highway Route 1, Pescadero-as Lime Point Lighthouse
• Sir Francis Drake Hotel, 450 Powell Street, Union Square District-restaurant
• Marine Hospital, 1801 Wedemeyer Street, Presidio, Golden Gate National Recreation Area-hospital exterior

Finian's Rainbow
1968, Warner Brothers
A leprechaun tries to retrieve a crock of gold from a wanderer who has taken it to the U.S.

Director: Francis Ford Coppola
Screenwriters: E. Y. Harburg, Fred Saidy
Authors: E. Y. Harburg, Fred Saidy (book)
Production Designer: Hilyard M. Brown
Cinematographer: Philip H. Lathrop
Partial Cast: Fred Astaire, Petula Clark

- Golden Gate Bridge
- Sacramento River Delta
- San Francisco-Oakland Bay Bridge
- Intersection of Bodega Highway and Bodega Lane, Bodega

The First 20 Million Is Always the Hardest
2002, 20th Century Fox
A successful marketing executive decides to chuck his non-stop, upwardly-mobile lifestyle when he realizes that he wants to be a creator instead of a seller.

Director: Mick Jackson
Screenwriters: Jon Favreau, Gary Tieche
Author: Po Bronson (novel)
Production Designer: William Sandell
Art Directors: Bruce Crone, Brad Ricker
Cinematographer: Ronald Victor Garcia
Partial Cast: Adam Garcia, Rosario Dawson, Jake Busey

- Columbus Avenue, North Beach District
- Baker Beach, Presidio, Golden Gate National Recreation Area
- Earl Warren State Office Building, 350 McAllister Street, Civic Center
- San Francisco Ferry Terminal, 1 Ferry Building, The Embarcadero

Fisherman's Wharf
1939, RKO Radio Pictures
The relationship of a boy and his foster father is upset by the arrival of relations on their fishing boat.

Director: Bernard Vorhaus
Screenwriters: Bernard Schubert, Ian McLellan Hunter, Herbert Clyde Lewis
Art Director: Lewis J. Rachmil
Cinematographer: Charles Edgar Schoenbaum
Partial Cast: Bobby Breen, Leo Carillo, Rosina Galli, Lee Patrick, Henry Armetha

- San Francisco Bay
- Fisherman's Wharf District
- Filbert Street Steps, Telegraph Hill District
- Golden Gate Bridge
- Treasure Island
- Alcatraz Island, Golden Gate National Recreation Area
- Fisherman's Grotto Restaurant, 9 Fisherman's Wharf, Fisherman's Wharf District

THE ROCK

One of the Bay Area's most popular tourist destinations has a varied history. During the 22.5-acre island's history it has been a nesting area for white and brown pelicans (Spanish explorers named it Isla de Alcatraces, island of pelicans), a military fort (established in 1859) and on October 12, 1933 a federal civil prison. Closed in 1963 it became part of the Golden Gate National Recreation Area in 1973. The original lighthouse (the first in San Francisco Bay) was built in 1854 with the current one having been built in 1909 was overshadowed by neighboring structures. On March 8, 1964 five Sioux Indians took over the island using an 1868 treaty with the Sioux Nation to claim the island theirs as "unoccupied government land." Another American Indian occupation started in 1969 until removal by U.S. Marshals on June 11, 1971.

The Five Pennies
1959, Paramount
A musician falls on difficult times when his daughter contracts polio.

Director: Melville Shavelson
Screenwriters: Robert Smith, Jack Rose, Melville Shavelson
Art Directors: Tambi Larsen, Hal Pereira
Cinematographer: Daniel Fapp
Partial Cast: Danny Kaye, Barbara Bel Geddes, Louis Armstrong, Bob Crosby, Harry Guardino, Tuesday Weld, Ray Anthony

- Mark Hopkins Hotel, 999 California Street, Nob Hill District-porte cochere

5 Star Day
2010, Breaking Glass Pictures
AKA: Five Star Day
A young man's journey to disprove the theory of astrology.

Director: Danny Buday
Screenwriter: Danny Buday
Production Designer: Megan Hutchison
Art Director: Mark Achilles White
Cinematographer: Jason Oldak

Partial Cast: Jena Malone, Cam Gigandet, Will Yun Lee

• Hass School of Business, University of California Campus, Berkeley, Berkeley
• San Francisco-Oakland Bay Bridge
• Cable car on 700 block of California Street, Nob Hill District
• Skyline Boulevard, Oakland-driving

The Five-Year Engagement
2012, Universal Pictures
When a couple is engaged, problems are revealed in their relationship.

Director: Nicholas Stoller
Screenwriters: Jason Segal, Nicholas Stoller
Production Designer: Julie Berghoff
Art Director: John B. Josselyn
Cinematographer: Javier Aguirresarobe
Partial Cast: Jason Segal, Emily Blunt, Chris Pratt

• San Francisco-Oakland Bay Bridge
• Ferry Building, The Embarcadero
• Chinatown
• The Embarcadero
• Beltane Ranch, 11175 Sonoma Highway, Glen Ellen-as Drunken Pig
• California Street Cable Car
• Palace of Fine Arts, 3601 Lyon Street, Marina District
• Marina Green, Marina District
• Golden Gate Bridge
• Fulton Street with view to San Francisco City Hall, Western Addition District
• Alamo Square, Western Addition District-wedding site

Flashback
1990, Paramount Pictures
An FBI agent escorts a counter culture hero to prison after his 20-years on the run.

Director: Franco Amurri
Screenwriter: David Loughery
Production Designer: Vincent M. Cresciman
Art Director: James Terry Welden
Cinematographer: Stefan Czapsky
Partial Cast: Dennis Hopper, Keifer Sutherland, Carol Kane

• City Lights Bookstore, 261 Columbus Street, Jackson Square District

Flatliners
1990, Columbia and Tri-Star
Life after death is studied by a group of medical students.

Director: Joel Schumacher
Screenwriter: Peter Filardi
Production Designer: Eugenio Zanetti
Art Director: Jim Dultz
Cinematographer: Jan de Bont
Partial Cast: Kiefer Sutherland, Julia Roberts, Kevin Bacon

• Maffia Dairy Ranch, 6700 Gravenstein Highway, State Highway Route 116, Cotati

The Fleet's In
1942, Paramount
An on-leave sailor takes a bet that he will kiss the glamorous singer at a swank night club.

Director: Victor Schertzinger
Screenwriters: Monte Brice, Walter DeLeon, Kenyon Nicholson, Charles Robinson, J. Walter Ruben, Sid Silvers, Ralph Spence
Art Directors: Hans Drier, Ernst Fegté
Cinematographer: William C. Mellor
Partial Cast: Dorothy Lamour, William Holden, Eddie Bracken, Betty Hutton, Jimmy Dorsey, Helen O'Connell, Leif Erickson

• San Francisco-Oakland Bay Bridge
• Pier north of the San Francisco-Oakland Bay Bridge, The Embarcadero

LEIF ERICKSON

The swarthy figure of Leif Erickson was born in 1911 as William Y. Wycliffe Anderson to his Alameda-based parents. His father was a ship's commander and his mother a newspaperwoman. William studied at the University of Southern California and went on to sing and play the trombone with the Ted Fio Rito Orchestra. His first film appearance was in 1933 in *The Sweetheart of Sigma Chi* billed as Glenn Erickson for Monogram Pictures. He served for four years as a Navy combat photographer during the Second World War. During that time he served as an instructor, was shot down twice and wounded on both occasions. One of his notable roles was as Deborah Kerr's macho husband in *Tea and Sympathy*. Beside appearing as Jake in *The Fleet's In* his other filmed in the Bay Area work is *Kiss Them for Me* (1957). He was married to actress Francis Farmer for five years starting in 1936, was briefly married to Margaret Hayes in 1942, but finally settled down with Ann Diamond in 1945 until his death in 1986.

Flight of the Navigator
1986, Buena Vista
AKA: *The Navigator*
In 1978, a boy is transported eight years into the future and while there has an adventure with an alien ship.

Director: Randal Kleiser
Screenwriters: Mark H. Baker, Michael Burton, Matt MacManus
Production Designer: William J. Creber
Art Director: Michael Novothy
Cinematographer: James Glennon
Partial Cast: Joey Cramer, Paul Reubens, Veronica Cartwright, Sarah Jessica Parker, Howard Hesseman

• Golden Gate Bridge

Flower Drum Song
1961, Universal International
AKA: *Rogers and Hammerstein's Flower Drum Song*
Romantic problems occur among the immigrants of Chinatown.

Director: Henry Koster
Screenwriter: Joseph Fields
Author: C. Y. Lee *The Flower Drum Song* (novel)
Art Directors: Alexander Golitzen, Joseph C. Wright
Cinematographer: Russell Metty
Partial Cast: Nancy Kwan, James Shigeta, Benson Fong, Jack Soo, Juanita Hall, Miyoshi Umeki

• Golden Gate Bridge
• Panorama of San Francisco from San Francisco Bay

The Flower Thief
1960, Filmmakers Distribution Center
Idylls of the beats in the Beat Generation scene of San Francisco's North Beach District.

Director: Ron Rice
Screenwriter: Ron Rice
Partial Cast: Taylor Mead, Barry Clark, Heinz Ellsworth

• Telegraph Hill District

Flubber
1997, Walt Disney Pictures
AKA: *Disney's Flubber: The Absent Minded Professor*
A scatterbrained professor invents a substance with special anti-gravity properties.

Director: Les Mayfield
Screenwriters: John Hughes, Bill Walsh
Author: Samuel W. Taylor "A Situation of Gravity" (short story)
Production Designer: Andrew McAlpine
Art Director: James E. Tocci
Cinematographer: Dean Cundey
Partial Cast: Robin Williams, Marcia Gay Harden

• Kohl Mansion, 2750 Adeline Drive, Burlingame-school exterior
• 1962 University Avenue, San Jose-professor's residence
• Residences along Funston Avenue, Presidio, Golden Gate National Recreation Area
• San Jose State University, Washington Square Hall, One Washington Square, San Jose-tiered science room
• Roscoe Maples Pavilion, Stanford University, 655 Campus Drive, Stanford-basketball pavilion exterior
• 345 Park Avenue, San Jose-office tower and flying car
• Mountain View Cemetery, Gothic Chapel, 5000 Piedmont Avenue, Oakland-church interior
• Open Door Christian Church, 16 Fifth Street, Petaluma-church exterior

The Fog
1979, Avco Embassy
A small town is invaded by the ghosts of mariners wrecked on the coast a hundred years earlier.

Director: John Carpenter
Screenwriters: John Carpenter, Debra Hill
Production Designer: Tommy Lee Wallace
Art Director: Craig Stearns
Cinematographer: Dean Cundey
Partial Cast: Adrienne Barbeau, Hal Holbrook, John Houseman, Janet Leigh, Jamie Lee Curtis, Tom Atkins

• Pt. Reyes Lighthouse, Pt. Reyes National Seashore
• Pt. Reyes Station-as Antonio Bay
• Drake's Beach, Pt. Reyes National Seashore
• Inverness, Tomales Bay-house
• Tides Restaurant and dock, 835 Shoreline Highway, State Highway Route 1, Bodega Bay
• Stinson Beach, Golden Gate National Recreation Area

Fog Over Frisco
1934, Warner Brothers
Half-sisters from a respected family
have polar opposite life styles.

Director: William Dieterle
Screenwriters: Robert N. Lee, George Dyer,
Eugene Solow
Art Director: Jack Okey
Cinematographer: Tony Gaudio
Partial Cast: Bette Davis, Don Woods, Margaret
Lindsay, Robert Barrat, Douglas Dumbrille, Henry
O'Neill, Irving Pichel, Alan Hale

• Irwin Mansion, 2180 Washington Street, Pacific
Heights District

Follow the Fleet
1936, RKO Radio Pictures
While on shore leave, a sailor tries to
rekindle a romance with the woman
he loves.

Director: Mark Sandrich
Screenwriters: Allan Scott, Dwight Taylor
Author: Hubert Osborne *Shore Leave* (play)
Art Director: Van Nest Polglase
Cinematographer: David Abel
Partial Cast: Fred Astaire, Ginger Rogers,
Randolph Scott, Betty Grable, Lucille Ball, Tony
Martin

• San Francisco-Oakland Bay Bridge-under
construction

TONY MARTIN

A romantic balladeer who was most
popular during the 1940s and 50s,
Martin was born Alvin Morris on December 25, 1912 in San Francisco.
His parents, who soon after moved to
Oakland, were Edward and Hattie
(Smith) Morris who were well-to-do
Jewish immigrants from Poland. They
divorced when Alvin was young and
his mother then married Meyer Meyers, who he considered his father. He
attended Oakland Technical High
School in the late 1920s where he
formed his first band. During the early
1930s he attended St. Mary's, a Christian Brothers college in Moraga, as his
parents suggested he become a lawyer. But his interest in music led him
on a different path; he worked with
Woody Herman in Tom Gerun's band

in Oakland. His uncredited work as a
sailor in *Follow the Fleet*, that starred
Fred Astaire and Ginger Rogers, was
his first feature film appearance. Service in World War II interrupted his
music career where he served briefly
the U.S. Navy, but with rumors that he
tried to buy a commission, he
switched to the U.S. Army. Restarting
his career after wartime service was
difficult due to the bad, and unfound-
ed, publicity. He and actress Alice
Faye married in 1937 but they divorced after three years and in 1948
he married actress and dancer Cyd
Charisse who he remained with until
her death in 2008. After working in
various television, radio and concerts
he landed his own variety television
program during 1954 through 1956.
Over his long career, which lasted into
the 21st century, he appeared in more
than 30 films and had numerous hit
audio recordings. Martin succumbed
to natural causes in 2012—at age 98
in West Los Angeles.

Fools
1970, Cinerama
An unsuccessful actor falls for the
much younger wife of an attorney.

Director: Tom Gries
Screenwriter: Robert Rudelson
Cinematographer: Michael Hugo
Partial Cast: Jason Robards, Katharine Ross,
Scott Hylands

• Cable Car Barn, 2101 Mason Street, Chinatown
District

Force of Darkness
1985, AFC Home Video
The infamous Alcatraz Federal Prison
is again full of violence and terror.

Director: Alan Hauge
Screenwriter: Jack Baylam
Art Director: Karl Shields
Cinematographer: Darrell Davenport
Partial Cast: Mel Novak, Douglas Alan Shanklin,
Loren Cedar, Mark Milan

• Alcatraz Federal Prison, Alcatraz Island, Golden
Gate National Recreation Area

Forever Young
1992, Warner Brothers
AKA: *Return of Daniel*
A test pilot asks his best friend to use him in a cryogenics experiment in 1939 and he awakens in 1992.

Director: Steve Miner
Screenwriter: J. J. Abrams
Production Designer: Gregg Fonseca
Cinematographers: Russell Boyd, Christian Santiago
Partial Cast: Mel Gibson, Jamie Lee Curtis, Elijah Wood, George Wendt

• Sonoma County Airport, Airport Boulevard, Santa Rosa
• Aerial view of the mouth of the Russian River, Jenner

Forrest Gump
1994, Paramount Pictures
A man, while not intelligent, has accidentally been present at many historic moments, but his true love eludes him.

Director: Robert Zemeckis
Screenwriter: Eric Roth
Author: Winston Groom (novel)
Production Designer: Rick Carter
Art Directors: Leslie McDonald, William James Teegarden
Cinematographer: Don Burgess
Partial Cast: Tom Hanks, Robin Wright, Gary Sinise, Sally Field

• Palace of Fine Arts, 3601 Lyon Street, Marina District-as background where Forrest presents medal

40 Days and 40 Nights
2002, Miramax
After a brutal breakup, a young man vows to stay celibate during the 40 days of Lent, but finds the girl of his dreams and is unable to do anything about it.

Director: Michael Lehmann
Screenwriter: Rob Perez
Art Directors: Yvonne J. Hurst, Nanci Noblett
Cinematographer: Elliot Davis
Partial Cast: Josh Hartnett, Shannyn Sossamon, Paulo Costanzo

• Golden Gate Bridge
• Crepes on Cole, 100 Carl Street, Haight-Ashbury District
• Muni yard, 2630 Geary Boulevard, Laurel Heights District

• Baker Beach, Presidio, Golden Gate National Recreation Area
• Pier 9, The Embarcadero-dotcom workspaces
• Pier 3, The Embarcadero
• Walden House, 815 Buena Vista West, Haight-Ashbury District-as St. Joseph's

48 Hours
1982, Paramount Pictures
A San Francisco cop is stuck with a paroled criminal who helps him to track a killer.

Director: Walter Hill
Screenwriters: Roger Spottiswoode, Walter Hill, Larry Gross, Steven E. de Sousa, Jeb Stuart
Production Designer: John Vallone
Cinematographer: Ric Waite
Partial Cast: Nick Nolte, Eddie Murphy, Annette O'Toole, Frank McRae, James Renar

• 1369 Hyde Street, Nob Hill District
• Muni/BART station, Market Street at Church Street, Eureka Valley District

Foul Play
1978, Paramount Pictures
AKA: *Killing Lydia*
A woman accidentally comes across a plot to murder the Pope.

Director: Colin Higgins
Screenwriter: Colin Higgins
Production Designer: Alfred Sweeney
Cinematographer: David M. Walsh
Partial Cast: Goldie Hawn, Chevy Chase, Burgess Meredith
Local Cast: Chief of Protocol Cyril Magnin, ACT Founder William Ball

• Belvedere Island, Richardson Bay-party venue
• State Highway Route 1, Marin County
• Conzelman Road, Marin Headlands, Golden Gate National Recreation Area-aerial view
• Hallidie Plaza, Market Street at Powell Street-cable car turnaround
• San Pedro Road, San Rafael, Glenwood District
• 430 Vallejo Street, Telegraph Hill District-Gloria's residence
• 2245 Jones Street, Russian Hill District-Sarah B. Cooper Elementary School
• Black Point Park, Fort Mason Center, Golden Gate National Recreation Area
• Lombard Street, Marina District
• 15 Yellow Ferry Harbor, Gate 6 Road, Waldo Point Harbor, Sausalito-houseboat
• Intersection of Filbert Street and Jones Street, Russian Hill District-phone booth
• 1691 Laguna Street, Pacific Heights-gas station
• Hayes Valley Market, 580 Hayes Street, Hayes Valley-car crash site
• San Francisco City Hall, 1 Carlton B. Goodlett Place, Civic Center District-rotunda as Opera House entry

• War Memorial Opera House, 301 Van Ness and War Memorial Performing Arts Center and Veterans Building, 401 Van Ness, Civic Center

Four Christmases
2008, New Line Cinema
A couple struggles to visit all four of their divorced parents on Christmas Day.

Director: Seth Gordon
Screenwriters: Matt Allen, Caleb Wilson, Jon Lucas, Scott Moore
Production Designer: Sheperd Frankel
Art Directors: Michael Atwell, Oana Bogdan
Cinematographer: Jeffrey L. Kimball
Partial Cast: Vince Vaughn, Reese Witherspoon, Mary Steenburgen, Robert Duvall, Sissy Spacek, Jon Voight

• Fluid Ultra Lounge, 662 Mission Street, South of Market District
• Columbus Avenue, North Beach District
• Financial District
• Union Square, 333 Post Street
• U.S. Highway Route 101, South San Francisco
• Golden Gate Bridge
• San Francisco-Oakland Bay Bridge

Freebie and the Bean
1974, Warner Brothers
Two police detectives pursue a gangster.

Director: Richard Rush
Screenwriter: Robert Kaufman
Author: Floyd Mutrux (story)
Art Director: Hilyard M. Brown
Cinematographer: László Kovács
Partial Cast: Alan Arkin, James Caan, Loretta Swit, Valerie Harper

• 525 Market Street, Financial District
• Robert C. Levy Tunnel, Broadway, Russian Hill District
• Candlestick Park, 602 Jamestown Avenue, Bayview District
• City Lights Bookstore, 261 Columbus Street, Jackson Square District
• Embarcadero Freeway, South of Market District
• Exchange Barbershop, 435 Pine Street, Financial District
• Hotel St. Moritz, 190 O'Farrell Street, Tenderloin District
• Huntington Park, Nob Hill District
• Hyatt Regency Hotel, 5 Embarcadero Center, Embarcadero District
• Old Transamerica Building, 701 Montgomery Street, Financial District
• Potrero Hill District
• Red Coach Motor Lodge, 700 Turk Street, Tenderloin District
• Stockton Street tunnel, Chinatown District
• Sidney Walton Square, Front Street near

intersection of Pacific Avenue, Golden Gateway
• Transamerica Pyramid, 600 Montgomery Street, Financial District

The Front Page
1974, Universal International
A reporter finds mayhem during his last day on the job in 1929 Chicago.

Director: Billy Wilder
Screenwriters: Billy Wilder, I. A. L. Diamond
Authors: Ben Hecht, Charles MacArthur (play)
Art Director: Henry Bumstead
Cinematographer: Jordan Crowenweth
Partial Cast: Jack Lemmon, Walter Matthau, Susan Sarandon, Vincent Gardenia, Austin Pendleton, Carol Burnett

• Earl Warren State Office Building, 350 McAllister Street, Civic Center

Fruitvale Station
2013, Weinstein Company
AKA: *Fruitvale*
The last day in the life of Oakland resident Oscar Grant who was shot by BART police in the early morning hours of New Years Day in 2009.

Director: Ryan Coogler
Screenwriter: Ryan Coogler
Production Designer: Hannah Beachler
Cinematographer: Rachel Morrison
Partial Cast: Michael B. Jordan, Chad Michael Murray, Kevin Durand, Octavia Spencer, Ahna O'Reilly

• Fruitvale BART station, 3301 East 12th Street, Oakland
• San Quentin State Prison, San Quentin

RYAN COOGLER

Fruitvale Station is the feature film debut of Richmond-based director Ryan Coogler. The film premiered at the 2013 Sundance Film Festival where it won two important awards. Ryan was born in Oakland on May 23, 1986. He attended St. Mary's College of California, Moraga on a football scholarship. After the school canceled its football program, he received another scholarship to attend Sacramento State University where he majored in finance and took film classes. He graduated in 2012 from the University of Southern California School of Cinematic Arts where made a series of short films that gave him a portfolio. Ryan's other profession is as a counselor of incarcerated youth at San Francisco's Juvenile Hall.

Funny Lady
1975, Columbia and Rastar
The story of comedian/singer Fanny Brice's tempestuous relationship with showman Billy Rose.

Director: Herbert Ross
Screenwriters: Jay Presson Allen, Arnold Schulman
Production Designer: George Jenkins
Cinematographer: James Wong Howe
Partial Cast: Barbra Streisand, James Caan, Omar Sharif

• Oakland Central Train Station, intersection of 16th Street and Wood Street, Oakland-as Cleveland, Ohio train station waiting room

Funnyman
1967, Korty Films
A comedian decides he needs to get away from it all for awhile.

Director: John Korty
Screenwriters: Peter Bonerz, John Korty
Cinematographer: John Korty
Partial Cast: Peter Bonerz, Sandra Archer, Carole Androsky

• Intersection of Union Street and Calhoun Terrace, Telegraph Hill District
• The Committee Theater, 622 Broadway, Telegraph Hill District
• Broadway, Telegraph Hill District
• Alta Street, Telegraph Hill District
• Montgomery Street Stairs, Montgomery Street near Green Street, Telegraph Hill District
• Fisherman's Wharf District
• Ocean Beach, Golden Gate National Recreation Area
• Golden Gate Park
• Stockton Street Tunnel, Nob Hill District
• St. Francis Hotel, 335 Powell Street, Union Square District
• Alcatraz Federal Prison, Alcatraz Island, Golden Gate National Recreation Area
• Golden Gate Bridge
• State Highway Route 1, Stinson Beach
• Bolinas Lagoon, Bolinas
• Stinson Beach, Gate National Recreation Area
• Studio of artist Arthur Okamura, Bolinas

Funny People
2009, Universal

A famous comic doesn't give much thought to how he treats people until a doctor gives him news about his health.

Director: Judd Apatow
Screenwriter: Judd Apatow
Production Designer: Jefferson Sage
Art Director: James F. Truesdale
Cinematographer: Janusz Kaminski
Partial Cast: Adam Sandler, Seth Rogen, Leslie Mann

• International Terminal, San Francisco International Airport
• Bridgeway, Sausalito
• Orpheum Theater, 1192 Market Street, Civic Center District
• ACT and Curran Theaters, 415 and 445 Geary Street, Union Square District-exteriors

Further Tales of the City
2001, Showtime
AKA: *Armistead Maupin's Further Tales of the City*
In this second sequel Mary Ann tries to advance her career, among other episodes.

Director: Pierre Gang
Screenwriters: James Lecesne, Armistead Maupin
Author: Armistead Maupin (book)
Cinematographer: Serge Ladouceur
Partial Cast: Jackie Borroughs, Bill Campbell, Henry Czerny, Olympia Dukakis, Barbara Garrick, Joel Grey, Laura Linney, Mary Kay Place
Local Cast: Author Armistead Maupin

• Golden Gate Bridge
• Intersection of Macondray Lane Steps and Taylor Street, Russian Hill District
• Conservatory of Flowers, 100 JFK Drive, Golden Gate Park
• Lily Pond, Golden Gate Park
• Australian Tree Fern Dell, Main Drive, Golden Gate Park
• Devil's Slide, State Route Highway 1, Pacifica
• St. Mary's Cathedral, 111 Gough Street, Cathedral Hill District
• Twin Peaks
• California Academy of Sciences, 55 Music Concourse Drive, Golden Gate Park

The Game
1997, PolyGram
AKA: *Rincon Point*
A birthday present from a wealthy man's brother turns into a nightmare.

Director: David Fincher
Screenwriters: John D. Brancato, Michael Ferris
Production Designer: Jeffrey Beecroft
Art Director: Steve Saklad
Cinematographer: Harris Savides
Partial Cast: Michael Douglas, Sean Penn, Deborah Kara Unger, James Rebhorn, Peter Donat, Carroll Baker, Anna Katarina, Armin Mueller-Stahl

• Filoli Estate and Gardens, 86 Cañada Road, Woodside-mansion
• City Club of San Francisco, 155 Sansome Street, Financial District
• Century Place, Financial District-alley
• West Pacific Avenue, Presidio, Golden Gate National Recreation Area-driveway to mansion
• 111 Sutter Street, Financial District-Little Baer Publishing
• Merchant Exchange, 465 California Street, Financial District
• Nikko Hotel, 222 Mason Street, Union Square District
• Ritz-Carlton, 600 Stockton Street, Nob Hill District
• Sheraton Palace Hotel, 2 New Montgomery Street, South of Market District-exterior entry, Garden Court Restaurant and other interior spaces
• Lion House, San Francisco Zoo, 1 Zoo Road, Parkside District
• Letterman Hospital, Presidio, Golden Gate National Recreation Area-cafeteria

THE RITZ

The classical elegance of The Ritz-Carlton on San Francisco's Nob Hill was originally home to the West Coast offices of the Metropolitan Life Insurance Company of New York. Perched on the east side of the hill with spectacular vistas, the glazed terra cotta-clad building was constructed in four stages to the design of various architectural teams between 1909 (the same year the company's iconic "The Light That Never Fails" headquarters building opened in New York City) and 1952. The building then became home to Cogswell College between 1974 and 1985. In a major transformation the office building was repurposed into a hotel with 336 guest rooms that opened it doors in 1991. The original building is San Francisco Landmark 167.

Gates of Heaven
1978, New Yorker Films

A documentary about a pet cemetery in California and the people who have animals buried there.

Director: Errol Morris
Cinematographer: Ned Burgess
Partial Cast: Lucille Billingsley, Zella Graham, Cal Harberts

• Bubbling Well Pet Memorial Park, 2462 Atlas Peak Road, Napa

Gattaca
1997, Columbia
AKA: The Eighth Day
An outsider poses as a genetically superior citizen.

Director: Andrew Niccol
Screenwriter: Andrew Niccol
Production Designer: Jan Roelfs
Art Director: Sarah Knowles
Cinematographer: Salwomir Idziak
Partial Cast: Ethan Hawke, Uma Thurman, Jude Law

• Marin County Civic Center, 3501 Civic Center Drive, San Rafael-as aerospace company

The General's Daughter
1999, Paramount
AKA: The General's Daughter: Elizabeth Campbell
When the daughter of a popular commander is murdered, an undercover detective is summoned to look into the matter.

Director: Simon West
Screenwriters: Christopher Bertolini, William Goldman
Author: Nelson DeMille (novel)
Production Designer: J. Dennis Washington
Art Directors: Ann Harris, Thomas T. Taylor
Cinematographer: Peter Menzies Jr.
Partial Cast: John Travolta, Madeleine Stowe, James Cromwell, Timothy Hutton

• Steamboat Slough, near Isleton, Sacramento River Delta

Georgia Rule
2007, Universal Studios
An uncontrollable teenager is sent off by her dysfunctional mother to spend the summer with her grandmother and

they discover buried family secrets and a lot more.

Director: Garry Marshall
Screenwriter: Mark Andrus
Production Designer: Albert Brenner
Art Director: Norman Newberry
Cinematographer: Karl Walter Lindenlaub
Partial Cast: Jane Fonda, Lindsay Lohan, Felicity Huffman

• Coit Tower, Pioneer Park, 1 Telegraph Hill Boulevard, Telegraph Hill District

George of the Jungle
1997, Disney
A man grows up in the jungle where he is raised by apes.

Director: Sam Weisman
Screenwriters: Jay Ward, Dance Olsen, Audrey Wells
Production Designer: Stephen Marsh
Art Directors: David M. Haber, Mark Zuelzke
Cinematographer: Thomas E. Ackerman
Partial Cast: Brendan Fraser, Leslie Mann, Thomas Hayden Church, Richard Roundtree, John Cleese
Local Cast: Mayor Willie J. Brown Jr., TV anchor Pete Giddings, TV anchor Terilyn Jo

• Columbus Avenue, North Beach District
• The Tamalpais Apartments, 1201 Greenwich Street, Russian Hill District
• Neiman Marcus, 150 Stockton Street, Union Square District
• Clay Street, Nob Hill District
• 550 Montgomery Street, Financial District-as Stanhope Bank
• Powell/Hyde Cable Car
• Fairmont Hotel, 950 Mason Street, Nob Hill District
• San Francisco-Oakland Bay Bridge
• Crookedest Street in the World, 1000 block of Lombard Street, Russian Hill District
• Filoli Estate and Gardens, 86 Cañada Road, Woodside-interiors

Getting Even With Dad
1994, Metro Goldwyn Mayer
A criminal trying to reform is forced to endure the most humiliating punishment of all—hanging out with his son.

Director: Howard Deutch
Screenwriters: Tom S. Parker, Jim Jennewein
Production Designer: Virginia L. Randolph
Art Director: Clayton Hartley
Cinematographer: Tim Suhrotedt
Partial Cast: Macaulay Culkin, Ted Danson, Glenne Headly, Saul Rubinek, Gailard Sartain, Hector Elizondo

• San Francisco-Oakland Bay Bridge
• Veterans Building, 401 Van Ness Avenue, Civic Center District-chute
• Panorama of San Francisco from San Francisco Bay
• 1000 Jackson Street, Nob Hill District
• California Academy of Sciences, Steinhart Aquarium, 55 Music Concourse Drive, Golden Gate Park
• Candlestick Park, 602 Jamestown Avenue, Bayview District
• Stow Lake, Golden Gate Park
• Ice rink, Berkeley
• Chinatown
• Maiden Lane, Union Square District
• de Young Museum, 50 Hagiwara Tea Garden Way, Golden Gate Park
• Neiman Marcus, 150 Stockton Street, Union Square District
• Washington Square, North Beach District
• Saints Peter and Paul Church, 666 Filbert Street, North Beach District
• Conservatory of Flowers, 100 JFK Drive, Golden Gate Park
• BART/Muni station at The Embarcadero
• Transbay Transit Terminal, 425 Mission Street, South of Market District
• Chinatown Branch, San Francisco Public Library, 1135 Powell Street, Chinatown District
• Old Main Public Library, 200 Larkin Street, Civic Center District-upper lobby
• Scandia Family Fun Center, 5301 Redwood Drive, Rohnert Park
• Paramount's Great America Amusement Park, 4701 Great America Parkway, Santa Clara

The Gift of Love
1958, Metro Goldwyn Mayer
Facing the possibility of an early death, a wife hopes that her husband will be consoled by the orphan they adopt.

Director: Jean Negulesco
Screenwriters: Luther Davis, Nelia Gardner White
Art Directors: Lyle R. Wheeler, Mark-Lee Kirk
Cinematographer: Milton R. Krasner
Partial Cast: Lauren Bacall, Robert Stack, Evelyn Rudie, Lorne Greene, Anne Seymour, Edward Platt, Joseph Kearns, Scatman Corothers

• San Francisco-Oakland Bay Bridge
• James Lick Freeway, U.S. Highway 101, South of Market District
• 450 Sutter Street, Union Square District

Gimme Shelter
1970, Cinema 5
A harrowing documentary of the Rolling Stones' 1969 tour, with much of the focus on the tragic concert at the Altamont Speedway.

Directors: Albert Maysles, David Maysles

Cinematographers: Albert Maysles, David Maysles, Gary Weis
Partial Cast: Mick Jager, Keith Richards, Mick Taylor, Charlie Watts, Bill Wyman, Jefferson Airplane
Local Cast: Attorney Melvin Belli

• Altamont Speedway, 17001 Midway Road, Tracy

MELVIN BELLI SR.

Dubbed the "King of Torts" Melvin Belli (1907-1996) was a flamboyant and influential lawyer whose biggest claim to fame was as an innovator in personal injury law. A native of the Gold Country's town of Sonora he graduated from the University of California's prestigious Boalt Hall in Berkeley. His flair for courtroom theatrics was recorded in a 1954 article that appeared in *Life* magazine penned by Robert Wallace, which was followed by a book about the lawyer by the same author. Belli represented some of Hollywood's most notable royalty including Mae West, Lana Turner, Tony Curtis, and Errol Flynn. His most notable case was as criminal defense of Jack Ruby for the murder of Lee Harvey Oswald, assassin of President John F. Kennedy. Echoing the marriage pattern of his Tinseltown clients he was married six times, the last just 13 months before his death at age 88. He also appeared in NBC's *Lady of the House* (1978) and *Ground Zero* (1973), among several other top-rated TV shows. His work in the Zodiac serial murder case was recounted in the 2007 eponymous movie where Brian Cox portrayed Belli.

Gloria
1999, Columbia
A streetwise moll who stands up against a mob shows her soft side when she takes an orphaned boy under her wing.

Director: Sidney Lumet
Screenwriters: Steve Antin, John Cassavetes
Production Designer: Mel Bourne
Art Director: Carlos Menéndez
Cinematographer: David Watkin

Partial Cast: Sharon Stone, Jean-Luke Figueroa, Jeremy Northam

• Dunsmuir House and Gardens, 2960 Peralta Oaks Court, Oakland-driveway of school

The Gnome-Mobile
1967, Buena Vista
An eccentric millionaire and his grandchildren are involved in the troubles of some forest gnomes who are searching for the rest of their tribe.

Director: Robert Stevenson
Screenwriter: Ellis Kadison
Author: Upton Sinclair (book)
Art Directors: Carroll Clark, William H. Tuntke
Cinematographer: Edward Colman
Partial Cast: Walter Brennan, Matthew Garber, Karen Dotrice, Richard Deacon, Tom Lowell, Sean McClory, Ed Wynn

• Golden Gate Bridge

The Godfather
1972, Paramount Pictures
AKA: *Mario Puzo's The Godfather*
The aging patriarch of an organized crime dynasty transfers control of his clandestine empire to his reluctant son.

Director: Francis Ford Coppola
Screenwriters: Mario Puzo, Francis Ford Coppola
Author: Mario Puzo (novel)
Production Designer: Dean Tavoularis
Art Director: Warren Clymer
Cinematographer: Gordon Willis
Partial Cast: Al Pacino, Marlon Brando, Diane Keaton, Robert Duvall, James Caan, Sterling Hayden, Rick Conte

• Ross Elementary School, 9 Lagunitas Road, Ross

Golden Gate
1994, Samuel Goldwyn
A brash young FBI agent trumps up charges of communist spying against a Chinese laundryman; ten years later he wants to make amends to the man.

Director: John Madden
Screenwriter: David Henry Hwang
Production Designer: Andrew Jackness
Art Director: Edward L. Rubin
Cinematographer: Bobby Bukowski
Partial Cast: Matt Dillon, Joan Chen, Elizabeth Morehead, Bruno Kirby, Teri Polk

- San Francisco-Oakland Bay Bridge
- Chinatown District
- Lands End, Outer Richmond District
- San Francisco City Hall, 1 Carlton B. Goodlett Place, Civic Center District
- Marin Headlands, Golden Gate Recreation Area
- Lighthouse Café, 1311 Bridgeway, Sausalito
- Deserted office building, Oakland-FBI office scenes

ETHNIC FAUX PAS

While filming in San Francisco's Chinatown some set dressing was slated to transform shops reflecting the 1950s and 60s time period of the script. The location liaison was made aware by community members that installing one sign over another and changing the business type was considered a jinx by the Chinese community. The faux pas was solved by replacing the signs with others that stated that the same business occurred at those locations.

Golden Gate Girl
1941, Golden Gate
AKA: *Tears in San Francisco*
The romantic exploits of a disobedient shopkeeper's daughter.

Director: Esther Eng
Screenwriter: Moon Quan
Cinematographer: J. Sunn
Partial Cast: Liu Nom, Moon Quan, Luk Won Fee, Hok Sing Wong, Tso Yee Man, Bruce Lee (uncredited)

- Chinatown
- Scenes taken of the 1941 Rice Bowl Party were integrated into the script

Golden Girl
1951, 20th Century Fox
The life of Gold Rush-era entertainer Lotta Crabtree.

Director: Lloyd Bacon
Screenwriters: Walter Bullock, Gladys Lehman, Albert Lewis, Arthur Lewis, Charles O'Neal, Edward Thompson
Art Directors: Leland Fuller, Lyle R. Wheeler
Cinematographer: Charles J. Clarke
Partial Cast: Mitzi Gaynor, Dale Robertson, Dennis Day

- Panorama of Financial District skyline
- Lotta's Fountain, intersection of Kearny Street and Market Street, Financial District

LOTTA CRABTREE

Born on November 7, 1847 to British immigrant parents John and Mary Ann Crabtree in New York City, Lotta Mignon Crabtree's first appearance on stage was as a song-and-dance entertainer at the age of eight in California's Gold Country town of Rough and Ready. Taught by a talented neighbor, actress and dancer Lola Montez, the quick learning child learned the art of performance. The dark eyed, red haired captivating moppet would cavort much to the delight to miners hungry for entertainment. Many admired her work and she toured various mining camps in the area with her mother who was her manager. In 1856 her family moved to San Francisco and in 1859 she appeared there at McGuire's Opera House. Later she performed in New York City gaining an international recognition – then retired at age 45. Her final performance was at "Lotta Crabtree Day" at the 1915 Pan Pacific International Exposition in San Francisco. She gave the fountain located on Market Street in 1875 to the City of San Francisco. In 1924, at age 76, she died a wealthy woman who bequeathed her fortune to a charitable trust to benefit veterans, actors and animals.

Good Deeds
2012, Lionsgate
AKA: *Tyler Perry's Good Deeds*
A businessman finds a way out of his scripted life when he meets a woman on the cleaning crew in his office building.

Director: Tyler Perry
Screenwriter: Tyler Perry
Production Design: Ina Mayhew
Art Director: Gentry L. Akens II
Cinematographer: Alexander Gruszynski
Partial Cast: Tyler Perry, Gabrielle Union, Thandie Newton

- Panorama of waterfront with Ferry Building
- Cable car at intersection of Powell Street and California Street, Nob Hill District
- San Francisco-Oakland Bay Bridge
- Muni F Line streetcar
- St. Anthony Dining Room, 45 Jones Street, Tenderloin District-exterior
- Golden Gate Bridge
- San Francisco International Airport-exterior

Good Morning, Babylon

1987, Vestron Pictures

AKA: *Good Morning Babilonia*
Two brothers emigrate to America to make their fortunes.

Directors: Paolo Taviani, Vittorio Taviani
Screenwriters: Tonino Guerra, Paolo Taviani, Vittorio Taviani
Production Designer: Gianni Sbarra
Art Director: Lorenzo D'Ambrosio
Cinematographer: Giuseppe Lanci
Partial Cast: Vincent Spano, Joaquin de Alemida, Greta Scacchi, Desiree Nosbusch

- Film clip of the 1915 Panama-Pacific International Exposition, Marina District
- Alamo Square, Western Addition District
- Haslett Warehouse, 680 Beach Street, San Francisco Maritime National Historic Park, Golden Gate National Recreation Area
- Hyde Street Pier, San Francisco Maritime National Historic Park, Golden Gate National Recreation Area
- Aquatic Park, San Francisco Maritime National Historic Park, Golden Gate National Recreation Area

Good Neighbor Sam

1964, Columbia Pictures

A wholesome family man's professional life in an advertising firm gets a boost when he is assigned an account that turns out to complicate his personal life.

Director: David Swift
Screenwriters: James Fritzell, Everett Greenbaum, David Swift
Author: Jack Finney (novel)
Production Designer: Dale Hennesy
Cinematographer: Burnett Guffey
Partial Cast: Jack Lemmon, Romy Schneider, Dorothy Provine, Mike Connors, Lewis Nye, Bernie Kopell, Edward G. Robinson, Charles Lane

- Golden Gate Bridge
- Marina Boulevard, Marina District
- Tommy's Joynt Restaurant, 1101 Geary Boulevard, Cathedral Hill District

- Fairmont Hotel, 950 Mason Street, Nob Hill District-lobby and Crown Room Restaurant
- St. Mary's Square Garage, 433 Kearny Street, Financial District
- Union Square, 333 Post Street
- Crookedest Street in the World, 1000 block of Lombard Street, Russian Hill District

CHARLES LANE

Charles Lane was a ubiquitous character actor who appeared in hundreds of films and television sitcoms in his long career—uncredited in many earlier films. You probably didn't know his name but you did know the face and voice of the scowly character he was usually cast as. Lane was born as Charles Gerstle Levinson in San Francisco in 1905 to parents Alice (Gerstle) and Jacob B. Levison who resided at 2420 Pacific Avenue in the tony Pacific Heights District. His family escaped the 1906 earthquake and fire when his father chartered a tugboat to ferry the family and servants to their country home in San Rafael. His father rose up through and ultimately became the president of the Fireman's Fund Insurance Company. In Charles's early twenties he was an insurance agent with Levison Brothers that included his two brothers John G. and Robert M. Levison. He had some amateur acting experience but in 1928 he joined the Pasadena Playhouse for training where he appeared in scores of plays. His movie debut was in 1931. Lane married Ruth Covell in 1932 and they had a son Tom and daughter Alice. He interrupted his acting career during WW II when he served in the U.S. Coast Guard. Besides appearing in *Good Neighbor Sam* he also appeared in the Bay Area made movies *The Gnome-Mobile* (1967), *It's a Mad, Mad, Mad, Mad, World* (1963), *The Sniper* (1952), *Riding High* (1950), *Race Street* (1948), *The Farmer's Daughter* (1947), *They All Come Out* (1939), and *Broadway Bill* (1934). He died in 2007 at age 102—only a year after his final appearance as the narrator in the short film *The Night Before Christmas*.

The Goonies
1985, Warner Brothers
A group of kids embark on a wild adventure after finding a pirate treasure map.

Director: Richard Donner
Screenwriter: Chris Columbus
Author: Steven Spielberg (story)
Production Designer: J. Michael Riva
Art Director: Rick Carter
Cinematographer: Nick McLean
Partial Cast: Sean Astin, Josh Brolin, Jeff B. Cohen, Corey Feldman, Martha Plimpton, Kerri Green, Ke Huy Quan, Mary Ellen Trainor

• Bodega Bay
• Sonoma Coast State Beach, Goat Rock, State Highway Route 1, Jenner

The Graduate
1967, United Artists
A woman seduces a younger man who falls for her daughter.

Director: Mike Nichols
Screenwriter: Calder Willingham
Author: Charles Webb (novel)
Production Designer: Richard Sylbert
Cinematographer: Robert Surtees
Partial Cast: Anne Bancroft, Dustin Hoffman, Katharine Ross, Murray Hamilton, William Daniels, Elizabeth Wilson

• San Francisco-Oakland Bay Bridge
• San Francisco Zoo, 1 Zoo Road, Parkside District
• Sproul Plaza, University of California Campus, Berkeley
• Caffe Mediterraneum, 2475 Telegraph Avenue, Berkeley-restaurant
• Theta Delta Chi House, 2647 Durant Avenue, Berkeley-frat house
• 2404 Dana Street, Berkeley-boarding house

KATHARINE ROSS

Although Katharine Juliet Ross was Hollywood born in 1940 she primarily grew up in the Bay Area's suburbs of Palo Alto and later in Walnut Creek. She attended Los Lomas High School in Walnut Creek graduating in 1957 and then attended Santa Rosa Junior College where she was exposed to acting. Out on her own in San Francisco she lived on Stockton Street and began her acting career in earnest when she studied at the San Francisco Actor's Workshop. Her performance as daughter Elaine Robinson in The Graduate garnered her an Oscar nomination and she was also awarded a Golden Globe as the "Most Promising Newcomer." Besides The Graduate, Ross also appeared in the Bay Area film production of Fools (1970). She was married four times for short periods but finally married actor Sam Elliott in 1984 and they have a daughter Cleo Rose.

A Great Wall
1986, Orion Classics
AKA: Beijing Story and The Great Wall Is a Great Wall
A Chinese-American family visits family in Peking on their summer vacation and find clashing customs.

Director: Peter Wang
Screenwriters: Shirley Sun, Peter Wang
Production Designer: Wing Lee
Cinematographers: Robert Primes, Peter Stein
Partial Cast: Peter Wang, Sharon Iwai, Kelvin Han Yee

• Golden Gate Bridge
• Dr. Roy W. Leeper residence, 166 Palo Alto Avenue, Twin Peaks District-urban residence
• Silvar Lisco Company, 1080 Marsh Road, Menlo Park

PETER WANG

Director Peter Wang was born in Beijing, China and was raised in Taiwan after his family fled the Chinese Revolution in 1949. At age 18 he dreamed of joining a traveling acting troupe, however his father persuaded Peter to study electrical engineering instead. He followed his father's wishes and attended Taiwan University. Later he moved to the United States where he attended the University of Pennsylvania, Philadelphia, earning a doctorate in electro-optics. After a fling with teaching and a job with "Big Blue" IBM he turned to the theater. In the early 1970s he co-founded the Asian Living Theater in San Francisco where he wrote and staged many productions. He turned to film later in the decade appearing in Chan is Missing (1982) as a short order cook. *A Great Wall* received widespread acclaim and was the first American feature film to be produced by the People's Republic of China.

Groove
2000, Sony Classic Pictures
A look into the San Francisco underground rave scene.

Director: Greg Harrison
Screenwriter: Greg Harrison
Production Designer: Chris Ferreira
Cinematographer: Matthew Irving
Partial Cast: Chris Ferreira, Elizabeth Sun, Steve Van Wormer

• Bethlehem Shipyard, 900 Illinois Street, Potrero Hill District-parking lot
• Fort Mason Center, Pier One, Golden Gate National Recreation Area
• The Endup, 401 Sixth Street, South of Market District
• Power Station A, 23rd Street near Illinois Street, Waterfront
• San Francisco-Oakland Bay Bridge, Oakland-toll plaza

Ground Zero
1973, BDB and Pattinson-Burrowes
AKA: *The Golden Gate Is Ground Zero*
A terrorist organization attaches a nuclear device to the top of the Golden Gate Bridge and an agent is sent to disarm it.

Director: James T. Flocker
Screenwriter: Samuel Newman
Cinematographer: Dave Flocker
Partial Cast: Ron Casteel, Gary Adams, Ernest Arasta
Local Cast: Attorney Melvin Belli

• Wells Fargo Bank, Petaluma
• Petaluma River
• Golden Gate Bridge

GOLDEN GATE BRIDGE

This often-used establishing shot for San Francisco, the Golden Gate Bridge is an icon the world over. The historic landmark 6,450-foot-long international orange-colored suspension span has appeared in scores of mov-ies. However, models and special effects have replicated or manipulated the structure in several motion pictures. Carrying tens of thousands of commuters each day, the bridge provides a critical north to south link in Northern California. The bridge, designed by Joseph P. Strauss, was built during 1933-1937 with two towers that are each 746-feet high. Fort Point spanned by the south anchorage, is a Civil War-era fortification of brick and granite that was completed in 1861 and was designated a National Historic Site in 1970.

Guess Who's Coming to Dinner
1967, Columbia
A white woman takes her black fiancé to meet her parents and ask for their absolute approval of the marriage.

Director: Stanley Kramer
Screenwriter: William Rose
Production Designer: Robert Clatworthy
Cinematographer: Sam Leavitt
Partial Cast: Katharine Hepburn, Spencer Tracy, Sidney Poitier, Katharine Houghton, Cecil Kellaway, Roy E. Glenn Sr., Beah Richards, Isabel Sanford, Virginia Christine

• Aerial panorama of San Francisco
• San Francisco International Airport
• James Lick Freeway, South of Market District
• Maxwell Galleries, 551 Sutter Street, Union Square District
• Intersection of Normandie Terrace and Broadway, Pacific Heights District
• Mel's Drive-In Restaurant, 5199 Mission Street, Crocker Amazon District

The Guilt Trip
2012, Paramount
An inventor and his mother hit the road together so he can sell his latest invention.

Director: Anne Fletcher
Screenwriter: Dan Fogelman
Production Designer: Nelson Coates
Art Director: David Lazan
Cinematographer: Oliver Stapleton
Partial Cast: Barbra Streisand, Seth Rogen, Yvonne Strahovski, Adam Scott, Danny Pudi

• San Francisco-Oakland Bay Bridge

Guinevere
1999, Miramax Films
A coming of age 21-year old discovers love and life through an older man.

Director: Audrey Wells
Screenwriter: Audrey Wells
Production Designer: Stephen McCabe
Cinematographer: Charles Minsky
Partial Cast: Sarah Poley, Stephen Rea, Jean Smart

• Chinatown District
• Spec's Twelve Adler Museum Café, 12 Saroyan Place, Telegraph Hill District
• San Francisco General Hospital, 1001 Potrero Avenue, Mission District
• Midtown Loan Office, 39 Sixth Street, South of Market District-as pawn shop
• City Lights Bookstore, 261 Columbus Street, Jackson Square District
• Potrero Hill District
• 2636 Vallejo Street, Pacific Heights District-parent's home
• 208 Utah Street, South of Market District-as warehouse
• The Embarcadero-south of San Francisco-Oakland Bay Bridge

Guyana: Cult of the Damned
1979, Universal
AKA: *Guyana: Crime of the Century*
A deluded reverend of an independent church in Guyana, South America orders his followers to commit suicide. Based on the historical story of Jim Jones and the Peoples Temple.

Director: René Cardona Jr.
Screenwriters: René Cardona Jr., Carlos Valdemar
Cinematographer: Leopoldo Villaseñor
Partial Cast: Stuart Whitman, Gene Barry, John Ireland, Joseph Cotten, Jennifer Ashley, Bradford Dillman

• Golden Gate Bridge
• Fisherman's Wharf District
• View to Telegraph Hill from Russian Hill
• 1000 block of Grant Avenue, Chinatown District
• Powell/Hyde Street Cable Cars, 2500 block of Hyde Street, Russian Hill District
• Peoples Temple, 1859 Geary Boulevard, Western Addition District

STUART WHITMAN

Born with the middle name of Maxwell, Whitman's parents were Cecilia (Gold) and Joseph, a realtor. He was the elder of the couple's two sons and was born in San Francisco on February 1, 1928. His parents moved frequently but he graduated from high school in Los Angeles. After the Second World War, in 1948, he spent three years with the Army Corps of Engineers. After his discharge he attended Los Angeles City College where he gained an interest in acting and then went on to study at the Los Angeles Academy of Dramatic Art. His first film role was an uncredited actor in *When Worlds Collide* in 1951. He garnered an Academy Award nomination for his leading role in *The Mark* (1961) portraying a child molester. He is probably best known for starring as Marshal Jim Crown in the western themed TV series *Cimarron Strip* that aired in 1967. His other filmed in the Bay Area movies include *Shadow of a Woman* (1946) and *Crime of Passion* (1957).

Haiku Tunnel
2001, Sony Pictures Classics
A temporary office worker suffers a crisis of commitment.

Directors: Jacob Kornbluth, Josh Kornbluth
Screenwriters: Jacob Kornbluth, Josh Kornbluth, John Bellucci
Production Designer: Chris Farmer
Art Director: Chad Owens
Cinematographer: Don Matthew Smith
Partial Cast: Josh Kornbluth, Warren Keith, Helen Shumaker

• Cable Cars
• Washington Square, North Beach District
• BART station
• Airtouch Communications, 1 California Street, Financial District
• Cypress Club, 500 Jackson Street, Telegraph Hill District
• Triton Hotel, 342 Grant Street, Union Square District
• BART entrance, Mission District

JOSH KORNBLUTH

Berkeley resident Josh Kornbluth, not your average talent, has been described as a comedic autobiographical monologuist. He was born in the Long Island suburban town of Roslyn, New

York on May 21, 1959. His parents were Paul K. Kornbluth, a public school teacher, and Bernice (Selden) who divorced early in Josh's life and each set up households in the urban landscape of Manhattan. Josh entered Princeton University in 1976 and walked at his class graduation in 1980 but technically dropped out by virtue of not submitting his thesis—he's still considering finishing it. Afterward he lived in Boston for a time working as a copy editor but his pivotal move was to San Francisco in 1987 where lived in a Mission District basement studio with the hope of launching a career in theater. Initially he worked as a temp secretary in San Francisco law firms. By 1991 he had three monologues in his repertoire. In the meantime he married Sara, a public school teacher, and they have a child, Guthrie. He hosted *The Josh Kornbluth Show* on San Francisco's PBS channel 9 between 2005 and 2007, which was a talk show with a variety of guests including Berkeley-based actress/singer Rita Moreno, among many others. He was commissioned by the Contemporary Jewish Museum of San Francisco to do a piece which became *Andy Warhol: Good for the Jews?* that he performed in 2010. Kornbluth has also appeared in locally filmed *Jack* (1996), a Francis Ford Coppola project, as a pack of cigarettes, *Bartleby* (2001), and *The Darwin Awards* (2006). In April of 2012 he returned to Princeton, this time to perform one of his works.

His younger half-brother, Jacob "Jake" Kornbluth, is a gifted screenwriter who shares the credits for *Haiku Tunnel* and is an occasional Bay Area resident.

Half Past Dead
2002, Sony Pictures
AKA: *Lockdown, The Rock*
A man goes undercover in a high-tech prison where he stumbles onto a plot involving a death-row inmate and his $200 million stash of gold.

Director: Don Michael Paul
Screenwriter: Don Michael Paul
Art Director: Andreas Olshausen
Production Designer: Albrecht Konrad
Cinematographer: Michael Slovis
Partial Cast: Steven Segal, Morris Chestnut, Ja Rule, Nia Peeples, Tony Plana

• Alcatraz Federal Prison, Alcatraz Island, Golden Gate National Recreation Area

The Hamiltons
2006, Lionsgate
A seemingly normal family is sadistic behind closed doors.

Directors: Mitchell Altieri, Phil Flores (The Butcher Brothers)
Screenwriters: Mitchell Altieri, Phil Flores, Adam Weis
Art Director: Andrew Casden
Cinematographer: Michael Maley
Partial Cast: Cory Knauf, Samuel Child, Joseph McKelheer, Mackenzie Firgens, Rebekah Hoyle

• Two Rock Ranch, 1051 Walker Road, Petaluma-family ranch
• U.S. Highway Route 101, Redwood Highway bridge over Petaluma River, Petaluma
• 500 block of First Street, Petaluma
• Dairyman's Feed and Supply Company, 323 East Washington Street, Petaluma-industrial building
• 200 Oak Street, Petaluma-house
• Hunt & Beherens, 30 Lakeville Street, Petaluma-industrial building
• Walnut Park, Petaluma
• U.S. Post Office, 120 Fourth Street, Petaluma-phone booth

"Let me tell you a story first. You like stories don't ya?"

Hammett
1982, Orion and Warner Brothers
Novelist Dashiell Hammett is involved in the investigation of the mysterious disappearance of a beautiful cabaret actress during the Prohibition era.

Director: Wim Wenders, Francis Ford Coppola (uncredited)
Screenwriters: Joe Gores, Dennis O'Flaherty, Thomas Pope, Ross Thomas

Production Designers: Dean Tavoularis, Eugene Lee
Art Directors: Leon Ericksen, Angelo P. Graham
Cinematographer: Joseph F. Biroc
Partial Cast: Frederic Forrest, Peter Boyle, Marilu Henner, Roy Kinnear, Elisha Cook Jr., Sylvia Sidney

• Intersection of Hastings Terrace Alley and Hyde Street, Russian Hill District-as Sun Wu Laundry
• 920 Sacramento Street, Chinatown-Occidental Board Presbyterian Mission
• House of Shields Bar, 39 New Montgomery Street, South of Market District
• Intersection of Stevenson Street and New Montgomery Street, South of Market District
• San Francisco Public Library, 200 Larkin Street-glass floor book stacks
• Top-O'-the-Hill Market, 1096 Union Street, Russian Hill District
• San Francisco City Hall, 1 Carlton B. Goodlett Place, Civic Center District-rotunda
• 1101 Leavenworth Street, Russian Hill District-Deco apartment building
• 2930 Vallejo Street, Pacific Heights District-exterior entry

DASHIELL HAMMETT

Author of hard-boiled detective novels and short stories, screenplay writer, and political activist Samuel Dashiell Hammett was born May 27, 1894 on a farm in St. Mary's County, Maryland to Mary B. (Dashiell) and Richard T. Hammett. The second of three children, he grew up in Philadelphia and Baltimore. He left the Baltimore Polytechnic Institute at age 13 and after a series of odd jobs went to work as a detective for the Pinkerton Agency starting in 1915. With World War I raging he enlisted in the U.S. Army in 1918 but was discharged the next year after contracting tuberculosis—something that would plague him for the rest of his life. Now on the West Coast he joined the San Francisco branch of Pinkerton's, based in the Flood Building on Market Street. But due to ill health he quit the agency and tried his hand at writing after taking a course on the subject. In San Francisco he and Josephine Dolan, a nurse, were married in 1921 and they went on to have two children. His first published story appeared in an upscale society magazine *The Smart Set* in 1922. He worked as an advertising copywriter for the venerable Albert Samuels Jewelry store until July 1926. Meanwhile he lived in residence hotels on Eddy and Post Streets and ate at John's Grille on Ellis Street. Around 1926 doctors recommended he not live with his family full time due to the potential of exposing the children to TB—this signaled the decline of his marriage. His move to New York City by 1930 started Hammett's best period. His most famous book *The Maltese Falcon* was published in 1930 at the beginning of the Great Depression. Like *Falcon* he used San Francisco as a setting in many of his stories. Soon after he was called by Hollywood as a screenwriter where he met playwright Lillian Hellman. He conducted a tempestuous affair with her starting in 1931 that would last through the course of his life. He returned to New York in 1931 when he introduced the fictional detective character Sam Spade, which would be filmed in 1931 and again in 1936 as *Satan Met a Lady*, but the 1941 version starring Humphrey Bogart got it right. "The Thin Man," a magazine serial that was published in 1933, spawned a series of movies staring the tony and comic charms of Nick (William Powell) and Nora (Myrna Loy) Charles that were filmed between 1934 through 1947. In 1934 he wrote his last novel, devoting much of the balance of his life to left-wing activism. He and Josephine were divorced in 1937. With World War II under way he again enlisted in the Army in 1942, at age 48, where he remained for three years. Around 1951 he retreated to a small cottage in New York State's Westchester County town of Katonah. During this time he was pulled into the McCarthy investigations and ultimately blacklisted. He died on January 10, 1961 in New York City and is buried in Arlington National Cemetery in Arlington, Virginia.

Happily Even After
2004, Hotbed Media

The lives of two siblings after their parents' death.

Director: Unsu Lee
Screenwriter: Rebecca Sonnenshine
Production Designer: Jim Edelhauser
Cinematographer: Jeffrey Chu
Partial Cast: Jason Behr, Marina Black, Fay Masterson, Michael A. Goorjian, Samuel Weaver
Local Cast: Mayor's spouse, Kimberly Guilfoyle Newsom

• San Rafael
• Golden Gate Bridge
• Crissy Field, Presidio, Golden Gate National Recreation Area
• Alameda

Happy Land
1943, Twentieth Century Fox
A pharmacist in a small Iowa town is lunching with his wife when a telegram arrives notifying them that their only child has been killed in action during the Second World War.

Director: Irving Pichel
Screenwriters: Julien Josephson, MacKinlay Kantor, Kathryn Scola
Art Directors: James Basevi, J. Russell Spencer
Cinematographer: Joseph LaShelle
Partial Cast: Don Ameche, Frances Dee, Harry Carey, Ann Rutherford, Cara Williams, Henry Morgan, Richard Crane, Dickie Moore, Minor Watson, Mary Wickes, Natalie Wood

• Bailey Field, 1501 Mendocino Avenue, Santa Rosa
• McDonald Avenue, Santa Rosa
• Healdsburg Plaza, Healdsburg

Hardcore
1979, Columbia
AKA: The Hardcore Life
A conservative Midwest businessman ventures into the underworld of pornography in California to look for his runaway teenage daughter.

Director: Paul Schrader
Screenwriter: Paul Schrader
Production Designer: Paul Sylbert
Art Director: Edwin O'Donovan
Cinematographer: Michael Chapman
Partial Cast: George C. Scott, Peter Boyle, Season Hubley

• 1133 Kearny Street, Telegraph Hill District
• Intersection of Broadway and Kearny Street, Telegraph Hill District
• Garden of Eden, 529 Broadway, Telegraph Hill District
• 487 Broadway, Telegraph Hill District

Hard to Hold
1984, Universal
A pop-rock star tries to win the love of a woman he meets in a car accident.

Director: Larry Peerce
Screenwriter: Thomas Hedley Jr.
Authors: Thomas Hedley Jr., Richard Rothstein (story)
Production Designer: Peter Wooley
Cinematographer: Richard H. Kline
Partial Cast: Rick Springfield, Janet Eilber, Patti Hansen

• Fairmont Hotel, 950 Mason Street, Nob Hill District

Harold and Maude
1971, Paramount
A 79-year-old woman teaches a young man the art of living—and dying.

Director: Hal Ashby
Screenwriter: Colin Higgins
Production Designer: Michael D. Haller
Cinematographer: John A. Alanzo
Partial Cast: Ruth Gordon, Bud Cort, Vivian Pickles, Cyril Cusack, Charles Tyner, Ellen Geer,

Eric Christmas, G. Wood, Judy Engles, Shari Summers

• Holy Cross Cemetery, Section J, 1500 Old Mission Road, Colma-scene with car is at Hillside Boulevard gate
• Sutro Heights Park, Great Highway at Point Lobos Avenue, Outer Richmond District
• Sutro Baths ruins, 1000 Point Lobos Avenue, Golden Gate National Recreation Area
• Dumbarton Bridge, State Highway Route 84, Newark
• Golden Gate National Cemetery, 1300 Sneath Lane, San Bruno
• St. Thomas Aquinas Church, 751 Waverly, Palo Alto-church interior and exterior funeral
• Hall of Justice and Records, 401 Marshall Street, (400 Courthouse Square) Redwood City
• Rosecourt Mansion, 10 Stacey Court, Hillsborough-Harold's home
• 11891 Half Moon Bay Road, State Highway Route 92, Half Moon Bay-speeding car goes off road
• Oyster Point Boulevard at Eccles Avenue, Oyster Point, South San Francisco-railroad car site
• San Carlos Auto Wreckers, (near San Carlos Airport) San Carlos
• Intersection of State Highway Routes 80 and 580, Emeryville-mudflats with stick sculptures
• Guadalupe Canyon Parkway, San Bruno Mountain, Brisbane
• Southern Pacific Railroad Yard, Bayshore Yard, South San Francisco-artist studio
• Sand Hill Road, Menlo Park-field with coast live oak trees
• Peninsula Hospital, 1783 El Camino Real, Burlingame-hospital
• Mori Point, Pacifica-car goes off cliff

RAILROAD CAR

Maude's railroad car home is a Western Pacific lounge type car, built in 1931, which was leased from the Western Railway Museum (5848 State Highway Route 12, Suisun City) for the filming. The car can be seen today in the museum's car barn number 3. It was built by the Pullman Co, lot 4101, as a 16-section sleeping car named "Holton." In May 1931, Pullman rebuilt the car into a buffet lounge car for the Western Pacific where it lost its name and was renamed as number 653.

ROSECOURT MANSION

The elegant two-story, 17-room Rosecourt was built for George and Helen Cameron on a seven and one-half acre site purchased from the Crocker family. Architect Louis P. Hobart fashioned its grand pink stucco exterior using a style reminiscent of a French country house. The cobblestone courtyard came from Pacific Height's California Street in front of what had been Michael H. de Young's residence, Mrs. Cameron's *San Francisco Chronicle* publisher father. The 24-foot high ceiling music room was added about 1925 using elements from a 15th century castle located near Seville, Spain. The property's original grand wrought iron entry gate, at the intersection of Redington Road and Eucalyptus Avenue, is now separated from the house because the estate was broken into smaller parcels. In its heyday, Rosecourt hosted the likes of the Duke and Duchess of Windsor and maestro Arturo Toscanini. The butler in the movie, played by Henry Diekoff, was the estate's actual butler.

Harrison Montgomery
2008, Divisadero Pictures
The chronicle of a down-at-the-heels apartment building's occupants, which is also where an elder man waits for his final message.

Director: Daniel Davila
Screenwriters: Karim Ahmad, Daniel Davila, Cliff Traiman
Production Designer: Lisa Roxanne Hyden
Art Director: Joshua Sankar
Cinematographer: Ben Kutchins
Partial Cast: Octavio Gómez Berríos, Martin Landau, Melora Walters

• Hibernia Bank Building, One Jones Street, Tenderloin District
• Boyd Hotel-Tenderloin Housing Clinic, 41 Jones Street, Tenderloin District-apartment building
• Piper's Jewelers, 1066 Market Street, Tenderloin District
• Pitco Market, 488 Ellis Street, Tenderloin District
• Intersection of Golden Gate Avenue and Jones Street, Tenderloin District-parking lot with mural
• 1308 Kobbe Avenue, Presidio, Golden Gate National Recreation Area-father's residence

Head
1968, Columbia
AKA: *Changes*

The band, The Monkees, are tossed about in a psychedelic, surrealist, plotless, bit of fun fluff.

Director: Bob Rafelson
Screenwriters: Bob Rafelson, Jack Nicholson
Art Director: Sydney Z. Litwack
Cinematographer: Michel Hugo
Partial Cast: Peter Tork, Davey Jones, Micky Dolenz, Michael Nesmith, Annette Funicello

• Golden Gate Bridge

Heart and Souls
1993, Universal Studios
Four people who perish in a Muni bus crash are in limbo until they resolve their unfinished lives.

Director: Ron Underwood
Screenwriters: Gregory Hansen, Erik Hansen, Brent Maddock, S. S. Wilson
Production Designer: John Muto
Art Director: Dan Webster
Cinematographer: Michael W. Watkins
Partial Cast: Robert Downey Jr., Alfre Woodard, Charles Grodin, Kyra Sedgwick, Elizabeth Shue, Tom Sizemore, David Palmer

• Stockton Street Tunnel, south portal, Nob Hill District
• Conservatory of Flowers, 100 JFK Drive, Golden Gate Park
• 2810 Pacific Avenue, Pacific Heights District-house
• 3365-3371 25th Street, Mission District

NOB HILL TUNNEL

The 911 foot-long Stockton Street Tunnel, which runs two blocks, was opened in 1914 to assist faster transportation between the north and south areas of the San Francisco for the upcoming Pan Pacific International Exposition of 1915. Unlike most city tunnels it has sidewalks for pedestrian traffic. Four years of haggling by the assessment Districts it would benefit preceded the start of construction. The concept is credited to Dr. Hartland Law who presented his essay "The Open Door to North Beach" to the Downtown Association, which in turn, convinced the City's Board of Supervisors to proceed with the civic project. It was designed under the hand of "the Chief" City Engineer Michael O'Shaughnessy and work com-

menced in June 1913. It cost $656,000 to construct that included $195,000 in various damage claims including foundation settling of the Metropolitan Life Insurance Company building that sits above the tunnel. It was inaugurated at high noon on December 29, 1914 with Mayor "Sunny Jim" Rolph at the wheel of the first streetcar to pass through the tunnel.

Heart Beat
1980, Orion and Warner Brothers
Fictionalized account of the friendship between writers Neal Cassady and Jack Kerouac, members of the Beat Generation of the late 1950s.

Director: John Byrum
Screenwriter: John Byrum
Production Designer: Jack Fisk
Cinematographer: László Kovács
Partial Cast: Nick Nolte, Sissy Spaceck, John Heard

• City Lights Bookstore, 261 Columbus Street, Jackson Square District
• San Francisco Art Institute, 800 Chestnut Street, Russian Hill District
• Washington Square Bar and Grill, 1707 Powell Street, North Beach District

Heartbreak Kid
2007, Paramount Pictures
A newlywed learns his bride is a total nightmare but finds the girl of his dreams.

Directors: Bobby Farrelly, Peter Farrelly
Screenwriters: Scot Armstrong, Leslie Dixon, Bobby Farrelly, Peter Farrelly, Kevin Barnett
Authors: Bruce Jay Friedman "A Change of Plan" (short story), Neil Simon (1972 screenplay)
Production Designers: Sydney J. Bartolomew Jr., Arlan Jay Vetter
Cinematographer: Matthew F. Leonetti
Partial Cast: Ben Stiller, Michelle Monaghan, Malin Akerman, Jerry Stiller, Carlos Mencia, Rob Corddry

• Golden Gate Bridge
• Embarcadero waterfront
• Coit Tower, Pioneer Park, 1 Telegraph Hill Boulevard, Telegraph Hill District
• Ferry Building, Embarcadero
• Cable Car, California Street, Chinatown District

• Intersection of 18th Street and Missouri Street, Potrero Hill District
• Intersection of Hyde Street and Green Street, Russian Hill District-laundry
• Cable Car, Hyde Street, Russian Hill District
• Mario's Bohemian Cigar Store Cafe, 566 Columbus Avenue, North Beach District
• Vallejo Street Steps, near Montgomery Street, Telegraph Hill District
• Lincoln Boulevard, below Doyle Drive, Presidio-on bicycles
• Crows Nest coastal trail, near intersection of 32nd Avenue and Camino Del Mar, Lincoln Park, Outer Richmond District
• Pier 7, The Embarcadero
• San Francisco-Oakland Bay Bridge
• Altamont Pass, U.S. Highway Route 680, Livermore
• Intersection of Union Street and Black Place, Russian Hill District

The Hearse
1980, Crown International Pictures

A woman fresh from a messy divorce decides to stay in her deceased aunt's house for the summer and encounters strange situations.

Director: George Bowers
Screenwriters: William Bleich, Mark Tenser
Art Director: Keith Michl
Cinematographer: Mori Kawa
Partial Cast: Trish Van Devere, Joseph Cotton, David Gautreaux

• Panorama of San Francisco
• Garfield Elementary School, 420 Filbert Street, Telegraph Hill District
• 712 Steiner Street, Western Addition District
• California Street Cable Car, 800 Block of California Street, Nob Hill District
• Golden Gate Bridge

Heat and Sunlight
1987, Silverlight Pictures

A troubled photojournalist is dumped by his girlfriend and in the hours following he desperately attempts to salvage their relationship.

Director: Rob Nilsson
Screenwriter: Rob Nilsson
Production Designer: Hildy Burns, Steve Burns
Cinematographer: Tomas Tucker
Partial Cast: Bill Bailey, Don Bejema

• Gnoss Field, 451 Airport Road, Novato
• Golden Gate Bridge
• BART
• Robert C. Levy Tunnel, Broadway, Russian Hill District

Heaven Can Wait
1978, Paramount Pictures

An inept angel prematurely summons a pro football player.

Directors: Warren Beatty, Buck Henry
Screenwriters: Elaine May, Warren Beatty, Robert Towne
Author: Harry Segall (play)
Production Designer: Paul Sylbert
Art Director: Edwin O'Donovan
Cinematographer: William A. Fraker
Partial Cast: Warren Beatty, Julie Christie, James Mason, Jack Warden, Dyan Cannon, Buck Henry, Vincent Gardenia

• Filoli Estate and Gardens, 86 Cañada Road, Woodside-interiors and exteriors

FILOLI

Filoli, whose name stems from "fight for a just cause, love your fellow man, live a good life," was created for water and mining baron William B. Bourne II, president of the Spring Valley Water Company. The 43-room Georgian Revival style brick mansion, one of the first designed with seismic bracing as the site straddles the San Andreas Fault, sits among a 650-acre wooded estate. The building was designed by architect Willis Polk in 1915 in concert with Bruce Porter who did the interiors and Isabella Worn the gardens. Crystal Springs Reservoir, originally owned by the Spring Valley Water Company, in the distance to the north is the well head of the Hetch Hetchy Aqueduct that flows from the Sierra Nevada Mountains. Open to the public only by appointment, Filoli is a California Historic Landmark.

Hell on Frisco Bay
1955, Warner Brothers

AKA: *The Darkest Hour*, *Hell on the Dock*

When an ex-cop is released from San Quentin State Prison after five years, his only thoughts are of revenge on the men who framed him for manslaughter.

Director: Frank Tuttle
Screenwriters: Sydney Boehm, William P.
McGivern, Martin Rackin
Art Director: John Beckman
Cinematographer: John F. Seitz
Partial Cast: Alan Ladd, Edward G. Robinson,
Joanne Dru, Paul Stewart, William Demarest,
Fay Wray, Jayne Mansfield

• William H. Martin Residence, southwest corner
of intersection of Franklin Street and Jackson
Street-site of fist fight

Hemingway and Gellhorn

2012, HBO Films
The romance between Ernest
Hemingway and World War II
correspondent Martha Gellhorn who
inspired *For Whom the Bell Tolls*.

Director: Philip Kaufman
Screenwriters: Jerry Stahl, Barbara Turner
Production Design: Geoffrey Kirkland
Art Director: Nanci Noblett
Cinematographer: Rogier Stoffers
Partial Cast: Nicole Kidman, Clive Owen

• China Camp State Park, North San Pedro
Road, San Rafael-as dock in Key West
• Stanley Ranch, 4400 North Livermore Road,
Livermore-as Spanish landscape
• Ross Alley, Chinatown District-as street market
in China
• Swedenborgian Church, 2107 Lyon Street,
Pacific heights District-fireplace and snow scene
• Herbst Theater and upper lobby, War Memorial
Opera House, 301 Van Ness Avenue, Civic
Center
• Oakland Central Train Station, intersection of
16th Street and Wood Street, Oakland-as Hotel
Florida
• SS *Jeremiah O'Brien*-as hospital ship

Her Best Move

2007, Metro Goldwyn Mayer
A teen girl soccer prodigy might join
the U.S. National Team but must
juggle a lot of priorities.

Director: Norm Hunter
Screenwriters: Norm Hunter, Tony Vidal
Production Designer: Dwane Platt
Cinematographer: Paul Ryan
Partial Cast: Leah Pipes, Daryl Sabara, Lisa Darr

• San Andreas High School, 240 Doherty Drive,
Larkspur-soccer field
• Coldstone Creamery, 1010 Court Street, San
Rafael
• San Francisco Botanical Garden at Strybing
Arboretum, 1199 Ninth Avenue, Golden Gate
Park-as Delliah's (sculpture) Garden

• Best Western Corte Madera, 56 Madera
Avenue, Corte Madera-conference site

Herbie Rides Again

1974, Buena Vista
The living Volkswagen Beetle helps
an elder woman protect her home
from a corrupt developer.

Director: Robert Stevenson
Screenwriters: Gordon Buford, Bill Walsh
Art Directors: John B. Mansbridge, Walter H.
Tyler
Cinematographer: Frank Phillips
Partial Cast: Helen Hayes, Ken Barry, Stefanie
Powers, Keenan Wynn, John McIntire

• Garden Court Restaurant, Sheraton Palace
Hotel, 2 New Montgomery Street, South of
Market District
• Fisherman's Wharf District-restaurant
• Mason O'Farrell Garage, 325 Mason Street,
Union Square District
• Golden Gate Bridge-car riding cables of bridge

RAYMOND BAILEY

The gruff character actor who often
played authoritative roles was born as
Raymond Thomas Bailey (1904–
1980) in San Francisco to William and
Alice (O'Brien) Bailey. The family was
poor, and Ray dropped out of school
in the tenth grade to work and shore
up the family finances. In his teens he
traveled to Hollywood with the intention of becoming a movie star—but
stardom eluded him and he ended up
working a variety of jobs, including
banker and stockbroker. Later he went
to New York City with no luck in secur-
ing any acting roles and became a
crewman on a freighter that sailed to
various parts of the globe. He returned
to Hollywood again in 1938 and secured a few roles, mostly during 1939,
but with the outbreak of World War II
he joined the Merchant Marine. His
locally filmed work was in *They All
Come Out* (1939), where he was seen
by audiences as an uncredited actor.
At the war's end he went back to Hollywood and started landing character
roles, and he really caught on in the
early 1950s. His roles from then on
were in film, stage, and television. His
other locally filmed work included *Vertigo* (1958), where he played a doctor;

I Want to Live! (1958) as the warden of San Quentin Prison, *The Lineup* (1958) as Phil Dressler, *Al Capone* (1959) as a lawyer, and *Herbie Rides Again* (1974) as a lawyer. He is widely recognized as the penny-pinching banker Milburn Drysdale in the popular comedy television series *The Beverly Hillbillies* during its run from 1962 through 1971.

Hereafter
2010, Warner Brothers
Supernatural thriller about three people and their differing responses to death.

Director: Clint Eastwood
Screenwriter: Peter Morgan
Production Designer: James J. Murakami
Art Director: Tom Brown
Cinematographer: Tom Stern
Partial Cast: Matt Damon, Cécile De France, Thierry Neuvic

• C & H Sugar Factory, 830 Loring Avenue, Crockett
• Emeryville-street
• Aerial view of Ferry Building, The Embarcadero
• Crissy Field, Presidio, Golden Gate National Recreation Area
• International Terminal, San Francisco International Airport

Here Comes the Navy
1934, Warner Brothers
A brash guy joins the Navy for the wrong reason but finds romance and twice is cited for his heroism.

Director: Lloyd Bacon
Screenwriters: Earl Baldwin, Ben Markson
Author: Ben Markson (story)
Art Director: Esdras Hartley
Cinematographer: Arthur Edeson
Partial Cast: James Cagney, Pat O'Brien, Dorothy Tree, Gloria Stuart, Frank McHugh, Robert Barrat

• Hangar 1, Moffett Field, Mountain View-USS *Macon* airship

Heroes
1977, Universal Pictures
A troubled war veteran escapes from an asylum and heads to California to start a worm farm.

Director: Jeremy Paul Kagan
Screenwriters: James Carabatsos, David Freeman
Production Designer: Charles Rosen
Cinematographer: Frank Stanley
Partial Cast: Henry Winkler, Sally Field, Harrison Ford, Val Avery

• Transbay Transit Terminal, 425 Mission Street, South of Market District-bus depot
• Intersection of Kentucky Street and Western Avenue, Petaluma
• Intersection of 4th Street and C Street, Petaluma-bus depot
• Sonoma-Marin Fairgrounds, 100 Fairgrounds Drive, Petaluma-racetrack
• 515 Walnut Street, Petaluma

The High and the Mighty
1954, Warner Brothers
On a flight from Honolulu to San Francisco, a plane develops engine trouble and the passengers take stock of their lives.

Director: William A. Wellman
Screenwriter: Ernest K. Gann
Author: Ernest K. Gann (novel)
Art Director: Alfred Ybarra
Cinematographer: Archie Stout
Partial Cast: John Wayne, Claire Trevor, Laraine Day, Robert Stack, Jan Sterling, Robert Newton

• San Francisco-Oakland Bay Bridge
• Runway 28 Right, San Francisco Airport-landing scene

SAN FRANCISCO-OAKLAND BAY BRIDGE

Simply known to most people as the Bay Bridge, the silver-colored less-glamorous, but more used of the two bridges from San Francisco has appeared in scores of movies. The 8 ½-mile-long span consists of two different portions linked together by a double height tunnel through Yerba Buena Island in San Francisco Bay. The west end has two suspension types and the east side a combination of cantilevered, truss, and deck spans. Construction started on July 9, 1933 with opening day on November 12, 1936. The replacement of the eastern span with a highly photogenic and strikingly contemporary white suspension span is bound to change the se-

High Anxiety
1978, 20th Century Fox
A doctor becomes the new
administrator of a mental health
institute and discovers some
suspicious events.

Director: Mel Brooks
Screenwriters: Mel Brooks, Ron Clark, Rudy De
Luca, Barry Levinson
Production Designer: Peter Wooley
Cinematographer: Paul Lohmann
Partial Cast: Mel Brooks, Madeline Kahn, Cloris
Leachman, Harvey Korman, Ron Carey, Howard
Morris, Dick Van Patten, Barry Levinson, Albert
Whitlock, Darrell Zwerling

• Golden Gate Bridge
• Fort Point National Historic Site, Marine Drive,
Golden Gate National Recreation Area
• Hyatt Regency Hotel, 5 Embarcadero Center,
The Embarcadero
• San Francisco International Airport

HYATT REGENCY HOTEL

Opened in 1973 as part of the large
Embarcadero Center development,
the Hyatt Regency San Francisco site
was part of a redevelopment project
that removed many smaller, older
buildings of the wharfside merchants
district. The hotel's 802 guest rooms
are aimed at the convention and business traveler. The theatrical gravity-
defying angle of the 17-story atrium
and acrophobia-inducing glass eleva-
tors were a symbol of their Atlanta-
based architect, John Portman. Built,
in part with David Rockefeller monies,
the design set the tone for many hotel
designs in the following years. Portman stated that the design was inspired by the 1936 H. G. Wells' sci-fi
movie *Things to Come*.

High Crimes
2002, 20th Century Fox
A woman finds out that her husband is
not who he said he was and, a trial for
murder follows.

Director: Carl Franklin
Screenwriters: Joseph Finder, Yuri Zeltser, Cary
Bickley
Production Designer: Paul Peters
Art Director: Gary Kosko
Cinematographer: Theo Van De Sande
Partial Cast: Ashley Judd, Morgan Freeman, Jim
Caviezel, Adam Scott, Amanda Peet, Bruce
Davison

• Aerial view of Paradise Cay, Tiburon
• Golden Gate Bridge
• Union Square, 333 Post Street
• Maiden Lane, Union Square-FBI takedown
• San Francisco City Hall, 1 Carlton B. Goodlett
Place, Civic Center District-front steps
• Crown Zellerbach Building, 1 Bush Street,
Financial District-lawyer's offices
• Vesuvio Cafe, 255 Columbus, Jackson Square
District
• Intersection of Broadway and Columbus
Avenue, Telegraph Hill District
• Philip Burton Federal Building, 450 Golden Gate
Avenue, Civic Center
• Bank of America Building, 555 California Street,
Financial District-front steps
• Civic Center District
• 500 Pensacola Road, Naval Air Station
Alameda, Alameda Island-house
• 391 19th Street, Potrero Hill District-Freeman's
residence

High Fidelity
2000, Buena Vista
A record store owner and compulsive
list maker recounts his top five
breakups, including the one in
progress.

Director: Stephen Frears
Screenwriters: D. V. DeVincentis, Steve Pink,
John Cusack, Scott Rosenberg
Author: Nick Hornby (book)
Production Designers: David Chapman, Thérèse
DePrez
Art Director: Nicholas Lundy
Cinematographer: Seamus McGarvey
Partial Cast: John Cusack, Tim Robbins, Joan
Cusack, Catherine Zeta-Jones

• Cesar Chavez Park, Berkeley

The Hippie Revolt
1967, Headliner Productions
AKA: *Something's Happening*
Documentary chronicling the youth
movement of the late 1960s San
Francisco's Haight-Ashbury District.

Director: Edgar Beatty
Partial Cast: Muhammad Ali, General Hershey
Bar, Carl Franzoni

- Panhandle, Golden Gate Park
- Haight Street, Haight-Ashbury District
- Intersection of Stanyan Street and Haight Street, Haight-Ashbury District

Home Alone 3
1997, 20th Century Fox
A young boy fends off thieves who seek a top-secret chip to support a North Korean terrorist organization's next deed.

Director: Raja Gosnell
Screenwriter: John Hughes
Production Designer: Henry Bumstead
Art Director: Jack G. Taylor Jr.
Cinematographer: Julio Macat
Partial Cast: Alex D. Linz, Olek Krupa, Rya Kihlstedt

- Transamerica Pyramid, 600 Montgomery Street, Financial District

Homegrown
1998, TriStar and Sony
Three inept people, who work on a marijuana farm, try to manage the contraband business themselves when the owner is killed.

Director: Stephen Gyllenhaal
Screenwriters: Nicholas Kazan, Stephen Gyllenhaal
Authors: Jonah Raskin, Stephen Gyllenhaal (story)
Production Designer: Richard Sherman
Cinematographer: Greg Gardiner
Partial Cast: Billy Bob Thornton, Hank Azaria, Ryan Phillippe, Kelly Lynch

- Aerial panorama of Financial District
- Crissy Field, Presidio, Golden Gate National Recreation Area
- Golden Gate Bridge
- Intersection of Columbus Avenue and Broadway, Telegraph Hill District
- State Highway Route 1, Jenner
- Henry Cowell Redwoods State Park, 101 North Big Trees Park Road, Felton
- Forest of Nisene Marks State Park, Aptos Creek Road, Aptos

Homeward Bound II: Lost in San Francisco
1996, Buena Vista
Three pets separated from their keepers face urban dangers.

Director: David R. Ellis
Screenwriters: Chris Hauty, Julie Hickson

Author: Shelia Burnford *The Incredible Journey* (novel)
Production Designer: Michael S. Bolton
Art Director: Eric Fraser
Cinematographer: Jack Conroy
Partial Voice Cast: Michael J. Fox, Sally Field, Ralph Waite, Al Michaels, Tommy Lasorda

- Intersection of 19th Street and Wisconsin Street, Potrero Hill District
- San Francisco International Airport
- Friedel Klussmann Memorial Cable Car Turnaround, Aquatic Park, San Francisco Maritime National Historic Park
- Panorama from Russian Hill to Alcatraz Island
- Pier 39, The Embarcadero
- Alamo Square, Western Addition District
- Golden Gate Bridge
- Coit Tower, Pioneer Park, 1 Telegraph Hill Boulevard, Telegraph Hill District

Homeward Bound: The Incredible Journey
1993, Buena Vista
Three pets search through the wilderness for their keepers.

Director: Duwayne Dunham
Screenwriters: Caroline Thompson, Linda Woolverton
Author: Shelia Burnford *The Incredible Journey* (novel)
Production Designer: Roger Cain
Art Director: Dan Self
Cinematographer: Reed Smoot
Principal Voice Cast: Michael J. Fox, Sally Field, Don Ameche

- Aerial of San Francisco skyline
- Intersection of Frederick Street and Clayton Street, Haight-Ashbury District

Honkytonk Man
1982, Warner Brothers
An aging alcoholic country singer turns to his rural family for help in the 1930s.

Director: Clint Eastwood
Screenwriter: Clancy Carlile
Author: Clancy Carlile (novel)
Production Designer: Edward C. Carfagno
Cinematographer: Bruce Surtees
Partial Cast: Clint Eastwood, Kyle Eastwood, John McIntire, Verna Bloom, Alexa Kenin, Matt Clark

- Birds Landing, Solano County

The House Across the Bay
1940, United Artists

A wife has her husband convicted of income tax evasion to protect him from his enemies.

Director: Archie Mayo
Screenwriters: Myles Connolly, Kathryn Scola
Art Directors: Alexander Golitzen, Richard Irvine
Cinematographer: Merritt B. Gerstad
Partial Cast: Joan Bennett, George Raft, Lloyd Nolan, Walter Pidgeon, Gladys George

• Alcatraz Island, Golden Gate National Recreation Area

LLOYD NOLAN

Lead character actor Lloyd Benedict Nolan, born in 1902 of Irish parents, first came to the attention of *San Francisco Examiner* newspaper readers at age 13. The young man garnered second prize in the paper's story contest, and a large portrait of the teen graced the page. He was the youngest of three children whose father was James C. Nolan Jr. and mother Margaret who resided in the upper flat at 1116 Fulton Street across from Alamo Square. Nolan's father was a shoe manufacturer and hoped his son would continue in his footsteps, but that was not Lloyd's dream, although he served as secretary in the family business for a while. Lloyd's mother took him to the local theaters quite often, which gave him exposure to the acting medium. He wanted to be a journalist and initially attended Santa Clara College and then went on to Stanford University, where he flunked out as he didn't focus on his studies. Although his initial love was the stage, where he performed for the prestigious Pasadena Community Playhouse starting in 1927, he found a better fiscal basis in film starting in 1934. By the next year, he appeared in five movies for Paramount. He and Mary Elizabeth Efird, known as Mell, were married in 1933 and they had two children. He remained with Paramount until 1940 appearing in mostly gangster films. Roles as a private detective, government agent, or police detective followed. In 1950 he entered the new market of television, which ultimately accounted for half of his long career. He had two TV series,

Martin Kane (1949) and *Special Agent 7* (1958). Over time he was seen in other San Francisco themed movies including *Wells Fargo* (1937), *King of Alcatraz* (1938), and *Susan Slade* (1961). Mell died in 1981 and two years later he married Virginia Dabney who only enjoyed two years of their marriage before Nolan's death in 1985.

House of Numbers
1957, Metro Goldwyn Mayer
A man falls in love with his sister-in-law while planning his twin brother's prison escape.

Director: Russell Rouse
Screenwriters: Don Mankiewicz, Russell Rouse
Author: Jack Finney (novel)
Cinematographer: George J. Folsey
Partial Cast: Jack Palance, Barbara Lang, Harold J. Stone, Edward Platt

• San Quentin State Prison, San Quentin

House of Sand and Fog
2003, Dreamworks SKG
A woman's house is seized and a sheriff's deputy tries to help her get the house back.

Director: Vadim Perelman
Screenwriters: Vadim Perelman, Shawn Lawrence Otto
Author: Andre Dubus III (novel)
Production Designer: Maia Javan
Art Director: Drew Boughton
Cinematographer: Roger Deakins
Partial Cast: Jennifer Connelly, Ben Kingsley, Ron Eldard, Francis Fisher, Kim Dickens, Shohreh Aghdashloo, Jonathan Ahout

• Golden Gate Bridge
• The Portside, 38 Bryant Street, Embarcadero
• San Francisco-Oakland Bay Bridge
• Intersection of 16th Street and Albion Alley, Mission District
• State Highway Route 1, Devil's Slide, Pacifica
• Municipal Pier, 2100 Beach Boulevard, Pacifica

House of Women
1962, Warner Brothers
A wrongly implicated woman is sent to prison where she faces deplorable conditions.

Director: Walter Doniger
Screenwriter: Crane Wilbur
Art Director: Leo K. Kuter
Cinematographer: Harold Stine
Partial Cast: Shirley Knight, Andrew Duggan, Constance Ford

• San Quentin State Prison, San Quentin

The House on Telegraph Hill
1951, 20th Century Fox
A woman takes the identity of another and plans to marry for money but things go astray.

Director: Robert Wise
Screenwriters: Dan Lyon, Elick Moll, Frank Partos
Art Directors: John De Cuir, Lyle Wheeler
Cinematographer: Lucien Ballard
Partial Cast: Richard Basehart, Valentina Cortese, William Lundigan, Fay Baker, Gordon Gebert, Steve Geray

• Coit Tower, Pioneer Park, 1 Telegraph Hill Boulevard, Telegraph Hill District-south lawn
• New Union Grocery, 301 Union Street, Telegraph Hill
• Larry Garage, 493 Broadway, Telegraph Hill District
• Crocker Building, One Post Street, Financial District
• Yacht Basin, Marina District-harbormaster

Howard the Duck
1986, Universal
AKA: *Howard, A New Breed of Hero*
An alien is brought to Earth and greed threatens its life.

Director: Willard Huyck
Screenwriters: Willard Huyck, Gloria Katz
Author: Steve Gerber (comic book character)
Production Designer: Peter Jamison
Art Directors: Mark Billerman, Blake Russell
Cinematographer: Richard H. Kline
Partial Cast: Lea Thompson, Jeffrey Jones, Tim Robbins

• California Academy of Sciences, 55 Music Concourse Drive, Golden Gate Park
• Rio Vista
• Petaluma waterfront
• Hamilton Field, Hamilton Air Force Base, Novato
• Nicasio Reservoir, Nicasio Valley Road, Nicasio
• Fireman's Fund Building complex, 777 San Marin Drive, Novato

Howl
2010, Oscilloscope Pictures

As Beat Poet Allen Ginsberg talks about his life and art, his most famous poem is illustrated in animation and the obscenity trial of the work is dramatized.

Directors: Rob Epstein, Jeffrey Friedman
Screenwriters: Rob Epstein, Jeffrey Friedman
Production Designer: Thérèse DePrez
Art Director: Russell Barnes
Cinematographer: Edward Lachman
Partial Cast: James Franco, Todd Rotondi, Jon Prescott, Aaron Tveit, David Strathaim, Jon Hamm, Andrew Rogers

• City Lights Bookstore, 261 Columbus Street, Jackson Square District
• Golden Gate Bridge

How Stella Got Her Groove Back
1998, 20th Century Fox
A successful investment analyst and divorced mother does something totally out of character for her age.

Director: Kevin Rodney Sullivan
Screenwriters: Terry McMillan, Ronald Bass
Author: Terry McMillan (novel)
Art Director: Marc Dabe
Cinematographer: Jeffrey Jur
Partial Cast: Angela Bassett, Taye Diggs, Whoppi Goldberg, Regina King, Suzanne Douglass

• San Francisco International Airport
• Golden Gate Bridge
• Waterfront Restaurant, Seven Pier 7, The Embarcadero-exterior

TERRY MCMILLAN

Danville author Terry McMillan's first book was *Mama*, published in 1989, which described a proud black woman with five children and the woman's progress from despair to hope. McMillan's background was not dissimilar having been born in Port Huron, Michigan in 1951 to a working-class family. Her parents divorced when she was 13 and her father died three years later. She attended the University of California, Berkeley earning a B.A. in journalism. Her third novel *Waiting to Exhale* (1992) hit a nerve with African American women and the best seller was subsequently made into a hit movie in 1995. With stars Whitney

Houston and Angela Bassett, the story told of four strong black women and their lives and loves. Her works, although considered by many to be pop, have inspired a generation of Black readers.

How the West Was Won
1962, Metro Goldwyn Mayer
The life of the daughter of a pioneering family is chronicled from youth to old age.

Directors: John Ford, Henry Hathaway, George Marshall, Richard Thorpe
Screenwriters: James R. Webb, John Gay
Author: James R. Webb (magazine series)
Art Directors: George W. Davis, William Ferrari, Addison Hehr
Cinematographers: William H. Daniels, Milton R. Krasner, Charles Lang, Joseph LaShelle
Partial Cast: James Stewart, John Wayne, Gregory Peck

• Golden Gate Bridge

Hulk
2003, Universal Pictures
AKA: *The Hulk*
Marvel comic's story about an accident that leaves him with the tendency to turn into a giant green brute with superhuman strength when under stress.

Director: Ang Lee
Screenwriters: James Schamus, John Turman, Michael France
Authors: Stan Lee, Jack Kirby (comic book series)
Production Designer: Rick Heinrichs
Art Directors: John Dexter, Greg Papalia
Cinematographer: Frederick Elmes
Partial Cast: Eric Bana, Jennifer Connelly, Nick Nolte, Sam Elliott, Josh Lucas

• Intersection of Vallejo Street and Sansome Street, Telegraph Hill District
• Intersection of Vallejo Street Steps and Montgomery Street, Telegraph Hill District
• Building 180, Treasure Island-as New York's East side
• Casa de la Vista, 271 Avenue of Palms, Treasure Island-as restaurant
• 410 Avenue of Palms, Building 1, Treasure Island-semi-circular building interior with murals

• Lawrence Berkeley National Laboratory, 1 Cyclotron Road, University of California Campus, Berkeley

• Berkeley Hills
• Golden Gate Bridge
• San Francisco-Oakland Bay Bridge

Hurlyburly
1998, Fine Line Features
Hollywood movers and shakers dissect their own personal lives when everything seems to clash together.

Director: Anthony Drazan
Screenwriter: David Rabe
Production Designer: Michael D. Haller
Art Director: Derek R. Hill
Cinematographer: Changei Gu
Partial Cast: Sean Penn, Kevin Spacey, Robert Wright, Chazz Palminteri, Garry Shandling, Anna Paquin, Meg Ryan
Local Cast: TV anchor Elaine Corral-Kendall, TV anchor Frank Somerville

• The Oakland Hills-as the hills of Hollywood

If I Had My Way
1940, Universal Pictures
A bridge construction worker looks after a 12-year old girl after her father is killed in a construction accident leaving her an orphan.

Director: David Butler
Screenwriters: David Butler, William M. Conselman, James V. Kern
Art Director: Jack Otterson
Cinematographer: George Robinson
Partial Cast: Bing Crosby, Gloria Jean

• Panoramic view of San Francisco from Twin Peaks
• Golden Gate Bridge (under construction)
• San Francisco-Oakland Bay Bridge

I Know What You Did Last Summer
1997, Columbia
Four teenagers are in great danger after their car hits a stranger whose body they dump in the sea.

Director: Jim Gillespie
Screenwriters: Lois Duncan, Kevin Williamson
Production Designer: Gary Wissner
Art Director: John J. Rutchland III
Cinematographer: Denis Crossan

Partial Cast: Jennifer Love Hewitt, Sarah Michelle Gellar, Ryan Phillippe, Freddie Prinze Jr.

• State HighwayRoute 1, Jenner
• Campbell Cove, Bodega Bay
• Kolmer Cove, north of Fort Ross
• Schoolhouse Beach, Carmet

Illusion
2004, Entitled Entertainment
AKA: *The Illusion*
A dying filmmaker is shown some of the course of his estranged son's life.

Director: Michael A. Goorjian
Screenwriters: Tressa DiFiflia, Michael A. Goorjian, Chris Horvath, Ron Marasco
Author: Pierre Corneille *L'Illusion Comique* (play)
Production Designer: Lisa Clark
Art Directors: Peter Mayer, Joe Schlick
Cinematographer: Robert Humphreys
Partial Cast: Kirk Douglas, Michael A. Goorjian, Karen Tucker, Bryan Cranston, Richard Arquette, Ron Marasco

• Intersection of Market Street and Sansome Street, Financial District-driving car
• San Francisco-Oakland Bay Bridge
• Intersection of Sansome Street and Halleck Street, Financial District
• Pan of waterfront from San Francisco Bay
• Embarcadero Four, Embarcadero Center-as Isabel's office interior
• St. Mary Cemetery, 4529 Howe Street, Oakland
• Roxie Theater, 3117 16th Street, Mission District-projection booth
• Bishop O'Dowd High School, 9500 Stearns Avenue, Oakland
• Route 29, Napa Valley-rail tracks
• Napa Valley Olive Oil Co., 800 Allison Avenue, St. Helena-boarding house
• Doug's Auto Repair, 1020 Foothill Boulevard, Calistoga-garage
• Gordon's Café, 6770 Washington Street, Yountville
• Alley, between 1310 and 1353 Lincoln Street, Calistoga-knife attack site
• Several spots along Lincoln Avenue, between Cedar Street and Washington Street, Calistoga-bus stop
• Golden Gate Bridge

MICHAEL A. GOORJIAN

The director, writer, producer and actor Michael Antranig Goorjian was born in Oakland in 1971 and reared in an artsy loft. His father, a physicist for NASA, and his mother, a nurse, are of Armenian extraction. He started his acting career at age 13 performing in local theater productions at the Contra Costa Musical Theater Company, the Berkeley Shakespeare Company, and

San Francisco's American Conservatory Theater. In 1989 he graduated from Oakland's Bishop O'Dowd High School and went to Los Angeles to attend UCLA and study theater arts. He has been seen in other locally filmed movies including *Forever Young* (1992) with Mel Gibson and, *Happily, Even After* (2004).

In Harm's Way
1965, Paramount
The U.S. Navy retaliates on Japan after the bombing of Pearl Harbor.

Director: Otto Preminger
Screenwriters: James Bassett, Wendell Mayes
Production Designer: Lyle Wheeler
Cinematographer: Loyal Griggs
Partial Cast: John Wayne, Kirk Douglas, Patricia Neal, Tom Tryon, Paula Prentiss, Dana Andrews,

• View from top of Crookedest Street in the World, 1000 block of Lombard Street, Russian Hill District
• Army and Navy YMCA, 166 The Embarcadero-interior
• Naval Air Station Alameda, Alameda Island

NAVAL AIR STATION ALAMEDA

Commissioned in 1940, the 2,527-acre site was the largest of its kind in the world with 300 buildings and was home to 271 trades for the manufacturing, maintenance and repair of naval aircraft. The base closed in 1997.

"In this world you turn the other cheek and you get hit with a lug wrench."

Impact
1949, United Artists
A woman and her lover plan the murder of her rich husband.

Director: Arthur Lubin
Screenwriters: Jay Dratler, Dorothy Reid
Art Director: Rudi Feld

Cinematographer: Ernest Laszlo
Partial Cast: Brian Donlevy, Ella Raines, Charles Coburn, Helen Walker, Anna May Wong

• Fairmont Hotel, 950 Mason Street, Nob Hill District
• Fisherman's Wharf District
• Old Hall of Justice, 750 Kearny Street, Financial District-exterior and courtroom
• Ferry Building, Herb Caen Way, Embarcadero District
• 700 and 800 blocks of Market Street
• Chinatown District
• Brocklebank Apartments, 1000 Mason Street at Sacramento, Nob Hill District-as Bayview Apartments
• Pacific Union Club, 1000 California Street, Nob Hill District
• Plaza Vina del Mar, Bridgeway, Sausalito
• Larkspur Volunteer Fire Department, 420 Magnolia Street, Larkspur

PLAZA VINA DEL MAR

The area of the charming triangular-shaped Plaza Vina del Mar was originally a vile and stagnant backwash of Richardson Bay. Filled-in through the efforts of Mayor Jacques Thomas; a simple drinking fountain was dedicated to honor his efforts in 1912 after his death. Resident architect William B. Faville designed the fountain that originally stood as part of the Palaces of Education and of Food Products at the 1915 Panama-Pacific International Exposition in San Francisco. The pair of flag poles surmounting elephants were in the PPIE's Court of the Universe. The transplant to Sausalito was funded through the generosity of several Sausalito citizens. The two elephants, known as Pee Wee and Jumbo, and the tiered fountain were officially dedicated in a ceremony on Flag Day in 1916. The sculptures seen today are cast stone copies of the originals that deteriorated over time. The plaza's name is derived from one in Sausalito's sister city of Valparaiso, Chile.

Impulse
1984, 20th Century Fox
After an earthquake a small town is menaced by a mysterious subterrane-

an substance that makes the citizens self-destructive.

Director: Graham Baker
Screenwriters: Bart Davis, Don Carlos Dunaway, Nicholas Kazan
Production Designer: Jack T. Collis
Cinematographer: Thomas Del Ruth
Partial Cast: Tim Matheson, Meg Tilly, Hume Cronyn, John Karlen, Amy Stryker

• Rio Vista-town
• Petaluma-farm

The Indestructible Man
1956, Allied Artists
Scientific experiments accidentally revive an executed criminal and make him impervious to harm.

Director: Jack Pollexfen
Screenwriters: Vy Russell, Sue Dwiggins
Art Director: Ted Holsopple
Cinematographer: John L. Russell
Partial Cast: Lon Chaney Jr., Max Showalter, Marian Carr

• Panoramic view of downtown San Francisco

Indiana Jones and the Last Crusade
1989, Paramount
The wiley adventurer squares off against bloodthirsty Indian cultists.

Director: Steven Spielberg
Screenwriter: Jeffrey Boam
Authors: George Lucas, Menno Meyjes (story)
Production Designer: Elliot Scott
Cinematographer: Douglas Secombe
Partial Cast: Harrison Ford, Sean Connery, Denholm Elliott, Alison Doody, John Rys-Davies

• 410 Avenue of Palms (Building One), Treasure Island-as Berlin's Tempelhof Airport

Indiana Jones and the Temple of Doom
1984, Paramount
AKA: *Indiana Jones and the Temple of Death*
After arriving in India, Indiana Jones is asked by a desperate village to find a mystical stone. His search reveals a secret cult plotting a terrible plan.

Director: Steven Spielberg
Screenwriters: Willard Huyck, Gloria Katz

Author: George Lucas (story)
Production Designer: Elliot Scott
Art Directors: Roger Cain, Alan Cassie
Cinematographer: Douglas Slocombe
Partial Cast: Harrison Ford, Kate Capshaw

• Hamilton Field, Hamilton Air Force Base,
Novato-as Shanghai airport hangars

In Love and War
1958, 20th Century Fox
Three marines are on shore leave in
San Francisco during World War II.

Director: Phillip Dunne
Screenwriter: Edward Anhalt
Author: Anton Myrer *The Big War* (novel)
Art Directors: George W. Davis, Lyle R. Wheeler
Cinematographer: Leo Tover
Partial Cast: Jeffrey Hunter, Robert Wagner,
Bradford Dillman, Dana Wynter, Hope Lange,
Sheree North, Veronica Cartwright

• San Francisco-Oakland Bay Bridge
• Potrero Hill District
• Spreckels Mansion, 2080 Washington Street,
Pacific Heights District
• Hoover Tower, Stanford University, Stanford
• Memorial Church, Stanford University, Stanford
• Golden Gate Bridge

BRADFORD DILLMAN

Longtime 49ers fan Bradford Dillman
was born in San Francisco in 1930.
His father, Dean, worked as a stockbroker for A. O. Slaughter, Anderson
and Fox and later E. F. Hutton in San
Francisco, and his mother Josephine
was a homemaker at their 3857 Clay
Street residence. His maternal grandfather, Charles C. Moore, was president of the Pan Pacific International
Exposition in 1915. Dillman credits his
first inkling about acting to an experience while attending Pacific Height's
tony Town School for Boys; there the
chubby third grader performed a part
as an angel. Later he gained movement experience attending Alys Miller's Children's Dance Studio near the
school. He was exposed to the film
entertainment medium during his
grammar school years when Dillman
went to the movies every Saturday at
The Warfield Theater on Market
Street. One of four children, Brad's
parents separated when he was 12
and later they divorced. Attending

boarding schools in New England
including Connecticut's venerable
Hotchkiss School he then attended
nearby Yale University graduating in
1951. During the Korean War he entered the United States Marines.
Steeped in New England by then he
left his hometown for good in 1953 to
try his luck in New York, the city of the
Great White Way. His talent was
showcased in Twentieth Century
Fox's *Francis of Assisi* (1961) and the
Italian-location film's 1961 gala premiere was appropriately held in his
hometown of San Francisco at the
Warfield. He married actress Suzy
Parker in 1963 who appeared in the
Bay Area-filmed *Kiss Them for Me*
(1957). Dillman also appeared in the
locally filmed *The Enforcer* (1976),
Guyana: Cult of the Damned (1979),
and *Sudden Impact* (1983).

Innerspace
1987, Warner Brothers
An Air Force flyer is miniaturized and
injected into the body of a grocery
store clerk.

Director: Joe Dante
Screenwriters: Jeffrey Boam, Chip Proser
Production Designer: James H. Spencer
Art Director: William F. Matthews
Cinematographer: Andrew Laszlo
Partial Cast: Dennis Quaid, Martin Short, Meg
Ryan, Kevin McCarthy, Fiona Lewis

• Mark Hopkins Hotel, 999 California Street, Nob
Hill District
• Golden Gate Bridge

Inside Moves
1980, Lionsgate
A man is crippled after a failed suicide
and he makes friends in a bar with
other interesting misfits.

Director: Richard Donner
Screenwriters: Valerie Curtin, Barry Levinson
Author: Todd Walton (novel)
Production Designer: Charles Rosen
Cinematographer: László Kovács
Partial Cast: John Savage, David Morse, Amy
Wright

• Oakland Coliseum, 7000 Coliseum Way,
Oakland

The Insider

1999, Buena Vista

AKA: *60 Minutes, Man of the People*

A research chemist comes under personal and professional attack when he decides to appear in a CBS TV *60 Minutes* expose about the business of Big Tobacco.

Director: Michael Mann
Screenwriters: Eric Roth, Michael Mann
Author: Marie Brenner (article)
Production Designer: Brian Morris
Art Director: Margie Stone McShirley
Cinematographer: Dante Spinotti
Partial Cast: Al Pacino, Russell Crowe, Christopher Plummer

• 505 Montgomery Street, Financial District-office building lobby
• Telegraph Avenue, Berkeley
• Santa Barbara Road, Berkeley-residence

The Internship

2013, Twentieth Century Fox

Two salesmen, whose careers have been torpedoed by the digital age, find their way into a coveted internship at Google. There they must compete with a group of young, tech-savvy geniuses for a shot at employment.

Director: Shawn Levy
Screenwriters: Vince Vaughn, Jared Stern
Author: Vince Vaughn (story)
Production Designer: Tom Meyer
Cinematographer: Jonathan Brown
Partial Cast: Owen Wilson, Vince Vaughn, John Goodman

• Google Campus, 1600 Amphitheatre Parkway, Mountain View

Invasion of the Body Snatchers

1978, United Artists

A group of people discover that humans are being replaced by emotionless clones.

Director: Philip Kaufman
Screenwriter: W. D. Richter
Author: Jack Finney *The Body Snatchers* (novel)
Production Designer: Charles Rosen
Cinematographer: Michael Chapman
Partial Cast: Donald Sutherland, Brooke Adams, Leonard Nimoy, Veronica Cartwright, Jeff Goldblum, Art Hindle, Lelia Goldoni, Kevin McCarthy, Don Siegel

• Golden Gate Bridge
• 1227 Montgomery Street, Telegraph Hill District-Bennell residence
• Intersection of Filbert Street Steps and Napier Lane, Telegraph Hill District
• Alamo Square, Western Addition District-playground
• 720 Steiner Street, Alamo Square, Western Addition District-Howell residence
• Market Street
• Department of Public Health, 101 Grove Street, Civic Center
• Grant Street, Chinatown District-laundry
• Civic Center Plaza, Civic Center District
• Embarcadero Center
• Alcoa Building, One Maritime Plaza, 300 Clay Street, Golden Gateway-escalator
• Intersection of Eddy Street and Leavenworth Street, Tenderloin District-pedestrian hit
• Union Square, 333 Post Street
• Cable Car Turnaround, intersection of Powell Street and Market Street-phone booth
• Pier 33 dock, The Embarcadero
• Pier 70, The Embarcadero-fire
• PSA San Franciscan Hotel, 1231 Market Street, South of Market District

Inventing the Abbotts
1997, Twentieth Century Fox
Two brothers court three sisters of a well-heeled family.

Director: Pat O'Conner
Screenwriters: Sue Miller, Ken Hixon
Production Designer: Gary Frutkoff
Art Director: William V. Ryder
Cinematographer: Kenneth MacMillan
Partial Cast: Liv Tyler, Joaquin Phoenix, Billy Crudup, Jennifer Connelly

• Intersection of American Alley and Western Avenue, Petaluma
• Mystic Theater, McNear Building, 15-23 Petaluma Boulevard, Petaluma-as bus stop
• Santa Rosa High School, 1235 Mendocino Avenue, Santa Rosa
• 18 Western Avenue, Petaluma-as Lily's Apparel
• 12820 Sir Francis Drake Boulevard, Inverness-as boathouse
• Healdsburg Fire Station, 601 Healdsburg Avenue, Healdsburg-as feed store
• 600 Healdsburg Avenue, Healdsburg-gas station
• 15 Western Avenue, Petaluma-as Iron Skillet Restaurant

Interview with the Vampire: The Vampire Chronicles
1994, Warner Brothers
AKA: *Interview with the Vampire*
A vampire tells his epic life story about love, betrayal, loneliness, and hunger.

Director: Neil Jordan
Screenwriter: Anne Rice
Author: Anne Rice (novel)
Production Designer: Dante Ferretti
Art Director: Malcolm Middleton
Cinematographer: Philippe Rousselot
Partial Cast: Tom Cruise, Brad Pitt, Antonio Banderas, Stephen Rea, Christian Slater

• Golden Gate Bridge
• Aerial view from Bay looking to Ferry Building and Market Street beyond
• Intersection of Market Street and Sixth Street, Tenderloin District
• 1024 Market Street, Tenderloin District-as St. Martin Hotel

The Invisible Circus
1999, New Line Cinema
A girl pursues why her Paris-based sister died and falls for her sister's boyfriend.

Director: Adam Brooks
Screenwriter: Adam Brooks
Author: Jennifer Egan (novel)
Production Designer: Robin Standefer
Art Director: Stephen Alesch
Cinematographer: Henry Braham

Partial Cast: Jordana Brewster, Christopher Eccleston, Cameron Diaz, Blythe Danner
• Golden Gate Bridge
• 3837 Clay Street, Pacific Heights District

I Remember Mama
1948, RKO Radio Pictures
A novelist recounts growing up with her Norwegian-American family.

Director: George Stevens
Screenwriter: DeWitt Bodeen
Author: Kathryn Forbes *Mama's Bank Account* (novel)
Art Directors: Caroll Clark, Albert S. D'Agostino
Cinematographer: Nicholas Musuraca
Partial Cast: Irene Dunne, Barbara Bel Geddes, Oscar Homolka, Phillip Dorn, Edgar Bergen, Rudy Vallee

• Ferry Building, Herb Caen Way, The Embarcadero
• Intersection of Noe Street and Liberty Street, Eureka Valley District
• Intersection of Leavenworth Street and Francisco Street Steps, Russian Hill District
• Cable car, intersection of Hyde Street and Chestnut Street, Russian Hill District
• Fairmont Hotel, 950 Mason Street, Nob Hill District-hotel lobby

KATHRYN FORBES

Born Kathryn Anderson in 1909, the San Francisco native was the daughter of Leon Ellis and Della (Jesser) Anderson. Kathryn attended Lowell High School in San Francisco but graduated from another unknown high school in 1925. The next year she married contractor Robert McLean and they went on to have two sons, Robert Jr. and Richard. They resided at 910 Edgehill Drive in Burlingame. Her writing career started in 1938 after she parlayed her voluntary publicity work into a career with the publication of her first story. The book on which the movie is based, *Mama's Bank Account*, was published in 1943. It was a fictionalized memoir about an immigrant Norwegian's family's life of assimilation in San Francisco during the 1920s. The book was turned into a play that was staged on Broadway in 1944 and then the story had another life as a popular CBS TV series between 1949 and 1957. This was followed by two versions of musicals staged in the 1970s. Forbes died in 1966 in San Francisco and is buried in Holy Cross Catholic Cemetery in Colma.

GEORGE STEVENS

During his long career George Cooper Stevens was a cinematographer, director, producer, and screenwriter working with the top studios and actors. Stevens was Oakland-born in 1904 to actor parents Landers Stevens and Georgie Cooper. They ran their own theater in Oakland named Ye Liberty Playhouse, worked in other Bay Area theaters, and were on the West Coast Orpheum circuit in vaudeville. Stevens had two brothers, Jack and Ashton. The family left the Bay Area in 1922, when Stevens was in his late teens and moved to Glendale to work in the movie industry. He joined the Hal Roach Studio as an assistant cameraman. He married actress Yvonne Howell, in 1930 and they had a son George Stevens Jr. who went on to be a large player in the movie industry. Stevens began his directorial career in 1930, working mostly in film shorts. He came into his own later in the decade with such movies as *Alice Adams* (1935) with Katharine Hepburn and in 1942 he again directed Hepburn in *Woman of the Year*. With WW II in full swing, Stevens joined the Army Signal Corps where he headed a combat motion picture unit from 1944 through 1946. He received the coveted Irving G. Thalberg Memorial Award in 1953 for maintaining a consistent level of high-quality production. In that decade he received the Oscar for Best Director for *A Place in the Sun* (1951) and *Giant* (1956), both with Elizabeth Taylor.

During 1958 and 1959 he was president of the Academy of Motion Pictures. Ultimately he became one of America's finest filmmakers; he is credited for creating a style that revealed a character's true human side. Stevens died in 1975 after a distinguished career.

It Came from Beneath the Sea

1955, Columbia
The City of San Francisco is attacked by a gigantic octopus.

Director: Robert Gordon
Screenwriters: George Worthing Yates, Harold Jacob Smith
Author: George Worthing Yates (story)
Art Director: Paul Palmentola
Cinematographer: Henry Freulich
Partial Cast: Kenneth Tobey, Faith Domergue, Donald Curtis, Ian Keith

• Crissy Field, Presidio, Golden Gate National Recreation Area
• Waterfront-piers
• Intersection of Market Street and Stockton Street, Union Square District

YOU CAN'T DO THAT WITH OUR BRIDGE!

The City of San Francisco would not allow Columbia Pictures to use actual footage of the Golden Gate Bridge being destroyed by a gargantuan octopus due to possible loss of public confidence in the structure, so a miniature model was used. The six-legged creature was an animated model intercut with newsreel and stock footage.

It's a Mad, Mad, Mad, Mad World

1963, United Artists
The dying words of a thief spark a madcap cross-country rush to find treasure.

Director: Stanley Kramer
Screenwriters: William Rose, Tania Rose

Production Designer: Rudolph Sternad
Art Director: Gordon Gurnee
Cinematographer: Ernest Laszlo
Partial Cast: Spencer Tracy, Jimmy Durante,
Milton Berle, Sid Caesar, Ethel Merman, Buddy
Hackett, Mickey Rooney, Dick Shawn, Phil
Silvers, Terry-Thomas

• Sonoma County Airport, Airport Boulevard,
Santa Rosa-airplane flies through open plane
hangar

I Want to Live
1958, United Artists
A vagrant prostitute goes to the gas
chamber despite growing doubts
about her guilt.

Director: Robert Wise
Screenwriters: Nelson Gidding, Don Mankiewicz
Authors: Ed Montgomery (news articles), Barbara
Graham (letters)
Cinematographer: Lionel Lindon
Partial Cast: Susan Hayward, Simon Oakland,
Virginia Vincent, Theodore Bikel, Wesley Lau,
Philip Coolidge

• San Quentin State Prison, Main Street, San
Quentin-main gate

BARBARA GRAHAM

Susan Hayward won an Academy
Award as Best Actress for her portrayal of the locally born woman gone
bad. Barbara Elaine Graham was pro-
nounced dead at 11:42 a.m. on June
3, 1955 in front of 37 witnesses. The
toxic combination of sulfuric acid and
cyanide completed Graham's capital
punishment; her body was buried at
Mt. Olivet Cemetery in San Rafael.
"Bonnie," as she was known in her
childhood, was born to Oakland un-
wed mother Hortense Wood in 1923.
Mother and daughter were never
close, and ultimately Barbara was
placed in a reformatory just as Hortense had been in her earlier years.
The cunning Barbara used her looks
to attract men and eventually turned to
a life as a hooker and undertaking
other shady dealings in Oakland, San
Diego, Long Beach, and San Francisco. Vacillating between a loose life
and then going straight, she married
three times. Her final marriage was to
Henry Graham, with whom she shared
a son named Tommy. Sadly, mother
and son both ended up sharing a heroin habit.

Jack
1996, Hollywood Pictures
A boy has an unusual aging disorder.

Director: Francis Ford Coppola
Screenwriters: James De Monaco, Gary Nadeau
Production Designer: Dean Tavoularis
Art Director: Angelo P. Graham
Cinematographer: John Toll
Partial Cast: Robin Williams, Diane Lane, Brian
Kerwin, Bill Cosby, Jennifer Lopez
Local Cast: TV anchor Terence McGovern

• 8 Redwood Drive, Ross-Jack's house
• Marin General Hospital, 250 Bon Air Road,
Greenbrae
• Ross Elementary School, 9 Lagunitas Road,
Ross-as Nathaniel Hawthorne School
• St. Helena Elementary School, 1325 Adams
Street, St. Helena
• Mountain Theater, Mt. Tamalpais Park, Golden
Gate National Recreation Area-graduation

FRANCIS FORD COPPOLA

Coppola was born on April 7, 1939,
the middle of three children in Detroit.
His family moved to New York two
years after his birth, and he grew up in
Queens. Coppola's father Carmine
was a composer and musician while
his mother Italia (Pennino) was an
actress. This gene combination contributed to Francis's multi-faceted talents as composer, writer, producer,
and director. He briefly attended the
New York Military Academy but graduated from Great Neck North High
School. He obtained an undergraduate degree in drama from Hofstra University in Hempstead, New York in
1959 and went on to UCLA where he
graduated in 1967 with an M.F.A. in
Film Production. Rising through the
ranks, he won his first Oscar for co-
writing the screenplay of Patton in
1970. He abandoned Hollywood for
San Francisco in 1969 and co-
created, with George Lucas, the independent production company called
American Zoetrope. In 1971 he acted
as executive producer for the ground-
breaking film THX-1138. That same

year, Lucas left the partnership to form his own company. Coppola and his wife Eleanor (Neil), a set decorator, were married in 1963 and had three children. They reside in Rutherford on the grounds of the venerable Inglenook Winery where *This Earth is Mine* (1959) was primarily filmed. He has directed several films that were entirely or partially shot in the Bay Area, including *Finian's Rainbow* (1968), *Peggy Sue Got Married* (1986), *Tucker: The Man and His Dream* (1988), and *Jack* (1996). He has been both screenwriter (or co-screenwriter) and director in the following: *The Godfather* (1972), *The Conversation* (1974), and *The Rainmaker* (1997). In a salute to his work the Academy of Motion Picture Arts and Sciences awarded Coppola the prestigious Irving G. Thalberg Memorial Award in 2010 recognizing Coppola's consistent high quality motion picture production.

Jack London
1943, United Artists
AKA: The *Adventures of Jack London*, *The Life of Jack London*, *The Story of Jack London*
An episodic story of the adventures in the novelist's life.

Director: Alfred Santell
Screenwriter: Issac Don Levine
Author: Charmian London *The Book of Jack London* (book)
Art Director: Bernard Herzbrun
Cinematographers: John W. Boyle, Lee Garnees
Partial Cast: Michael O'Shea, Susan Hayward, Virginia Mayo, Louise Beavers

• Opening is newsreel footage of the launch of Liberty Ship 1237 SS *Jack London* in Sausalito on July 16, 1943, which was the last Liberty Ship launched at the Marinship shipyard.

JACK LONDON

John Griffith "Jack" London was born on January 12, 1876 on Third Street in San Francisco. His parents, Flora Wellman and William H. Chaney, were unmarried. Later that year Flora married John London, a machinist who was a partially disabled Civil War veteran who worked at the Risdon Iron and Locomotive Works. The family moved around the Bay Area finally settling in Oakland where London completed grade school but also worked a variety of odd jobs. In 1894 he set out to tramp about the United States. He finished his secondary education at Oakland High School and later attended the University of California, Berkeley but did not finish due to a lack of funds. Being an adventurer he went to Alaska's Klondike in 1897. His experiences up to that time were grist for his writing and the prestigious publications *Overland Monthly* and *Atlantic Monthly* began printing his work. His first marriage was to Bess Maddern in 1900; they had two daughters. But the marriage foundered and, after divorcing Bess, Jack married Charmian Kittredge in 1905. London served several stints as a journalist, one in 1904 for the *San Francisco Examiner*. In 1905 he purchased land in Sonoma County's town of Glen Ellen, land that would eventually become 1,400 acres of what he dubbed "Beauty Ranch." In 1907 the couple sailed to Hawaii on their schooner *Snark*. The voyage was to have lasted for several years, but due to Jack's health the couple was back on the ranch just 27 months later. Here he had constructed his dream home, which he called "Wolf House," but the almost completed building burned in 1913, just before the Londons were to move in; it was never rebuilt. London died three years later, on November 22, 1916, due to kidney failure. Charmian's 1921 book, *The Book of Jack London* was the basis of the movie *Jack London*. The film was a disappointment to Charmian. Many of London's stories and novels have been captured on film. The first was *For Love of Gold* (1908), a short by D. W. Griffith; others include *Call of the Wild*, *The Sea Wolf*, and *White Fang*, which have each been put on film at various times.

Jack the Bear
1993, 20th Century Fox
A widower begins to drink heavily as he tries to cope with his two sons and an unbalanced neighbor.

Director: Marshall Herskovitz
Screenwriters: Dan Call, Steven Zaillian
Production Designer: Lilly Kilvert
Art Director: John Warnke
Cinematographer: Fred Murphy
Partial Cast: Danny DeVito, Robert J. Steinmiller Jr., Miko Hughes, Gary Sinise, Art LaFleur, Julia Louis-Dreyfus, Reese Witherspoon

• Fort Baker, Marin Headlands, Golden Gate National Recreation Area
• Golden Gate Bridge

Jade
1995, Paramount Pictures
An assistant district attorney investigates the murder of a wealthy citizen and finds a friend to be a prime suspect.

Director: William Friedkin
Screenwriter: Joe Eszterhas
Production Designer: Alex Tavoularis
Art Director: Charles Breen
Cinematographer: Andrzej Bartkowiak
Partial Cast: David Caruso, Linda Fiorentino, Chazz Palminteri, Michael Biehn, Richard Crenna
Local Cast: former San Francisco Police Department Inspector Kenny King

• Chinatown District
• Dolphin Swimming and Boating Club, 502 Jefferson Street, Waterfront
• Hall of Justice, 850 Bryant Street, South of Market District
• Getty Residence, 2896 Broadway, Pacific Heights District
• Saints Peter and Paul Church, 666 Filbert Street, North Beach District
• Fior d'Italia Restaurant, 601 Union Street, North Beach District
• Garden Court Restaurant, Sheraton Palace Hotel, 2 New Montgomery Street, South of Market District
• 8520 Cabrillo Highway, State Highway Route 1, Montara-beach house

VICTOR WONG

Born as Yee Victor Keung Wong on July 31, 1927 in San Francisco's Chinatown, Wong's parents were first-generation Chinese immigrants. His father was a scholar of Confucian studies. Wong attended the University of California, Berkeley, where he studied political science and journalism and then went to the University of Chicago to study theology. He also attended the San Francisco Art Institute to learn painting. He worked for six years at the PBS affiliate KQED TV station, where he was an Emmy-winning journalist covering San Francisco's Chinatown and other big stories like the 1968 Democratic Convention and the Patty Hearst/SLA case. He broke into acting in his late 50s, with an appearance on television in the soap opera *Search for Tomorrow*. Wong's first film appearance was in local director Wang Wang's movie *Dim Sum: A Little Bit of Heart* (1985); he later appeared in *Eat a Bowl of Tea* (1989) and *Life is Cheap... but the toilet paper is expensive* (1990). He was memorable in his offbeat role as the Chinese wizard Egg Shen in *Big Trouble in Little China* (1986) that starred Kurt Russell. He also appeared in the locally filmed Amy Tan story *The Joy Luck Club* that debuted on the silver screen in 1993. The veteran character actor died in 2001 at his home near the historic Central Valley town of Locke, founded by Chinese immigrants.

Jagged Edge
1985, Columbia
A lawyer defends a newspaper publisher who may or may not be guilty.

Director: Richard Marquand
Screenwriter: Joe Eszterhas
Production Designer: Gene Callahan
Art Director: Peter J. Smith
Cinematographer: Matthew F. Leonetti
Partial Cast: Glenn Close, Beau Bridges, Peter Coyote

• 2898 Broadway, Pacific Heights District
• Golden Gate Bridge
• San Francisco City Hall, 1 Carlton B. Goodlett Place, Civic Center District-rotunda and steps
• Pier 39 public parking garage, intersection of Powell Street and Beach Streets, Waterfront-roof

Jobs
2013, Open Road Films

The story of Steve Jobs' rise from college dropout to one of the most revered creative entrepreneurs of the twentieth century.

Director: Joshua Michael Stern
Screenwriter: Matt Whiteley
Production Designer: Freddy Waff
Art Director: Bruce Robert Hill
Cinematographer: Russell Carpenter
Partial Cast: Aston Kutcher, Amanda Crew, Matthew Modine, James Woods, Josh Gad, Leslie Ann Warren

• Palo Alto
• 2066 Crist Drive, Los Altos-childhood home

Johnny Get Your Hair Cut

1927, Metro Goldwyn Mayer

When an orphan is adopted by a racehorse owner he decides to pay back his benefactor by training to ride the horse so he can win an important race.

Directors: B. Reeves Eason, Archie Mayo
Screenwriters: Gerald Beaumont, Florence Ryerson, Ralph Spence
Cinematographer: Frank B. Good
Partial Cast: Jackie Coogan, Harry Carey, James Corrigan

• Tanforan Racetrack, El Camino Real, San Bruno

FOR WHOSE BENEFIT?

In 1925, a grand 12.5-acre, 375,000-gallon freshwater artificial lake with boathouse was proposed for the site of the current soccer fields in the west end of San Francisco's Golden Gate Park. Intended to double as a reservoir, the lake was to have been named for Park Superintendent John McLaren. One step to finance the lake's estimated $100,000 cost was a fundraiser held at the Tanforan Racetrack in San Bruno on Sunday, September 19, 1926. During the benefit, filming took place for an upcoming movie as well. All the city newspapers ran stories to build up the event, and San Francisco Mayor James "Sunny Jim" Rolph Jr. officially proclaimed that Sunday "John McLaren Day" at the racetrack. Two days before the

event, a parade on Market Street, from the Ferry Building to City Hall, featured 12-year-old film star Jackie Coogan wearing racing silks. (The MGM silent film *Johnny Get Your Hair Cut* involved horses and was Coogan's last film as a child star. He was later known best for his role of Uncle Fester in television's *The Addams Family*.) Despite great fanfare, with 10,000 attendees and the raising of some $10,000 the lake was not built. A park was later named for McLaren in the Visitacion Valley District of southern San Francisco.

The Joy Luck Club

1993, Buena Vista and Hollywood Pictures

The recollection of relationships between four Chinese-American daughters and their Chinese mothers.

Director: Wayne Wang
Screenwriter: Amy Tan
Author: Amy Tan (novel)
Production Designer: Donald Graham Burt
Art Director: Diana Kunce
Cinematographer: Amir M. Mokri
Partial Cast: Tsai Chin, Kieu Chinh, Ming-Na Wen, Tamyln Tomita, France Nuyen, Lauren Tom, Lisa Lu, Rosalind Chao

• 884 Union Street, Russian Hill District
• 180 Manchester Street, Bernal Heights District-contemporary interior

AMY TAN

Sausalito-based writer Amy Tan originally hails from Oakland where she was born on February 19, 1952. Her father, John Tan, was an electrical engineer and Baptist Minister who fled to the United States to escape the Chinese Civil War; her mother was Daisy (Li) Tan who escaped from Shanghai before the communist takeover in 1949. Amy's family moved on several occasions before settling in Santa Clara. In Tan's mid-teens her father and brother died of brain tumors within a year of each other. Amy's mother moved the remaining family to Switzerland, where the teen finished high school in Montreau. Back in the United States she graduated from San Jose State University with both bachelors and masters degrees in linguistics. Later she attended the University of California, Santa Cruz and then the University of California, Berkeley. Originally conceived as a collection of short stories, *The Joy Luck Club* was ultimately published as a novel in 1989 by G. P. Putnam's Sons. This was Amy's first novel; she has since written several other well-received novels, non-fiction books and children's books have come from her pen since. Her 2001 novel *The Bonesetter's Daughter* was adapted into an opera that was staged by the San Francisco Opera in 2008. On her less-serious side she was the vocalist in the charity-minded rock group, which consists of well-known writers (even occasionally Stephen King) that were known as The Rock Bottom Remainders who disbanded in 2012.

Julie
1956, Metro Goldwyn Mayer
A terrified wife tries to escape from her insanely jealous husband who is bent on killing her.

Director: Andrew L. Stone
Screenwriter: Andrew L. Stone
Cinematographer: Fred Jackman Jr.
Partial Cast: Doris Day, Louis Jourdan, Barry Sullivan

• Taloa Academy of Aeronautics, Oakland Municipal Airport-plane interior
• Transocean Air Lines, Oakland Municipal Airport

Julie and Jack
2003, Golden Gate Pictures
A computer chip salesman subscribes to an on-line dating service.

Director: James Nguyen
Screenwriters: James Nguyen, Joe Bright
Production Designer: James Nguyen
Cinematographer: James Nguyen
Partial Cast: Jenn Gotzon, Justin Kunkle, Tippi Hedren

• Golden Gate Bridge
• 900 Lombard Street, Russian Hill District
• 180 Baytech Drive, San Jose-as Stellachip Corporation
• U.S. Grant Monument, Music Concourse, Golden Gate Park
• California Palace of the Legion of Honor, Lincoln Park
• Fort Point National Historic Site, Marine Drive, Golden Gate National Recreation Area
• Coit Tower, Pioneer Park, 1 Telegraph Hill Boulevard, Telegraph Hill District
• California Street Cable Car at Market Street
• La Bocca's Corner, 957 Columbus Avenue, North Beach District-bar
• Muni car in front of Federal Reserve Bank, 101 Market Street, South of Market District
• Muir Woods National Monument, Muir Woods Road, Golden Gate National Recreation Area
• Muir Beach, Golden Gate National Recreation Area, State Highway Route 1, Muir Beach
• Chinatown Restaurant, 744 Washington Street, Chinatown District
• Portsmouth Square, Chinatown District
• Palace of Fine Arts, 3601 Lyon Street, Marina District
• Washington Square, North Beach District
• Rose Garden, JFK Drive, Golden Gate Park
• Mission Dolores, 320 Dolores Street, Mission District
• San Jose State University, San Jose
• Panorama of Bodega Bay

Junior
1994, Universal Pictures
As part of a fertility research project, a male scientist agrees to carry a pregnancy in his own body.

Director: Ivan Reitman
Screenwriters: Kevin Wade, Chris Conrad
Production Designer: Stephen J. Lineweaver
Art Director: Gary Wissner
Cinematographer: Adam Greenburg
Partial Cast: Arnold Schwarzenegger, Danny DeVito, Emma Thompson, Frank Langella, Jan Yanehire, Dennis O'Donnell

• 722 Steiner Street, Alamo Square, Western Addition District
• Fairmont Hotel, 950 Mason Street, Nob Hill District
• 2552 Hyde Street, Russian Hill District
• Rochester Big and Tall, 700 Mission Street, South of Market District
• Valley Life Sciences Building, University of California Campus, Berkeley

Just Like Heaven
2005, Dreamworks SKG
AKA: *If Only It Were True*
A lonely landscape architect falls for the spirit of beautiful woman who used to live in his new apartment.

Director: Mark S. Waters
Screenwriters: Ronald Bass, Bob Dolman, Marc Levy, Peter Tolan
Author: Marc Levy *If Only It Were True* (novel)
Production Designer: Cary White
Art Director: Maria L. Baker
Cinematographer: Daryn Okada
Partial Cast: Donal Logue, Mark Ruffalo, James D. Weston II, Reese Witherspoon, Dina Waters, Ben Shenkman, Jon Heder, Ivana Milicevic

• 1660 Mason Street, Russian Hill District-apartment building
• Intersection of Taylor Street and Green Street, Russian Hill District
• Washington Square, North Beach District
• 425 Liberty Street, Mission District
• Abandoned Planet, 518 Valencia Street, Mission District-bookstore
• Caffe Trieste, 609 Vallejo Street, North Beach District-café
• Mission Dolores Park, Mission District
• Muddy Waters Café, 521 Valencia Street, Mission District-café
• Moose's Restaurant, 1652 Stockton Street, North Beach District
• Golden Gate Bridge
• Arkansas Street, Potrero Hill District
• 3857 20th Street, Potrero Hill District
• San Francisco General Hospital Medical Center, 1001 Potrero Avenue, Mission District
• The Saloon, 1232 Grant Avenue, Telegraph Hill District-bar

Just One Night
2000, First Look Pictures
AKA: *S.F.O.*
On his wedding eve a man loses his shoe and spends the rest of the night searching for it.

Director: Alan Jacobs
Screenwriter: Alan Jacobs
Production Designer: Claire Jenora Bowin
Cinematographer: John J. Campbell
Partial Cast: Timothy Hutton, Don Novello
Local Cast: Mayor Willie J. Brown Jr.

• Bally of Switzerland, 250 Stockton Street, Union Square District
• San Francisco International Airport
• Ferry Building, Herb Caen Way, Embarcadero District
• Hotel Beresford, 635 Sutter Street, Union Square District

Key to the City
1950, Metro Goldwyn Mayer
At a mayors' convention, two mayors get involved in several escapades.

Director: George Sidney
Screenwriters: Albert Beich, Robert Riley Crutcher

Art Directors: Cedric Gibbons, Hans Petters
Cinematographer: Harold Rosson
Partial Cast: Clark Gable, Loretta Young, Frank Morgan, Raymond Burr, Pamela Britton

• San Francisco-Oakland Bay Bridge
• Stanford Court Hotel, 905 California Street, Nob Hill District-lightwell view to Mark Hopkins Hotel

RAYMOND BURR

Most people remember Burr for his starring roles in the television dramas *Perry Mason* (1957–1966) and *Ironside* (1967–1975), which garnered him two Emmys and seven further nominations, but his early career included roles on the Broadway stage and radio. Canadian Raymond William Stacey Burr was born in New Westminster, British Columbia on May 21, 1917 to parents Minerva (Smith) and William Burr. His early years were spent traveling; at one point his trade-agent father took the family to China. His mother was a concert pianist and music teacher. After returning to Canada Raymond's parents separated; the mother and three children moved to Vallejo. Raymond attended school in Berkeley at Willard Jr. High School and graduated from Berkeley High School. In 1937 he made his acting debut at the Pasadena Playhouse. He had a prolific career in TV during the 1950s, this while also acting in many movies as well. He and his life partner, Robert Benevides, purchased property in the Sonoma Valley, which is now known as Raymond Burr Vineyards in Healdsburg. Burr died in Healdsburg in 1993 at age 76. Burr's life as a Canadian in Hollywood was commemorated by his home country in a postage stamp issued by the Canadian government in 2008. He also appeared in locally filmed noir movies *San Quentin* (1946), *Raw Deal* (1948), *Walk a Crooked Mile* (1948), *Red Light* (1949), and *Crime of Passion* (1957).

The Killer Elite
1975, United Artists

A private crime fighting organization handles cases that the CIA prefers not to consider.

Director: Sam Peckinpah
Screenwriters: Marc Norman, Robert Rostand, Stirling Silliphant
Production Designer: Ted Haworth
Cinematographer: Philip H. Lathrop
Partial Cast: James Caan, Robert Duvall, Arthur Hill

• Intersection of Drumm Street and Sacramento Street, The Embarcadero-building explosion
• Richmond-San Rafael Bridge
• Southern Pacific Hospital, 1509 Hayes Street, North of Panhandle District
• Filbert Street Steps, Telegraph Hill District
• Portsmouth Square, Chinatown District
• Intersection of Union Street and Montgomery Street, Telegraph Hill District
• San Francisco-Oakland Bay Bridge
• San Francisco International Airport
• Ferry Building, Herb Caen Way, The Embarcadero
• 46 Waverly Place, Chinatown District
• 18th Street Bridge over Interstate Highway Route 280, John F. Foran Freeway, Potrero Hill District-car bomb
• Golden Gate Yacht Club, 1 Yacht Road, Marina District-bar
• Bethlehem Shipyard, 900 Illinois Street, Potrero Hill District-pier
• Marin Headlands, Golden Gate National Recreation Area
• Suisun Reserve Fleet, Suisun Bay-rafted ships
• Benicia Bridge, Suisun Bay

Killer's Delight
1978, Intercontinental
A detective tracks a serial killer.

Director: Jeremy Hoenack
Screenwriter: Maralyn Thoma
Art Direction: Martin Speer
Cinematographer: Arthur. R. Botham
Partial Cast: James Luisi, Susan Sullivan, John Karlen

• Palace of Fine Arts, 3601 Lyon Street, Marina District
• Aerial views of Financial District
• Golden Gate Bridge
• Conzelman Road, Marin Headlands, Golden Gate National Recreation Area
• Aerial view of Broadway nightlife, Telegraph Hill District
• Aerial view of Coit Tower, Pioneer Park, 1 Telegraph Hill Boulevard, Telegraph Hill District
• Aerial view of Hall of Justice, 850 Bryant Street, South of Market District

The Killing
1956, United Artists

AKA: *Bed of Fear*, *Clean Break*, *Day of Violence*
A racetrack becomes the focus of an ex-convict's scheme to steal $2 million.

Director: Stanley Kubrick
Screenwriter: Stanley Kubrick
Author: Lionel White *Clean Break* (novel)
Art Director: Ruth Sobotka
Cinematographer: Lucien Ballard
Partial Cast: Sterling Hayden, Coleen Gray, Vince Edwards, Marie Windsor, Elisha Cook Jr.

• Bay Meadows Racetrack, El Camino Real, San Mateo-as Lansdowne Park Racetrack

Kinjite: Forbidden Subjects
1989, Cannon
A pimp, who specializes in child prostitution, is hunted by a cop.

Director: J. Lee Thompson
Screenwriter: Harold Rebenzal
Art Director: Whitney Brook Wheeler
Cinematographer: Gideon Porath
Partial Cast: Charles Bronson, Perry Lopez

• Muni Metro/BART station-as a Tokyo subway station

Kiss Them for Me
1957, 20th Century Fox
Three navy pilots go AWOL in San Francisco.

Director: Stanley Donen
Screenwriters: Luther Davis, Julius J. Epstein
Author: Fredric Wakeman *Shore Leave* (book)
Art Directors: Maurice Ransford, Lyle R. Wheeler
Cinematographer: Milton R. Krasner
Partial Cast: Cary Grant, Jayne Mansfield, Suzy Parker, Ray Walston, Larry Blyden, Leif Erickson, Werner Klemperer, Jack Mullaney, Richard Deacon, Nancy Kulp
Local Cast: Jeweler Sidney Mobell

• Aerial shots of Russian Hill and Nob Hill Districts
• Fairmont Hotel, 950 Mason Street, Nob Hill District
• California Street and Powell/Mason Street cable cars
• San Francisco-Oakland Bay Bridge
• Crookedest Street in the World, 1000 block of Lombard Street, Russian Hill District

The Kite Runner
2007, Paramount Vantage

After spending years in California, a man returns to his homeland in Afghanistan to help his old friend whose son is in trouble.

Director: Marc Forster
Screenwriter: David Benioff
Author: Khaled Hosseini (novel)
Production Designer: Carlos Conti
Art Director: Karen Murphy
Cinematographer: Roberto Schaefer
Partial Cast: Khalid Abdalla, Atossa Leoni, Shaun Toub

- Berkeley Marina, Berkeley
- BART, Fremont
- Oakland-cemetery
- Piedmont-cemetery
- Treasure Island-graduation ceremony
- San Francisco-Oakland Bay Bridge

Knife Fight
2012, IFC Films
A political strategist juggling three clients questions whether or not to take the high road.

Director: Bill Guttentag
Screenwriters: Bill Guttentag, Chris Lehane
Production Designer: Michael E. Goldman
Cinematographer: Stephen Kazmiershi
Partial Cast: Rob Lowe, Julie Bowen, Saffron Burrows, Jamie Chung, David Harbour
Local Cast: journalist Malou Nubla

- Intersection of California Street and Powell Street, Nob Hill District
- Various Financial District streets-driving in vehicle
- Jim Georgies Donuts, 2799 16th Street, Mission District
- Sutter Stockton Garage, 444 Stockton Street, Union Square District-roof parking
- Avenue of Palms, Treasure Island
- Osgood Place, Telegraph Hill District
- 440 Pacific Avenue, Telegraph Hill District
- Civic Center Plaza, Civic Center District
- Broadway Showgirls Cabaret, 412 Broadway, Telegraph Hill District
- Millennium Tower, 301 Mission Street, South of Market District-lawyer's office
- San Francisco National Cemetery, 1 Lincoln Boulevard, Presidio, Golden Gate National Recreation Area
- KPIX TV Channel 5, 855 Battery Street, Telegraph Hill District-conference room
- The Warfield Theater, 982 Market Street, Tenderloin District-office and roof
- 310 Valencia Street, Mission District-Penelope's campaign headquarters
- Intersection of Pacific Avenue and Montgomery Street, Jackson Square District
- Haight Ashbury Free Clinic, 1735 Mission Street, Mission District

- Caffe Roma, 526 Columbus Avenue, North Beach District
- Ida B. Wells High School, 1099 Hayes Street, Western Addition District
- The Embarcadero-driving in vehicle

The Kremlin Letter
1970, 20th Century Fox
An American intelligence undercover team is sent to Moscow to retrieve a mistakenly signed arms treaty.

Director: John Huston
Screenwriters: Noel Behn, Gladys Hill, John Huston
Production Designer: Ted Haworth
Art Director: Elven Webb
Cinematographer: Edward Scaife
Partial Cast: George Saunders, Max Von Sydow, Orson Welles, Bibi Anderson, Richard Boone, Nigel Green, Dean Jagger

- Golden Gate Bridge

Kuffs
1992, Universal
A high school dropout inherits his murdered brother's P.I. business and sets out to avenge his death.

Director: Bruce A. Evans
Screenwriters: Bruce A. Evans, Raynold Gideon
Production Designers: Armin Ganz, Victoria Paul
Art Director: Tom Davick
Cinematographer: Thomas Del Ruth
Partial Cast: Christian Slater, Lilla Jovovich, Bruce Boxleitner

- Golden Gate Bridge
- San Francisco National Cemetery, 1 Lincoln Boulevard, Presidio, Golden Gate National Recreation Area
- MacArthur BART station, 555 40th Street, Oakland
- Intersection of Grant Avenue and Green Street, Telegraph Hill District
- Baker Beach, Presidio, Golden Gate National Recreation Area
- Columbus Avenue, North Beach District
- 1101 Leavenworth Street, Russian Hill District-Deco apartment building
- Palace of Fine Arts, 3601 Lyon Street, Marina District
- San Francisco-Oakland Bay Bridge
- 1321-1323 Waller Street, Haight-Ashbury District-residence
- North Beach Garage, 735 Vallejo Street, North Beach District-view to Washington Square

Kung Phooey!
2002, Kung Phooey Productions

A monk tries to find a mysterious lost Fountain of Youth in the form of a magic peach.

Director: Darryl Fong
Screenwriter: Darryl Fong
Production Designer: Mulan Chan
Art Director: Katho Baer
Cinematographer: Cliff Traiman
Partial Cast: Michael Chow Man-Kin, Joyce Thi Brew, Jones Chan

• Stow Lake, Golden Gate Park
• Japanese Tea Garden, 75 Hagiwara Tea Garden Way, Golden Gate Park
• Strybing Arboretum, 1199 Ninth Avenue, Golden Gate Park
• Yet Wah Restaurant, 2140 Clement Street, Richmond District
• Joy Luck Restaurant, 327 8th Street, Oakland
• Silver Dragon Restaurant, 835 Webster Street, Oakland
• Wah Hung Market, 415 9th Street, Oakland
• San Yick Market, 362 8th Street, Oakland
• Lucasey Manufacturing, 2744 East 11th Street, Oakland
• Lionel Wilson Building, 150 Frank Ogawa Plaza, Oakland

Ladies They Talk About

1933, Warner Brothers
A member of a bank robbery gang goes to prison where there's trouble.

Directors: Howard Bretherton, William Keighley
Screenwriters: Brown Holmes, William McGrath, Sidney Sutherland
Authors: Dorothy Mackaye, Carlton Miles (play)
Art Director: Esdras Hartley
Cinematographer: John F. Seitz
Partial Cast: Barbara Stanwick, Preston Foster, Lyle Talbot

• Aerial view of San Quentin State Prison, San Quentin

The Lady from Shanghai

1948, Columbia
AKA: *Black Irish*, *The Girl from Shanghai*, *Take This Woman*
A seaman becomes involved with a lawyer and his homicidal wife.

Director: Orson Welles
Screenwriters: Orson Welles, William Castle, Charles Lederer, Fletcher Markle
Author: Sherwood King *If I Die Before I Wake* (novel)

Art Directors: Sturges Carne, Stephen Goosson
Cinematographers: Charles Lawton Jr., Rudolphe Maté, Joseph Walker
Partial Cast: Orson Welles, Rita Hayworth, Everett Sloane, Glenn Anders, Ted de Corsia, Erskine Sanford

• California Academy of Sciences, Steinhart Aquarium, 55 Music Concourse Drive, Golden Gate Park
• Golden Gate Bridge
• Brocklebank Apartments, 1000 Mason Street, Nob Hill District
• Hall of Justice, 750 Kearny Street, Financial District
• Portsmouth Square, Chinatown District
• Shanghai Low Restaurant, 532 Grant Avenue, Chinatown District
• Playland-at-the-Beach, 4800 Cabrillo Street, Outer Richmond District
• Valhalla Restaurant, 201 Bridgeway, Sausalito

HALL OF JUSTICE

The exterior and courtroom scenes of *The Lady From Shanghai* took place in the Classically-styled former Hall of Justice that was located on the east side of Portsmouth Square, the original civic nucleus of San Francisco. This was the second Hall of Justice building constructed on this site, the first building was destroyed in the 1906 Earthquake and Fire. The newer building was completed in 1911 at a cost of $1.1 million and was designed by City Architect Newton K. Tharp. The iconic half-round fourth-floor windows, as seen from the interior, inspired their use in many courtroom and detective movies and TV series of the mid-20th century. The building site is currently occupied by a hotel that was originally constructed as a Holiday Inn with a bridge to Portsmouth Square.

Lady of the House

1978, National Broadcasting Company
The life of madame Sally Stanford after she adopted Sausalito as her hometown.

Directors: Ralph Nelson, Vincent Sherman
Screenwriter: Ron Koslow
Author: Sally Stanford (book)
Art Director: Sydney Z. Litwack

Cinematographer: Robert L. Morrison
Partial Cast: Dyan Cannon, Armande Assante, Johra Lampert, Jesse Dizon
Local Cast: Attorney Melvin Belli

• Golden Gate Bridge
• Fairmont Hotel, 950 Mason Street, Nob Hill District
• Japanese Tea Garden, 75 Hagiwara Tea Garden Way, Golden Gate Park
• Spreckels Temple of Music, Golden Gate Park
• Koshland Mansion, 3800 Washington Street, Presidio Heights Ditrict
• Cogswell College, 600 Stockton Street, Nob Hill District
• San Francisco Waterfront
• San Francisco-Oakland Bay Bridge
• McLaren Lodge, 501 Stanyan Street, Golden Gate Park
• Palace of Fine Arts, 3601 Lyon Street, Marina District
• Valhalla Restaurant, 201 Bridgeway, Sausalito
• Bank of America, 750 Bridgeway, Sausalito

SALLY STANFORD

Two years after the release of *Lady of the House*, the building known as Valhalla, originally used as a liquor-running spot during Prohibition, was redecorated and turned into a restaurant. The new owner was none other than San Francisco's most notorious madame Sally Stanford, who decided to have a legitimate business in her newly adopted town of Sausalito. Years later, in 1976, the legendary character was elected mayor of Sausalito. After she left office she was made "vice mayor for life," a wink-of-the-eye honor by locals.

La Mission

2009, Five Stick Films
AKA: Mission Street Rhapsody
A proud Latino learns how to accept his son's sexuality.

Director: Peter Bratt
Screenwriter: Peter Bratt
Production Designer: Keith Neely
Art Director: Garrett Lowe
Cinematographer: Hiro Narita
Partial Cast: Benjamin Bratt, Alex Hernandez, Christopher Borgzinner

• New Mission Theater, 2550 Mission Street, Mission District
• Mission High School, 3750 18th Street, Mission District
• 923 Valencia Street, Mission District-as garage

• Pedestrian bridge over James Lick Freeway, U.S. Highway Route 101, Potrero Hill District
• Intersection of Castro Street and Market Street, Eureka Valley District
• 299 Santa Paula Avenue, St. Francis Wood District
• Columbus Avenue, North Beach District
• San Francisco General Hospital, 1001 Potrero Avenue, Mission District
• Nicasio Reservoir, Nicasio

THE BRATT BROS

Brothers Peter Weirich (born 1962) and Benjamin G. (born 1963) are the sons of San Francisco's Peter Sr., a sheet metal worker, and Eldy (Banda) Bratt, a nurse. The two sons have three other siblings. Benjamin attended Lowell High School in San Francisco, graduating in 1982, and later attended the University of California, Santa Barbara, where he earned a B.F.A. in 1986. He was accepted at San Francisco's American Conservatory Theater's M.F.A. program but landed a part in the television series *Juarez* before graduating. The TV project did not go forward but his first appearance on television was in 1988 in the short-lived series *Knightwatch*. A pivotal step in his career was joining the cast of TV's *Law and Order* for its sixth season in 1995. Playing Detective Renaldo Rey Curtis, he landed an Emmy nomination in 1999 for that role, the year he left the series. He later appeared as Dr. Jake Reilly in 23 episodes of *Private Practice* from 2011 through 2012. Still a San Francisco resident, he married actress Talisa Soto in 2002; they have two children, Sophia and Mateo.

While Benjamin has been the more noticed of the two brothers, Peter has come into his own as a director/screenwriter. He wrote and directed the critically acclaimed 1996 film *Follow Me Home*. He is also a commissioner with the San Francisco Film Commission.

Larger Than Life
1996, United Artists

AKA: *Large as Life, Nickel and Dime*
A motivational speaker discovers that the inheritance from his father is in the form of an elephant.

Director: Howard Franklin
Screenwriters: Pen Densham, Garry Williams, Roy Blount Jr.
Production Designer: Marcia Hinds-Johnson
Art Directors: Bo Johnson, Stephen Reece
Cinematographer: Elliot Davis
Partial Cast: Bill Murray, Matthew McConaughey, Jerry Adler, Harve Presnell

• San Jose International Airport, 1701 Airport Boulevard, San Jose

The Last Gangster

1937, Metro Goldwyn Mayer
AKA: *Another Public Enemy*
A gangster is released from Alcatraz Federal Prison and plans revenge on his wife who deserted him.

Director: Edward Ludwig
Screenwriters: Robert Carson, John Lee Mahin, William A. Wellman
Art Director: Cedric Gibbons
Cinematographer: William H. Daniels
Partial Cast: Edward G. Robinson, Rose Stradner, James Stewart, John Carradine, Louise Beavers

• Alcatraz Federal Prison, Alcatraz Island, Golden Gate National Recreation Area
• San Francisco-Oakland Bay Bridge

The Laughing Policeman

1973, 20th Century Fox
AKA: *An Investigation of Murder*
A mad man eludes San Francisco Police while he shoots up the town.

Director: Stuart Rosenberg
Screenwriter: Thomas Rickman
Authors: Per Wahlöö, *Maj Sjöwall Den skrattande polisen* (novel)
Cinematographer: David M. Walsh
Partial Cast: Walter Matthau, Bruce Dern, Louis Gossett Jr., Anthony Zerbe, Cathy Lee Crosby

• Transbay Transit Terminal, 425 Mission Street, South of Market District
• Portsmouth Square, Chinatown District
• Golden Gate Bridge
• Hall of Justice, 850 Bryant Street, South of Market District
• Garden of Eden, 529 Broadway, Telegraph Hill District
• Enrico's Sidewalk Cafe, 504 Broadway, Telegraph Hill District

• Washington Square, North Beach District
• La Palma, 2884 24th Street, Mission District
• San Francisco Art Institute, 800 Chestnut Street, Russian Hill District
• Filbert Street Steps, Telegraph Hill District
• Embarcadero Center
• The Ramrod Bar, 1225 Folsom Street, South of Market District
• San Francisco-Oakland Bay Bridge and approaches
• Daly City

The Lemon Drop Kid

1934, Paramount
A gangster forces a bookie to locate the money he lost on a horse due to the bookie's incompetence.

Director: Marshall Neilan
Screenwriters: Howard J. Green, J. P. McEvoy, Damon Runyon
Art Directors: Hans Drier, John B. Goodman
Cinematographer: Henry Sharp
Partial Cast: Lee Tracy, Helen Mack, William Frawley

• Tanforan Racetrack, El Camino Real, San Bruno

Lenny

1974, United Artists
Biographical look at the career of comedian Lenny Bruce and his struggles.

Director: Bob Fosse
Screenwriter: Jullian Barry
Production Designer: Joel Schiller
Cinematographer: Bruce Surtees
Partial Cast: Dustin Hoffman, Valerie Perrine

• Ann's 440 Club, 440 Broadway, Telegraph Hill District

Leonard Part VI

1987, Columbia
A retired secret agent is called back to service to save mankind from an evil doer.

Director: Paul Weiland
Screenwriters: Bill Cosby, Jonathan Reynolds
Production Designer: Geoffrey Kirkland
Art Director: Blake Russell
Cinematographer: Jan DeBont
Partial Cast: Bill Cosby, Tom Courtenay, Joe Don Baker, Moses Gunn, Pat Colbert, Gloria Foster

• Golden Gate Bridge
• Safeway, 850 La Playa Street, Outer Richmond District
• Outer Richmond District

• Potrero Hill District
• Conzelman Road, Marin Headlands, Golden Gate National Recreation Area
• Dunsmuir House and Gardens, 2980 Peralta Court, Oakland-interiors

DUNSMUIR HOUSE

Built in 1899 this late Victorian Colonial Revival-style, 37-room mansion is set in a 50-acre wooded estate. Three levels of the building have undergone preservation and are furnished. Its curious three-column entry (historically an even, versus an odd, quantity would have been used) is unique forcing the visitor to go around the center column to enter the bi-lateral symmetrically placed front door. The architect was San Franciscan Eugene Freeman who designed the mansion for Alexander Dunsmuir, the son of a wealthy Canadian coal magnate. Dunsmuir had the residence built as a present for his bride, but the groom died while on their honeymoon. She took up residence in the mansion, but died two years later. The mansion and grounds are open to the public from late spring through early fall with special events during the Christmas season.

Life
1999, MCA and Universal Pictures
Two criminals discover the value of life after being sentenced to life imprisonment.

Director: Ted Demme
Screenwriters: Robert Ramsey, Matthew Stone
Production Designer: Dan Bishop
Art Director: Jeff Knipp
Cinematographer: Geoffrey Simpson
Partial Cast: Eddie Murphy, Martin Lawrence, Obba Babatundé

• Main Street, Locke
• Bridge over Steamboat Slough on River Road, State Highway Route 160, north of Isleton, Sacramento River Delta

The Lineup
1958, Columbia

A psychotic gunman and drug contact is hunted by the San Francisco Police.

Director: Don Siegel
Screenwriter: Stirling Silliphant
Art Director: Ross Bellah
Cinematographer: Hal Mohn
Partial Cast: Warner Anderson, Robert Keith, Eli Wallach, Richard Jaeckel, Mary LaRoche, William Leslie

• Piers 41 and 43, Embarcadero
• The Embarcadero (interlaced with Belt Line Train tracks)
• Old Hall of Justice, 750 Kearny Street, Financial District
• San Francisco City Hall, 1 Carlton B. Goodlett Place, Civic Center District
• Opera House, 301 Van Ness Avenue, Civic Center District-exterior and interior
• U.S. Custom House, 555 Battery Street, Financial District-exterior
• 11 Kent Street, Russian Hill District
• San Francisco-Oakland Bay Bridge-from Pacific Dock south of bridge
• Intersection of Mary Teresa Street and Megan Drive, Visitacion Valley District-residence on hill
• Whittier Mansion, 2090 Jackson Street, Pacific Heights District
• Army and Navy YMCA, 166 The Embarcadero-Seaman's Club entry and lobby
• Golden Gate Bridge-aerial shot with United Airlines plane
• San Francisco Airport-main terminal building exterior
• Mark Hopkins Hotel, 999 California Street, Nob Hill District
• California Academy of Sciences, Steinhart Aquarium, 55 Music Concourse Drive, Golden Gate Park-interior and exterior
• Sutro Baths, 1000 Point Lobos Avenue, Golden Gate National Recreation Area-exterior and interiors
• Gas tank on current Safeway site with gas company building in foreground, Marina District
• Embarcadero Freeway, South of Market District

Little City
1997, Miramax Films
A man who is an artist has complications with the opposite sex.

Director: Roberto Benabib
Screenwriter: Roberto Benabib
Production Designer: Don De Fina
Art Director: Bill McGirr
Cinematographer: Randall Love
Partial Cast: Jon Bon Jovi, Penelope Ann Miller, Josh Charles, Annabella Sciorra, JoBeth Williams

• San Francisco-Oakland Bay Bridge
• San Remo Hotel Bar, 2237 Mason Street, North Beach District
• Balboa Café, 3199 Fillmore Street, Cow Hollow District
• United Commercial Bank Building, 555 Montgomery Street, Financial District-as

psychiatrist's office
• Golden Gate Bridge
• Crissy Field, Presidio, Golden Gate National Recreation Area-fishing pier
• San Francisco Art Institute, 800 Chestnut Street, Russian Hill District
• Little City Antipasti Bar, 673 Union Street, North Beach District
• Harbor Court Hotel, 165 Steuart Street, South of Market District-as Harry Denton's
• Fort Baker, Marin Headlands, Golden Gate National Recreation Area
• 21 Baker Street, Haight-Ashbury District-residence
• Alta Square, Pacific Heights District
• Acorn Books, 1436 Polk Street, Polk Gulch District
• Washington Square, North Beach District
• 37-39 Salmon Street, Russian Hill District
• Marina Green, Waterfront
• Victorian Park, San Francisco Maritime National Historic Park, Golden Gate National Recreation Area

Little Fauss and Big Halsy

1970, Paramount

A pair of motorcycle racers team up and roam the country having rough adventures.

Director: Sidney J. Furie
Screenwriter: Charles Eastman
Art Director: Lawrence G. Paull
Cinematographer: Ralph Woolsey
Partial Cast: Robert Redford, Michael J. Polard, Lauren Hutton

• Sears Point Speedway, State Highway Route 29, Sonoma

ROBERT REDFORD

Charles Robert Redford Jr. was born in Santa Monica, California to parents Martha (Hart) and Charles Robert Redford Sr., a milkman-turned-accountant, on August 18, 1936. The Redford family moved to Van Nuys, where Robert attended the local high school. His upper education includes the University of Colorado for a year and a half but he was asked to leave because of his bad boy behavior. Following this, he spent time living in Europe. With his European tour behind him he then studied painting at Brooklyn's Pratt Institute and took classes at the American Academy of Dramatic Arts in New York City. He

made his screen debut in *War Hunt* (1962) set during the last days of the Korean War. Highlights of his film career include *Butch Cassidy and the Sundance Kid* (1969) with co-star Paul Newman and *The Way We Were* (1973) with Barbra Streisand. His directorial debut was with the acclaimed *Ordinary People* (1980), which won him an Academy Award for Best Director. His other locally filmed projects are *The Candidate* (1972) and *Sneakers* (1992). He has an estate, a second home, in Calistoga that he purchased in 2001.

Little Miss Marker

1980, Universal

A Depression-era story about a tot who is left as collateral on a bet.

Director: Walter Bernstein
Screenwriters: Damon Runyon, Walter Bernstein
Production Designer: Edward C. Carfagno
Cinematographer: Phillip H. Lathrop
Partial Cast: Walter Matthau, Julie Andrews, Tony Curtis, Bob Newhart, Sara Stimson, Lee Grant, Brian Dennehy

• Sonoma County Fairgrounds, 1350 Bennett Valley Road, Santa Rosa-as race track

Lolita

1997, Samuel Goldwyn

A middle-aged professor becomes smitten with a 14-year-old girl.

Director: Adrian Lyne
Screenwriters: Vladimir Nabokov, Stephen Schiff
Production Designer: Jon Hutman
Art Director: Chris Shriver
Cinematographers: Howard Atherton, Stephen Smith
Partial Cast: Jeremy Irons, Melanie Griffith, Frank Langella, Dominique Swain, Suzanne Sheperd

• Petaluma Boulevard North, D Street Bridge, Petaluma
• Mystic Theater, McNear Building, 15-23 Petaluma Boulevard, Petaluma
• Seaview Ridge, near Fort Ross
• Filoli Estate and Gardens, 86 Cañada Road, Woodside

The Lost Coast

2008, Year Zero Pictures

A group of friends wander on

Halloween night and two of them confront their unspoken sexual history.

Director: Gabriel Fleming
Screenwriter: Gabriel Fleming
Cinematographer: Nils Kenaston
Partial Cast: Ian Scott McGregor, Lucas Alifano, Lindsay Benner

• 2300 block of Market Street, Eureka Valley District-street party
• 5 Fulton Muni bus
• Clark Pillars Gate, intersection of Fulton Street and Arguello Boulevard, Golden Gate Park
• Rainbow Falls, JFK Drive, Golden Gate Park
• Lincoln Boulevard, Sunset District
• Ocean Beach, Golden Gate National Recreation Area

The Love Bug
1969, Buena Vista
AKA: *Car-Boy-Girl*
Herbie is a Volkswagen Beetle with a life of its own even on the racetrack.

Director: Robert Stevenson
Screenwriters: Gordon Buford, Bill Walsh
Art Directors: Carroll Clark, John B. Mansbridge
Cinematographer: Edward Colman
Partial Cast: Dean Jones, Michelle Lee, Buddy Hackett, Joe Flynn, Andy Granatelli, Joe E. Ross

• Crookedest Street in the World, 1000 block of Lombard Street, Russian Hill District
• Golden Gate Bridge
• Hyde Street Cable Car
• 44 Montgomery Street, Financial District

The Lusty Men
1952, RKO Radio Pictures
An injured rodeo star returns to his hometown and coaches a fellow ranch hand to ride.

Director: Nicholas Ray
Screenwriters: David Dortort, Horace McCoy
Author: Claude Stanush (novel)
Art Directors: Albert S. D'Agostino, Alfred Herman
Cinematographer: Lee Garmes
Partial Cast: Robert Mitchum, Susan Hayward, Arthur Kennedy

• Livermore Stockmen's Rodeo Association Arena, Robertson Park Road, Livermore-rodeo scenes

Machine Gun McCain
1968, Columbia

After a dozen years in prison a tough criminal hooks up with his son who has devised a daring caper.

Director: Guiliano Montaldo
Screenwriters: Giuliano Montaldo, Mino Roli
Author: Ovid Demaris "Candyleg" (story)
Production Designer: Flavio Mogherini
Art Directors: Emilio Baddelli, Roberto Velocchio
Cinematographer: Erico Menczer
Partial Cast: John Cassavetes, Brit Ekland, Peter Falk, Gabriele Ferzetti
Local Cast: Stripper Carol Doda

• Alcoa Building, One Maritime Plaza, 300 Clay Street, Golden Gateway
• Intersection of El Camino del Mar and Seacliff Avenue, Seacliff District
• Golden Gate Bridge
• Panorama of Telegraph Hill from Russian Hill
• San Quentin State Prison, San Quentin
• California Street cable car
• Intersection of Columbus Avenue and Kearny Street, Telegraph Hill District
• Clown Alley Restaurant, 42 Columbus Avenue, Telegraph Hill District
• 400 and 500 blocks of Broadway, Telegraph Hill District
• Varni's Roaring Twenties Club, 807 Montgomery Street, Telegraph Hill District
• Union Square, 333 Post Street
• Saints Peter and Paul Church, 666 Filbert Street, North Beach District
• Fisherman's Wharf District

The Mack
1973, Cinerama
AKA: *The Mack and His Pack*
Five years in prison have little effect on a man who becomes the king of pimping.

Director: Michael Campus
Screenwriter: Robert J. Poole
Cinematographer: Ralph Woolsey
Partial Cast: Max Julien, Don Gordon, Richard Pryor

• Various Oakland street locations

Made in America
1993, Warner Brothers
A black teen, born by artificial insemination, discovers that her father is a white car salesman.

Director: Richard Benjamin
Screenwriters: Marcia Brandwynne, Nadine Schiff, Holly Goldberg Sloan
Production Designer: Evelyn Sakash
Cinematographer: Ralf D. Bode

Partial Cast: Whoppi Goldberg, Ted Danson, Will Smith, Nia Long, Paul Rodriguez, Jennifer Tilly, Peggy Rae, Clyde Kusatsu

• Sather Gate, University of California Campus, Berkeley
• H. Tulanian & Sons Rug Company, 2998 College Avenue, Berkeley-as African Queen Bookstore
• Oakland Technical High School, 4351 Broadway, Oakland
• Lake Merritt, Oakland
• Parking lot, intersection of 14th Street and Madison Street, Oakland-car dealership

Mad City

1997, Warner Brothers

A normal guy blows his top, and a news reporter turns into a national spectacle.

Director: Costa-Gavras
Screenwriters: Tom Matthews, Eric Williams
Production Designer: Catherine Hardwicke
Art Director: Ben Morahan
Cinematographer: Patrick Blossier
Partial Cast: Dustin Hoffman, John Travolta, Mia Kirshner, Alan Alda, Robert Prosky, Blythe Danner, William Atherton, Ted Levine

• San Jose Athletic Club, 196 North Third Street, San Jose-as Taylor County Natural History Museum
• Intersection of South Market Street and Post Street, San Jose

The Magic of Lassie

1978, Lassie Productions

The collie dog is taken far away from her keeper but eventually finds her way home.

Director: Don Chaffey
Screenwriters: Jean Holloway, Richard M. Sherman, Robert B. Sherman
Cinematographer: Michael D. Margulies
Partial Cast: Lane Davies, Gene Evans, Alice Faye, Mickey Rooney, James Stewart, Stephanie Zimbalist, Pernell Roberts, Robert Lussier, Mike Mazurki

• Hop Kiln Winery, 6050 Westside Road, Healdsburg
• Glen Ellen Grocery, 13710 Arnold Drive, Glen Ellen
• Charles J. Poppe Building, 13750 Arnold Drive, Glen Ellen

Magnum Force

1973, Warner Brothers

A police inspector has to track down his partner who is slaughtering gangsters.

Director: Ted Post
Screenwriters: Harry Julien Fink, Rita M. Fink, John Milius, Michael Cimino
Art Director: Jack Collis
Cinematographer: Frank Stanley
Partial Cast: Clint Eastwood, Hal Holbrook, Mitch Ryan, Felton Perry, David Soul, Suzanne Somers

• San Francisco City Hall, 1 Carlton B. Goodlett Place, Civic Center District-rotunda
• Southern Freeway, Federal Highway Route 280, Potrero Hill
• 18th Street Bridge over Interstate Highway Route 280, John F. Foran Freeway, Potrero Hill District
• 2190 Washington Street, Pacific Heights District
• Hall of Justice, 850 Bryant Street, South of Market District
• Oakland International Airport, 1 Airport Drive, Oakland
• 2200 Sacramento Street, Pacific Heights District
• Cost Plus Imports, 2552 Taylor Street, Fisherman's Wharf District
• Fairmont Hotel, 950 Mason Street, Nob Hill District
• Golden Gate Bridge
• Marin Headlands, Golden Gate National Recreation Area
• Pier 30-32, The Embarcadero
• Pier 70, The Embarcadero
• San Francisco International Airport
• Centro West Street, Tiburon-murder at house with pool
• Robert C. Levy Tunnel, Broadway, Russian Hill District
• Embarcadero Freeway, Waterfront
• Potrero Hill District
• Vermont Street, between 20th and 22nd Streets, Potrero Hill District-curvy street
• Third Street Bridge, China Basin District
• Bethlehem Shipyard, 900 Illinois Street, Potrero Hill District
• Macondray Lane, Russian Hill District
• Point Molate, Richmond

SUZANNE SOMERS

Suzanne Marie Mahoney was born in the Peninsula city of San Bruno on October 16, 1946 to parents Marion (Turner), a medical secretary, and Frank Mahoney, a boxcar laborer and gardener; she was one of the couple's four children. She graduated from San Bruno's Capuchino High School in 1964 and was accepted to Lone Mountain College, but her schooling was interrupted by pregnancy. She married Bruce Somers in 1965 and they had one child; the couple divorced in 1968. Her film work in other

Bay Area projects include *Bullitt* (1968), *Daddy's Gone A-Hunting* (1969), *Fools* (1970), as a topless girl in the dramatic pool murder scene in *Magnum Force* (1973), and *American Graffiti* (1973)—most of her performances were uncredited. Years later, in 1977, she married again, to Alan Hamel, who was a game show host on a TV show that she had worked on. The eight-year run (1976 to 1984) of the comedy TV show *Three's Company* is her most enduring legacy; she appeared in 89 episodes as the not-so-ditzy blond character Chrissy Snow between 1977 through 1981. She went on to be a Las Vegas entertainer during the 1980s, an author, and a spokesperson for a variety of products.

Malaya
1949, Metro Goldwyn Mayer
AKA: *Operation Malaya*
A newspaperman convinces government officials of a plan to obtain rubber for the war effort by stealing it out from under the Japanese.

Director: Richard Thorpe
Screenwriter: Frank Fenton
Author: Manchester Boddy (story)
Art Directors: Cedric Gibbons, Malcolm Brown
Cinematographer: George J. Folsey
Partial Cast: Spencer Tracy, James Stewart, Valentina Cortese, Sydney Greenstreet

• Alcatraz Federal Prison, Alcatraz Island, Golden Gate National Recreation Area

The Maltese Falcon
1931, Warner Brothers
AKA: *Dangerous Female*
A woman employs the services of a private detective, who is quickly caught up in the mystery and intrigue of a statuette.

Director: Roy Del Ruth
Screenwriters: Maude Fulton, Brown Holmes
Author: Dashiell Hammett
Art Director: Robert M. Haas
Cinematographer: William Rees
Partial Cast: Ricardo Cortez, Bebe Daniels

• Panorama from San Francisco Bay to Ferry Building
• Panorama from mid-Market Street moving to north

"Don't be sure I'm as crooked as I'm supposed to be."

The Maltese Falcon
1941, Warner Brothers
A detective searches for a very special statuette and has many adventures along the way.

Director: John Huston
Screenwriters: John Huston
Author: Dashiell Hammett
Art Director: Robert M. Haas
Cinematographer: Arthur Edeson
Partial Cast: Humphrey Bogart, Mary Astor, Gladys George, Peter Lorre, Barton MacLane, Lee Patrick, Sydney Greenstreet, Ward Bond, Jerome Cowan, Elisha Cook Jr.

• San Francisco-Oakland Bay Bridge
• Ferry Building, Herb Caen Way, Embarcadero District
• Coit Tower, Pioneer Park, 1 Telegraph Hill Boulevard, Telegraph Hill District-view from lawn to south

The Manitou
1978, AVCO and Embassy
A fake spiritualist finds his girlfriend is possessed by a 400-year-old American Indian demon.

Director: William Girdler
Screenwriters: William Girdler, Jon Cedar, Thomas Pope
Author: Graham Masterton (book)
Production Designer: Walter Scott Herndon
Cinematographer: Michael Hugo
Partial Cast: Tony Curtis, Susan Strasberg, Michael Ansora, Stella Stevens, Ann Sothern, Burgess Meredith

• City scene from Twin Peaks lookout
• Westin St. Francis Hotel, 335 Powell Street, Union Square District
• Japanese Tea Garden, 75 Hagiwara Tea Garden Way, Golden Gate Park
• Hyde Street cable car
• International Building, 601 California Street, Financial District
• Golden Gate Bridge
• San Francisco-Oakland Bay Bridge

THE CABLE CARS: A MUNICIPAL ROLLER COASTER

The early form of public transportation in San Francisco was developed by Andrew Smith Hallidie and engineer William Eppelsheimer to negotiate San Francisco's steep hills. The first line opened on Clay Street in 1873. The cable travels on a pulley system within an underground slot at a constant speed of 9.5 miles per hour driven by a 510 horsepower electric motor. Each of the line's cables are powered from the cable car barn and powerhouse located at the intersection of Washington and Mason Streets on Nob Hill. At their peak, there were 23 cable car lines in San Francisco, but with the development of less expensive electric streetcars in the 1890s, the number of cable cars lines quickly declined. In 1947 there was a move to close two more of the remaining lines but a battle led by citizen Friedel Klussmann stopped the closure. By 1979 the system had become unsafe and was shut down for urgent repairs; subsequently, between 1982 and 1984, the whole system was shut down and all of the infrastructure replaced or repaired. Currently there are three lines, the Powell-Hyde line, Powell-Mason line, and the California line, which cater mostly to the tourist trade. The system was made a National Historic Landmark in 1964 and is the only mobile National Monument in the world.

Beware of motorized fake cable cars used by local tour companies that appear in movies such as *Metro* (1997). For *Metro*, faux cable car tracks were painted on Nob Hill's Jones Street from California Street to Colin Alley. This method of filming is more convenient and less expensive than tying up the cable car system for a film shoot and allows flexibility in what appears in the location's background.

The Man Who Cheated Himself
1950, 20th Century Fox

A bad cop falls for a bad woman who kills her husband and they try to cover it up, but her accomplice's brother figures out the plot.

Director: Felix Feist
Screenwriters: Philip McDonald, Seton I. Miller
Production Designer: Van Nest Polglase
Cinematographer: Russell Harlan
Partial Cast: Lee J. Cobb, John Dall, Jane Wyatt, Lisa Howard

• Intersection of Washington Street and Kearny Street, Financial District
• Intersection of Eddy Street and Gough Street, Western Addition District
• Jefferson Square Park, Western Addition District
• 1100 block of Turk Street, Western Addition District
• Lafayette Park, Pacific Heights District
• Golden Gate Bridge toll booth
• Golden Gate Bridge
• Intersection of Union Street and Montgomery Street, Telegraph Hill District
• Wentworth Street, Chinatown District
• Intersection of Castle Alley and Green Street, Telegraph Hill District
• Old Hall of Justice, 750 Kearny Street, Financial District
• Café in 700 block of Kearny Street, Financial District
• Intersection of Seacliff Avenue and El Camino del Mar, Seacliff District
• Doyle Drive, Presidio
• Fort Point National Historic Site, Marine Drive, Golden Gate National Recreation Area

WELL MEANING REDEVELOPMENT

The scene driving the 1100 block of Turk Street captures a time and place in 1950 that was soon to change. It is a poignant lesson in today's view of cultural and building preservation. Not one building shown in that scene exists today as most of the Western Addition was wiped clean by the San Francisco Redevelopment Agency starting in the late 1950s in what was a wholesale removal of the African American and Japanese populations that lived there. The stated intent was to return the population to the same area but in new housing stock and infrastructure. Some 4,700 households were displaced, 800 businesses

shuttered and 2,500 Victorian buildings demolished. Decades passed
before housing was rebuilt, but many
residents went elsewhere in the
meantime never to reestablish the
homes they once occupied—or the
community that once flourished there.
By the mid-1970s there was a change
in plan to move some Victorian buildings that were in good condition rather
than demolish them. Many were
moved to the western edge of the
Redevelopment Agency's jurisdiction
in the area near the intersection of
Scott Street and Ellis Street.

Many Rivers to Cross
1955, Metro Goldwyn Mayer
A footloose frontiersman and trapper
in the early American West winds up
being pursued by a tomboyish girl who
has decided her marriage to him will
save her from spinsterhood.

Director: Roy Rowland
Screenwriters: Harry Brown, Guy Trosper
Author: Steve Frazee (book)
Art Directors: Cedric Gibbons, Hans Peters
Cinematographer: John F. Seitz
Partial Cast: Robert Taylor, Eleanor Parker,
Victor McLaglen, Jeff Richards, Rosemary De
Camp, Russell Johnson

• Russian River, Cloverdale
• Russian River, Preston

Man's Favorite Sport?
1964, Universal
A star fishing tackle salesman's bluff
is called when he has to enter a
fishing competition.

Director: Howard Hawks
Screenwriters: John Fenton Murray, Steve
McNeil
Author: Pat Frank "The Girl Who Almost Got
Away" (short story)
Art Directors: Alexander Golitzen, Tambi Larsen
Cinematographer: Russell Harlan
Partial Cast: Rock Hudson, Paula Prentiss, Maria
Perschy, Charlene Holt, John McGiver, Roscoe
Karns

• Fairmont Hotel, 950 Mason Street, Nob Hill
District

Man-Trap
1961, Paramount
An honest man is lured by a Marine
buddy into a highjack attempt that
leads to the death of his wife.

Director: Edmond O'Brien
Screenwriter: Ed Waters
Author: John D. MacDonald *Taint of the Tiger*
(novel)
Art Director: Hal Pereira
Cinematographer: Loyal Griggs
Partial Cast: Jeffrey Hunter, David Jansen, Stella
Stevens, Hugh Sanders

• San Francisco International Airport
• Fisherman's Wharf District

Marnie
1964, Universal
A rich man marries a pathological liar
but finds there is a nightmare in her
past.

Director: Alfred Hitchcock
Screenwriter: Jay Presson Allen
Author: Winston Graham (novel)
Cinematographer: Robert Burks
Production Designer: Robert F. Boyle
Partial Cast: Tippi Hedren, Sean Connery, Diane
Baker

• Diridon Railroad Station, 65 Cahill Street, San
Jose-as Union Station, Hartford
• Pier 50, The Embarcadero with SS *Grover
Cleveland*-as ship

The Master
2012, The Weinstein Company
The relationship between a
charismatic intellectual whose faith-
based organization begins to catch on
in America, and a young drifter who
becomes his right-hand man.

Director: Paul Thomas Anderson
Screenwriter: Paul Thomas Anderson
Production Designers: David Crank, Jack Fisk
Cinematographer: Mihai Malaimare Jr.
Partial Cast: Joaquin Phoenix, Philip Seymour
Hoffman, Amy Adams, Laura Dern

• USS *Hornet*, 707 West Hornet Avenue,
Alameda-as below deck in yacht
• USS *Potomac*, Jack London Square, Oakland-
yacht on San Francisco Bay
• Golden Gate Bridge
• Mare Island Base Hospital, Mare Island
• 619 Winslow Street, Crockett

• Quarters B, Captain's Mansion, intersection of Walnut Avenue and Tenth Street, Mare Island, Vallejo
• Hillside School, 1581 Leroy Avenue, Berkeley

The Matrix Reloaded
2003, Warner Brothers
AKA: *The Matrix 2*
Freedom fighters stage a revolt against machines.

Directors: Andy Wachowski, Lana Wachowski
Screenwriters: Andy Wachowski, Lana Wachowski
Production Designer: Owen Paterson
Art Director: Hugh Bateup
Cinematographer: Bill Pope
Partial Cast: Keanu Reeves, Laurence Fishburne, Carrie-Anne Moss

• 16th Street, Oakland-car chase
• 5th Street, Oakland-car chase
• Latham Square Building, 1611 Telegraph Avenue, Oakland-garage exit
• Webster Tube, Oakland-car chase
• Naval Air Station Alameda, Alameda Island-runways 07/25 and 13/31 as freeway

Maxie
1985, Orion
AKA: *Free Spirit*
An eccentric landlady tells new tenants of a young girl's ghost.

Director: Paul Aaron
Screenwriters: Jack Finney, Patrick Resnick
Production Designer: John J. Lloyd
Cinematographer: Fred Schuler
Partial Cast: Glenn Close, Mandy Patinkin, Ruth Gordon
Local Cast: TV anchor Leeza Gibbons, TV anchor Evan White, Chief of Protocol Cyril Magnin

• 722 Steiner Street, Western Addition District-house
• San Francisco Public Library, 200 Larkin Street, Civic Center
• 625 Kearny Street, Financial District
• Grace Cathedral Parsonage, 1100 California Street, Nob Hill District
• Crocker Galleria, 50 Post Street, Financial District

Medicine for Melancholy
2008, IFC Films
The tentative relationship of a minority couple in a gentrifying city.

Director: Barry Jenkins

Screenwriter: Barry Jenkins
Cinematographer: James Laxton
Partial Cast: Wyatt Cenac, Tracey Heggins

• Corona Heights Park, Corona Heights District
• XO Café, 1799 Church Street, Noe Valley District-breakfast
• Dolores Street, Noe Valley District-cab ride
• Marina District
• 709 Geary Street, Tenderloin District-Micha's studio
• Stephen Wirtz Gallery, 49 Geary Street, Financial District
• Intersection of Market Street and Third Street, South of Market District
• Martin Luther King Memorial, Yerba Buena Gardens, South of Market District
• Carousel, Yerba Buena Gardens, South of Market District
• Rainbow Grocery, 1745 Folsom Street, South of Market District
• The Knockout Bar, 3223 Mission Street, Mission District

Memoirs of a Geisha
2005, Sony Pictures Entertainment
A woman tells how she became one of Japan's most celebrated geisha.

Director: Rob Marshall
Screenwriter: Robin Swicord
Author: Arthur Golden (book)
Production Designer: John Myhre
Art Directors: Patrick M. Sullivan Jr., Tomas Voth
Cinematographer: Dion Beebe
Partial Cast: Ziyi Zhang, Ken Watanabe, Michelle Yeoh

• Seal Cove, Moss Beach-exteriors
• Hakone Gardens, 21000 Big Basin Way, Saratoga
• Japanese Tea Garden, 75 Hagiwara Tea Garden Way, Golden Gate Park
• Muir Beach overlook, Muir Beach

Memoirs of an Invisible Man
1992, Warner Brothers
The victim of a freak accident becomes invisible and turns into a potential commodity for the CIA.

Director: John Carpenter
Screenwriters: Robert Collector, Dana Olsen, William Goldman
Author: H. F. Saint (book)
Production Designer: Lawrence J. Paull
Art Director: Bruce Crone
Cinematographer: William A. Fraker
Partial Cast: Chevy Chase, Daryl Hannah, John Carpenter, Patricia Heaton
Local Cast: TV anchor Elaine Corral

- Panorama of San Francisco skyline from Bank of America Building
- San Francisco-Oakland Bay Bridge
- Market Street
- Adolph Gasser photographic materials, 181 Second Street, South of Market District
- California Street, Financial District
- University Club, 800 Powell Street, Nob Hill District-as Academy Club exterior
- Sacramento Street at Powell Street, Nob Hill District
- St. Elizabeth Apartments, 901 Powell Street, Nob Hill District-as Nick's residence
- Sacramento Street at Jones Street, Nob Hill District
- Hallidie Plaza, Market Street at Powell Street-cable car turnaround
- John's Grille, 63 Ellis Street, Union Square District-exterior
- Grace Cathedral Close, 1100 California Street, Nob Hill District
- Huntington Park, Nob Hill District
- Golden Gate Bridge-toll booths
- Flood Building, 870 Market Street

The Men's Club
1986, Atlantic Releasing
Friends nearing forty years of age convene and discuss their lives.

Director: Peter Medak
Screenwriter: Leonard Michaels
Production Designer: Ken Davis
Art Director: Laurence Bennett
Cinematographer: John Fleckenstein
Partial Cast: Roy Scheider, Frank Langella, Harvey Keitel, Treat Williams, Richard Jordan, David Dukes, Craig Wasson, Stockard Channing, Jennifer Jason Leigh

- Waterfront, Berkeley
- Treasure Island
- 2800 Vallejo Street, Pacific Heights District

Men of San Quentin
1942, Producers Releasing Corporation
When a jailhouse guard is promoted to warden, his skills are put to the test.

Director: William Beaudine
Screenwriters: Martin Mooney, Ernest Booth
Cinematographer: Clark Ramsey
Partial Cast: J. Anthony Hughes, Eleanor Stewart, Dick Curtis, Charles Middleton

- San Quentin State Prison, San Quentin-various exterior scenes

Merlin's Shop of Mystical Wonders
1995, Herton Films

A wizard time travels and opens a magic shop, which serves as the backdrop for two horror tales.

Director: Kenneth J. Berton
Screenwriter: Kenneth J. Berton
Production Designers: Melodie Ennist, Lee Sjostrom
Cinematographers: Michael Gfelner, Tony Martin
Partial Cast: Ernest Borgnine, George Milan, Bunny Summers

- 32 Kentucky Street, Petaluma-shop
- 312 Maple Drive, Petaluma

Metro
1997, Touchstone and Caravan Pictures
A hostage negotiator and his new partner hunt for a psychopath.

Director: Thomas Carter
Screenwriter: Randy Feldman
Production Designer: William A. Elliott
Art Director: Greg Papalia
Cinematographer: Fred Murphy
Partial Cast: Eddie Murphy, Kim Miyori, Art Evans, James Carpenter, Michael Rapaport, Donal Logue, Jeni Chau
Local Cast: TV anchor Frank Somerville, journalist Malou Nubla, Diva Val Diamond

- San Francisco-Oakland Bay Bridge
- Panorama of waterfront including Ferry Building from San Francisco Bay
- Hibernia Bank, One Jones Street, Tenderloin District
- 1000 block of Market Street
- 520-522A Green Street, Telegraph Hill District
- Golden Gate Fields, 1100 East Shore Frontage Road, Berkeley-race track
- Shreve and Company, 200 Post Street, Union Square District-jewelry store
- 400 block of Grant Avenue, Chinatown District
- Jack Kerouac Alley, Telegraph Hill District
- Postrio Restaurant, 545 Post Street, Union Square District
- Mare Island, Vallejo

The Midnight Story
1957, Universal International Pictures
AKA: *Appointment with a Shadow*
A priest is murdered and his cop friend takes a hiatus to solve the mystery.

Director: Joseph Pevney
Screenwriters: Edwin Blum, John Robinson
Art Directors: Alexander Golitzen, Eric Orbom
Cinematographer: Russell Metty
Partial Cast: Tony Curtis, Marisa Pavan, Gilbert

Rowland, Jay C. Flippen, Argentina Brunetti, Ted de Corisa, Richard Monda, Kathleen Freeman

• All Hallows Church, 1490 Newhall Street, Bayview District
• Mt. St. Joseph's by the Sisters Orphanage, 1700 Newhall Street, Bayview District
• Fisherman's Wharf District
• 1227 Montgomery Street, Telegraph Hill District-as home
• Intersection of Union Street and Calhoun Alley, Telegraph Hill District
• Washington Square, North Beach District

Milk
2008, Focus Features
The life of gay San Francisco Supervisor Harvey Milk from 1970 through 1978 when he was assassinated.

Director: Gus Van Sant
Screenwriter: Dustin Lance Black
Production Designer: Bill Groom
Art Director: Charley Beal
Cinematographer: Harris Savides
Partial Cast: Sean Penn, Josh Brolin, Emile Hirsch, James Franco
Local Cast: Politician Tom Ammiano, Politician Carol Ruth Silver

• San Francisco City Hall, 1 Carlton B. Goodlett Place, Civic Center District
• Building 3, Treasure Island
• 573-575 Castro Street, Eureka Valley District-as Castro Camera
• Golden Gate Bridge
• Intersection of Castro Street and Market Street, Eureka Valley District
• Castro Theatre, 429 Castro Street, Eureka Valley District
• 50 United Nations Plaza, Civic Center-main lobby, hall of doorways on 4th floor, and toilet room

JAMES FRANCO

Best known for his breakthrough-starring TV role in NBC's Freaks and Geeks (1999), local actor James Edward "Ted" Franco was born in Palo Alto, California on April 19, 1978. Ted was the eldest of three sons, and his parents are writer and editor Betsy (Verne), and Douglas Franco (now deceased) who ran a non-profit agency as well as a shipping container security company. Franco graduated from Palo Alto High School in 1996 where he got some acting experience. A talented mathematician, Franco interned at Lockheed Martin Aero-space then attended the University of California, Los Angeles for a brief time where he studied English and drama. He dropped out in his freshman year to pursue the acting profession. He later returned to UCLA where he earned his undergraduate degree in 2008. Moving to New York City, he attended Columbia University and New York University's Tisch School for the Arts to study filmmaking. He also received an M.F.A. in writing from Brooklyn College. He received rigorous training in a 15-month intensive study at Playhouse West, in North Hollywood under the direction of Robert Carnegie. He received a brief part in Never Been Kissed (1999) that starred Drew Barrymore, which introduced Franco to movie audiences, followed by a more substantial exposure in Whatever It Takes in 2000. His first blockbuster movie was the 2002 comic book superhero flick Spider-Man, where he played opposite Tobey Maguire; that same year he garnered a Golden Globe for Best Actor in the TNT movie James Dean. He won the Independent Spirit Award's Best Supporting Actor for his role as Scott Smith in Milk (2008). He then appeared in the locally shot film Howl (2010) where he performed the role of beat poet Allen Ginsberg. He played a starring role in Rise of the Planet of the Apes (2011), although the computer-generated apes upstaged the movie's human stars. His most recent locally filmed work was in About Cherry, which was released in 2012.

A Millionaire for Christy
1951, 20th Century Fox
A legal secretary is sent to inform a man that he has inherited $2 million.

Director: George Marshall
Screenwriters: Ken Englund, Robert Harari
Art Director: Boris Leven
Cinematographer: Harry Stradling Sr.
Partial Cast: Fred MacMurray, Eleanor Parker

• Various vistas of San Francisco

Million Dollar Weekend
1948, Eagle-Lion Films
Two people running from desperate situations are blackmailed by another.

Director: Gene Raymond
Screenwriters: Charles Belden, Matty Kemp, Gene Raymond
Art Director: Lewis Creber
Cinematographer: Paul Ivano
Partial Cast: Gene Raymond, Osa Massen, Francis Lederer

• Golden Gate Bridge
• St. Francis Hotel, 335 Powell Street, Union Square District
• Sheraton Palace Hotel, 2 New Montgomery Street, South of Market District
• Fairmont Hotel, 950 Mason Street, Nob Hill District
• Mark Hopkins Hotel, 999 California Street, Nob Hill District

Mrs. Doubtfire
1993, 20th Century Fox
A desperate, divorced father disguises himself as a nanny to be near his children.

Director: Christopher Columbus
Screenwriters: Randi Mayem Singer, Leslie Dixon
Author: Anne Fine *Alias Madame Doubtfire* (novel)
Production Designer: Angelo P. Graham
Art Director: Steven W. Graham
Cinematographer: Don McAlpine
Partial Cast: Robin Williams, Sally Field, Pierce Brosnan, Harvey Fierstein, Polly Holiday, Lisa Jakub, Matthew Lawrence, Mara Wilson, Martin Mull

• City College, Chinatown branch, 940 Greenwich Street, Russian Hill District-school
• 2640 Steiner Street, Pacific Heights District-exterior only
• 520/522A Green Street, North Beach District-Daniel's apartment
• 1200 Washington Street, Nob Hill District-Frank's apartment
• The Claremont Hotel and Spa, 41 Tunnel Road, Berkeley-pool
• Old San Mateo Courthouse, 777 Hamilton Street, Courtroom A, Redwood City
• KTVU Channel 2 TV studios, Jack London Square, Oakland
• Bridges Restaurant, 44 Church Street, Danville

ROBIN WILLIAMS

A Tiburon waterfront residence is home to improvisational comic sensation and actor Robin McLaurim Williams. Williams was born in Chicago in 1951, the son of Laura (Smith) and Robert F. Williams, a senior executive at the Ford Motor Company. The family resided in the exclusive city of Bloomfield Hills, Michigan, but when Robin was at 16 years old his family moved to Woodacre in Marin County, where he attended Redwood High School. Before graduating in 1969, he got some initial training in his future profession at the school's drama department. This was followed by his occasional attendance at Southern California's Claremont Men's College. He intended to train for the foreign-service, but his studies were derailed by an elective in theater. After taking a course in acting at the College of Marin in Kentfield and then he got serious about his future and went on to New York's Julliard School under the hand of veteran actor John Houseman. Williams' second wife and manager Marsha Garces was his producer for *Patch Adams* and *Doubtfire*; they have since divorced. He married Susan Schneider in 2011. Williams has been in many Bay Area films, including *Being Human* (1993), *Mrs. Doubtfire* (1993), *Nine Months* (1995), *Jack* (1996), *Fathers' Day* (1997), *Patch Adams* (1998), *What Dreams May Come* (1998), *Bicentennial Man* (1999), and *August Rush* (2007).

Mission
2000, Vanguard
AKA: *City of Bars*
A young New York City writer moves to San Francisco where he dabbles in the life of the dot-com-era Mission District.

Director: Loren Marsh
Screenwriter: Loren Marsh
Production Designer: Suzanne Wang
Cinematographer: Matthew Uhry
Partial Cast: Chris Coburn, Joshua Leonard, Sandrine Holt, Adam Arkin

• Pillar Point, Half Moon Bay
• California Pacific Medical Center, Davies Campus, 45 Castro Street, Duboce Triangle District

- 3605 23rd Street, Mission District-as house
- 500 Club Bar, 500 Guerrero Street, Mission District
- The Abandoned Planet bookstore, 518 Valencia Street, Mission District
- Golden Gate Bridge
- Conzelman Road, Marin Headlands, Golden Gate National Recreation Area
- Kirby Cove Beach, Marin Headlands, Golden Gate National Recreation Area
- Sutro Tower, Mt. Sutro District
- Women's Building, 3543 18th Street, Mission District
- Dolores Park, Mission District
- Bean There Café, 201 Steiner Street, Dolores Park District
- Great Highway, Outer Richmond District
- Ocean Beach, Golden Gate National Recreation Area

Mr. Billion
1977, 20th Century Fox
AKA: *The Windfall*
An Italian man will become heir to a fortune if he can get to San Francisco in time.

Director: Jonathan Kaplan
Screenwriters: Ken Friedman, Jonathan Kaplan
Art Director: Richard Berger
Cinematographer: Matthew F. Leonetti
Partial Cast: Terence Hill, Valerie Perrine, Jackie Gleason, Slim Pickins, William Redfield, Chill Wills
Local Cast: Artist and puppeteer Ralph Chessé

- Sonoma-Marin Fairgrounds, 175 Fairgrounds Drive, Petaluma
- Sonoma County Developmental Center, 15000 Arnold Drive, Eldridge

Mr. Moto Takes a Vacation
1939, 20th Century Fox
Mr. Moto chases a robber who took the crown of the Queen of Sheba.

Director: Norman Foster
Screenwriters: Philip MacDonald, Norman Foster
Author: John P. Marquand (character)
Art Directors: Bernard Herzbrun, Heldane Douglas
Cinematographer: Charles G. Clarke
Partial Cast: Peter Lorre, Joseph Schildkraut, Lionel Atwill, Virginia Field

- View from Russian Hill to San Francisco-Oakland Bay Bridge

Mr. Ricco
1975, Metro Goldwyn Mayer

An attorney is hired to defend a black militant who is accused of murder.

Director: Paul Bogart
Screenwriters: Robert Hoban, Ed Harvey, Francis Kiernan
Art Director: Herman A. Blumenthal
Cinematographer: Frank Stanley
Partial Cast: Dean Martin, Eugene Roche, Thalmus Rasulala

- Hall of Justice, 850 Bryant Street, South of Market District
- 2229 Divisadero Street, Pacific Heights District
- 251-253 Cervantes Boulevard, Marina District
- Fisherman's Wharf District
- Berkeley Museum of Art/Pacific Film Archive, 2626 Bancroft Way, Berkeley
- Stewart Memorial Presbyterian Church, 1074 Guerrero Street, Mission District

Mr. Wong, Detective
1938, Monogram
A detective uncovers an international spy ring that is trying to steal a formula for poison gas.

Director: William Nigh
Screenwriter: Houston Branch
Author: Hugh Wiley (characters)
Cinematographer: Harry Neumann
Partial Cast: Boris Karloff, Grant Withers, Maxine Jennings

- Various shots of San Francisco
- Golden Gate Bridge

Mistress of Spices
2005, Rainbow Films U.S.A.
An enchanting Indian orphan learns to harness the magical properties of spices.

Director: Paul Mayeda Berges
Screenwriters: Gurinder Cgadha, Paul Mayeda Berges
Author: Chintra Banerjee Divakaruni *Mistress of Spices* (novel)
Production Designer: Amanda McArthur
Cinematographer: Santosh Sivan
Partial Cast: Aishwarya Rai, Dylan McDermott, Nitin Ganatra, Adewale Akinnuoye-Agbaje

- Legogo Trading Company, 811 Washington Street, Oakland
- EZ Ship, 815 Washington Street, Oakland-taqueria
- Lake Merritt, Oakland-joggers and murals

Mondo Topless
1966, RM Films

AKA: *Mondo Girls, Mondo Top*
Pseudo documentary about the lives of strippers and the day-to-day realities of their work.

Director: Russ Meyer
Cinematographer: Russ Meyer
Partial Cast: Babette Bardot, Pat Barrington, Sin Lenee, Darlene Grey, Diane Young, Darla Paris, Donna "X"

• Golden Gate Bridge
• Nob Hill District
• Jack Tar Hotel, 1101 Van Ness Avenue, Cathedral Hill District
• California Street, Nob Hill District
• Cliff House, 1090 Point Lobos Avenue, Golden Gate National Recreation Area

Moneyball
2011, Columbia
The story of Oakland A's general manager successful attempt to put together a baseball club on a budget by employing computer-generated analysis to draft his players.

Director: Bennett Miller
Screenwriters: Steven Zaillian, Aaron Sorkin
Author: Michael Lewis *Moneyball: The Art of Winning an Unfair Game* (book)
Production Designer: Jess Gonchor
Art Directors: Brad Ricker, David Scott
Cinematographer: Wally Pfister
Partial Cast: Brad Pitt, Robin Wright, Jonah Hill

• Oakland Coliseum, 7000 Coliseum Way, Oakland

Monster in the Closet
1986, Troma Entertainment
After several people and a dog are found dead in their closets, a reporter, a college professor, her son, and a befuddled professor band together to uncover the mystery.

Director: Bob Dahlin
Screenwriter: Bob Dahlin
Production Designer: Linda Cohen
Cinematographer: Ronald W. McLeish
Partial Cast: Claude Akins, Howard Duff, Henry Gibson, Donald Moffat, John Carradine, Stella Stevens

• Transamerica Pyramid, 600 Montgomery Street, Financial District
• Chinatown District

Moonraker
1979, United Artists

Agent 007 James Bond investigates the mid-air theft of a space shuttle and discovers a plot to commit global genocide.

Director: Lewis Gilbert
Screenwriter: Christopher Wood
Author: Ian Fleming (novel)
Production Designer: Ken Adam
Art Directors: Charles Bishop
Cinematographer: Jean Tournier
Partial Cast: Roger Moore, Lois Chiles, Michael Lonsdale, Richard Kiel

• High in the skies above Pope Valley-opening scenes as Bond is pushed from a private jet with Lake Berryessa in the background

More American Graffiti
1979, Universal
AKA: *Purple Haze*
College graduates deal with the Vietnam War and other issues of the late 1960s.

Director: Bill L. Norton
Screenwriters: George Lucas, Gloria Katz, Willard Huyck, Bill L. Norton
Art Director: Ray Storey
Cinematographer: Caleb Deschanel
Partial Cast: Candy Clark, Bo Hopkins, Ron Howard, Paul le Mat, Mackenzie Phillips, Cindy Williams

• Baylands Raceway Park, 44333 Christy Street, Fremont
• Various sites in San Francisco
• Macedonia Baptist Church, 2135 Sutter Street, Lower Pacific Heights District-rooftop
• Library Building, Cal State University, 25800 Carlos Bee Boulevard, Hayward-protest site
• Australian Tree Fern Dell, JFK Drive, Golden Gate Park-desertion site

More Tales of the City
1998, Channel Four Films
AKA: *Armistead Maupin's: More Tales of the City*
More episodic adventures of the residents of Barbary Lane.

Director: Pierre Gang
Screenwriters: Armistead Maupin, Nicholas Wright
Author: Armistead Maupin (novel)
Production Designer: Normand Sarazin
Cinematographer: Serge Ladouceur
Partial Cast: Olympia Dukakis, Laura Linney, Colin Ferguson, Bill Campbell, Barbara Garrick, Paul Hopkins, Jackie Borroughs, Whip Hubley, Diana Leblanc, Thomas Gibson, Swoozie Kurtz

• Alcatraz Island, Golden Gate National Recreation Area
• Brocklebank Apartments, 1000 Mason Street, Nob Hill District
• Union Square, 333 Post Street
• California Palace of the Legion of Honor, Lincoln Park, Outer Richmond District
• Palace of Fine Arts, 3601 Lyon Street, Marina District
• Taylor Street, Nob Hill District
• Huntington Park, Nob Hill District

ARMISTEAD MAUPIN

Openly gay author Maupin called San Francisco his home for a number of decades until moving to Santa Fe in 2012. He was born in Washington, DC in 1944 and grew up in Raleigh, North Carolina. He graduated from that state's university and served as a naval officer in the Mediterranean as well as with the River Patrol Force in Vietnam. Later he volunteered to return to Southeast Asia, this time as a civilian, to build housing for disabled Vietnamese veterans. His journalism career started as a newspaper reporter in Charleston, South Carolina. In 1971 he was assigned to the Associated Press's San Francisco bureau. His "Tales of the City" was serialized in the *San Francisco Chronicle* newspaper that captured the spirit of 1970s San Francisco; his interweaving of gay and straight characters made the stories appealing readers. Many follow-up books based on *Tales* followed. He also wrote the narration for *The Celluloid Closet* (1995), a documentary that garnered many awards for its exposure of GLBT lifestyles as seen in the movies. The musical *Tales of the City* debuted in 2011 at the American Conservatory Theater in San Francisco.

Mother
1996, Paramount
A divorced son moves back in with his mother in hopes of discovering why she dislikes him.

Director: Albert Brooks
Screenwriters: Albert Brooks, Monica McGowan Johnson

Production Designer: Charles Rosen
Art Director: Charles Butcher
Cinematographer: Lajos Koltai
Partial Cast: Debbie Reynolds, Albert Brooks, Paul Collins, Laura Weekes, John C. McGinley

• Devil's Slide, State Highway Route 1, Montara
• Golden Gate Bridge
• Central Avenue, Sausalito
• Molly Stone's Market, 100 Harbor Way, Sausalito
• Magnolia Avenue, Larkspur
• Bridgeway, Sausalito

Mumford
1999, Touchstone
In the small town of Mumford, a psychologist of the same name moves in and quickly becomes very popular, despite a questionable past.

Director: Lawrence Kasdan
Screenwriter: Lawrence Kasdan
Production Designer: Jon Hutman
Art Director: W. Steven Graham
Cinematographer: Eric Core
Partial Cast: Loren Dean, Hope Davis, Jason Lee, Alfre Woodard, Martin Short, Ted Danson

• Intersection of State Highway Route 1, Shoreline Highway, and Dillon Beach Road, Tomales
• 1300 block of Main Street, State Highway Routes 29 and 128, St. Helena
• 113 Plaza Street, Healdsburg-as Lily's Restaurant
• 237 Liberty Street, Petaluma-as Mumford's residence
• Old Main Street Saloon, 153 North Main Street, Sebastopol-bar
• Rex Tomasini's Ace Hardware, 313 B Street, Petaluma-as hardware store
• U.S. Coast Guard Training Center, Colorado Avenue at Arizona Avenue, Petaluma-as Panda Modem headquarters
• 347 Walnut Street, Petaluma-as Sophie's residence
• Guerneville Pedestrian Bridge across Russian River, Guerneville
• Intersection of Western Avenue and American Alley, Petaluma
• Astro Motel, 323 Santa Rosa Avenue, Santa Rosa
• Analy High School, 6950 Analy Avenue, Sebastopol-nude classroom scene and high school graduation
• Napa County Courthouse, 825 Brown Street, Napa-as courtroom

Murder in the First
1994, Warner Brothers
An attorney represents a brutalized inmate of Alcatraz Federal Prison.

Screenwriter: Dan Gordon
Production Designer: Kirk M. Petruccelli
Art Director: Michael Rizzo
Cinematographer: Fred Murphy
Partial Cast: Christian Slater, Kevin Bacon, Gary Oldman, Embeth Davidz, William H. Macy

• Alcatraz Island, Golden Gate National Recreation Area
• Cable cars
• Maritime Museum, Sala Burton Building, 900 Beach Street, San Francisco Maritime National Historic Park, Golden Gate National Recreation Area
• Golden Gate Bridge
• San Francisco City Hall, 1 Carlton B. Goodlett Place, Civic Center District-interiors and exteriors
• Fort Point National Historic Site, Marine Drive, Golden Gate National Recreation Area

Mutiny on the Bounty
1935, Metro Goldwyn Mayer
A British naval vessel sets off for South America but during a mutiny the captain is set adrift.

Director: Frank Lloyd
Screenwriters: Talbot Jennings, Jules Furthman
Authors: Charles Nordoff, James Norman Hall (book)
Art Director: Cedric Gibbons
Cinematographers: Arthur Edeson, Charles G. Clarke, Sidney Wagner
Partial Cast: Charles Laughton, Clark Gable, Franchot Tone, Donald Crisp, Spring Byington

• San Francisco Maritime National Historic Park, Balclutha, Hyde Street wharf, Golden Gate National Recreation Area
• The ship Ellen, Sailing Ship Restaurant, Pier 42, Embarcadero-as the Bounty

THE BALCLUTHA

The 300-foot-plus long deepwater vessel Balclutha unfurled her sails in 1857 with a cargo of coal during a voyage from the Atlantic-facing coastal port of Cardiff, Wales to San Francisco—a long trip of 140 days at sea, despite the ship's well-regarded fast pace. This, her maiden trans-Atlantic voyage, began many years of service. The name recalls the fortified town on the banks of Scotland's Clutha, or Clyde River. The square-rigged three-masted ship was designed to ply the often-difficult waters around usually stormy Cape Horn with a crew of 26. In 1904 the 22.7-foot draft proved too much and the windjammer ran aground. Purchased as-is for $500 by the Alaskan Packers Association, she was renamed Star of Alaska to augment the company's fish cannery operations. The ship, now carrying 200 or more sailors, was used regularly until she was retired in 1930. Yet another name change occurred, this time to the Pacific Queen in 1933, when Frank Kissinger purchased the vessel of a bygone era. While the ship was anchored of Catalina Island, filming took place for the movie Mutiny. The San Francisco Maritime Museum purchased the vessel in 1954, paying $25,000 for her and with restoration returned her initial name. She is said to have appeared in some 39 other movies as well.

My Favorite Brunette
1947, Paramount Pictures
A photographer gets mixed up with mobsters.

Director: Elliott Nugent
Screenwriters: Edmund Beloin, Jack Rose
Art Directors: Hans Dreier, A. Earl Hedrick
Cinematographer: Lionel Lindon
Partial Cast: Bob Hope, Dorothy Lamour, Peter Lorre, Lon Chaney Jr.

• San Quentin State Prison, San Quentin
• Intersection of California Street and Stockton Street, Chinatown District-photography studio

My Name is Kahn
2010, Fox Searchlight Pictures
A Muslim man with Asperger syndrome inspires others with his unique outlook on life.

Director: Karan Johar
Screenwriters: Shibani Bathija, Niranjan Lyengar
Production Designer: Sharmishta Roy
Cinematographer: Ravi K. Chandran
Partial Cast: Shanrukh Kahn, Kajol

• International Terminal, San Francisco International Airport-exterior and interior
• San Francisco-Oakland Bay Bridge
• Hallidie Plaza, Market Street at Powell Street-cable car turnaround
• Pacific Telephone and Telegraph Building, 140 New Montgomery Street, South of Market District-exterior and interior as offices
• Fortune Wok Restaurant, 1358 Mason Street, Nob Hill District-as salon

- Spreckels Lake, Golden Gate Park
- Ida B. Wells High School, 1099 Hayes Street, Western Addition District
- Dolores Park, Mission District
- Coit Tower, Pioneer Park, One Telegraph Hill Boulevard, Telegraph Hill District
- Women's Building, 3543 18th Street, Mission District
- Golden Gate Pavilion, Strawberry Island, Stow Lake, Golden Gate Park
- Jetty at Wave Organ, Marina District
- Corona Heights Park, Corona Heights District
- Palace of Fine Arts, 3601 Lyon Street, Marina District
- dePietro Todd Salon, 2239 Fillmore Street, Pacific Heights District

My Six Convicts
1952, Columbia
A psychologist joins a prison staff and gains the trust of some inmates.

Director: Hugo Fregonese
Screenwriter: Michael Blankfort
Author: Donald Powell Wilson (novel)
Art Direction: Edward L. Iiou
Cinematographer: Guy Rose
Partial Cast: Millard Mitchell, Gilbert Rowland, John Beal, Harry Morgan

- San Quention State Prison, San Quentin

The Mystery of Mr. Wong
1939, Monogram
A detective tries to solve the murder of antiques collector who was in possession of a famous jewel.

Director: William Nigh
Screenwriter: Scott Darling
Author: Hugh Wiley "James Lee Wong" series (stories)
Art Director: E. R. Hickson
Cinematographer: Harry Neumann
Partial Cast: Boris Karloff, Grant Withers, Dorothy Tree

- San Francisco-Oakland Bay Bridge

Neon Maniacs
1986, Castle Hill Productions
A group of teenagers discover a nest of homicidal monsters and when they try to tell authorities, no one believes them.

Director: Joseph Mangine
Screenwriter: Mark Patrick Cardicci
Art Director: Katherine Vallin

Cinematographers: Joseph Mangine, Oliver Wood
Partial Cast: Clyde Hayes, Leilani Sarelle, Donna Locke
- Golden Gate Bridge
- BART car

The Net
1995, Columbia Pictures
A mysterious diskette endangers a computer expert's life.

Director: Irwin Winkler
Screenwriters: John D. Brancato, Michael Ferris
Production Designer: J. Dennis Washington
Art Director: Thomas T. Taylor
Cinematographer: Jack N. Green
Partial Cast: Sandra Bullock, Jeremy Northam, Dennis Miller
Local Cast: TV anchor Evan White, TV anchor Elaine Corral

- Golden Gate Bridge
- McKesson Building, 600 Market Street, Financial District-as Cathedral offices
- Moscone Convention Center, 747 Howard Street, South of Market District-as Pan-Pacific Computer Convention venue

Never Die Twice
2001, Scott and Kelly Films
Two female San Francisco police detectives find their own dead bodies; they have four days to investigate before it happens again.

Director: Sean Scott
Screenwriters: Nancy L. Kelly, Sean Scott
Production Designer: Evan Cecil
Cinematographer: Greg Merkes
Partial Cast: Claudia Christian, Patricia Tallman, Steven Anthony Jones

- Painted Ladies, 700 block of Steiner Street, Western Addition District

Never the Twain Shall Meet
1931, Metro Goldwyn Mayer
A young lawyer falls for a South Sea island girl.

Director: W. S. Van Dyke
Screenwriters: Edwin Justus Mayer, Ruth Cummings, John Lynch
Author: Peter B. Kyne (novel)
Art Director: Cedric Gibbons
Cinematographer: Merritt B. Gerstad
Partial Cast: Leslie Howard, Conchita Montenegro, C. Aubrey Smith

• Ferry Building, Herb Caen Way, The Embarcadero

A Night Full of Rain (the end of the world in our usual bed in a night full of rain)
1978, Warner Brothers
The relationship between a chauvinist Italian journalist and a feminist American photographer.

Director: Lina Wertmuller
Screenwriter: Lina Wertmuller
Art Director: Gianni Giovagnoni
Cinematographer: Giuseppe Rotunno
Partial Cast: Giancarlo Giannini, Candice Bergen

• San Francisco Chronicle Newspaper Building, 901 Mission Street, South of Market District

Night Into Morning
1951, Metro Goldwyn Mayer
A professor adjusts to the tragic death of both his wife and son.

Director: Fletcher Markle
Screenwriters: Karl Tunberg, Leonard Spigelass
Cinematographer: George J. Folsey
Partial Cast: Ray Milland, John Hodiak, Nancy Davis

• University of California Campus, Berkeley

Night of Henna
2005, Illuminare Entertainment
A Pakistani daughter learns that a marriage has been arranged for her.

Director: Hassan Zee
Screenwriter: Hassan Zee
Production Designer: Phyllis Bowie
Cinematographer: Hiro Narita
Partial Cast: Pooja Kumar, Girja Shankar, Suhail Tayeb, Craig Marker

• International Terminal, San Francisco International Airport
• Intersection of 19th Avenue and Lincoln Way, Inner Sunset District
• Stow Lake, Golden Gate Park
• Caffe D'Melanio, 1314 Ocean Avenue, Ingleside District
• Grace Cathedral, 1100 California Street, Nob Hill District
• Huntington Park, Nob Hill District
• City College of San Francisco, 50 Phelan Avenue, Sunnyside District

• Stow Lake Boathouse, 50 Stow Lake Drive, Golden Gate Park
• Cat Club, 1190 Folsom Street, South of Market, District
• Pacific-Union Club, 1000 California Street, Nob Hill District
• Twin Peaks lookout, Twin Peaks District

Nightmare in Blood
1977, Xeromega
An actor who plays a vampire role is, in fact, one of the undead.

Director: John Stanley
Screenwriters: Ken Davis, John Stanley
Cinematographer: Charles Rudnick
Partial Cast: Jerry Walter, Dan Caldwell, Barrie Youngfellow

• Marin Headlands, Golden Gate National Recreation Area-sword fight
• Panorama of downtown San Francisco
• KTVU Channel 2 TV station, Jack London Square, Oakland-sign with logo
• Lincoln Park Golf Course, Outer Richmond District
• Sir Francis Drake Hotel, 450 Powell Street, Union Square District-Starlight Roof entry marquee

Night of the Quarter Moon
1959, Metro Goldwyn Mayer
AKA: *Flesh and Flame, The Color of Her Skin*
A boy marries a racially-different girl and others are very concerned about their union.

Director: Hugo Haas
Screenwriters: Franklin Coen, Frank Davis
Art Directors: Malcolm Brown, William A. Horning
Cinematographer: Ellis W. Carter
Partial Cast: Julie London, John Drew Barrymore, Anna Kashfi, Dean Jones, Agnes Moorehead, Nat "King" Cole, Jackie Coogan, Charles Chaplin Jr., Cathy Crosby

• Golden Gate Bridge
• Yerba Buena Island
• San Francisco-Oakland Bay Bridge
• Angel Island, Golden Gate National Recreation Area
• Alcatraz Federal Prison, Alcatraz Island, Golden Gate National Recreation Area
• Fisherman's Wharf District
• Lighthouse, Marina District
• Russian Hill District
• Chinatown District
• Burlingame

Nina Takes a Lover

1994, Triumph Releasing Corporation

A lonely young wife starts an affair with a married photographer.

Director: Alan Jacobs
Screenwriter: Alan Jacobs
Production Designer: Don De Fina
Cinematographer: Philip Parmet
Partial Cast: Laura San Giacomo, Paul Rhys, Michael O'Keefe, Fisher Stevens

• San Francisco-Oakland Bay Bridge
• 409 Vallejo Street, Telegraph Hill District-rooftop
• 3998 Cesar Chavez Street, Noe Valley District-as Café Sanchez
• 333 Parkview Terrace, Oakland-residence
• 465 Ninth Street, Oakland-shoe shop
• Music Concourse, Golden Gate Park-park benches
• Arbor, intersection of Lakeshore Avenue and El Embarcadero, Lake Merritt, Oakland

Nine Months

1995, 20th Century Fox

An easygoing man suddenly has to deal with the issues of fatherhood.

Director: Chris Columbus
Screenwriter: Chris Columbus
Author: Patrick Braoude *Neuf mois* (movie)
Production Designer: Angelo P. Graham
Cinematographer: Donald McAlpine
Partial Cast: Hugh Grant, Julianna Moore, Joan Cusack, Tom Arnold, Jeff Goldblum, Robin Williams
Local Cast: Diva Val Diamond

• Crissy Field Beach, Presidio, Golden Gate National Recreation Area
• Aquatic Park, San Francisco Maritime National Historic Park, Golden Gate National Recreation Area-fishing pier
• Napa Valley
• Guaymas Restaurant, 5 Main Street, Tiburon-deck at dock
• 1801 Bush Street, Pacific Heights District
• Stars Bar and Dining, 555 Golden Gate Avenue, Civic Center
• Alta Plaza Park, Pacific Heights District
• 1360 Montgomery Street, Telegraph Hill District
• Saint's Peter and Paul Church, 666 Filbert Street, North Beach District
• Golden Gate Bridge
• Alcatraz Island, Golden Gate National Recreation Area
• Tiburon downtown and waterfront
• Veteran's Memorial Building, 200 Grand Avenue, Oakland
• Los Medanos Community Hospital, 2311 Loveridge Road, Pittsburg
• San Francisco General Medical Center, 1001 Potrero Avenue, Mission District
• 60 Spear Street, South of Market District
• Jack Kerouac Alley, Telegraph Hill District
• Showplace Square, 2 Henry Adams Street, South of Market District
• The Wasteland, 1600 Haight Street, Haight-Ashbury District
• Marathon Plaza, 303 Second Street, South of Market District
• Serramonte Ford, 999 Serramonte Boulevard, Colma
• Talbot's Toyland, 445 South B Street, San Mateo

School of the Arts where he studied film. He and Monica Devereaux were married in 1983 and they have four children. His script for *Gremlins* (1984) caught the eye of Amblin Entertainment's Steven Spielberg after many others passed on the script; the movie became a huge financial success. His other Bay Area filmed projects include writing the screenplay for *The Goonies* (1985); directing *Mrs. Doubtfire* (1993); as directing/producing *Bicentennial Man* (1999) with Robin Williams; and as directing/producing *Rent* (2005), the smash Broadway hit. Columbus helped launch the wildly successful *Harry Potter* series of films that debuted in 2001.

Nine to Five

1980, 20th Century Fox
AKA: *9 to 5*
Three women office workers scheme to eliminate their offensive boss.

Director: Colin Higgins
Screenwriters: Colin Higgins, Patricia Resnick
Production Designer: Dean Mitzner
Art Director: Jack G. Taylor Jr.
Cinematographer: Renaldo Villobos
Partial Cast: Jane Fonda, Dolly Parton, Lily Tomlin, Dabney Coleman, Sterling Haden, Elizabeth Wilson, Henry Jones
Local Cast: Fashion twins Vivian A. and Marian B. Brown

• Albert P. Samuels clock, 856 Market Street

No Escape

1953, United Artists
AKA: *City On a Hunt*
When the available evidence in a murder case points to a young woman as the main suspect, her boyfriend, a police detective, arranges for a struggling songwriter to be blamed for the crime.

Director: Charles Bennett
Screenwriter: Charles Bennett
Authors: George Goodchild, Frank Witty *No Exit* (play)
Cinematographer: Benjamin H. Kline
Partial Cast: Lew Ayres, Sonny Tufts, Marjorie Steele, Lewis Martin, Gertrude Michael, Charles Cane, Renny McEvoy

• Golden Gate Bridge

Nora Prentiss

1947, Warner Brothers
AKA: *The Sentence*
A married doctor falls for a café singer —with a tragic result.

Director: Vincent Sherman
Screenwriter: N. Richard Nash
Authors: Paul Webster, Jack Sobell (story)
Cinematographer: James Wong Howe
Partial Cast: Ann Sheridan, Kent Smith, Bruce Bennett, Robert Alda, Rosemary de Camp
Local Cast: newspaper columnist Herb Caen (uncredited)

• Hallidie Plaza, Powell and Market Streets-cable car turnaround
• Ferry Building, Herb Caen Way, The Embarcadero
• Hall of Justice, 750 Kearny Street, Financial District
• Seacliff District
• The Belgravia, 795 Sutter Street, Nob Hill District-doctor's office
• San Francisco-Oakland Bay Bridge
• Palace of Fine Arts, 3601 Lyon Street, Marina District
• Chinatown District
• Union Square, 333 Post Street
• St. Joseph's Hospital, 355 Buena Vista East Avenue, Buena Vista District
• Cliff House, 1090 Point Lobos Avenue, Golden Gate National Recreation Area
• Ocean Beach, Golden Gate National Recreation Area

HERB CAEN

Widely known as the master of three-dot journalism and considered a San Francisco institution, the Pulitzer Prize winning Herb Caen (1916–1997) often wrote about visiting celebrities. Although appearing uncredited in *Nora Prentiss* (1947) as a news reporter, Caen authored many articles about movies being made in San Francisco for his long running column.

North Beach

2000, Leo Films
A slacker's infidelity enrages his girlfriend, which only prompts a bizarre cast of characters to comment on the situation in a San Francisco neighborhood.

Directors: Jed Mortenson, Richard Speight Jr.
Screenwriter: Casey Peterson
Cinematographer: Mark Herzig
Partial Cast: Casey Peterson, Jennifer Milmore, Richard Speight Jr., Jim Hanna, Hopwood DePree, Barrow Davis

• 1412 Grant Avenue, North Beach District-as North End Café
• Savoy Tivoli Café, 1434 Grant Avenue, North Beach District
• Washington Square, North Beach District
• 400 and 500 blocks of Broadway, Telegraph Hill District
• Grant Avenue, North Beach District

No Small Affair
1984, Columbia
A teenager falls for a girl in a photo and tracks her down.

Director: Jerry Schatzberg
Screenwriters: Craig Bolotin, Terrence Mulcahy
Author: Craig Bolotin (story)
Production Designer: Robert F. Boyle
Art Director: Frank Richwood
Cinematographer: Vilmos Zsigmond
Partial Cast: Jon Cryer, Demi Moore, George Wendt, Elizabeth Daily, Peter Frechette, Tim Robbins, Jeffrey Tambor

• San Francisco Maritime Museum, Hyde Street Wharf, Waterfront
• War Memorial Opera House, 301 Van Ness Avenue, Civic Center
• Saks Fifth Avenue, 384 Post Street, Union Square District
• 100 Broderick Street, Haight-Ashbury District-Charles' residence
• 500 block of Broadway, Telegraph Hill District-night clubs
• California Academy of Sciences, Steinhart Aquarium, 55 Music Concourse Drive, Golden Gate Park
• James Lick Middle School, 1220 Noe Street, Noe Valley District
• Agriculture Building, 101 The Embarcadero-Laura's loft
• Mitchell Brothers O'Farrell Theatre, 895 O'Farrell Street, Tenderloin-mural of whales
• Fisherman's Wharf District
• I. Magnin and Co., 135 Stockton Street, Union Square District
• Fort Point National Historic Site, Marine Drive, Golden Gate National Recreation Area
• Caffe Trieste, 609 Vallejo Street, North Beach District
• San Francisco International Airport

Nowhere to Run
1992, Columbia
An escaped convict takes on ruthless developers who are determined to evict a widow and her children.

Director: Robert Harmon
Screenwriters: Joe Eszterhas, Randy Feldman, Leslie Bohem
Authors: Joe Eszterhas, Richard Marquand (story)
Production Designer: J. Dennis Washington
Art Director: Joseph P. Lucky
Cinematographer: David Gribble
Partial Cast: Jean-Claude Van Damme, Rossana Arquette, Kieran Culkin, Ted Levine, Joss Ackland, Tiffany Taubman, Edward Blatchford, Anthony Starke

• 17235 Coleman Valley Road, Occidental-farmhouse

Obstacles
2002, Shot Films
AKA: *City of Crime: Obstacles*
Bad happenings in the city of Oakland.

Directors: D-Shot, Hunter McCann, Harry Mok
Art Directors: Ellie Basler, Bobby Mickey Kwan
Cinematographer: Joachim Hanwright
Partial Cast: E-40, D-Shot, Brian Hooks

• San Francisco-Oakland Bay Bridge
• Center Street, Oakland
• Phat Fades Barber Shop, 2621 Martin Luther King Jr. Way, Oakland
• San Quentin State Prison, San Quentin
• Dan Foley Park, 1498 North Camino Alto, Vallejo
• Oakland City Hall, One Frank H. Ogawa Plaza, Oakland
• Port of Oakland, Waterfront
• 11925 Skyline Boulevard, Oakland-residence

Olly, Olly, Oxen Free
1978, Sanrio Films
AKA: *The Great Balloon Adventure, The Great Balloon Race*
Two young children launch a broken-down hot-air balloon with the help of a junkyard owner.

Director: Richard A. Colla
Screenwriter: Eugene Poinc
Production Designer: Peter Wooley
Cinematographer: Gayne Rescher
Partial Cast: Katharine Hepburn, Kevin McKenzie, Dennis Dimster

• Bale Grist Mill, State Route 29, Calistoga-junkyard
• Southern Pacific Railroad Depot, 1520 Railroad Avenue, St. Helena
• Lyman Park, Railroad Avenue, St. Helena-park with bandstand
• Spottswoode Wine Cellar, 1902 Madrona Avenue, St. Helena-stone winery building
• Lincoln Street, Calistoga
• San Francisco-Oakland Bay Bridge

• Golden Gate Bridge
• Painted Ladies, 700 block of Steiner Street, Western Addition District

On the Road
2012, American Zoetrope and MK2 Productions
Two young men of the Beat Generation live in the here and now during the 1950s. Their search for "It" results in a fast-paced roller coaster ride throughout the United States.

Director: Walter Salles
Screenwriter: Jose Rivera
Author: Jack Kerouac (novel)
Production Designer: Carlos Conti
Art Director: Martin Gendron
Cinematographer: Eric Gautier
Partial Cast: Garrett Hedlund, Sam Riley, Kristen Stewart

• San Francisco-Oakland Bay Bridge
• Intersection of Filbert Street and Leavenworth Street, Russian Hill District
• 2019 23rd Street, Potrero Hill District

Once a Thief
1965, Metro Goldwyn Mayer
AKA: *Scratch a Thief*
A cop, bent on revenge, hounds an ex-convict.

Director: Ralph Nelson
Screenwriter: Zekial Marko
Author: Zekial Marko *Scratch a Thief* (novel)
Art Directors: George W. Davis, Paul Groesse
Cinematographer: Robert Burks
Partial Cast: Alain Delon, Ann-Margret, Van Heflin, Jack Palance, John Davis Chandler

• Big Al's, 556 Broadway, Telegraph Hill District

One Is a Lonely Number
1972, Metro Goldwyn Mayer
AKA: *Two Is a Happy Number*
After her husband leaves her a woman has a difficult time coping but ultimately finds salvation.

Director: Mel Stuart
Screenwriter: David Seltzer
Author: Rebecca Morris (story)
Art Director: Walter M. Simonds
Cinematographer: Michel Hugo
Partial Cast: Trish Van Devere, Monte Markham, Janet Leigh, Melvin Douglas

• 1800 Stockton Street, North Beach District-residence
• 3157 Fillmore Street, Marina District-produce store
• Podium level, One Embarcadero Center-circular stair and bridge
• 801-823 Market Street-as employment agency office interior
• Mission Playground, intersection of Linda Street and 19th Street, Mission District-as pool and park
• San Francisco Art Institute, 800 Chestnut Street, Russian Hill District-artist venue
• Magic Pan Restaurant, 900 Northpoint Street, Ghirardelli Square, Waterfront-as outdoor Sea Witch Restaurant
• Intersection of Fillmore Street and Vallejo Street, Pacific Heights District
• San Francisco City Hall, 1 Carlton B. Goodlett Place, Civic Center District-rotunda

One on Top of the Other
1969, Gadabout Gaddis Productions
AKA: *Perversion Story*
The wife of a doctor is murdered.

Director: Lucio Fulci
Screenwriters: Lucio Fulci, Roberto Gianviti
Authors: Lucio Fulci, Roberto Gianviti "Una Sull'altra" (story)
Production Designer: Neelo Azzini
Cinematographer: Alejandro Ulloa
Partial Cast: Jean Sorel, Marisa Mell

• Crookedest Street in the World, 1000 block of Lombard Street, Russian Hill District
• San Mateo Bridge
• Golden Gate Bridge
• San Quentin State Prison, San Quentin

One Way Passage
1932, Warner Brothers
AKA: *SS Atlantic*
A terminally ill socialite falls for a convict on his way to prison.

Director: Tay Garnett
Screenwriters: Wilson Mizner, Joseph Jackson
Author: Robert Lord (story)
Art Director: Anton Grot
Cinematographer: Robert Kurrle
Partial Cast: William Powell, Kay Francis

• San Francisco skyline from San Francisco Bay
• Alcatraz Island, Golden Gate National Recreation Area

On the Beach
1959, United Artists

Doomsday story placed in 1964 about an atomic-powered submarine that sails to investigate the consequences of an atomic blast.

Director: Stanley Kramer
Screenwriters: John Paxton, James Lee Barrett
Author: Nevil Shute (novel)
Production Designer: Rudolph Sternad
Art Director: Fernando Carrere
Cinematographers: Donald L. Frapp, Giuseppe Rotunno
Partial Cast: Gregory Peck, Ava Gardner, Fred Astaire, Anthony Perkins, Donna Anderson, John Tate, Lola Brooks

• Golden Gate Bridge
• Waterfront scenes-from periscope of submarine in San Francisco Bay looking at deserted streets including Ferry Building, Pacific Heights and Fort Mason/gas tank, 350 Bay Street, Marina District-now site just south of Marina Safeway

TRAFFIC JAM

On May 8, 1959 a 15-man crew arrived at the Golden Gate Bridge before sunrise. Their job was to film a sequence where a submarine went under the bridge right at sunrise. But fog delayed the shoot until much later —well into the morning commute. Consequently, until the fog lifted the submarine needed to cruise around the bay, which must have been an unusual sight. Curious drivers were distracted by the filming, and a which created a monumental traffic jam spread well beyond Marin's Waldo Grade Tunnel, much to the dismay of commuters. Today, heavy traffic in this area is commonplace without filming, but it was not well received by commuters at the time.

On the Edge
1985, Skouras Pictures

An aging sidelined runner is determined to compete in, and win, a venerable grueling footrace.

Director: Rob Nilsson
Screenwriters: Roy Kissin, Rob Nilsson
Production Designer: Don DeFina
Art Director: Steve Burns
Cinematographer: Stefan Czapsky
Partial Cast: Bruce Dern, Pam Grier, John

Marley, Bill Bailey, Jim Haynie, Marty Liquori
Local Cast: TV anchor Mike Cerre

• San Francisco waterfront from San Francisco Bay-aboard commuter ferry
• Mt. Tamalpais Park, Golden Gate National Recreation Area-all over mountain including lookout tower
• 2 AM Club, 380 Miller Avenue, Mill Valley-as 'Till Two Bar
• Tamalpais High School, 700 Miller Avenue, Mill Valley-football field grandstand
• Western Drive, Richmond-Chevron petroleum refinery tanks in background
• Pt. Molate, Richmond-houseboat
• KRON TV Channel 4 TV studios, 1001 Van Ness Avenue, Cathedral Hill District
• California Academy of Sciences, Steinhart Aquarium, 55 Music Concourse Drive, Golden Gate Park-fish roundabout
• Bolinas Street, Manzanita District, Marin City-start of foot race
• San Francisco Bay Trail, Marin City to Mill Valley
• Stinson Beach, Golden Gate National Recreation Area-end of foot race

DIPSEA RUN: THE REAL FOOTRACE

The "Cielo-Sea Race" recounted in On the Edge is based on a real annual foot race run over Marin County's Mt. Tamalpais, whose highest peak is 2,567 feet above sea level. The race has its roots with the first official Dipsea run on November 19, 1905. What became an annual event started the previous year when several members of San Francisco's Olympic Club gathered to take a ferry to Sausalito, where they transferred to a train that took them to the starting point at Mill Valley's railroad depot. The challenge was who could make it first to the newly opened Dipsea Inn in Stinson Beach's Seadrift District, some 12 grueling miles. The group found this event so exciting that they decided to make it an annual event, and it has carried on to this day without interruption. Head starts that based on age were instituted in 1965. Although the Dipsea was technically a men-only race, women had participated since 1950 and were officially allowed to compete starting in 1971. Limits on the total number of entrants allowed were adopted in 1977, since the race squeezes through some narrow trails.

The Organization
1971, United Artists
The San Francisco Police Department combats an international drug smuggling gang.

Screenwriter: James R. Webb
Art Director: George B. Chan
Cinematographer: Joseph F. Biroc
Partial Cast: Sidney Poitier, Barbara McNair, Sheree North, Raul Julia

• The Icehouse, 151 Union Street, Embarcadero
• BART/Muni station and tunnel, Market Street
• Taj Mahal houseboat, Pier A, Berths 840/841, Richardson Bay, Sausalito

The Other End of the Line
2008, Metro Goldwyn Mayer
An Indian call-center employee travels to San Francisco to be with a guy she falls for over the phone.

Director: James Dodson
Screenwriter: Tracey Jackson
Production Designer: Minal D. Rath
Art Director: Jim Edelhauser
Cinematographer: Harlan Bosmajian
Partial Cast: Jesse Metcalfe, Sara Foster, Anupam Kher

• Golden Gate Bridge
• Hyde Street Cable Car at intersection of Lombard Street, Russian Hill-as Hawksin Hotel site
• Intersection of California Street and Sansome Street, Financial District-as New York City with full moon
• Intersection of Montgomery Street and Sacramento Street, Financial District-as New York City
• U.S. Highway Route 280, Mission Bay District-limo scene
• Alcatraz Island, Golden Gate National Recreation Area
• 2100 block of Union Street, Cow Hollow District
• San Francisco International Airport
• San Francisco-Oakland Bay Bridge
• Intersection of California Street and Mason Street with cable car, Nob Hill District
• Fisherman's Wharf District
• Aquatic Park, San Francisco Maritime National Historic Park, Golden Gate National Recreation Area-beach
• Intersection of Montgomery Street and Vallejo Street, Telegraph Hill District
• Pier 7, The Embarcadero
• U.S. Highway Route 280 intersection

The Other Sister
1999, Touchstone
A mentally disabled young woman finds her way in life much against her mother's wishes.

Director: Garry Marshall
Screenwriters: Garry Marshall, Bob Brunner
Production Designer: Stephen J. Lineweaver
Art Director: Clayton Hartley
Cinematographer: Dante Spinotti
Partial Cast: Diane Keaton, Tom Skerritt, Juliette Lewis, Hector Elizondo, Givanni Ribisi, Poppy Montgomery, Sarah Paulson, Juliet Mills, Dina Merrill

• St. Francis of Assisi Church, 610 Vallejo Street, North Beach District-church scenes and interiors
• Palace of Fine Arts, 3601 Lyon Street, Marina District
• San Francisco-Oakland Bay Bridge
• 177 Caledonia Street, Sausalito
• Golden Gate Bridge

Out
1982, Echo Bridge Home Entertainment
A self-styled urban guerrilla is sent on various assignments across the U.S.

Director: Eli Hollander
Screenwriters: Ronald Sukenick, Eli Hollander
Author: Ronald Sukenick (novel)
Production Designer: Antony Chapman
Cinematographer: Robert Ball
Partial Cast: Peter Coyote, O-Lan Jones, Jim Haynie

• San Gregorio General Store, 7615 Stage Road, San Gregorio

Outbreak
1995, Warner Brothers
A lethal virus is somehow imported into the U.S. and a small town is quarantined.

Director: Wolfgang Petersen
Screenwriters: Laurence Dwort, Robert Roy Pool
Production Designer: William Sandell
Art Directors: Nancy Patton, Frances J. Pezza
Cinematographer: Michael Ballhaus
Partial Cast: Dustin Hoffman, Rene Russo, Morgan Freeman Jr., Kevin Spacey, Cuba Gooding Jr., Donald Sutherland

• Golden Gate Bridge
• 666 Folsom Street, South of Market District- helicopter lands on top of building
• Travis Air Force Base, Fairfield

"I never saw her in the daytime. We seemed to live by night. What was left of the day went away like a pack of cigarettes you smoked."

Out of the Past
1947, RKO Radio Pictures
AKA: *Build My Gallows High*
A private eye falls in love with his quarry who turns out to be the homicidal girlfriend of a thug.

Director: Jacques Tourneur
Screenwriter: Daniel Manwaring
Author: Daniel Manwaring *Build My Gallows High* (novel)
Cinematographer: Nicholas Musuraca
Partial Cast: Kirk Douglas, Robert Mitchum, Jane Greer, Rhonda Fleming, Dickie Moore, Paul Valentine, Virginia Huston, Richard Webb, Ken Niles

• San Francisco-Oakland Bay Bridge-view to east down Broadway from Russian Hill District
• 962-966 Broadway, Russian Hill District-house

Out on a Limb
1992, Universal Studios
AKA: *Buzzsaw*

Two adults who are jealous of each other don't know how to resolve their conflict.

Director: Francis Veber
Screenwriters: Daniel Goldin, Joshua Goldin
Production Designer: Stephen Marsh
Cinematographer: Donald E. Thorin
Partial Cast: Matthew Broderick, Jeffrey Jones, Heidi Kling, John C. Reilly, Marian Mercer

• Lockheed Aerospace, Sunnyvale
• Falkirk Cultural Center, 1408 Mission Avenue, San Rafael

Pacific Heights
1990, 20th Century Fox
A landlord couple rent part of their house to a tenant who turns out to be deranged.

Director: John Schlesinger
Screenwriter: Daniel Payne
Production Designer: Neil Spisak
Art Directors: Gershon Ginsburg, Sharon Seymour
Cinematographer: Amir M. Mokri
Partial Cast: Melanie Griffith, Matthew Modine, Michael Keaton

• 1243 19th Street, Potrero Hill District-house
• Riding Stables, Officer James W. Bloesch Road, Golden Gate Park

The Pack
1977, Warner Brothers
AKA: *The Long, Dark Night*
Vacationers to an island are terrified by a wild pack of dogs.

Director: Robert Clouse
Screenwriter: Robert Clouse
Author: Dave Fisher (novel)
Cinematographer: Ralph Woolsey
Partial Cast: Joe Don Baker, Hope Alexander Willis, Richard B. Schull, R. G. Armstrong

• Bodega Bay
• Hendren Ranch, 18900 Coleman Valley Road, Occidental

Pal Joey
1957, Columbia Pictures
Musical about a nightclub entertainer's rising career and his tendency to be a not-so-nice guy.

Director: George Sidney
Screenwriter: Dorothy Kingsley
Author: John O'Hara (novel)

Art Director: Walter Holscher
Partial Cast: Rita Hayworth, Frank Sinatra, Kim Novak

• Oakland Mole with San Francisco bound ferry
• San Francisco-Oakland Bay Bridge
• Panoramic view of downtown San Francisco from San Francisco Bay
• Ferry Building, Herb Caen Way, Embarcadero District
• International Settlement Gateway, Pacific Avenue at Columbus Avenue, Telegraph Hill District
• 500 block of Pacific Avenue, Telegraph Hill District
• Spreckels Mansion, 2080 Washington, Pacific Heights District-as exterior of Chez Joey nightclub on Nob Hill
• Presidio Avenue, California and Market Streets Cable Car at intersection of Washington Street and Taylor Street, Nob Hill District
• Coit Tower, Pioneer Park, 1 Telegraph Hill Boulevard, Telegraph Hill District-south lawn and walkways
• 1250 Taylor Street, Nob Hill District-boarding house
• Marina Green roadway, Marina District-berth of yacht *Vera*
• Golden Gate Bridge

Panther
1995, Gramercy Pictures
Semi-historic look at the origins of the Black Panther Party of Self-Defense during a three-year period in Oakland.

Director: Mario Van Peebles
Screenwriter: Melvin Van Peebles
Author: Melvin Van Peebles (book)
Production Designer: Richard Hoover
Art Directors: Bruce Robert Hill, Carol Lavoie
Cinematographer: Edward J. Pei
Partial Cast: Kadeem Hardison, Bokeem Woodbine, Joe Don Baker, Courtney B. Vance, Angela Bassett, Chris Rock, Dick Gregory, Melvin Van Peebles, Mark Curry

• San Francisco-Oakland Bay Bridge
• Berkeley
• Alameda County Courthouse, 1225 Fallon Street, Oakland

MARK CURRY

Oakland resident Curry was born on June 1, 1961, the youngest of eight children. He graduated from St. Joseph Notre Dame High School in Alameda in 1979. He then attended California State University, Hayward majoring in journalism. He dropped out before graduating to manage an Oakland drugstore—where he discovered his talent for keeping people in stitches. In 1987 he debuted his first comedy act in an Oakland club that launched his professional career just two years later. His first film role was alongside Martin Lawrence in *Talkin' Dirty After Dark* (1991). The next year he would star in TV's *Hangin' with Mr. Cooper*, a role where he played an NBA player-turned-substitute-teacher and gym coach. Beyond starring in the series that aired until 1997, he was executive and creative consultant shaping the scripts with material from his own life experiences in Oakland. In 1996 he starred in the HBO comedy special *Mark Curry-The Other Side*, which was filmed at Oakland's Paramount Theatre. He continues to work on a variety of TV shows and films, ranging from being a guest to hosting various shows. Most recently, he appeared in the Nick at Nite's live-action family comedy TV show *See Dad Run* as Scott Baio's friend Marcus.

The Parent Trap
1998, Buena Vista
Long separated twins conspire to reunite their estranged parents.

Director: Nancy Meyers
Screenwriter: David Swift
Author: Erich Kästner *Das Doppelte Lottchen* (book)
Production Designer: Dean Tavoularis
Art Director: Alex Tavoularis
Cinematographer: Dean Cundey
Partial Cast: Lindsay Lohan, Dennis Quaid, Natasha Richardson, Polly Holliday, Joanna Barnes

• 410 Avenue of Palms, Treasure Island-as Stafford Hotel
• Pier 7, The Embarcadero
• San Francisco Maritime Museum, Sala Burton Building, 900 Beach Street, Aquatic Park, San Francisco Maritime National Historic Park, Golden Gate National Recreation Area
• Staglin Family Vineyards, 1570 Bella Oaks Lane, Rutherford-residence

Passport to Alcatraz
1940, Columbia
AKA: *Alien Sabotage*
A sharp police investigator is assigned to run down those who dynamited a munitions plant.

Director: Lewis D. Collins
Screenwriter: Albert DeMond
Cinematographer: James S. Brown Jr.
Partial Cast: Jack Holt, Noah Beery Jr., Cecila
Callejo, Max "Slapsie Maxie" Rosenbloom

• Alcatraz Federal Prison, Alcatraz Island, Golden
Gate National Recreation Area

Patch Adams
1998, Universal
An unconventional doctor uses the
power of laughter to heal his patients
who otherwise don't respond to
medical treatment.

Director: Tom Shadyac
Screenwriter: Steve Oedekerk
Authors: Hunter A. Doherty, Maureen Mylander
Gesundheit: Good Health is a Laughing Matter
(book)
Production Designer: Linda DeScenna
Art Director: James Nedza
Cinematographer: Phedon Papamichael
Partial Cast: Robin Williams, Monica Potter,
Phillip Seymour Hoffman, Bob Gunton, Peter
Coyote

• LeConte Hall, University of California Campus,
Berkeley
• Pt. Richmond
• Glen Alpine Road, Piedmont
• Sheraton Palace Hotel, 2 New Montgomery
Street, South of Market District
• Naval Hospital, Mare Island, Vallejo

MARE ISLAND NAVAL SHIPYARD

Mare Island Naval Shipyard in Vallejo
was the first of its kind facility on the
West Coast. Sited on 4,351 acres, the
996-building yard was opened in 1854
by Naval Commander David G. Far-
ragut. The yard became famous for its
record-breaking construction sched-
ules, highlighted by the creation of the
destroyer USS *Ward* in just 17 and a
half days during 1918. At its height
during World War II, the shipyard em-
ployed 46,000 people, both civilian
and enlisted. Of the wide variety of
512 vessels constructed there, 17
were submarines. Its last launch occurred in 1970, and the yard was decommissioned in April of 1996.

Pat And Mike
1952, Metro Goldwyn Mayer

Romance blooms between a female
athlete and her manager.

Director: George Cukor
Screenwriters: Ruth Gordon, Garson Kanin
Art Directors: Cedric Gibbons, Urie McCleary
Cinematographer: William Daniels
Partial Cast: Katharine Hepburn, Spencer Tracy,
Aldo Ray
Local Cast: Tennis star Alice Marble

• San Francisco-Oakland Bay Bridge

Patty Hearst
1988, Atlantic Entertainment
True story of an heiress who is
kidnapped by a revolutionary group
and joins their terrorist activities.

Director: Paul Schrader
Screenwriter: Nicholas Kazan
Authors: Patricia Campbell Hearst, Alvin Moscow
Every Secret Thing (book)
Production Designer: Jane Musky
Cinematographer: Bojan Bazelli
Partial Cast: Natasha Richardson, William
Forsyth, Ving Rhames, Francis Fisher

• Alamo Square, Western Addition District
• Bank of America, 3701 Balboa Street, Outer
Richmond District
• San Francisco-Oakland Bay Bridge
• Sproul Plaza, University of California Campus,
Berkeley
• Oakland

PATTY HEARST

Newspaper-family heiress Patricia
Hearst was violently kidnapped from
her Berkeley apartment on February
2, 1974. A captive of the radical terrorist group, self-proclaimed as the Symbionese Liberation Army, Hearst was
held for $6 million ransom and later
claimed she was brainwashed by her
captors. On the following April 15, she
was recorded on a security camera
during a brazen holdup in the Hibernia
Bank (now Bank of America) at 2325
Noriega Street, San Francisco. On
September 18 of the following year,
San Francisco police and the FBI arrested Hearst and four other SLA
members. After Patty served 21
months of her seven-year sentence,
President Jimmy Carter commuted
her sentence. In 1981 she wrote a
book about her life as "Tania," the
name she used during her captivity.

She married her bodyguard Bernard Shaw and now resides in Connecticut. Another chapter in the unfinished story surfaced on January 16, 2002 when four SLA figures were taken into custody. The four were key in the 1975 shooting of a Carmichael, California mother. Officials stated that new forensic technologies could be used to reevaluate 27-year-old evidence.

Peaceful Warrior

2006, Lions Gate Films

A chance encounter with a stranger changes the life of a college gymnast.

Director: Victor Salva
Screenwriter: Kevin Bernhardt
Author: Dan Millman *Way of the Peaceful Warrior* (novel)
Production Designer: Bernt Capra
Art Director: Anthony Tremblay
Cinematographer: Sharone Meir
Partial Cast: Scott Mechlowicz, Nick Nolte, Amy Smart

• Aerial view of University of California Campus, Berkeley
• Steps between Moses Hall and Stephens Hall, University of California Campus, Berkeley
• Sather Tower observation deck, University of California Campus, Berkeley

Peggy Sue Got Married

1986, TriStar Pictures

A disillusioned woman attends her high school's 25th reunion and relives her younger years.

Director: Francis Ford Coppola
Screenwriters: Jerry Leichtling, Arlene Sarner
Production Designer: Dean Tavoularis
Art Director: Alex Tavoularis
Cinematographer: Jordan Cronenweth
Partial Cast: Kathleen Turner, Nicolas Cage, Barry Miller, Catherine Hicks, Maureen O'Sullivan, Jim Carrey, Sofia Coppola, Barbara Harris, Helen Hunt, John Carradine

• Santa Rosa High School, 1235 Mendocino Avenue, Santa Rosa
• Petaluma Boulevard North, Petaluma
• Lena's Restaurant, Santa Rosa
• Saturday Afternoon Club, 430 Tenth Street, Santa Rosa
• Millie's Chili Bar, 600 Petaluma Boulevard South, Petaluma-as The Donut Hole
• 1006 D Street, Petaluma-boyfriend's home
• 226 Liberty Street, Petaluma-Peggy Sue's home

SOFIA COPPOLA

Sofia Carmina Coppola is one of three children born to director/producer Francis Ford and Eleanor (Neil) Coppola, a costume and stage designer. Sofia was born in Manhattan on May 14, 1971, and her exposure to film came very early the next year when her father cast her as an infant boy being christened in the first of Mario Puzo's crime boss smash trilogy movies *The Godfather*. She appeared in the other two *Godfather* films as well in 1974 and 1990. The French fashion house of Chanel took her on as an intern at age 15; around the same time she was cast in *Peggy Sue Got Married* playing Nancy Kelcher, the sister of the lead character portrayed by Kathleen Turner. Coppola graduated from St. Helena High School in 1990. With an interest in the visual arts she went to Mills College in Oakland, where she studied photography; she also attended the California Institute of the Arts in Valencia to study painting. Her film *Lost in Translation* (2003) brought her the Oscar for the Best Original Screenplay at the 2004 Academy Awards. More importantly was her nomination for Best Director of the same movie as she was the first American woman to receive a nod for the coveted Oscar. Today she resides in Paris with husband Thomas Mars and their two children. She is co-owner of the San Francisco-based American Zoetrope film studio with her brother Roman, which was founded by her famous father and George Lucas.

Pete 'n Tillie

1972, Universal Pictures

An eccentric pair marry with tragic results.

Director: Martin Ritt
Screenwriter: Julius J. Epstein
Author: Peter de Vries *Witch's Milk* (book)
Art Director: George C. Webb
Cinematographer: John A. Alonzo

Partial Cast: Walter Matthau, Carol Burnett, Geraldine Page, Barry Nelson, Rene Auberjonois, Lee Montgomery, Henry Jones

• Golden Gate Bridge
• Golden Gate Bridge-toll booth
• Garden Court Restaurant, Sheraton Palace Hotel, Two New Montgomery Street, South of Market District

BARRY NELSON

Barry Nelson was born Robert Haakon Nielson in San Francisco on April 16, 1917. His Scandinavian-heritage parents, Betsy (Christophsen) and Trygve Nielsen, raised him in Oakland. He graduated from the University of California, Berkeley in 1941 and immediately landed work with Metro Goldwyn Mayer as a contract player. His screen debut was in the role of Paul Clark in *Shadow of the Thin Man* in 1941, which starred the comic detective characters played by Myrna Loy and William Powell. While serving in World War II, Barry appeared in the stage version of Moss Hart's play *Winged Victory* and then in the 1944 film version of the play. He is noted to have been the first actor to portray secret agent James Bond in a 1954 TV adaptation of Ian Fleming's *Casino Royale*—well before the launch of the 007 franchise we know today. He appeared in the hit Broadway play *Mary, Mary* and then reprised his role in the 1963 film version opposite Debbie Reynolds. He spent the majority of the rest of his career on television and on the stage in shows such as *Seascape, The Norman Conquests,* and *The Act,* which earned him a Tony nomination. He married actress Teresa Celli in 1951, but they divorced in 1965. Retired by the early 1990s, he again married in 1992 to Nansilee Hoy. He died in 2007 at age 90.

Petulia

1968, Warner Brothers
AKA: *Me and the Arch-Kook Petulia*
A doctor meets an unusual girl with family problems.

Director: Richard Lester
Screenwriter: Barbara Turner
Author: John Haase *Me and the Arch-Kook Petulia* (novel)
Production Designer: Tony Walton
Cinematographer: Nicholas Roeg
Partial Cast: George C. Scott, Julie Christie, Richard Chamberlain, Arthur Hill, Joseph Cotton, Rene Auberjonois, Jerry Garcia, Shirley Knight, Bobby Weir

• Fairmont Hotel, 950 Mason Street, Nob Hill District-lobby
• 307 Filbert Street Steps, Telegraph Hill District
• Cala Foods, 1095 Hyde Street, Nob Hill District
• Varni's Roaring Twenties Club, 807 Montgomery Street, Telegraph Hill District
• Fort Point National Historic Site, Marine Drive, Golden Gate National Recreation Area
• Waybur House, 3232 Pacific Avenue, Presidio Heights District
• Talbot-Dutton House, 1782 Pacific Avenue, Pacific Heights District
• Belvedere Island

Phantasm

1979, Avco and Embassy
Nightmares that seem to come true haunt a young man.

Director: Don Coscarelli
Screenwriter: Don Coscarelli
Art Director: David Gavin Brown
Production Designer: Kate Coscarelli
Cinematographer: Don Coscarelli
Partial Cast: Michael Baldwin, Bill Thronbury, Reggie Bannister, Angus Scrimm

• Dunsmuir House and Gardens, 2980 Peralta Court, Oakland

Phenomenon

1996, Touchstone Pictures
A man witnesses a falling star and suddenly finds himself with super-intelligence and telekinesis.

Director: Jon Turteltaub
Screenwriter: Gerald Di Pego
Production Designer: Garreth Stover
Art Director: Bruce Allen Miller
Cinematographer: Phedon Papamichael
Partial Cast: John Travolta, Kyra Sedgwick, Forest Whitaker, Robert Duvall

• Santa Rosa Junior College, 1501 Mendocino Avenue, Santa Rosa-as U.C. Berkeley Campus
• Two Rock Ranch, 1051 Walker Road, Petaluma
• Mache Brothers Dairy ranch, 14100 Bodega Highway, Bodega
• Pozzi Ranch, Valley Ford
• Thompson Residence, 5421 Blank Road, Sebastopol
• Wagon Wheel Saloon, 3320 Mendocino Avenue, Santa Rosa

The Picasso Summer
1969, Warner Brothers
An architect and his wife embark on a journey to France in search of the famous artist.

Directors: Serge Bourguignon, Robert Sallin
Screenwriters: Edwin Boyd, Ray Bradbury
Art Director: Damien Lanfranchi
Cinematographer: Vilmos Zsigmond
Partial Cast: Albert Finney, Yvette Mimeieux

• San Francisco-Oakland Bay Bridge
• Aerial panorama of South of Market District and Financial District
• Alcoa Building, One Maritime Plaza, 300 Clay Street, Golden Gateway
• Calhoun Terrace, Telegraph Hill District-party

P.K. and the Kid
1987, Castle Hill Productions
A girl runs away from home after her mother's boyfriend continues his unwanted advances.

Director: Lou Lombardo
Screenwriter: Neal Barbera
Production Designer: Chet Allen
Art Director: Bill Cornford
Cinematographer: Edmond L. Koons
Partial Cast: Paul Le Mat, Molly Ringwald, Alex Rocco

• Kentucky Street, Petaluma
• Petaluma Valley Hospital, 400 North McDowell Boulevard, Petaluma
• Sonoma-Marin Fairgrounds, 175 Fairgrounds Drive, Petaluma
• City Hall, 11 English Street, Petaluma
• Hide-Away Bar, 128 Kentucky Street, Petaluma

Playing Mona Lisa
2000, Buena Vista
AKA: *Two Goldsteins on Acid*
A young pianist is discouraged especially after her boyfriend drops her.

Director: Matthew Huffman
Screenwriters: Marni Freedman, Carlos De Los Rios
Author: Marni Freedman (play)
Production Designer: Frank Bollinger
Cinematographer: James Glennon
Partial Cast: Alicia Witt, Harvey Fierstein, Brooke Langton, Ivan Sergei, Johnny Galecki, Marlo Thomas, Elliott Gould, Estelle Harris

• Brooks House #2, Franklin Street, Fort Mason Center, Golden Gate National Recreation Area

• Momi Toby's Revolutionary Café, 528 Laguna Street, Hayes Valley District
• Conservatory of Flowers, 100 JFK Drive, Golden Gate Park
• Ferry Building, Herb Caen Way, The Embarcadero
• Dolores Park, Mission District
• Pier 7, The Embarcadero
• Transamerica Pyramid, 600 Montgomery Street, Financial District
• Fort Point National Historic Site, Marine Drive, Golden Gate National Recreation Area
• Aquatic Park, San Francisco Maritime National Historic Park, Golden Gate National Recreation Area
• Palace of Fine Arts, 3601 Lyon Street, Marina District
• Marin Headlands, Golden Gate National Recreation Area
• San Francisco Water Department, Sunset Reservoir, 28th Avenue and Ortega Street, Sunset District
• San Francisco Conservatory of Music, 1201 Ortega Street, Sunset District

> "My lawyer will call your lawyer."
> "I don't have a lawyer. Have him call my doctor."

Play It Again, Sam
1972, Paramount
AKA: *Aspirins for Three*
A neurotic film critic is abandoned by his wife and seems to invoke the spirit of Humphrey Bogart.

Director: Herbert Ross
Screenwriter: Woody Allen
Author: Woody Allen (play)
Production Designer: Ed Wittstein
Cinematographer: Owen Roizman
Partial Cast: Woody Allen, Diane Keaton, Tony Roberts, Jerry Lacy, Susan Anspach

• 15 Fresno Street, Telegraph Hill District-exterior of Allan's residence
• 1212 Lombard Street, Russian Hill District-Allan's residence interior
• San Francisco Museum of Modern Art, War Memorial Building, Civic Center
• Waldo Grade Tunnel, U.S. Highway Route 101, Sausalito
• Stinson Beach-beach house
• Music Concourse, Hagiwara Tea Garden Way, Golden Gate Park-benches
• Horizons Restaurant, 558 Bridgeway Avenue, Sausalito

• Ernie's Restaurant, 847 Montgomery Street, Telegraph Hill District
• Powell/Market Cable Car 517, intersection of Bay Street and Hyde Street, Russian Hill District

The Pleasure of His Company
1961, Paramount Pictures

A debutante is about to be married to a rancher and her estranged father appears for the wedding.

Director: George Seaton
Screenwriter: Samuel A. Taylor
Authors: Cornelia Otis Skinner, Samuel A. Taylor (play)
Art Directors: Tambi Larsen, Hal Pereira
Cinematographer: Robert Burks
Partial Cast: Fred Astaire, Lilli Palmer, Debbie Reynolds, Charles Ruggles, Tab Hunter, Gary Merrill, Harold Fong

• Golden Gate Bridge
• I. Magnin and Co., 233 Geary Street, Union Square
• San Francisco International Airport
• 2700 Vallejo Street, Pacific Heights District-house facade
• Coit Tower, Pioneer Park, 1 Telegraph Hill Boulevard, Telegraph Hill District-picnic
• Fisherman's Wharf District
• Norwegian Seaman's Church, 2454 Hyde Street, Russian Hill District-as Chez Alain
• Grace Cathedral, 1100 California Street, Nob Hill District

2700 VALLEJO STREET: MANSION BUT NO GARDEN

The imposing 2700 Vallejo Street residence was built in 1915 for Captain F. Olsen to the design of architect C. O. Clausen and currently is the residence of the Japanese Counsel General. The mansion also appeared in *Bullitt* (1968) and *The Towering Inferno* (1974). The rear façade has no such garden as shown in *The Pleasure of His Company* so a set was modeled on the property two blocks away at 2460 Lyon Street steps in the Pacific Heights District. George Lucas' former wife Marcia Griffin lived there for several years in the 1990s, and now Senator Dianne Feinstein and husband Richard Blum have relocated to the Lyon Street mansion that has panoramic views of San Francisco Bay.

Poetic Justice
1993, Columbia

Having witnessed the murder of her boyfriend, a girl loses her ambition but discovers a friend in a former foe.

Director: John Singleton
Screenwriter: John Singleton
Art Director: Kirk M. Petruccelli
Production Designer: Keith Brian Burns
Cinematographer: Peter Lyons Collister
Partial Cast: Janet Jackson, Tupac Shakur, Regina King, Joe Torry, Tyra Ferrell
Local Cast: Poet, among other things, Maya Angelou

• Gray Whale Cove, Devil's Slide, Pacifica
• 1720 Filbert Street, Oakland
• Alice's Restaurant, 17288 Skyline Boulevard, Woodside-as Lazy Josey Café
• Saeed Dobahi Market, 1000 18th Street, Oakland
• Lakeside Motel, 122 East 14th Street, Oakland
• Altamont Pass, Interstate Highway Route 580-windmills

MAYA ANGELOU

Maya Angelou was born Marguerite Annie Johnson on April 4, 1928 in St. Louis, Missouri. She was schooled in Stamps, Arkansas and later in San Francisco where she attended George Washington High School in the Outer Richmond District, graduating in 1945. The early lives of her and her brother were in constant flux as they were shuttled between various relatives. After she debuted as a dancer at the Purple Onion cabaret on Columbus Avenue in the Jackson Square District, she adopted the name of Maya Angelou. She was the first black, female streetcar conductor in San Francisco. At President Bill Clinton's inauguration in 1993 she recited a poem she wrote, "On the Pulse of Morning." She has garnered numerous awards for her work as poet, educator, historian, best-selling author, playwright, civil-rights activist, producer, and director. She has also received over thirty honorary doctoral degrees.

Point Blank
1967, Metro Goldwyn Mayer

A gangster becomes aware of his girlfriend's cheating and takes an elaborate reprisal.

Director: John Boorman
Screenwriters: Alexander Jacobs, David Newhouse, Rafe Newhouse
Author: Donald E. Westlake *The Hunter* (novel)
Art Directors: Albert Brenner, George W. Davis
Cinematographer: Philip H. Lathrop
Partial Cast: Lee Marvin, Angie Dickinson, Keenan Wynn, Carroll O'Connor

• Montgomery Street tunnel to Montgomery Muni and BART Station, Financial District
• Fisherman's Wharf District
• Alcatraz Federal Prison, Alcatraz Island, Golden Gate National Recreation Area
• Fort Point National Historic Site, Marine Drive, Golden Gate National Recreation Area

Pollyanna
1960, Buena Vista

An eternally optimistic orphan goes to live with a rich spinster aunt and has a surprising effect on her aunt's life.

Director: David Swift
Screenwriter: David Swift
Author: Eleanor H. Porter (novel)
Art Directors: Carroll Clark, Robert Clatsworthy
Cinematographer: Russell Harlan
Partial Cast: Hayley Mills, Jane Wyman, Richard Egan, Karl Malden, Adolphe Menjou, Agnes Moorehead, Nancy Olsen, Donald Crisp

• Sulphur Springs railroad trestle, St. Helena
• Southern Pacific Railroad Depot, 1520 Railroad Avenue, St. Helena
• Mableton House, 1015 McDonald Avenue, Santa Rosa-as exterior and grounds of Harrington Residence
• Bale Grist Mill, State Route 29, Calistoga
• Napa River, Napa
• Egan Ranch
• Gus Luer Ranch, Guerneville Road, Santa Rosa
• Stags' Leap Winery, 6150 Silverado Trail, Napa- as Pendergast House

TWO PROMINENT RESIDENCES

Located near the vertical palisades of the Vaca Mountain Range on the eastern side of the Napa Valley is the menacing Pendergast House which is sited among a grove of California oaks. Known as The Manor, it was completed in 1890 by Horace Blanchard Chase, son of a wealthy Chicago businessman. The 400-acre estate also included a coach house, a greenhouse, a guesthouse, and a winery originally called Stag's Leap, which commenced operation in 1893. The English-influenced house design features a round tower capped by a crenellated rampart. Construction was started the same year Chase married Mary "Minnie" Ysabel Mizner, whose prominent San Francisco father was a United States senator and envoy to Central America. The structure is built of native cut stone, but at some point someone added an oddly designed wood third story (shown in the movie), which has since been removed. The interior features fine wood paneling, a grand staircase, and an over-scaled fireplace in the living room. In 1913 Frances Grange acquired the property and transformed it into a working ranch and resort. The property later served several purposes including a temporary billet for military wives whose spouses were stationed at Mare Island. Having gained a seedy reputation, the property finally closed in the early 1950s. Reopened in 1979 by new owner Carl Doumani, it was he who had the later unfortunate appendages to the building demolished. And in a landmark case before the California Supreme Court the owner took on the subtly different moniker of Stags' Leap Winery when his neighbor (who got to use Stag's Leap Wine Cellars) and Doumani tussled over the appellation name. Beringer Wine Estates purchased the property in 1997.

The real story behind the creation of the residence that served as Aunt Polly's house is not far from that in the movie's storyline. Known as Mableton House, it was constructed for capitalist "Colonel" Mark L. McDonald during 1877–1878 for his wife Ralphine on Santa Rosa's most exclusive street. The area was known as McDonald's Addition, a 130-acre tract of exclusive property for high-profile wealthy merchant princes. The house served as the McDonalds' summer residence since they wintered in San Francisco. The house's design is said to be a replica of a Natchez, Mississippi home owned by the McDonald family prior to

Portrait in Black
1960, Universal International
Lovers carry out a murder scheme on the woman's cruel but wealthy husband and blackmail, guilt, and suspicion are the unanticipated results.

Director: Michael Gordon
Screenwriters: Ivan Goff, Ben Roberts
Art Director: Richard H. Riedel
Cinematographer: Russell Metty
Partial Cast: Lana Turner, Anthony Quinn, Richard Basehart, Anna May Wong, Lloyd Nolan, Sandra Dee, John Saxon, Ray Walston, Virginia Grey

• Aerial view of waterfront with Ferry Building, The Embarcadero
• I. Magnin and Co., 233 Geary Street, Union Square
• 2898 Broadway, Pacific Heights-house
• San Francisco Bay-speed boat ride
• Crocker Bank, One Montgomery Street, Financial District
• Japanese Tea Garden, 75 Hagiwara Tea Garden Way, Golden Gate Park
• Maiden Lane, Union Square District
• Devil's Slide, State Highway Route 1, Pacifica-car being pushed over edge

Predator 2
1990, 20th Century Fox
Amidst a territorial gang-war, a sophisticated alien hunter stalks the citizens of Los Angeles; and the only man between him and his prey is a veteran LAPD officer.

Director: Stephen Hopkins
Screenwriters: Jim Thomas, John Thomas
Production Designer: Lawrence G. Paull
Art Director: Geoff Hubbard
Cinematographer: Peter Levy

Partial Cast: Kevin Peter Hall, Gary Busy, Rube'n Blades

• BART car and tunnels

The Presidio
1988, Paramount Pictures
AKA: *The Presidio: The Scene of the Crime*
An Army provost helps solve the murder of a guard.

Director: Peter Hyams
Screenwriter: Larry Ferguson
Production Designer: Albert Brenner
Art Director: Kandy Stern
Cinematographer: Peter Hyams
Partial Cast: Sean Connery, Mark Harmon, Meg Ryan, Jack Warden

• San Francisco Bay with Ferry Building, The Embarcadero
• Officer's Club, Moraga Avenue, Presidio, Golden Gate National Recreation Area-murder location
• Golden Gate Bridge
• Fort Point National Historic Site, Marine Drive, Golden Gate National Recreation Area
• Unnamed private alley between Harrison Street and Main Street (between 426 and 450 Harrison with Pier 26 in the background-as bottled water warehouse
• Arguello Boulevard, Presidio, Golden Gate National Recreation Area
• 56 Presidio Boulevard, Presidio, Golden Gate National Recreation Area-residence
• San Francisco City Hall, 1 Carlton B. Goodlett Place, Civic Center District
• Intersection of Market Street and Front Street, Financial District-crash
• Intersection of Filbert Street Steps and Montgomery Street, Telegraph Hill District
• Building 35, 35 Keyes Avenue, Presidio, Golden Gate National Recreation Area
• Old Presidio Hospital, intersection of Funston Avenue and Lincoln Boulevard, Presidio, Golden Gate National Recreation Area
• San Francisco National Military Cemetery, Lincoln Boulevard, Presidio
• Crissy Field, Presidio, Golden Gate National Recreation Area
• 732 Vermont Street, Potrero Hill District
• San Francisco-Oakland Bay Bridge
• Building 87, 87 Graham Street, Presidio, Golden Gate National Recreation Area

• Galileo High School, 1150 Francisco Street, Russian Hill District-as high school courtyard
• Buildings 935 (Presidio Utilities and Sewer Department) and 937 (Wheeled and Tracked Branch) Crissy Field hangar, Presidio, Golden Gate National Recreation Area-as Falcon Sports rock climbing gym
• Hamlin School, 2120 Broadway, Pacific Heights District-as rooftop playground
• Musee Mecanique, Cliff House, 1090 Point Lobos Avenue, Golden Gate National Recreation Area
• Intersection of Broadway and Taylor Street, Russian Hill District-car/motorized cable car accident
• Baker Beach, Presidio, Golden Gate National Recreation Area
• Rustic Bridge, Stow Lake, Golden Gate Park

Pretty Woman
1990, Buena Vista
AKA: *$3000*
A man in a legal but hurtful business needs an escort for some social events and hires a beautiful prostitute he meets—only to fall in love.

Director: Garry Marshall
Screenwriter: J. F. Lawton
Production Designer: Albert Brenner
Art Director: David Haber
Cinematographer: Charles Minsky
Partial Cast: Richard Gere, Julia Roberts, Ralph Bellamy, Jason Alexander, Laura San Giacomo, Elinore Donahue, Hector Elizondo

• Aerial view of San Francisco waterfront at night

The Princess Diaries
2001, Buena Vista
AKA: *The Princess of Tribeca*
A teenage girl discovers she has royal roots.

Director: Garry Marshall
Screenwriters: Meg Cabot, Gina Wendkos
Production Designer: Mayne Schuyler Berke
Art Director: Caty Maxey
Cinematographer: Karl Walter Lindenlaub
Partial Cast: Julie Andrews, Anne Hathaway, Hector Elizondo, Heather Matasazzo, Mandy Moore, Sandra Oh
Local Cast: Mayor Willie J. Brown Jr., socialite Daru Kalwalkowski

• Golden Gate Bridge
• Firehouse, Engine #43½, 724 Brazil Street, Excelsior District-residence
• 2601 Lyon Street, Pacific Heights District-as school

The Principal
1987, TriStar Pictures
A teacher gets to be principal in a rough public school.

Director: Christopher Cain
Screenwriter: Frank Deese
Art Director: Mark Billerman
Cinematographer: Arthur Albert
Partial Cast: Jim Belushi, Lou Gossett Jr., Rae Dawn Chong, Michael Wright, J. J. Cohen

• Walnut Creek
• Merritt College Campus, 12500 Campus Drive, Oakland

Profession: Adventurers
1973, Les Films Cocinor
Two people who meet in a police station join forces to get rich quick and generally buck authority.

Director: Claude Mulot
Screenwriters: Albert Kantof, Claude Mulot
Author: François Ponthier (novel)
Art Director: Raymond Gabutti
Cinematographers: Jacques Assuérus, Roger Fellous
Partial Cast: Charles Southwood, Nathalie Delon, André Pousse

• Golden Gate Bridge

The Promise
1979, MCA and Universal Pictures
AKA: Face of a Stranger
A young man does not recognize his lost lover after an accident.

Director: Gilbert Cates
Screenwriters: Paul M. Heller, Fred Weintraub, Garry Michael White
Production Designer: William Sandell
Cinematographer: Ralph Woolsey
Partial Cast: Kathleen Quinlan, Stephen Collins, Beatrice Straight, Laurence Luckinbill, William Prince

• University of California Campus, Berkeley-various exteriors
• Maiden Lane, Union Square District
• Fitzgerald Marine Preserve, Seal Cove, Moss Beach
• Golden Gate Bridge
• Ralph K. Davies Medical Center, 45 Castro Street, Duboce Triangle District
• San Francisco International Airport
• Marina Boulevard, Marina District
• 2226 Union Street, Cow Hollow District-as front of gallery
• Cable car, California Street line
• Mark Hopkins Hotel, 999 California Street, Nob Hill District-porte cochere
• Alameda County Coliseum, 7000 Coliseum Way, Oakland
• Belvedere Island-doctor's home
• Sausalito-waterfront
• Engine Company Firehouse #21, 1152 Oak Street, Haight-Ashbury District-as rear of gallery

Psych-Out
1968, American International Pictures
AKA: *Revolt of the Flower People*
A deaf runaway goes to San Francisco's Haight-Ashbury District looking for her missing brother.

Director: Richard Rush
Screenwriters: Betty Tusher, Betty Ulius, E. Hunter Willett
Art Director: Leon Ericksen
Cinematographer: László Kovács
Partial Cast: Jack Nicholson, Susan Strasberg, Dean Stockwell, Bruce Dern, Adam Roarke, Garry Marshall

• Panhandle, Golden Gate Park
• Intersection of Masonic Avenue and Haight Street, Haight-Ashbury District
• Various Haight Street locations, Haight-Ashbury District
• Haight Theater, 1700 Haight Street, Haight-Ashbury District-roof scenes

Purpose
2002, First Look Home Entertainment
AKA: *Purpo$e*
A computer software developer becomes very wealthy and is distracted by fame, greed and power, then must save his invention and company from a hostile takeover.

Director: Alan Ari Lazar
Screenwriters: Ronnie Apteker, Alan Ari Lazar, Saki Missaikos, Thomas W. Roush
Production Designer: Franco-Giacomo Carbone
Art Director: John Zachary
Cinematographer: John Peters
Partial Cast: John Light, Jeffrey Donovan, Megan Doods, Peter Coyote, Archie Kao, Hal Holbrook, Mia Farrow

• Aerial shots of Financial District
• Golden Gate Bridge
• San Francisco-Oakland Bay Bridge
• U.S. Highway Route 101, Waldo Grade Tunnel, Sausalito
• Houseboats, Mission Creek, Mission Bay District
• Lincoln Park Golf Course, Lincoln Park, Outer Richmond District
• Pac Bell Park, 24 Willie Mays Plaza, South of Market District

Pursuit of Happyness
2006, Columbia Pictures
Chronicle of a salesman living on the edge who winds up on the streets after he and his five-year-old son are evicted from their apartment.

Director: Gabriele Muccino
Screenwriter: Steve Conrad
Cinematographer: Phedon Papamichael
Partial Cast: Will Smith, Jaden Smith, Thandie Newton, Brian Howe, James Karen
Local Cast: Reverend Cecil Williams

• 45 Upper Terrace, Buena Vista District
• Embarcadero Center
• Glide Memorial Church, 330 Ellis Street, Tenderloin District
• Transbay Terminal, 425 Mission Street, South of Market District
• Bank of America Building, 555 California Street, Financial District
• Crissy Field, Presidio, Golden Gate National Recreation Area-beach

JEFF MOSLEY

Local stunt actor Jeff Mosley has appeared in more than locally shot movies in addition to *Pursuit of Happyness*, plus a multitude of other movie and TV parts. His movie stunt career started in 1988, and his first appearance in a locally shot movie was in *Made in America* (1993). A resident of Concord, California, Mosley started a film project in 2010 with the intention of benefiting the beleaguered Mt. Diablo Unified School District. Called *Chasing Rodriquez*, the movie is the first project of 3 J Films, LLC, which has aspirations to produce family-friendly feature length films.

Quicksilver
1986, Columbia

A hot-shot stock market whiz kid makes a disastrous professional decision and joins a messenger firm that relies on bicycles to avoid traffic jams in San Francisco.

Director: Thomas Michael Donnelly
Screenwriter: Thomas Michael Donnelly
Production Designer: Charles Rosen
Art Director: James Shanahan
Cinematographer: Thomas Del Ruth
Partial Cast: Kevin Bacon, Jami Gertz, Laurence Fishburne

• War Memorial Opera House, 301 Van Ness Avenue, Civic Center
• Filbert Street, Russian Hill District
• Pacific Stock Exchange, 301 Pine Street, Financial District
• Citicorp Center, One Sansome Street, Financial District
• Embarcadero Freeway, Embarcadero

EMBARCADERO FREEWAY

The now gone San Francisco freeway was the child of another time when freeway development was at its zenith throughout the United States, as busses and trains were considered outmoded forms of transportation. The elevated double-decker Embarcadero Freeway, also known as State Highway Route 480, began at the approach to the San Francisco-Oakland Bay Bridge and ran north along the waterfront, most notably in front of the Ferry Building, ending in ramps at Broadway. The freeway opened to traffic in 1959, but by that time sentiment was running against the freeway as the San Francisco Board of Supervisors passed a resolution opposing its continuance along the waterfront to connect with the Golden Gate Bridge, which would have effectively cut off much of the waterfront from the city.

This and other freeway plans were met with what became popularly known as the Freeway Revolt. In 1985 the Board of Supervisors voted to tear down the 16-year-old structure, and the proposal put to a public vote two years later was defeated. Fate interceded, and the reviled auto artery was a casualty of the 1989 Loma Prieta Earthquake; the cast-in place concrete structure was slated for retrofitting by Caltrans, but instead it was torn down in 1991, reopening the waterfront and establishing numerous opportunities for development—many which have been carried out creating one of San Francisco's most vibrant areas for locals and tourists alike. The freeway appeared in several movies but its use in the pivotal final scenes of *The Lineup* (1958) was its film debut—before it was even opened to traffic.

Race Street
1948, RKO Radio Pictures
AKA: *Jackpot*

A bookie vows revenge when his pal is killed by an extortionist gang, then discovers that his girlfriend is married to the leader.

Director: Edwin L. Marin
Screenwriters: Maurice Davis, Martin Rackin
Art Directors: Darrell Silvera, Walter E. Keller
Cinematographer: J. Roy Hunt
Partial Cast: George Raft, William Bendix, Marilyn Maxwell, Henry Morgan

• Fitzhugh Building, 386 Post Street, Union Square-shop
• Stanford Court Apartments, 905 California Street, Nob Hill District
• Bay Meadows Racetrack, El Camino Real, San Mateo
• 1201 California, Nob Hill District-highrise apartment building
• Cliff House, 1090 Point Lobos Avenue, Golden Gate National Recreation Area
• Golden Gate Bridge
• RKO Radio Pictures, Golden Gate Theater, 1 Taylor Street, Tenderloin District

The Rack
1956, Metro Goldwyn Mayer

A Korean War veteran is

court-martialed for collaborating with the enemy while being tortured.

Director: Arnold Laven
Screenwriters: Rod Serling, Stewart Stern
Art Directors: Cedric Gibbons, Merrill Pye
Cinematographer: Paul C. Vogel
Partial Cast: Paul Newman, Walter Pidgeon, Edmund O'Brien, Anne Francis, Lee Marvin, Cloris Leachman, Wendell Corey, Dean Jones, Debbie Reynolds

• Presidio, Golden Gate National Recreation Area

Radio Flyer
1992, Columbia TriStar
Two brothers endure a life of abuse by their stepfather but discover how a wagon can transform their circumstances through vivid imagination.

Director: Richard Donner
Screenwriter: David M. Evans
Production Designer: J. Michael Riva
Art Director: David F. Klassen
Cinematographer: László Kovács
Partial Cast: Lorraine Bracco, John Heard, Adam Baldwin, Elijah Wood, Tom Hanks

• Hamilton Field, Hamilton Air Force Base, Novato
• Novato Theater, 924 Grant Avenue, Novato

TOM HANKS

Thomas Jeffrey Hanks was born on July 9, 1956 in Concord, California to Amos Hanks, an itinerant cook, and Janet (Frager) Hanks, a hospital worker. His parents divorced when he was four years old, and he remained with his father and two other siblings while his mother moved to Red Bluff with the family's youngest child. His father remarried in 1965 to Frances Wong which brought new siblings into his family. He attended Skyline High School in Oakland graduating in 1974. At Chabot College in Hayward, he studied theater for two years and then transferred to California State University, Sacramento. Hanks dropped out before graduating when he became an intern at the Great Lakes Theater Festival in Cleveland, Ohio for three years, learning all the aspects of the craft. He moved to New York City in

1979 and a year later he debuted before the camera in *He Knows You're Alone*. The public saw Hanks on TV the next year in the popular comedy *Bosom Buddies*. His work in the film *Philadelphia* (1993) won him an Academy Award for Best Actor and another came to him the next year for the film *Forrest Gump*. The East Bay's Emeryville-based Pixar Studio, in concert with Walt Disney, has used Hanks as the voice of Sheriff Woody in the digitally animated *Toy Story* series: *Toy Story* (1995), *Toy Story 2* (1999), and *Toy Story 3* (2010). The veteran actor continues to act in, produce, and direct movies.

The Raging Tide
1951, Universal International
A gangster stows away on a fishing trawler and redeems himself when he dies saving the life of a fisherman.

Director: George Sherman
Screenwriter: Ernest K. Gann
Author: Ernest K. Gann *Fiddler's Green* (novel)
Art Directors: Hilyard Brown, Bernard Herzbrun
Cinematographer: Russell Metty
Partial Cast: Richard Conte, Charles Bickford, Shelley Winters, Stephen McNally, Jesse White, John McIntire

• Golden Gate Bridge
• The Embarcadero-piers and waterfront
• Julius' Castle Restaurant, 1541 Montgomery Street, Telegraph Hill District
• Japanese Tea Garden, 50 Hagiwara Tea Garden Way, Golden Gate Park
• Sausalito-waterfront and hills

Raiders of the Lost Ark
1981, Paramount, Studios
AKA: *Indiana Jones and the Raiders of the Lost Ark*
An American archaeologist and explorer beats the Nazis to a priceless religious artifact.

Director: Steven Spielberg
Screenwriters: George Lucas, Philip Kaufman, Lawrence Kasdan
Production Designer: Norman Reynolds
Art Director: Leslie Dilley
Cinematographer: Douglas Slocombe
Partial Cast: Harrison Ford, Karen Allen, Paul Freeman, Ronald Lacey, John Rhys-Davies,

Alfred Molina, Wolf Kohler, Anthony Higgins, Denholm Elliott

• Golden Gate Bridge-flying west to Pacific Ocean
• San Francisco City Hall, 1 Carlton B. Goodlett Place, Civic Center District-rotunda and steps

The Rainmaker
1997, Constellation Films and Paramount
AKA: *John Grisham's The Rainmaker*
An idealistic young lawyer and his cynical partner take on a powerful law firm representing a corrupt insurance company.

Director: Francis Ford Coppola
Screenwriters: Francis Ford Coppola, Michael Herr
Author: John Grisham (novel)
Production Designer: Howard Cummings
Art Director: Robert Shaw
Cinematographer: John Toll
Partial Cast: Matt Damon, Danny De Vito, Claire Danes, Jon Voight, Dean Stockwell, Virginia Madsen, Mary Kay Place, Teresa Wright, Danny Glover

• Naval Air Station Alameda, Buildings 23 and 24, Webster Street, Alameda

Raising Cain
1992, Universal Studios
A psychologist develops multiple personalities including one who is a murderous twin brother.

Director: Brian De Palma
Screenwriter: Brian De Palma
Production Designer: Doug Kraner
Art Director: Mark Billerman
Cinematographer: Stephen H. Burum
Partial Cast: John Lithgow, Lolita Davidovich, Steven Bauer, Frances Sternhagen, Gregg Henry

• California Palace of the Legion of Honor, Lincoln Park, Outer Richmond District
• Stanford Shopping Center, intersection of El Camino Real and Sand Hill Road, Palo Alto
• Shoup Park, 400 University Avenue, Los Altos
• Old Stanford Children's Hospital, 520 Sand Hill Road, Palo Alto
• Mountain View City Hall, 500 Castro Street, Mountain View
• Best Western Riviera Motel, 15 El Camino Real, Menlo Park

"I told you he had a cash register mind. Rings every time he opens his mouth."

Raw Deal
1948, Reliance and Eagle-Lion
AKA: *Corkscrew Alley*
A convict escapes with the assistance of his girlfriend, and the police chase them across country.

Director: Anthony Mann
Screenwriters: Arnold B. Armstrong, Audrey Ashley, Leopold Atlas, John C. Higgins
Art Director: Edward L. Ilou
Cinematographer: John Alton
Partial Cast: Dennis O'Keefe, Claire Trevor, Marsha Hunt, John Ireland, Raymond Burr

• San Quentin State Prison, San Quentin
• San Francisco-Oakland Bay Bridge

Red Light
1949, United Artists
An industrialist tracks down his brother's murderer.

Director: Roy Del Ruth
Screenwriters: George Callahan, Charles Grayson
Art Director: F. Paul Sylos
Cinematographer: Bert Glennon
Partial Cast: George Raft, Virginia Mayo, Gene Lockhart, Raymond Burr, Harry Morgan, Barton Lane, William Frawley

• Old St. Mary's Church, 660 California Street, Chinatown
• San Francisco-Oakland Bay Bridge
• San Quentin State Prison, San Quentin

Red Tails
2012, 20th Century Fox
A crew of African American pilots, who have been grounded during WWII due to segregation, are called to take flight.

Director: Anthony Hemingway
Screenwriters: John Ridley, Aaron McGruder
Author: John B. Holway *Red Tails, Black Wings: The Men of America's Black Air Force* (book)

Production Designers: Michael Carlin, Nicholas Palmer
Art Directors: Milene Koubkova, Martina Ter-Akopowá
Cinematographer: John B. Aronson
Partial Cast: Cuba Gooding Jr., David Oyelowo, Andre Royo

• Hamilton Field, Novato

Rent
2005, Columbia Pictures
Bohemians struggle with life, love, and AIDS, as well as the impacts they have on America.

Director: Christopher Columbus
Screenwriters: Steve Chbosky, Chris Columbus, Jonathan Larson
Production Designer: Howard Cummings
Art Directors: Steve Carter, Keith P. Cunningham, Nanci Nobett
Cinematographer: Stephen Goldblatt
Partial Cast: Rosario Dawson, Taye Diggs, Wilson Jermaine Heredia, Jesse L. Martin, Idina Menzel, Adam Pascal, Anthony Rapp, Tracie Thoms

• 100 block of 6th Street, South of Market District
• Filoli Estate and Gardens, 86 Cañada Road, Woodside
• Oakland

The Return of Count Yorga
1971, Metro Goldwyn Mayer
A vampire moves into a mansion next to an orphanage to prey on the local community.

Director: Bob Kelljan
Screenwriters: Bob Kelljan, Yvonne Wilder
Cinematographer: Bill Butler
Partial Cast: Robert Quarry, Mariette Hartley, Roger Perry

• Golden Gate Bridge
• Powell-Hyde Street Cable Car, 2500 block of Hyde Street, Russian Hill District
• Friedel Klussmann Memorial Cable Car Turnaround, Aquatic Park, San Francisco Maritime National Historic Park, Golden Gate National Recreation Area
• Fisherman's Wharf District

Revenge of the Stolen Stars
1986, Six Stars Production
The bumbling heir to a remote island plantation searches for special rubies.

Director: Ulli Lommel
Screenwriters: Ben A. Hein, Ulli Lommel
Production Designer: Andrea Leone
Cinematographers: David Sperling, Jürg V. Walther
Partial Cast: Suzanna Love, Barry Hickey, Klaus Kinski

• Golden Gate Bridge
• Alcatraz Island, Golden Gate National Recreation Area
• Painted Ladies, 700 block of Steiner Street, Western Addition District
• Bill Graham Civic Auditorium, 99 Grove Street, Civic Center
• First Chinese Southern Baptist Church, 1255 Hyde Street, Nob Hill District

The Revolt of Mamie Stover
1956, 20th Century Fox
A dance hall girl goes to Honolulu and falls for a rich novelist.

Director: Raoul Walsh
Screenwriter: Sydney Boehm
Author: William Bradford Huie (novel)
Art Director: Mark-Lee Kirk, Lyle R. Wheeler
Cinematographer: Leo Tover
Partial Cast: Jane Russell, Richard Egan, Joan Leslie, Agnes Moorehead,

• Docks, Waterfront

RICHARD EGAN

Known by audiences for his distinctive voice, Egan was born in 1921 in San Francisco where he later went to St. Ignatius Preparatory School, a private Catholic school. In 1942 he enlisted in the U.S. Army and served as a judo, knife, and bayonet instructor, attaining the rank of captain. Back home he attended the University of San Francisco for undergraduate work followed by Stanford University for graduate studies in theater history and drama, where he received his M.A. in 1948. He also studied and then taught at Northwestern University in Evanston, Illinois. His first film role was a bit part in a locally filmed production of *The Story of Molly X* (1949). The Golden Globes presented him with Most Promising Newcomer award in 1954. In 1958 he and Patricia Hardy married; they went on to have five children. Beyond *The Revolt of Mamie*

Revolution

1968, Lopert Pictures Corporation

AKA: *Hippie Revolution*
Documentary about the hippie lifestyle as seen through many different eyes.

Director: Jack O'Connell
Screenwriters: Norman Martin, Jack O'Connell
Cinematographer: Bill Godsey
Partial Cast: Country Joe and the Fish, Louis Gottlieb, Daria Halprin, Kurt Hirschhorn, Today (Louise) Malone, Country Joe McDonald, Barry Melton, Steve Miller, Steve Miller Band, San Francisco Mime Troupe
Local Cast: Newspaper columnist Herb Caen, Reverend Cecil Williams, Chief of Police Thomas Cahill

• Mary B. Connally Playground, Golden Gate Park
• Carousel, Golden Gate Park
• Haight Street, Haight-Ashbury District
• Sharon Meadow, Golden Gate Park
• Hippie Hill, Golden Gate Park
• San Francisco General Hospital, 1001 Potrero Avenue, Mission District
• Golden Gate Bridge
• Drugstore Café, 1398 Haight Street, Haight-Ashbury District
• Mountain Theater, Mt. Tamalpais Park, Golden Gate National Recreation Area
• Morningstar Commune, Occidental
• Buena Vista Park, Haight-Ashbury District
• Ocean Beach, Golden Gate National Recreation Area

Riding High

1950, Paramount

An equine fancier forgoes marriage to money and lives a plainer life with the intent of winning an important derby.

Director: Frank Capra
Screenwriters: Melville Shavelson, Jack Rose
Author: Mark Hellinger (story)
Art Directors: Hans Dreier, Walter H. Tyler

Cinematographers: George Barnes, Ernest Laszlo
Partial Cast: Bing Crosby, Coleen Gray, Charles Bickford, William Demarest, Ward Bond, Percy Kilbride, Margaret Hamilton, Marjorie Lord

• Tanforan Racetrack, El Camino Real, San Bruno
• South San Francisco

in 1929 for Lindsay Howard the property was passed to his father Charles
Howard owner of the famous racehorse Seabiscuit. Crosby loved to bet
on the ponies and was an avid golfer;
he was a member of the nearby Bur-
lington County Club. Bing Crosby died
in 1977 in Spain, just after completing
a round of golf. He recorded more
than 1700 songs during the period of
1926 through 1977.

Kathryn Crosby, born in 1933 in Houston as Olive Kathryn Grandstaff, appeared in *Cell 2455, Death Row*
(1955) and *Storm Center* (1956),
which were filmed in the Bay Area.
She also hosted a local talk show on
KPIX-TV Channel 5 from 1972
through 1975, on which she inter-
viewed various personalities coming
through San Francisco. In 2010, Grant
was seriously injured in an automobile
accident in the Sierra Nevada that
killed her 85-year-old second husband, Maurice William Sullivan, whom
she married in 2000.

The Right Stuff

1983, Warner Brothers

Test pilots are recruited and trained to
be NASA astronauts.

Director: Philip Kaufman
Screenwriter: Philip Kaufman
Author: Tom Wolfe (novel)
Production Designer: Geoffrey Kirkland
Art Directors: W. Stewart Campbell, Richard
Lawrence, Peter R. Romero
Cinematographer: Caleb Deschanel
Partial Cast: Sam Shepard, Scott Glenn, Ed
Harris, Dennis Quaid, Fred Ward, Barbara
Hershey, Kim Stanley, Veronica Cartwright

• San Francisco City Hall, 1 Carlton B. Goodlett
Place, Civic Center District-fourth floor corridor as
Washington power center
• Cow Palace, 2600 Geneva Avenue, Daly City-
as Houston Coliseum
• Four-block stretch of Sansome Street, Financial
District-ticker tape parade
• Hamilton Field, Hamilton Air Force Base,
Novato-as Cape Canaveral, Florida
• Chevron Refinery, Richmond-as Russian
industrial complex
• NASA Ames Research Center, Moffett Field,
Mountain View-as Langley Air Force Base,
Virginia

• Half Moon Bay harbor, Half Moon Bay-capsule
splashdown

PHILIP KAUFMAN

Film director and screenwriter Philip
Kaufman heads the family production
company Walrus and Associates in
San Francisco. He hails from the north
side of Chicago, Illinois, where he was
born October 23, 1936. He graduated
from the University of Chicago and
spent a year at Harvard Law School,
but he returned to the University of
Chicago to begin a Master's degree
program in history. In 1958 he married
Rose Fisher (1939–2009), who col-
laborated with her husband on some
screenplays. His first film was *Goldstein* (1963), which won the Prix de la
Nouvelle Critique at the 1964 Cannes
Film Festival. Kaufman moved his
family to San Francisco in 1977, which
by then included son Peter who now
works with his father. Other movies
filmed in the Bay Area movies using
Kaufman's talents include directing
the remake of *Invasion of the Body
Snatchers* (1978), *Raiders of the Lost
Ark* (1981), where he is credited with
the original basic story line about the
search for the Ark of the Covenant,
the directing of *Twisted* (2004), and
Hemingway and Gellhorn (2012) for
HBO.

Rise of the Planet of the Apes

2011, 20th Century Fox

A man's experiments with genetic
engineering lead to the development
of ape intelligence that begets a
supremacy war.

Director: Rupert Wyatt
Screenwriters: Rick Jaffa, Jamie Moss, Amanda
Silver
Author: Pierre Boulle *La planete des singes*
(novel)
Production Designer: Claude Paré
Art Directors: Dan Hermansen, Helen Jarvis,
Grant Van Der Slagt
Cinematographer: Andrew Lesnie
Partial Cast: James Franco, Freida Pinto, John
Lithgow, Brian Cox, Andy Serkis

• Muir Woods National Monument, Muir Woods Road, Golden Gate National Recreation Area
• Panorama of San Francisco from Twin Peaks
• San Francisco Zoo, 1 Zoo Road, Parkside District
• 700 block of California Street, Nob Hill
• Old Mason Street, Crissy Field, Golden Gate National Recreation Area
• International Terminal, San Francisco International Airport

Road to Alcatraz
1945, Republic Pictures
A man cannot defend himself against accusations that he murdered his business partner, as he has no memory of the event.

Director: Nick Grinde
Screenwriters: Francis K. Allen, Dwight V. Babcock, Jerry Sackheim
Art Director: Lucius Croxton
Cinematographer: Ernest Miller
Partial Cast: Robert Lowery, June Storey, Grant Withers, Clarence Kolb, Charles Gordon

• Alcatraz Island, Golden Gate National Recreation Area

Road to Singapore
1940, Paramount
AKA: *Beach of Dreams*, *Road to Mandalay*
In this first of the *Road to* Series, a rich man trades his orderly life for a life with his adventure-seeking friend. In Singapore they both fall for an island beauty.

Director: Victor Schertzinger
Screenwriters: Frank Butler, Don Hartman
Author: Harry Hervey (book)
Art Directors: Hans Dreier, Robert Odell
Cinematographer: William C. Mellor
Partial Cast: Bing Crosby, Dorothy Lamour, Bob Hope, Charles Coburn, Judith Barrett, Anthony Quinn, Jerry Colonna

• Ferry Building and waterfront piers, The Embarcadero

Roaring City
1951, Lippert Pictures
A gritty gumshoe finds himself among those suspected of committing a string of murders involving boxers and petty gangsters.

Director: William Berke
Screenwriters: Julian Harmon, Victor West

Authors: Herbert Margolis, Louis Morheim (short story)
Art Director: F. Paul Sylos
Cinematographer: Jack Greenhalgh
Partial Cast: Hugh Beaumont

• Panorama of Financial District
• Fisherman's Wharf District
• Ferry Building, Herb Caen Way, Embarcadero District
• Pier 23, The Embarcadero

"If we receive launch authority, your mission is to complete thermal destruction of Alcatraz Island."

The Rock
1996, Buena Vista
Alcatraz Island terrorists threaten to gas San Francisco.

Director: Michael Bay
Screenwriters: David Weisburg, Douglas Cook, Mark Rosner
Production Designer: Michael White
Art Directors: Mark W. Mansbridge, Edward T. McAvoy
Cinematographer: John Schwartzman
Partial Cast: Sean Connery, Nicolas Cage, Ed Harris, John Spencer

• Fairmont Hotel, 950 Mason Street, Nob Hill District
• Pier 45, Fisherman's Wharf District
• Palace of Fine Arts, 3601 Lyon Street, Marina District
• Intersection of Jones Street and Pacific Avenue, Nob Hill District-exploding cable car
• Alcatraz Federal Prison, Alcatraz Island, Golden Gate National Recreation Area
• Golden Gate National Cemetery, 1300 Sneath Lane, San Bruno

Roger and Me
1989, Warner Brothers
AKA: *A Humorous Look at How General Motors Destroyed Flint, Michigan*
General Motors CEO Roger Smith is pursued to confront him about the harm he did to Flint, Michigan with his massive downsizing.

Director Michael Moore
Screenwriter: Michael Moore

Cinematographers: Chris Beaver, John Prusak, Kevin Rafferty, Bruce Schermer
Partial Cast: James Bond, Pat Boone, Anita Bryant, Bob Eubanks, Ronald Reagan, Robert Schuller

• Golden Gate Bridge
• Cable Car
• Chinatown streetscape
• Sweet Cakes, 4073 24th Street, Noe Valley District
• Just Desserts, 248 Church Street, Eureka Valley District
• Ultimate Cookie, 1409 Haight Street, Haight-Ashbury District
• Tart to Tart, 641 Irving Street, Inner Sunset District
• San Francisco-Oakland Bay Bridge

Rollerball

2001, Metro Goldwyn Mayer

The many hills of San Francisco traveled in the x-treme sport of street luging.

Director: John McTiernan
Screenwriters: Larry Ferguson, John Pogue
Author: William Harrison "Roller Ball Murder" (short story)
Production Designers: Norman Garwood, Dennis Bradford
Art Director: Helen Jarvis
Cinematographer: Steve Mason
Partial Cast: Chris Klein, Jean Reno, LL Cool J

• Twin Peaks Boulevard, Twin Peaks District
• Potrero Hill District
• Intersection of California Street and Mason Street, Nob Hill District
• Intersection of Grant Avenue and Sacramento Street, Chinatown District
• Intersection of Sacramento Street and Sansome Street, Financial District
• Adler Hotel, 175 Sixth Street, South of Market District

The Rookie

1990, Warner Brothers

An aging cop teaches his new young partner the ropes.

Director: Clint Eastwood
Screenwriters: Boaz Yakin, Scott Spiegel
Production Designer: Judy Cammer
Art Director: Ed Verreaux
Cinematographer: Jack N. Green
Partial Cast: Clint Eastwood, Charlie Sheen, Raul Julia, Tom Skerritt, Lara Flynn Boyle

• Villa Montalvo, 15400 Montalvo Road, Saratoga
• San Jose International Airport
• State Highway Route 680, San Jose

The Room

2003, Chloe and TPW

Lust and duplicity reign as the central character discovers that his fiancée is bedding with his best friend.

Director: Tommy Wiseau
Screenwriter: Tommy Wiseau
Production Designer: Mercedes Younger
Art Director: Kendra Hollaway
Cinematographer: Todd Barron
Partial Cast: Tommy Wiseau, Juliette Danielle, Carolyn Minnott

• Golden Gate Bridge
• Alcatraz Federal Prison, Alcatraz Island, Golden Gate National Recreation Area
• Palace of Fine Arts, 3601 Lyon Street, Marina District
• Painted Ladies, 700 block of Steiner Street, Western Addition District
• Ferry Building, Herb Caen Way, Embarcadero District
• Union Square, 333 Post Street

Rumor Has It...

2005, Warner Brothers

AKA: *Otherwise Engaged*

A complicated comedy about a woman who wants to know if her real father has anything to do with the story of the movie *The Graduate*.

Director: Rob Reiner
Screenwriter: Ted Griffin
Production Designer: Tom Sanders
Art Director: Thomas P. Wilkins
Cinematographer: Peter Deming
Partial Cast: Jennifer Aniston, Shirley MacLaine, Mark Ruffalo, Kevin Costner

• Sir Francis Drake Hotel, 450 Powell Street, Union Square District-hotel entry
• 600 block of Grant Avenue, Chinatown District

Saidoweizu

2009, 20th Century Fox

AKA: *Sideways*

A story of two old friends on a journey to rediscover their friendship, life, and themselves.

Director: Cellin Gluck
Screenwriters: Alexander Payne, Rex Pickett
Production Designer: Richard Lowe
Cinematographer: Garry Waller
Partial Cast: Fumiyo Kohinata, Katsuhisa Namase, Rinko Kikuchi, Kyôka Suzuki, Morgan Snyder, Jean-Christophe Lebert

- Golden Gate Bridge
- Enoteca Wine Shop, 1348 Lincoln Street, Calistoga
- Domaine Chandon Winery, 1 California Drive, Yountville
- Beringer Vineyards, 200 Main Street, St. Helena
- Darioush Winery, 4240 Silverado Trail, Napa
- Bistro Don Giovanni, 4110 Howard Lane, Napa
- Café Sarifornia, 1413 Lincoln Street, Calistoga
- Golden Haven Hot Springs, 1713 Lake Street, Calistoga
- Intersection of Lincoln Street and Washington Street, Calistoga
- Old Faithful Geyser, 1299 Tubbs Lane, Calistoga
- Silverado Pharmacy, 1348 Lincoln Street, Calistoga
- Newton Vineyard, 2555 Madrone Avenue, St. Helena
- Calistoga Village Inn and Spa, 1880 Lincoln Street, Calistoga-motel
- Frog's Leap Winery, 8815 Conn Creek Road, Rutherford
- Cal Mart, 11491 Lincoln Street, Calistoga-grocery store
- Kirkland Ranch Winery, 1 Kirkland Ranch Road, Napa
- Bar Vino, 1457 Lincoln Street, Calistoga
- Oakville Grocery Company, 7856 St. Helena Highway, Oakville

Salvador
1986, MGM and UA Artists
AKA: *Outpost Salvador*
The adventures of a photo journalist in Central America.

Director: Oliver Stone
Screenwriters: Oliver Stone, Rick Boyle
Production Designer: Bruno Rubeo
Cinematographer: Robert Richardson
Partial Cast: James Woods, James Belushi, Michael Murphy, John Savage

- Intersection of Broadway and Taylor Street, Russian Hill District
- San Francisco-Oakland Bay Bridge
- Embarcadero Freeway, South of Market District

San Franpsycho
2006, Pumpkin Patch Pictures
A serial killer is stalking the city of San Francisco. As the body count rises, two detectives, a reporter and a psychologist-priest relentlessly pursue the madman to end to his carnage.

Directors: Eduardo Quiroz, Jose Quiroz
Screenwriters: Eduardo Quiroz, Jose Quiroz
Cinematographer: Rocky Robinson
Partial Cast: Jose Estevez, Jose Rosete, Todd Bridges, Eleni C. Krinitsos, Victor Zaragoza, Elias Castillo, Chris Angelo

- Treasure Island-strangling scene
- Intersection of Market Street and Front Street, Financial District
- 500 block of Broadway, Telegraph Hill District-night clubs
- Intersection of Columbus Avenue and Broadway, Telegraph Hill District
- BART station
- MacArthur Tunnel, State Highway Route 1, Presidio, Golden Gate National Recreation Area
- Pier 39, Waterfront
- Alcatraz Island, Golden Gate National Recreation Area

San Quentin
1937, Warner Brothers
A former Army officer becomes prison warden and falls for a convict's sister.

Director: Lloyd Bacon
Screenwriters: John Bright, Humphrey Cobb, Peter Milne, Robert Tasker
Art Director: Esdras Hartley
Cinematographer: Sid Hickox
Partial Cast: Pat O'Brien, Humphrey Bogart, Ann Sheridan, Barton MacLane, Joe Sawyer, James Robbins

- San Quentin State Prison, San Quentin-various exterior scenes

SAN QUENTIN PRISON

San Quentin State Prison, also known as the Big House, originated as a private venture on San Quentin Point in 1852 to deal with the new state's teeming lawless immigrants. Now run by the State of California, the state's oldest penile institution houses some 6,000 male inmates and has the state's only gas chamber. A mini-city unto itself situated on 432 acres, the prison has its own TV station, hospital, fire station, police force, and zip code.

San Quentin
1946, RKO Radio Pictures
A convict starts a rehabilitation movement and gets caught up in a prison break scheme.

Director: Gordon Douglas
Screenwriters: Howard J. Green, Lawrence Kimble, Martin Mooney, Arthur A. Ross
Art Director: Lucius O. Croxton, Albert S. D'Agostino
Cinematographer: Frank Redman

Partial Cast: Laurence Tierney, Marian Carr, Barton MacLane, Carol Forman, Tom Keene, Raymond Burr

• San Quentin State Prison, San Quentin
• Alcatraz Island, Golden Gate National Recreation Area
• San Francisco-Oakland Bay Bridge

Sausalito

2000, Long Shong Entertainment Group
AKA: *Love at First Sight*
A single mother who drives a cab falls for an Internet mogul.

Director: Wai-keung Lau
Art Director: Patrick Ludden
Partial Cast: Maggie Cheung, Leon Lai, Scott Leung, Sasie M. Jang, Annie Scott Rogers

• Golden Gate Bridge
• San Francisco-Oakland Bay Bridge
• Financial District-various spots while driving
• 1600 block of Post Street, Japantown District
• Intersection of Market Street and Sutter Street, Financial District-news stand
• 358 10th Street, South of Market District-garage
• Marine Drive, Presidio, Golden Gate National Recreation Area
• 964 Natoma Street, South of Market District-loft
• U.N. Plaza, Civic Center-farmer's market
• Intersection of Bush Street and Montgomery Street-takedown
• Thailand Restaurant, 438 Castro Street, Eureka Valley District
• Marina Boulevard, Marina District-Sausalito sign
• Bridgeway, Sausalito
• Castro Theatre, 429 Castro Street, Eureka Valley District
• Oakland Hills, East Oakland-house
• Hotel Majestic, 1500 Sutter Street, Cathedral Hill District-tryst spot
• Market Street-various spots
• Marina Green, Marina District-promenade
• The Embarcadero
• 300 block of Pine Street, Financial District-flower bouquets

Scaramouche

1952, Metro Goldwyn Mayer
A young man disguises himself as an actor to avenge a friend's death by a wicked marquis.

Director: George Sidney
Screenwriters: Ronald Millar, George Froeschel
Author: Rafael Sabatini (novel)
Art Directors: Cedric Gibbons, Hans Peters
Cinematographer: Charles Rosher
Partial Cast: Stewart Granger, Eleanor Parker, Janet Leigh, Mel Ferrer, Nina Foch, Robert Coote, John Litel

• Rustic Bridge, Stow Lake, Golden Gate Park
• Music Concourse and Spreckels Temple of Music, Golden Gate Park
• Huntington Falls, Strawberry Hill Island, Golden Gate Park

Scream

1996, Dimension Films
An offbeat group of friends unlock a town's deadly secrets after a series of mysterious deaths.
AKA: *Scary Movie*

Director: Wes Craven
Screenwriter: Kevin Williamson
Production Designer: Bruce Alan Miller
Art Director: David Lubin
Cinematographer: Mark Irwin
Partial Cast: Drew Barrymore, Courtney Cox, David Arquette, Neve Campbell, Matthew Lillard, Rose McGowan, Skeet Ulrich, Henry Winkler

• 8171 Sonoma Mountain Road, Glen Ellen-as Casey's house
• Bradley Video, Town and Country Market, 3080 Marlow Road, Santa Rosa
• Healdsburg Plaza, Healdsburg
• Healdsburg Police Station, Healdsburg-as Woodsboro Police Station
• 1820 Calistoga Road, Santa Rosa-as Sidney's house
• Town and Country Market, 1465 Town and Country Drive, Santa Rosa
• 842 McDonald Avenue, Santa Rosa-as Deputy Dewey's and Tatem's house
• Sonoma Community Center, 276 East Napa Street, Sonoma-as high school
• 3871 Tomales-Petaluma Road, Tomales-final gore scenes

SCARY MOVIE

The good news was that Wes Craven's Los Angeles-based film company, Frightmare, Inc., was willing to pay the Santa Rosa school District $30,000 to use the Santa Rosa High School on Mendocino Street as a setting for this parody of a horror film; students would be paid as extras in the film. The bad news was that even though the deal had been struck, the school District's board ultimately pulled out of the agreement when board members learned more about the film's content. The board got cold feet after learning details about what Craven intended to show. The major points of concern were images of disemboweled students and a principal with a very foul mouth. (If the students had any say about this, it would have been a shoe in, but...) The classic building, also used in Francis Ford Coppola's nostalgic *Peggy Sue Got Married* (1986), is memorable for its 1925 Gothic Revival design of brick and cast concrete decoration by architect William H. Weeks. Its setting among green lawns and mature trees exemplifies the look of a special place. But, Craven had the last word when he included the following in the movie's credits: "No thanks whatsoever to the Santa Rosa City School District Governing Board."

The Second Coming of Suzanne
1973, American Video
AKA: *Suzanne*
A director is finally able to secure funds to make his longtime dream portraying Christ as a woman.

Director: Michael Barry
Screenwriter: Michael Barry
Art Director: Elayne Barbara Ceder
Cinematographer: Isidore Mankosky
Partial Cast: Sondra Locke, Richard Dreyfuss, Gene Barry

• Golden Gate Bridge and toll booths
• The Dock Restaurant, 25 Main Street, Tiburon
• Strybing Arboretum, 1199 Ninth Avenue, Golden Gate Park-pond
• Pulgas Water Temple, La Cañada Road, Woodside
• Waterfront pier interior, The Embarcadero
• Tiburon harbor, Tiburon
• V. C. Morris Gift Shop, 140 Maiden Lane, Union Square District
• Pioneer Log Cabin, 2 Stow Lake Drive, Golden Gate Park
• Jack Tar Hotel, 1101 Van Ness Avenue, Cathedral Hill District
• Alcoa Building, One Maritime Plaza, 300 Clay Street, Golden Gateway-building podium
• Tree and rock grouping in field, Sir Francis Drake Boulevard, Woodacre
• Ridgecrest Boulevard, Mt. Tamalpais, Golden Gate National Recreation Area
• Intersection of Sather Road and Bancroft Way, University of California Campus, Berkeley
• Embarcadero One Building, Embarcadero Center-circular staircase
• Mark Hopkins Hotel, 999 California Street, Nob Hill District
• Benjamin Lyford House, 376 Greenwood Beach Road, Tiburon

• Bank of America Building, 555 California Street, Financial District-interior office
• San Francisco City Hall, 1 Carlton B. Goodlett Place, Civic Center District-interior rotunda

Secret Service of the Air
1939, Warner Brothers
A Pacific Clipper pilot is recruited into the secret service and goes undercover to crack a ruthless gang that smuggles illegal aliens.

Director: Noel M. Smith
Screenwriters: Raymond L. Schrock, W. H. Moran
Art Director: Ted Smith
Cinematographers: Ted D. McCord, Arthur Edeson
Partial Cast: Ronald Reagan, John Litel, Ila Rhodes

• Golden Gate Bridge
• Ferry Building, Herb Caen Way, Embarcadero District
• San Francisco-Oakland Bay Bridge
• San Quentin State Prison, San Quentin-as Alcatraz Federal Prison

Serendipity
2001, Miramax
A man and a woman let fate determine their relationship.

Director: Peter Chelsom
Screenwriter: Marc Klein
Production Designer: Caroline Hanania
Art Director: Tracey Gallacher
Cinematographer: John de Borman
Partial Cast: Amita Balla, Kate Beckinsale, John Corbett, John Cusack

• Transamerica Pyramid, 600 Montgomery Street, Financial District
• Ferry Building, Herb Caen Way, Embarcadero District
• San Francisco-Oakland Bay Bridge

"These are exciting times aren't they? Gas is over a dollar a gallon and it's okay to be an asshole."

Serial
1980, Paramount

A well-healed suburban community goes through various cults and fashions.

Director: Bill Persky
Screenwriters: Rich Eustis, Michael Elias
Author: Cyra McFadden *The Serial: A Year in the Life of Marin* (novel)
Art Director: William Sandell
Cinematographer: Rexford L. Metz
Partial Cast: Martin Mull, Tuesday Weld, Sally Kellerman, Bill Macy, Peter Bonerez, Christopher Lee, Tom Smothers

• Houseboats, Sausalito
• Plaza Vina del Mar, Bridgeway, Sausalito
• *Harbor Emperor* ferry between Sausalito and San Francisco
• Intersection of California Street and Kearny Street-cable car stop
• One Market Plaza, South of Market District-atrium and tower interiors
• Mill Valley-downtown
• Fort Baker, Marin Headlands, Golden Gate National Recreation Area
• Army and Navy YMCA, 166 The Embarcadero
• Embarcadero Freeway, South of Market District
• Golden Gate Bridge

CYRA MCFADDEN

Cyra McFadden was born in 1939 to Pat (Montgomery), a vaudeville dancer, and Cy Taillon, known as the "dean of rodeo announcers" in Great Falls, Montana. The original story behind *Serial* was first published in the Marin County alternative newspaper the *Pacific Sun*. Fifty-two chapters lampooned the over-the-top lifestyles of Marin. At the time, McFadden lived in a modest tract house in Mill Valley with husband John—sans hot tub. She followed the newspaper stories with the novel version titled *The Serial: A Year in the Life of Marin*, published by Knopf in 1977 to popular acclaim. The book made the hot tubs, drugs, and wife-swapping of Marin infamous. She went on to join the *San Francisco Examiner* newspaper from 1985 through 1991 as a features writer and bi-weekly columnist. The Noe Valley resident has written for the *New York Times*, *Newsweek*, and *The Nation*. She wrote the *Serial* movie script's first draft—and was then fired. In 1979 she penned two scripts for the TV series *13 Queens Boulevard* and in 1986 she published *Rain or Shine*.

A Family Memoir, for which she received a Pulitzer Prize nomination.

TOM SMOTHERS

Tom, half of the perennial favorite Smothers Brothers comedy and music team, established Sonoma County's Remick (his grandfather's surname) Ridge Vineyards of Kenwood in 1977. There, 50 acres of Cabernet Sauvignon grapes ferment into award-winning wine. Born on Governor's Island in New York harbor in 1937, Smothers attended San Jose State University. His first professional appearance was in 1959 at the subterranean Purple Onion nightclub on Columbus Avenue in San Francisco's Jackson Square District. The guitar-playing Tom and brother Dick are best known for *The Smothers Brothers Comedy Hour*, which ran on CBS TV from 1967 through 1969. Known for their political satire and keen attention to politics, the two continue to tour together. Tom and wife Marcy Carriker have a son and daughter.

The Sessions
2012, Fox Searchlight
AKA: *The Surrogate*
A man in an iron lung who wishes to lose his virginity contacts a professional sex surrogate.

Director: Ben Lewin
Screenwriter: Ben Lewin
Author: Mark O'Brien "On Seeing a Sex Surrogate" (essay)
Production Designer: John Mott
Cinematographer: Geoffrey Simpson
Partial Cast: John Hawkes, Helen Hunt, William H. Macy

• California Street Cable Car at intersection of Stockton Street, Nob Hill District
• Sather Tower, University of California Campus, Berkeley
• Golden Gate Bridge

Seung sing gusi
1991, Alan and Eric Films Ltd.

Two childhood friends are reunited to find that they both want the affection of the same woman.

Director: Peter Chan
Screenwriters: Peter Chan, Chi-Ngai Lee, Barry Wong
Production Designer: Man-Wah Luk
Cinematographer: Jingle Ma
Partial Cast: Maggie Cheung, Michael Dingo, Paul Fonoroff

• Aerial flyover from San Francisco-Oakland Bay Bridge along Market Street to Civic Center
• Transbay Terminal, 425 Mission Street, South of Market District
• Market Street
• Haight Street, Haight-Ashbury District
• Westin St. Francis Hotel, 335 Powell Street, Union Square District
• St. Luke's Hospital, 3555 Cesar Chavez Street, Mission District
• Valhalla Restaurant, 201 Bridgeway, Sausalito
• Aquatic Park, San Francisco National Maritime Historical Park, Waterfront
• Ocean Beach, Golden Gate National Recreation Area
• Musee Mecanique, Cliff House, 1090 Point Lobos Avenue, Golden Gate National Recreation Area
• Pier 39, Waterfront
• Moore Road Pier, Fort Baker, Golden Gate National Recreation Area
• Alamo Square, Western Addition District

Seven Days Ashore
1944, RKO Pictures
A playboy on leave from the Merchant Marine asks two shipmates to help him by dating two surplus girlfriends.

Director: John H. Auer
Screenwriters: Edward Verdier, Irving Phillips, Lawrence Kimble
Author: Jacques Deval (story)
Art Directors: Albert S. D'Agostino, Lucius O. Croxton
Cinematographer: Russell Metty
Partial Cast: Wally Brown, Alan Carney, Marcy McGuire

• San Francisco skyline from San Francisco Bay

Seven Girlfriends
1999, Castle Hill Productions
A young man asks his former girlfriends what went wrong with the relationships.

Director: Paul Lazarus
Screenwriters: Paul Lazarus, Stephen Gregg
Production Designer: William Barclay
Art Director: Denise Domét
Cinematographer: Don E. FauntLeRoy

Partial Cast: Laura Leighton, Timothy Daly, Olivia d'Abo

• Golden Gate Bridge
• 1151-1153 Montgomery Street, Telegraph Hill District
• Intersection of Green Street and Montgomery Street, Telegraph Hill District

Seven Miles from Alcatraz
1942, RKO Radio Pictures
After Pearl Harbor, convicts at Alcatraz Federal Prison live in fear of bomb attacks, driving two men to a desperate escape attempt.

Director: Edward Dmytryk
Screenwriter: Joseph Krumgold
Author: John D. Klorer (story)
Art Directors: Albert S. D'Agostino, Field M. Gray
Cinematographer: Robert De Grasse
Partial Cast: James Craig, Bonita Granville, Frank Jenks

• Alcatraz Federal Prison, Alcatraz Island, Golden Gate National Recreation Area

Shadow of a Woman
1946, First National Pictures and Warner Brothers
A woman suspects her new husband of trying to murder his son by a former marriage.

Director: Joseph Santley
Screenwriters: Whitman Chambers, C. Graham Baker
Author: Virginia Perdue He Fell Down Dead (book)
Art Director: Hugh Reticker
Cinematographer: Bert Glennon
Partial Cast: Andrea King, Helmut Dantine

• Mark Hopkins Hotel, 999 California Street, Nob Hill District

"I want to send a telegram to Santa Rosa, California."
"That's right Santa Rosa, Santa Rosa, California."

Shadow of a Doubt
1943, Universal

A murderer hides out in plain sight with his sister's family.

Director: Alfred Hitchcock
Screenwriters: Gordon McDonell, Thornton Wilder, Sally Benson, Alma Reville
Art Director: John B. Goodman
Cinematographer: Joseph A. Valentine
Partial Cast: Joseph Cotten, Teresa Wright, Henry Travers, Patricia Collinge, Hume Croyn, Edna May Wonacott

• Dr. Clifford Carlson Residence, 904 McDonald Avenue, Santa Rosa-as Newton residence
• Santa Rosa Northwest Pacific Depot, 9 Fourth Street, Railroad Square, Santa Rosa
• Carnegie Library, intersection of Fourth Street and E Street, Santa Rosa
• Carnegie Library, 20 Fourth Street, Petaluma-library interior scenes
• American Trust Bank, Courthouse Square, at 4th Street and Mendocino Avenue, Santa Rosa
• 'Til Two Bar, 3rd Street at Santa Rosa Avenue, Santa Rosa
• Western Union Telegraph Office, 311 Mendocino Avenue, Santa Rosa
• Methodist Episcopal Church, 904 Mendocino Avenue, Santa Rosa
• Sonoma County Courthouse, Courthouse Square, Santa Rosa

Shadow of the Thin Man
1941, Metro Goldwyn Mayer
A private eye and his wife investigate murder and racketeering at a local racetrack.

Director: Maj. W. S. Van Dyke II
Screenwriters: Dashiell Hammett, Harry Kurnitz, Irving Brecher
Art Director: Cedric Gibbons
Cinematographer: William H. Daniels
Partial Cast: William Powell, Myrna Loy, Barry Nelson, Donna Reed, Sam Levene, Louise Beavers

• San Francisco-Oakland Bay Bridge
• Golden Gate Fields, 1100 Eastshore Highway, Berkeley

Shakedown
1950, Universal International Pictures
AKA: *The Magnetic Heel*
A ruthless press photographer becomes a blackmailer.

Director: Joe Pevney
Screenwriters: Nat Dallinger, Martin Goldsmith, Alfred Lewis Levitt, Don Martin

Art Directors: Robert Clatworthy, Bernard Hurzbrun
Cinematographer: Irving Glassberg
Partial Cast: Howard Duff, Brian Donlevy, Peggy Dow, Lawrence Tierney

• San Francisco-Oakland Bay Bridge
• 1225-1227 Clay Street, Nob Hill District

Shattered
1991, Metro Goldwyn Mayer
A car crash victim with amnesia hires a private eye to discover his past.

Director: Wolfgang Peterson
Screenwriters: Richard Neely, Wolfgang Peterson
Production Designer: Gregg Fonseca
Art Director: Bruce Alan Miller
Cinematographer: László Kovács
Partial Cast: Tom Berenger, Bob Hoskins, Theodore Bikel

• Transamerica Pyramid, 600 Montgomery Street, Financial District
• Marin County

Shoot the Moon
1981, Metro Goldwyn Mayer
A family is affected when well-healed parents separate.

Director: Alan Parker
Screenwriter: Bo Goldman
Production Designer: Geoffrey Kirkland
Art Director: Stu Campbell
Cinematographer: Michael Seresin
Partial Cast: Albert Finney, Diane Keaton, Karen Allen, Peter Weller, Dana Hill, Leora Dana

• 11540 Pt. Reyes-Petaluma Road, Nicasio-farmhouse
• Waterfront from San Francisco Bay with Ferry Building, The Embarcadero
• San Francisco-Oakland Bay Bridge
• Hyde-Powell Cable Car, Union Square District
• Fairmont Hotel, 950 Mason Street, Nob Hill District-exterior and Venetian Room
• Pine Cone Diner, 60 Fourth Street, Pt. Reyes Station
• West Marin Elementary School, 11550 Shoreline Highway, State Highway Route 1, Pt. Reyes Station
• Stinson Beach, Golden Gate National Recreation Area
• Wolf House ruins, Jack London State Park, Glen Ellen
• Nicasio Reservoir, Nicasio
• Carl's Jr., 3640 Industrial Drive, Santa Rosa

Shoot to Kill
1988, Buena Vista
AKA: *Deadly Pursuit*

An FBI agent and a guide track down a killer who is hiding in the mountains.

Director: Roger Spottiswoode
Screenwriters: Harv Zimmel, Michael Burton, Daniel Petrie Jr.
Production Designer: Richard Sylbert
Art Director: John Willett
Cinematographer: Michael Chapman
Partial Cast: Sidney Poitier, Kirstie Alley, Tom Berenger

• Powell-Hyde Street Cable Car
• 101 California Street, Financial District
• Ferry Building, Herb Caen Way, Embarcadero District
• San Francisco-Oakland Bay Bridge

The Show-Off
1946, Metro Goldwyn Mayer
A clerk with big thoughts woos a girl to marry him but his show-off manners get them in financial trouble.

Director: Harry Beaumont
Screenwriters: George Kelly, George Wells
Author: George Wells (play)
Art Directors: E. Preston Ames, Cedric Gibbons
Cinematographer: Robert H. Planck
Partial Cast: Red Skelton, Marilyn Maxwell, Marjorie Main

• First block of Turk Street through to Market Street continuing east to about Montgomery Street-site of car accident

Sibling Rivalry
1990, Columbia
A woman advises her unhappily married sister to have an affair—with complicated results.

Director: Carl Reiner
Screenwriter: Martha Goldhirsh
Production Designer: Jeannine C. Oppewall
Cinematographer: Reynaldo Villalobos
Partial Cast: Kirstie Alley, Scott Bakula, Sam Elliott, Carrie Fisher, Bill Pullman, Jami Gertz

• Marin County

Sid and Nancy
1986, New Line Cinema and Samuel Goldwyn Company
Gritty biopic about Sid Vicious of the British punk rock group the Sex Pistols and his junkie girlfriend.

Director: Alex Cox
Screenwriters: Alex Cox, Abbe Wool

Production Designers: Linda Burbank, J. Rae Fox, Andrew McAlpine
Art Director: J. Rae Fox
Cinematographer: Roger Deakins
Partial Cast: Gary Oldman, Chloe Webb, David Hayman, Debby Bishop, Andrew Schofield, Courtney Love

• Intersection of Buena Vista East and Duboce Street, Buena Vista District
• Dumbarton Bridge, San Francisco Bay

COURTNEY LOVE

Courtney Love was born in San Francisco on July 9, 1964 as Courtney Michelle Harrison. Her parents are Linda Carroll, a therapist, and Hank Harrison, a publisher, who was at one point a road manager for the Grateful Dead. They divorced when she was five and she lived with her mother in an Oregon commune. Love had a troubled childhood spending time in a reform school for shoplifting. She became a stripper at age 16, and later made a few attempts at college but ended up spending time traveling the globe. Her first foray into music was with the punk trio Sugar Baby Doll and later with Babes in Toyland in 1987. Her appearance in *Sid and Nancy* was her film debut. She founded the alternative rock band Hole in 1989, the same year she married James Moreland, but the marriage was brief. She and Nirvana grunge band's Kurt Cobain wed in 1992, and later that year the couple welcomed daughter Frances Bean into the family. Just two years later, Cobain committed suicide. Courtney Love's break out role was as Althea Flynt in *The People vs. Larry Flynt* (1996). Various dips in her career and life followed with drug-related arrest and probation violations. Her latest video work was a documentary *Hit So Hard* (2011).

Signal Seven
1983, Lorimar
AKA: *Signal 7*
Two best friends are down-on-their-luck taxi drivers who are also wannabe actors.

Director: Rob Nilsson
Screenwriter: Rob Nilsson
Art Directors: Hildy Burns, Steve Burns
Cinematographers: Geoffrey Schaaf, Tomas Tucker
Partial Cast: Bill Ackridge, Don Bejema, Dan Leegant, John Tidwell, Herb Mills

• 855 Geary Street, Tenderloin District-as DeSoto Cab Company
• Ferry Building, Herb Caen Way, The Embarcadero
• Clay Movie Theatre, 2261 Fillmore Street, Pacific Heights District
• San Francisco International Airport
• Robert C. Levy Tunnel, Broadway, Russian Hill District

Sincerely Yours
1955, Warner Brothers
A popular pianist becomes deaf, dashing his dream to play at Carnegie Hall.

Director: Gordon Douglas
Screenwriter: Irving Wallace
Author: Jules Eckert Goodman *The Silver Voice* (play)
Art Director: Edward Carrere
Cinematographer: William H. Clothier
Partial Cast: Liberace, Joanne Dru, Dorothy Malone

• Golden Gate Bridge
• Mark Hopkins Hotel, 999 California Street, Nob Hill District

Sister Act
1992, Buena Vista and Touchstone
A singer on the run from the Mafia hides out in a convent and transforms its choir.

Director: Emile Ardolino
Screenwriter: Joseph Howard
Production Designer: Jackson De Govia
Art Director: Eve Cauley
Cinematographer: Adam Greenberg
Partial Cast: Whoopi Goldberg, Maggie Smith, Harvey Keitel, Mary Wickes, Kathy Najimy, Wendy Makkena

• St. Paul's Catholic Church, 1660 Church Street, Noe Valley District

SAINT PAUL'S CATHOLIC CHURCH

Evoking a several-millennia-old European design, the design of St. Paul's Catholic Church is in the late Victorian Gothic Revival Style by architect

brothers Frank T. Shea and William D. Shea. The edifice was dedicated on May 29, 1911 by Archbishop Patrick Riordan after 14 years of construction. The exterior features a pair of steeples, a large rose window, and a triple Gothic arch entry; its exterior is clad in heavily rusticated stone. The church reopened in December of 2000 after a year-long seismic retrofit project.

Sister Act 2: Back in the Habit
1993, Buena Vista and Touchstone
Delores and her nun friends help save a school from closing.

Director: Bill Duke
Screenwriters: Joseph Howard, James Orr, Jim Cruickshank, Judi Ann Mason
Production Designer: John DeCuir Jr.
Art Director: Louis M. Mann
Cinematographer: Oliver Wood
Partial Cast: Whoopi Goldberg, Maggie Smith, Kathy Najimy, Mary Wickes, Barnard Hughes, Wendy Makkena, James Coburn

• Aerial panorama of waterfront with Ferry Building, The Embarcadero
• San Francisco-Oakland Bay Bridge
• 750 Eddy Street, Tenderloin District-as St. Francis School
• Willie "Woo Woo" Wong Playground, Sacramento Street at Waverly Place, Chinatown District
• Saints Peter and Paul Church, 666 Filbert Street, North Beach District

The Sisters
1938, Warner Brothers
The marriages of a trio of sisters who hail from a small Montana town.

Director: Anatole Litvak
Screenwriters: Milton Krims, Julius J. Epstein
Author: Myron Brinig (novel)
Art Director: Carl Jules Weyl
Cinematographer: Tony Gaudino
Partial Cast: Errol Flynn, Bette Davis, Anita Louise, Alan Hale, Lee Patrick

• Ferry Building, Herb Caen Way, The Embarcadero
• Market Street

'68
1988, Entertainment and New World Pictures
A year in the life of a family focusing on a father and his two sons in 1968.

Director: Steven Kovacs
Art Director: Joshua Koral
Cinematographer: Daniel Lacambre
Partial Cast: Shony Alex Braun, Elizabeth De Charaym, Mike Doukas, Anna Doukasz, Neil Young

• Top-O'-the-Hill Market, 1096 Union Street, Russian Hill District
• San Francisco-Oakland Bay Bridge
• California Palace of the Legion of Honor, Lincoln Park, Outer Richmond District
• SS *Jeremiah O'Brien*-ship
• Aquatic Park, San Francisco Maritime National Historic Park, Golden Gate National Recreation Area-fishing pier
• University of California Campus, Berkeley

Skidoo
1968, Paramount
Active and reformed gangsters get involved with hippies and preach universal love.

Director: Otto Preminger
Screenwriter: Doran William Cannon
Art Director: Robert Emmet Smith
Cinematographer: Leon Shamroy
Partial Cast: Frankie Avalon, Carol Channing, Jackie Gleason, Frank Gorshin, Groucho Marx, Burgess Meredith, Peter Lawford, Michael Constantine, George Raft, Caesar Romero

• Alcatraz Federal Prison, Alcatraz Island, Golden Gate National Recreation Area
• 947 Green Street, Russian Hill District

CAROL CHANNING

Indomitable, wide-eyed, animated, and with husky-voice that can belt out a song are apt descriptions of the bubbly comedienne, singer, and actress Carol Channing. Although born in 1921 in Seattle to parents George, a newspaper journalist, and executive secretary Adelaide Channing, Channing spent most of her childhood growing up in several districts of San Francisco. The family initially lived in the Richmond District followed by Miraloma Park, West Portal and finally (when Carol was a teenager) at two different Washington Street addresses on Nob Hill. An only child, and the daughter of a Christian Science lecturer father, Carol attended Commodore Sloat Grammar School, Aptos Junior High, and spent her senior high years at Lowell High School, graduating in 1938. She credited her Commodore Sloat for originating her passion for acting, when she was nominated to run for secretary of the class. During the campaign she imitated her teachers to the delight of classmates, and was elected to the position. (The auditorium at the original Lowell school building, now called John Adams Community College, is named in her honor.) She studied ballet with the San Francisco Opera Ballet School under the master and choreographer Adolph Bolm. At the age of 12, she was featured in a production of *Aida*. Her mother was influential by taking her to the California Palace of the Legion of Honor museum, and she often went to the Curran and Geary Theaters to see stage shows. Later she spent two years at Bennington College in Vermont before trying out in New York as an actress. She returned to San Francisco and worked at I. Magnin's department store for a while. In 1962 comedian George Burns selected Channing to be his sidekick after the death of his wife Gracie Allen. Her credits include an Oscar nominee, an Emmy Award, a Tony Award, and the prestigious Tony Lifetime Achievement Award. Curiously she was branded an enemy of the Senate Watergate Commission in 1973 (along with scores of others). She appeared on San Francisco stages several times starting in 1958 with an act at the Fairmont Hotel, 1959 in *Show Business*, 1965 *Hello Dolly*, and 1973 in *Lorelei*, both of the later productions were at the Curran Theater where she had seen many performances as a young girl.

Slaughterhouse Rock
1988, Sony Video

A man visits Alcatraz Prison after having dreams about all the people who died there.

Director: Dimitri Logothetis
Screenwriters: Nora Goodman, Ted Landon, Sandra Willard
Author: Dimitri Logothetis (story)
Production Designer: Peter Paul Raubertas
Cinematographer: Nicholas Josef von Sternberg
Partial Cast: Toni Basil, Nicholas Celozzi, Tom Reilly, Donna Denton, Hope Marie Carlton

• Alcatraz Federal Prison, Alcatraz Island, Golden Gate National Recreation Area

The Sleepy Time Gal
2001, Sundance Channel Home Entertainment
A woman who has terminal cancer spends her remaining time making up for missed opportunities.

Director: Christopher Münch
Screenwriters: Alice Elliott Dark, Christopher Munch
Art Directors: Jody Asnes, Jesse Epstein, Melissa Frankel, Bryan Hodge
Cinematographers: Marco Fargnoli, Rob Sweeney
Partial Cast: Jacqueline Bisset, Martha Plimpton, Seymour Cassel, Nick Stahl, Amy Madigan, Peggy Gormley

• 1186-1190 Fulton Street, Western Addition District
• Intersection of Hayes Street and Pierce Street, Western Addition District
• Oakland International Airport, 1 Airport Drive, Oakland
• San Francisco-Oakland Bay Bridge
• Point Bonita Lighthouse, Marin Headlands, Golden Gate National Recreation Area
• Battery Wallace, Marin Headlands, Golden Gate National Recreation Area
• Conzelman Road, Marin Headlands, Golden Gate National Recreation Area
• Golden Gate Bridge
• Huntington Falls, Golden Gate Park
• Battery Mendel, Marin Headlands, Golden Gate National Recreation Area
• Rustic Bridge, Stow Lake, Golden Gate Park

Slither
1972, Metro Goldwyn Mayer
An ex-con, some gangsters, and a few mobile homes are involved in a chase across California for hidden loot.

Director: Howard Zieff
Screenwriter: W. D. Richter
Cinematographer: László Kovács

Partial Cast: James Caan, Peter Boyle, Sally Kellerman, Louise Lasser

• U.S. Highway Route 101, Cloverdale
• Santa Rosa

Slow Moves
1983, Jon Jost Productions
Two ugly-ducklings enter an awkward courtship, live together with the usual problems of money and work, and take flight to an illusory freedom on the road.

Director: Jon Jost
Screenwriter: Jon Jost
Cinematographer: Jon Jost
Partial Cast: Marshall Gaddis, Roxanne Rogers, Bebe Bright

• Golden Gate Bridge
• Sutro Baths ruins, 1000 Pt. Lobos Avenue, Golden Gate National Recreation Area
• Camera Obscura, Cliff House, Golden Gate National Recreation Area
• Mission Rock
• Bank of America, 555 California Street, Financial District
• Walnut Grove

Smashing the Money Ring
1939, Warner Brothers and First National Pictures
A U.S. Secret Service agent infiltrates and nabs a counterfeiter.

Director: Terry O. Morse
Screenwriters: Anthony Coldeway, Raymond L. Schrock, Jonathan Finn
Art Director: Charles Novi
Cinematographer: James Van Trees, L. William O'Connell
Partial Cast: Ronald Reagan, Margot Stevenson, Eddie Foy Jr.

• San Quentin State Prison, San Quentin-as The Big House

Smile
1975, United Artists
A small California town hosts the Young American Miss beauty pageant.

Director: Michael Ritchie
Screenwriter: Jerry Belson
Cinematographer: Conrad L. Hall
Partial Cast: Bruce Dern, Barbara Feldon, Michael Kidd, Geoffrey Lewis, Nicholas Pryor

• Santa Rosa Veterans Memorial Auditorium, 1351 Maple Avenue, Santa Rosa
• Federal Highway Route 101, Redwood Highway, Santa Rosa
• Coddingtown Mall, Cleveland Avenue, Santa Rosa
• Sonoma County Airport, Airport Boulevard, Santa Rosa
• Sonoma Community Center, 276 East Napa Street, Sonoma
• United Airlines Terminal, Oakland International Airport, 1 Airport Drive, Oakland

A Smile Like Yours
1997, Paramount Pictures
A couple attempt to have a child.

Director: Keith Samples
Screenwriters: Kevin Meyer, Keith Samples
Production Designer: Garreth Stover
Art Director: Chris Cornwell
Cinematographer: Richard Bowen
Partial Cast: Greg Kinnear, Lauren Holly, Joan Cusack, Jill Hennessy, Jay Thomas, Christopher McDonald, Donald Moffat, France Nuyen, Shirley MacLaine

• Hotel Monaco, 501 Geary Boulevard, Union Square District-Grand Café
• Grace Cathedral, 1100 California Street, Nob Hill District
• California Street Cable car, Financial District
• 3-Com Park, Candlestick Point, Bayview District
• Park Hyatt Hotel, 333 Battery Street, Financial District
• TWA international gates, San Francisco International Airport
• Grove Café, 2250 Chestnut Street, Marina District
• Tadich Grill Building, 242 California Street, Financial District-as aromatherapy shop
• 3600 Washington Street, Presidio Heights District-mother's house
• San Francisco-Oakland Bay Bridge
• Saks Fifth Avenue, 384 Post Street, Union Square District
• San Francisco Towers, 1661 Pine Street, Pacific Heights District-construction site
• Hills Brothers Plaza, 2 Harrison Street, The Embarcadero-clinic
• Golden Gate Bridge
• Piers 30-32, The Embarcadero
• Naval Air Station Alameda, Alameda Island
• Justin Herman Plaza, The Embarcadero

Smooth Talk
1985, Nepenthe
Story of a teenage girl and her experiments with sexuality.

Director: Joyce Chopra
Screenwriter: Tom Cole
Author: Joyce Carol Oates "Where Are You Going, Where Have You Been?" (story)
Production Designer: David Wasco

Cinematographer: James Glennon
Partial Cast: Treat Williams, Laura Dern, Mary Kay Place

• China Camp State Park, North San Pedro Road, San Rafael-beach
• North San Pedro Road, San Rafael-road
• Richmond-San Rafael Bridge
• Frank's 24-Hour Mini Mart, State Highway Route 116, Gravenstein Highway, Cotati-drive-in diner
• 2150 Pleasant Hill Road, Sebastopol-family ranch
• Coddingtown Mall, Cleveland Ave., Santa Rosa
• Santa Rosa Plaza, Santa Rosa

Sneakers
1992, Universal Pictures
Recovery of an electronic device from a criminal mastermind involves a group of oddball experts.

Director: Phil Alden Robinson
Screenwriters: Phil Alden Robinson, Lawrence Lasker
Production Designer: Patrizia von Brandenstein
Art Director: Dianne Wager
Cinematographer: John Lindley
Partial Cast: Robert Redford, Dan Aykroyd, Ben Kingsley, Mary McDonnell, River Phoenix, Sidney Poitier, David Strathairn, James Earl Jones, Stephen Tobolowsky, Timothy Busfield

• Union Bank of California, 400 California Street, Financial District
• Hills Brothers Plaza, 2 Harrison Street, The Embarcadero
• Robert C. Levy Tunnel, Broadway, Russian Hill District
• Fox Theater, 1807 Telegraph Avenue, Oakland
• Villa Montalvo, 15400 Montalvo Road, Saratoga

The Sniper
1952, Columbia
A psychopath kills a succession of women with a high-powered rifle.

Director: Edward Dmytryk
Screenwriter: Harry Brown
Authors: Edna Anhalt, Edward Anhalt (story)
Production Designer: Rudolph Sternad
Art Director: Walter Holscher
Cinematographer: Burnett Guffey
Partial Cast: Arthur Franz, Aldolphe Menjou, Richard Kiley, Marie Windsor

• 36-52 Calhoun Terrace, Telegraph Hill District
• Spreckels Mansion, 2080 Washington Street, Pacific Heights District
• 460 Washington Street, Financial District
• Civic Center
• John McLaren Park, Portola District
• The Field of San Francisco Bar, 524 Union Street, North Beach District-as Paper Doll Bar

• Playland-at-the-Beach, 4800 Cabrillo Street, Outer Richmond District

So I Married an Axe Murderer
1993, TriStar Pictures
A commitment-wary poet fears his new girlfriend is a murderer.

Director: Thomas Schlamme
Screenwriter: Robbie Fox
Production Designer: John Graysmark
Art Director: Michael Rizzo
Cinematographer: Julio Macat
Partial Cast: Mike Myers, Nancy Travis, Anthony LaPagila, Amanda Plummer, Brenda Fricker, Matt Doherty, Charles Grodin, Phil Hartman

• San Francisco-Oakland Bay Bridge
• Ferry Building, Herb Caen Way, The Embarcadero
• Palace of Fine Arts, 3601 Lyon Street, Marina District
• Golden Gate Bridge
• Alcatraz Federal Prison, Alcatraz Island, Golden Gate National Recreation Area
• Fog City Diner, 1300 Battery Street, The Embarcadero
• Rococo Showplace, 165 10th Street, South of Market District-as Cafe Roads
• Philip Burton Federal Building, 450 Golden Gate Avenue, Civic Center
• R. Iacopi Meats, 1462 Grant Avenue, North Beach District-as Meats of the World butcher shop
• Vesuvio Cafe, 255 Columbus, Jackson Square District
• Aladdin Terrace, Russian Hill District

• Alamo Square Park, Western Addition District
• Friedel Klussmann Memorial Cable Car Turnaround, Aquatic Park, San Francisco Maritime National Historic Park, Golden Gate National Recreation Area
• Cloverdale Airport, 220 Airport Road, Cloverdale

• Golden Gate Bridge
• Dunsmuir House and Gardens, 2980 Peralta Court, Oakland-as honeymoon hotel

Song of the City
1937, Metro Goldwyn Mayer
A slacker falls overboard and is rescued by Italian fishermen who teach him about life.

Director: Errol Taggart
Screenwriter: Michael Fessier
Art Director: Cedric Gibbons
Cinematographer: Leonard Smith
Partial Cast: Margaret Lindsay, Jeffrey Dean, J. Carrol Naish, Nat Pendleton, Stanley Morner, Edward Norris

• Golden Gate Bridge
• Panorama of San Francisco
• Fisherman's Wharf District

Southside 1-1000
1950, Allied Artists
An undercover agent sleuths a counterfeit money ring.

Director: Boris Ingster
Screenwriters: Leo Townsend, Boris Ingster
Production Designer: Ted Haworth
Art Director: Dave Milton
Cinematographer: Russell Harlan
Partial Cast: Don DeFore, Andrea King, George Tobias, Barry Kelley, Morris Ankrum

• San Quentin State Prison, San Quentin

Space Is the Place
1974, North American Star System
This experimental film is a bizarre combination of social commentary, Blaxploitation, science fiction, and concert performance.

Director: John Coney
Screenwriters: Sun Ra, Joshua Smith
Production Designer: Whit Mather
Cinematographer: Seth Hill
Partial Cast: Sun Ra, Barbara Deloney, Raymond Johnson

- Aerial view of Mt. Tamalpais lookout, Golden Gate National Recreation Area
- Aerial view of Mt. Tamalpais radar domes, Golden Gate National Recreation Area
- Aerial view of Sutro Tower, Mt. Sutro District
- Aerial view of downtown San Francisco
- Potrero Hill Youth Development Program, 991 Wisconsin Street, Potrero Hill District-shoes scene
- Oakland
- Merritt College Campus, 12500 Campus Drive, Oakland
- Rosicrucian Museum, 1660 Park Avenue, San Jose-room with hieroglyphs
- Third Street Bridge, China Basin
- Pier, The Embarcadero

Sphere
1998, Warner Brothers
A spaceship is discovered at the bottom of the ocean.

Director: Barry Levinson
Screenwriters: Kurt Wimmer, Stephen Hauser, Paul Atlanasio
Author: Michael Crichton (novel)
Production Designer: Norman Reynolds
Art Directors: Mark W. Mansbridge, Jonathan McKinstry
Cinematographer: Adam Greenberg
Partial Cast: Dustin Hoffman, Sharon Stone, Samuel L. Jackson, Peter Coyote, Queen Latifah

- SS *Jeremiah O'Brien*, Vallejo
- Sports Center, Mare Island, Vallejo

BARRY LEVINSON

Acclaimed writer, director and producer Barry Levinson was born in Baltimore in 1942. He started his training in media, studied broadcast journalism, and went on to writing and acting. He attended American University in Washington, DC and later moved to Los Angeles to write for such high-profile television shows as *The Carol Burnett Show. High Anxiety* showcased his writing talent; he also appears in the movie as an over caffeinated bellboy in the *Psycho* parody scene. He received three Academy Award nominations as screenwriter and a host of other awards for his impact on the craft of filmmaking and television. In 1994 he moved his family and office to the Marin County town of Ross. His other locally filmed work is *Sphere* (1998).

Stablemates
1938, Metro Goldwyn Mayer
A broken-down veterinarian saves a stable boy's racehorse.

Director: Sam Wood
Screenwriters: Richard Maibaum, Reginald Owen, Leonard Praskins, Wilhelm Thiele
Art Director: Cedric Gibbons
Cinematographer: John F. Seitz
Partial Cast: Wallace Beery, Mickey Rooney, Margaret Hamilton, Minor Watson, Marjorie Gateson

- Tanforan Racetrack, El Camino Real, San Bruno

Stand by for Action
1942, Metro Goldwyn Mayer
An ivy-league graduate learns the realities of war on an old destroyer ship.

Director: Robert Z. Leonard
Screenwriters: George Bruce, John L. Balderston, Herman J. Mankiewicz
Authors: Harvey S. Haislip, R. C. Sherriff (story)
Art Director: Cedric Gibbons
Cinematographer: Charles Rosher
Partial Cast: Robert Taylor, Charles Laughton, Brian Donlevy, Walter Brennan

- San Francisco-Oakland Bay Bridge
- Golden Gate Bridge

Star Trek: The Motion Picture
1979, Paramount Pictures
An alien intruder nears Earth and the USS *Enterprise* mobilizes to intercept them.

Director: Robert Wise
Screenwriters: Alan Dean Foster, Harold Livingston, Leonard Nimoy, William Shatner
Author: Gene Roddenberry (TV series)
Production Designer: Harold Michelson
Art Directors: Leon Harris, Joseph R. Jennings, John Vallone
Cinematographer: Richard H. Kline
Partial Cast: William Shatner, Leonard Nimoy, DeForest Kelley

- Golden Gate Bridge

Star Trek IV: The Voyage Home
1986, Paramount

AKA: *The Voyage Home: Star Trek IV*
To save Earth from an alien probe, the captain and his crew go back in time to retrieve humpback whales, the only beings who can communicate with the probe.

Director: Leonard Nimoy
Screenwriters: Leonard Nimoy, Harve Bennett, Steve Meerson, Peter Kribes, Nicholas Meyer
Author: Gene Roddenberry (TV series)
Production Designers: Jack T. Collis, Peter Lansdown Smith
Art Directors: Joe Aubel, Nilo Rodis-Jamero, Peter Lansdown Smith
Cinematographer: Donald Peterman
Partial Cast: William Shatner, Leonard Nimoy, DeForest Kelley, Jane Wyatt

• Golden Gate Bridge
• Fort Point National Historic Site, Marine Drive, Golden Gate National Recreation Area
• Crissy Field, Presidio, Golden Gate National Recreation Area
• Marina Green, Marina District
• Intersection of Kearny Street and Columbus Avenue, Telegraph Hill District
• Naval Air Station Alameda, Alameda Island
• College of Marin, 835 College Avenue, Kentfield-swimming pool

ALIEN TOURISTS

In one San Francisco street scene of *Star Trek: The Voyage Home*, two time travelers from the twenty-third century crew of the USS *Enterprise* ask passerby's "We are looking for the nuclear vessels" (in a Russian language intonation). The scene was done *Candid Camera* style with non-actors and after several takes a young woman with long hair was selected for the scene; very seriously, and sincerely she replied "across the bay in Alameda." Her answer was a happy accident, chosen because it was blasé compared to the many others asked who gave quizzical looks.

Star Trek VI: The Undiscovered Country
1991, Paramount
Captain Kirk is accused of killing the Klingon chancellor.

Director: Nicholas Meyer
Screenwriters: Gene Roddenbery, Leonard

Nimoy, Lawrence Konner, Mark Rosenthal
Author: Gene Roddenbery (TV series)
Production Designer: Herman F. Zimmerman
Art Director: Nilo Rodis-Jamero
Cinematographer: Hiro Narita
Partial Cast: William Shatner, Leonard Nimoy, DeForest Kelley, James Doohan, Walter Konig, Nichelle Nichols, George Yakei, Kim Cantrall, Mark Lenard, Christopher Plummer

• Fireman's Fund Building complex, 777 San Marin Drive, Novato

Steelyard Blues
1973, Warner Brothers
AKA: *The Final Crash*
Black comedy about a group of misfits who try to escape from it all on a plane.

Director: Alan Meyerson
Screenwriter: David S. Ward
Production Designer: Vincent M. Cresciman
Cinematographers: László Kovács, Stevan Larner
Partial Cast: Donald Sutherland, Howard Hesseman, Peter Boyle, Jane Fonda

• Antioch Speedway, 1201 West 10th Street, Antioch
• Intersection of 20th Street and Broadway, Oakland
• Oakland Zoo, 9777 Golf Links Road, Oakland
• Oakland City Hall, One Frank H. Ogawa Plaza, Oakland
• Ephesian Church of God in Christ, 1709 Alcatraz Avenue, Berkeley
• The Scarlet Monk, 1950 San Pablo Avenue, Oakland
• Superburger, Fourth Street, Santa Rosa
• Julliard Park, 227 Santa Rosa Avenue, Santa Rosa
• Sonoma County Airport, Airport Boulevard, Santa Rosa

Stigmata
1999, Metro Goldwyn Mayer
AKA: *Toby's Story*
A Vatican priest goes to Brazil to investigate the appearance of the Virgin Mary's face on the side of a building.

Director: Rupert Wainwright
Screenwriters: Tom Lazarus, Rick Ramage
Production Designer: Waldemar Kalinowski
Art Director: Anthony R. Stabley
Cinematographer: Jeffrey L. Kimball
Partial Cast: Patricia Arquette, Gabriel Byrne, Jonathan Pryce

• Palace of Fine Arts, 3601 Lyon Street, Marina District

• Filoli Estate and Gardens, 86 Cañada Road, Woodside

Stop or My Mom Will Shoot

1992, Universal
A tough detective's mother comes to visit him and begins to meddle in his life and career.

Director: Roger Spottiswoode
Screenwriters: Blake Snyder, William Osborne, William Davies
Production Designer: Charles Rosen
Art Director: Diane Yates
Cinematographer: Frank Tidy
Partial Cast: Sylvester Stallone, Estelle Getty, Jo Beth Williams

• Santa Rosa Air Center, Finley Avenue, Santa Rosa

Storm Center

1956, Columbia
AKA: *The Library*, *The Librarian*, *Circle of Fire*
A small-town librarian is branded a communist by locals when she refuses to withdraw a controversial book from the library's shelves.

Director: Daniel Taradash
Screenwriters: Elick Moll, Daniel Taradash
Art Director: Cary Odell
Cinematographer: Burnett Guffey
Partial Cast: Bette Davis, Brian Keith, Kim Hunter

• Carnegie Library, Fourth and E Streets, Santa Rosa
• McMullen's Soda Fountain, Fourth Street, Santa Rosa
• Morissey's Restaurant, Rosenberg Building, intersection of Fourth Street and Mendocino Avenue, Santa Rosa
• City Hall, Santa Rosa

The Story of Molly X

1949, Universal International Pictures
AKA: *Tehachapi: The Story of Molly X*
A gangster's widow looks to find her husband's killer.

Director: Crane Wilbur
Screenwriter: Crane Wilbur
Art Directors: Bernard Herzbrun, Emrich Nicholson
Cinematographer: Irving Glassberg

Partial Cast: June Havoc, John Russell, Dorothy Hart

• Top of the Mark Bar, Mark Hopkins Hotel, 999 California Street, Nob Hill District

Stranded

1935, Warner Brothers
A woman who works for Travelers Aid meets an old school boyfriend.

Director: Frank Borzage
Screenwriters: Delmer Daves, Carl Erickson
Authors: Frank Wead, Ferdinand Reyher "Lady With a Badge" (story)
Art Directors: Anton Grot, Hugh Reticker, Arthur Gruenberger
Cinematographer: Sidney Hickox
Partial Cast: Kay Francis, George Brent, Patricia Ellis

• Golden Gate Bridge

The Strawberry Statement

1970, Metro Goldwyn Mayer
Student rebels occupy a university's administration building.

Director: Stuart Hagmann
Screenwriters: James Kunen, Israel Horovitz
Art Directors: Preston Ames, George W. Davis
Cinematographer: Ralph Woolsey
Partial Cast: Bruce Davison, Kim Darby, Bud Cort

• Washington Square, North Beach District
• High School of Commerce, 135 Van Ness Avenue, Civic Center District
• 1145 Montgomery Street, Telegraph Hill District
• San Francisco General Hospital Medical Center, 1001 Potrero Avenue, Mission District
• Alamo Square, Western Addition District
• San Francisco-Oakland Bay Bridge
• Broadway Tunnel, Russian Hill District
• Coit Tower, Pioneer Park, 1 Telegraph Hill Boulevard, Telegraph Hill District
• The Cannery, 2801 Leavenworth Street, Fisherman's Wharf District-courtyard
• Caffe Trieste, 609 Vallejo Street, North Beach District
• Market Street, Financial District

Street Music

1981, Specialty Films
The story of a hotel that is scheduled for demolition and its older residents trying to fight back against its closure.

Director: H. Anne Riley
Screenwriter: H. Anne Riley
Art Director: Don Di Fina

Cinematographer: Richard Bowen
Partial Cast: Elizabeth Daily, Larry Breeding, Ned Glass, Marjorie Eaton

• Hamlin Hotel, 385 Eddy Street, Tenderloin District
• The Hyde Out, 1068 Hyde Street, Nob Hill District

Street People
1976, American International Pictures
AKA: *The Sicilian Cross*
A lawyer teams up with his buddy to find the gangsters responsible for smuggling a million dollars worth of heroin hidden inside a cross.

Director: Maruizio Lucidi
Screenwriters: Roberto Leoni, Gianfranco Bucceri, Maurizio Lucidi, Randal Kleiser, Ernest Tidyman, Niccola Badalucco
Art Director: Gastone Carsetti
Cinematographer: Aiace Parolin
Partial Cast: Roger Moore, Stacey Keach, Ivo Garrani

• Pier 38, The Embarcadero
• Pioneer Park, 1 Telegraph Hill Boulevard, Telegraph Hill District
• 400 to 500 block of Broadway, Telegraph Hill District-nightlife
• San Francisco-Oakland Bay Bridge
• Pepo's Place, 1421 Stockton Street, North Beach District-billiards
• Columbus Avenue, between Lombard Street and Chestnut Street, North Beach District
• La Roca's Corner Tavern, 957 Columbus Avenue, North Beach District
• Ninth Circuit Court of Appeals and Post Office, 95 Seventh Street, South of Market District
• Stanford Court Hotel, 905 California Street, Nob Hill District
• Houseboats, Sausalito
• Conzelman Road, Marin Headlands, Golden Gate National Recreation Area
• Saints Peter and Paul Church, 666 Filbert Street, North Beach District
• Safeway, 690 Chestnut Street, North Beach District

Submarine Command
1951, Paramount Pictures
A submarine officer who considers himself a coward becomes a hero in Korea.

Director: John Farrow
Screenwriter: Jonathan Latimer
Art Directors: Henry Bumstead, Hal Pereira
Cinematographer: Lionel Lindon
Partial Cast: William Holden, Don Taylor, Nancy Olson, William Bendix, Jerry Paris

• Mare Island, Vallejo

JERRY PARIS

William Gerald Paris was born on July 25, 1925 in San Francisco. His father was a Russian immigrant. His mother Ester (Mohr) parted with Paris and married Milton Grossman when William was a small child. He attended both New York University and the University of California, Los Angeles. After service in World War II he studied at the Actor's Studio in New York City. He made his film debut in the locally filmed *D.O.A.* (1950) as an uncredited player portraying a bellboy. He played Sergeant Gentry in *Submarine Command* the following year. He and Ruth (Benjamin) were married in 1954 and they had three children. His most enduring legacy may be as Rob and Laura Petrie's dentist neighbor in television's *The Dick Van Dyke Show*. Paris began working on the show in 1961; producer Carl Reiner gave Paris the opportunity to direct the show starting in 1963 until it shut down production in 1966. Paris acted in scores of movies, and directed just as many, but also cast a wide net in the industry as a producer and writer. He was the director of the popular TV show *Happy Days* with Ron Howard between 1974 and 1984. He died in Los Angeles on March 31, 1986 of complications from brain surgery.

The Subterraneans
1960, Metro Goldwyn Mayer
The love affairs of some Bohemian urban residents.

Director: Ranald MacDougall
Screenwriter: Robert Thom
Author: Jack Kerouac (novella)
Art Directors: George W. Davis, Urie McCleary
Cinematographer: Joseph Ruttenberg
Partial Cast: Leslie Caron, George Peppard, Roddy McDowall, Jim Hutton, Arte Johnson, Andre Previn

• Aerial scenes of San Francisco
• San Francisco-Oakland Bay Bridge
• Golden Gate Bridge
• 1228 Montgomery Street, Telegraph Hill

District-Leo's residence
• Market Street
• 1453 Kearny Street, Telegraph Hill District-Mardou's residence
• Coit Tower, Pioneer Park, 1 Telegraph Hill Boulevard, Telegraph Hill District

Suckerfish
1999, Glass Eye Productions
At look at the wholesale pet supply business where two veteran salesmen try to squeeze out a new kid hired to take over a retiring competitor's lucrative route.

Director: Brien Burroughs
Cinematographer: Christopher Brown
Partial Cast: Dan Donovan, Tim Orr, Gerri Lawlor, Kurt Bodden

• 4455 18th Street, Eureka Valley District-as My Best Friend
• Rainbow Grocery Cooperative, 1745 Folsom Street, South of Market District-Trainor Street entry as warehouse truck dock
• Motel Capri, 2015 Greenwich Street, Cow Hollow District
• Pet World, 478 San Bruno Avenue, San Bruno
• Cal's Pet Supply, 5950 California Street, Outer Richmond District
• Cole Valley Pets, 910 Cole Street, Cole Valley District
• Sammy's Pet World, 1698 Bryant Street, Potrero Hill District
• Philosopher's Club, 824 Ulloa Street, West Portal District-bar
• Intersection of De Haro Street and Southern Heights Avenue, Potrero Hill District-park
• Lone Palm, 3394 22nd Street, Mission District-bar
• Club Deluxe, 1511, Haight Street, Haight-Ashbury District-bar
• Atlas Café, 3049 20th Street, Mission District
• Terry A. Francois Boulevard, near 16th Street, Mission Bay District

Sudden Fear
1952, RKO Radio Pictures
A con man tries to dupe an heiress out of her fortune.

Director: David Miller
Screenwriters: Lenore J. Coffee, Robert Smith
Author: Edna Sherry (novel)
Art Director: Boris Leven
Cinematographer: Charles Lang
Partial Cast: Joan Crawford, Jack Palance, Gloria Grahame, Bruce Bennett, Virginia Huston, Touch (Chuck) Conners

• 2800 Scott Street, Pacific Heights District
• The Tamalpais Apartments, 1201 Greenwich Street, Russian Hill District
• California Palace of the Legion of Honor,

Lincoln Park, Outer Richmond District-interior and colonnade
• Crookedest Street in the World, 1000 block of Lombard Street, Russian Hill District
• Market Street from Twin Peaks
• Golden Gate Bridge
• Le Cirque Nightclub, Fairmont Hotel, 950 Mason Street, Nob Hill District
• Tanforan Racetrack, El Camino Real, San Bruno
• 250 Beach Road, Belvedere-summer house

Sudden Impact
1983, Warner Brothers
A police detective goes after a killer, a woman who is avenging her rape.

Director: Clint Eastwood
Screenwriters: Harry Julian Fink, Rita M. Fink, Joseph Stinson, Earl E. Smith, Charles B. Pierce, Dean Rieser
Production Designer: Edward C. Carfagno
Cinematographer: Bruce Surtees
Partial Cast: Clint Eastwood, Sondra Locke, Pat Hingle, Bradford Dillman

• Burger Island, 695 Third Street, South of Market District
• Bowles Franklin Galleries, 765 Beach Street, Fisherman's Wharf District
• Civic Center Plaza, Civic Center District
• Hall of Justice, 850 Bryant Street, South of Market District
• Mark Hopkins Hotel, 999 California Street, Nob Hill District
• Pier 38-40, The Embarcadero
• Ferry Building, Herb Caen Way, Embarcadero District

CLINT EASTWOOD

Clint Eastwood's utterance of "Go ahead, make my day" in the fourth of the series of *Dirty Harry* films secured his role as the icon anti-hero cop. His father Clinton, a salesman at the Morris-Noble Company in Oakland, and mother M. Ruth resided at 637 Beacon Street in Oakland at his birth. Born in San Francisco's St. Francis Hospital on May 31, 1930, Clinton Eastwood Jr. eventually attended Oakland Technical High School and after graduation in 1949 took a job as a lumberjack in Oregon. He now resides not far away from his birthplace in Carmel-by-the-Sea where he was mayor for a period. His directorial debut was in 1971 with *Play Misty for Me*, filmed in the nearby Monterey County area. He won the prestigious

Irving G. Thalberg Memorial Award from the Academy of Motion Picture Arts and Sciences in 1995.

Superdad
1973, Buena Vista

A father is determined to control the life of his teenage daughter.

Director: Vincent McEveety
Screenwriters: Vincent McEveety, Harlan Ware
Art Directors: William J. Creber, John B. Mansbridge
Cinematographer: Andrew Jackson
Partial Cast: Bob Crane, Kurt Russell, Joe Flynn, Barbara Rush

• San Francisco Airport
• Alioto's Restaurant, 8 Fisherman's Wharf District
• The Embarcadero
• SS *Vallejo*, 36 Varda Landing, Sausalito-houseboat
• Cable car

Superman
1978, Warner Brothers

A baby saved from another planet grows up to use his special powers to fight evil.

Director: Richard Donner
Screenwriters: Mario Puzo, David Newman, Leslie Neuman, Robert Benton
Authors: Jerry Siegel, Joe Shuster (comic book character)
Production Designer: John Barry
Art Directors: Ernest Archer, Philip Bennet, Stuart Craig, Leslie Dilley, Norman Dorme, Tony Reading, Norman Reynolds
Cinematographer: Geoffrey Unsworth
Partial Cast: Christopher Reeve, Marlon Brando, Gene Hackman, Ned Beatty, Jackie Cooper, Glenn Ford, Trevor Howard, Margot Kidder, Valerie Perrine, Terence Stamp

• Golden Gate Bridge

Superman IV: The Quest for Peace
1987, Cannon

A man with special powers wants the planet to lay down its nuclear arms.

Director: Sidney J. Furie
Screenwriters: Christopher Reeve, Lawrence Konner, Mark Rosenthal
Authors: Jerry Siegel, Joe Shuster "Superman" (comic book character)

Production Designer: John Graysmark
Cinematographer: Ernest Day
Partial Cast: Christopher Reeve, Gene Hackman, Jackie Cooper, Marc McClure, San Wanamaker, Mariel Hemingway, Margot Kidder

• Golden Gate Bridge
• Ferry Building, Herb Caen Way, The Embarcadero

Susan Slade
1961, Warner Brothers

A pregnant teen allows her mother to pass off the baby as her own child.

Director: Delmer Daves
Screenwriters: Delmer Daves
Author: Doris Hume (novel)
Art Direction: Leo K. Kuter
Cinematographer: Lucien Ballard
Partial Cast: Troy Donahue, Connie Stevens, Dorothy McGuire, Lloyd Nolan

• Golden Gate Bridge
• Passenger Ship Terminal Piers, The Embarcadero
• Spreckels Mansion, 2080 Washington, Pacific Heights District

The Sweetest Thing
2002, Columbia Pictures

A young woman finds she is forced to educate herself on the etiquette of wooing the opposite sex when she finally meets Mr. Right.

Director: Roger Kumble
Screenwriter: Nancy Pimental
Production Designer: John Gary Steele
Art Director: Gershon Ginsburg
Cinematographer: Anthony B. Richmond
Partial Cast: Cameron Diaz, Christina Applegate, Thomas Jane, Selma Blair

• Huntington Park, intersection of California Street and Taylor Street, Nob Hill District
• Palace of Fine Arts, 3601 Lyon Street, Marina District
• 1151 Kearny Street, Telegraph Hill District-residence
• 501 Broadway, Telegraph Hill District-as entry to club
• Wilkes Bashford, 375 Sutter Street, Union Square District
• 800 block of Clay Street, Chinatown
• 1327 Grant Avenue, Telegraph Hill District-dry cleaner
• Golden Gate Bridge
• Pier 7, The Embarcadero-as restaurant
• Tunnel entry, intersection of Dorman Drive and South Garrard Boulevard, Pt. Richmond-as entry to town of Somerset
• Nicasio Reservoir, Nicasio Valley Road, Nicasio

• 114 Washington Avenue, Point Richmond-as Vera's House of Beauty
• 101 Park Place, Point Richmond-as café
• San Francisco-Oakland Bay Bridge

Sweet November
2001, Warner Brothers

A young woman begins a new romantic relationship each month, then helps him to evolve into a better and kinder human being before she moves on to the next partner.

Director: Pat O'Connor
Screenwriters: Herman Raucher, Paul Yurick, Kurt Voelker
Production Designer: Naomi Shohan
Art Director: Kevin Constant
Cinematographer: Edward Lachman
Partial Cast: Keanu Reeves, Charlize Theron, Jason Issacs, Frank Langella

• Transamerica Pyramid, 600 Montgomery Street, Financial District
• Intersection of Golden Gate Avenue and Jones Street, Tenderloin District-parking lot
• Christopher's Books, 1400 18th Street, Potrero Hill District-as Sara's place
• Crissy Field, Presidio, Golden Gate National Recreation Area
• Dolores Park, Muni stop, Mission District
• India Basin Shoreline Park, Hawes Street, Hunter's Point District-waterfront park
• Farley's Cafe, 1315 18th Street, Potrero Hill District
• Blooms Saloon, 1318 18th Street, Potrero Hill District
• Citicourt Cafe, One Sansome Street, Financial District
• San Francisco-Oakland Bay Bridge

KELVIN HAN YEE

Native San Franciscan Kelvin Han Lee's first film role was in *A Great Wall* (1986), which featured the Chinese-American in the first American feature film ever shot in the Republic of China. After being kicked out of high school he worked in the gritty dives and after-hours clubs of San Francisco's Tenderloin District—at one point as a bouncer. At the same time he was working in improv comedy with The National Theater of the Deranged. He acted in a variety of other local venues where he honed his career such as the Berkeley Repertory, San Jose Stage, and San Francisco Mime Troupe. He began his career as a company member of the American

Conservatory Theater, where he played in a wide variety of roles for six seasons. He has appeared in many other filmed-in-the-Bay-Area productions, including *Tales of the City* (1993), *So I Married an Axe Murderer* (1993), *Copycat* (1995), *Chalk* (1996), *Patch Adams* (1998), *True Crime* (1999), *Dumbarton Bridge* (1999), *Sweet November* (2001), *Cherish* (2002), and *Milk* (2008).

Swim Team
1979, Prism Pictures

A new swimming coach is hired to break a team's seven-year losing streak.

Director: James Polakof
Screenwriter: James Polakof
Cinematographer: Don Cirillo
Partial Cast: James Daughton, Richard Young, Stephen Furst, Buster Crabbe

• Campolindo Cabana Club, 3799 Campolindo Drive, Moraga-pool
• Orinda

BUSTER CRABBE

The athletic Buster Crabbe was born in Oakland on February 17, 1908 as Clarence Linden Crabbe. His father, Edward C. Crabbe, was a real estate broker and his mother Agnes Lucy (McNamara) a housewife. The family later moved to Hawaii where he graduated in 1927 from Honolulu's prestigious Punahou School. Back on the mainland he attended the University of Southern California and graduated in 1931. He had no formal training as an actor, but he appeared uncredited in his first film, MGM's *Good News* in 1930. An excellent swimmer he garnered a bronze medal for the 400-meter freestyle swimming event in the 1928 Olympic Games and a gold in 1932 for the 400-meter freestyle. He married his college sweetheart Adah Held in 1933 and they went on to have three children. His most famous film appearance was as the lead in the sci-fi serial *Flash Gordon* (1936), bringing to the screen the Alex Raymond com-

Swing
2003, Leprechaun Entertainment

A struggling young musician happens upon a nightclub that's frozen in time where he learns to follow his heart.

Director: Martin Guigui
Screenwriter: Mary Keil
Production Designer: Don Di Fina
Cinematographer: Massimo Zeri
Partial Cast: Constance Brenneman, Innis Casey, Tom Skerritt, Jonathan Winters, Nell Carter, Barry Bostwick, Jacqueline Bisset

• 644 Townsend Street, South of Market District- picnic venue
• Altenheim Senior Housing, 1720 MacArthur Boulevard, Oakland-senior home
• Dolores Street, Mission District
• Reilly Company, Goodwin & Scannell, 1598 Dolores Street, Mission District-funeral home
• Golden Gate Bridge
• 315 13th Street, Oakland-as Club Jimbo exterior
• Lodge Room, Regency Center, 1290 Sutter Street, Van Ness Corridor District- as Club Jimbo interior
• Velvet Lounge, 443 Broadway, Telegraph Hill District
• Broadway Studios, 435 Broadway, Telegraph Hill District
• G. B. Ratto & Co., 821 Washington Street, Oakland-as market
• Palace of Fine Arts, 3601 Lyon Street, Marina District
• Deja Nu, 1224 Fourth Street, San Rafael-as retro clothing store
• Crissy Field, Presidio, Golden Gate National Recreation Area
• Fort Point National Historic Site, Marine Drive, Golden Gate National Recreation Area

Swingin' Along
1961, Twentieth Century Fox
AKA: *Double Trouble*

A courier dreams of becoming a songwriter; his friend, a con artist, wants to enter the courier's original composition in a music competition.

Director: Charles Barton
Screenwriter: Jameson Brewer
Art Directors: Duncan Cramer, George Van Marter
Cinematographer: Arthur E. Arling
Partial Cast: Barbara Eden, Ray Charles, Peter Marshall, Roger Williams, Bobby Vee

• Powell Street near Market Street, Union Square District

1934 as Barbara Jean Morehead she spent most of her formative years in San Francisco. Eden's surname changed after her mother Alice was divorced from Barbara's father, Hubert Morehead, who was a telephone lineman. In 1945 her mother married Harrison Huffman. When she was 4-1/2 she and her mother moved to San Francisco to live at 1207 Bush Street. She attended Redding Elementary School and later Columbus Elementary in the Sunset District. By the time "BJ" graduated from the Sunset District's Abraham Lincoln High School, where she was a cheerleader and pop singer, the family lived nearby at 2434 45th Avenue. Barbara was crowned Miss San Francisco in the 1951 beauty pageant. She studied music at the San Francisco Conservatory of Music with thoughts of a singing career. Later she trained at the Elizabeth Holloway School of Theatre as she thought she was more suited to acting instead. Her agent changed her last name to Eden in 1956. She is most widely known for her appearance in the popular NBC television situation comedy show *I Dream of Jeannie* which ran from 1965 to 1970. She and current husband (number three), structural engineer Jon Eicholtz, were married in 1991 in Grace Cathedral, where she had been baptized and attended religious services as a child. (In her early years she had played in Huntington Park, across from the cathedral, after Sunday School.)

Take the Money and Run

1969, Palomar Studios

Pseudo documentary about an incompetent, petty criminal who is obsessed with bank robberies.

Director: Woody Allen
Screenwriters: Woody Allen, Mickey Rose
Art Director: Fred Harpman
Cinematographer: Lester Shorr
Partial Cast: Woody Allen, Janet Margolin, Marcel Hillaire

• Spreckels Lake, Golden Gate Park
• Hancock Grammar School, 940 Filbert Street, Russian Hill District
• Ernie's Restaurant, 847 Montgomery Street, Telegraph Hill District
• 2400 block of Mission Street, Mission District
• Bank of America, 801 Clement Street, Inner Richmond District
• San Quentin State Prison, San Quentin

Tales of the City

1993-1994, Channel 4 Films

AKA: *Armistead Maupin's Tales of the City*

Episodes about several colorful San Francisco residents as seen through the eyes of a tourist-turned-resident. Some of the characters are thinly veiled locals.

Director: Alastair Reid
Screenwriter: Richard Kramer
Author: Armistead Maupin (novel)
Production Designer: Victoria Paul
Art Director: Joyce Anne Gilstrap
Cinematographer: Walt Lloyd
Partial Cast: Olympia Dukakis, Donald Moffat, Chloe Webb, Laura Linney, Marcus D'Amico, Thomas Gibson, Barbara Garrick, Nina Foch, Edie Adams, Mary Kay Place

• Buena Vista Café, 2765 Hyde Street, Ghirardelli Square District
• Aquatic Park, San Francisco National Maritime Historical Park, Waterfront
• Macondray Lane Steps at Taylor Street, Russian Hill District-as Barbary Lane
• Intersection of California Street and Montgomery Street, Financial District
• Washington Square Bar and Grill, 1707 Powell Street, North Beach District
• Brocklebank Apartments, 1000 Mason Street, Nob Hill District-Day residence
• Painted Ladies, 700 block of Steiner Street, Western Addition District-park
• 3160 16th Street, Mission District-as Endup Bar
• 9 Scenic Way, Seacliff District-as D'or's Pacific Heights residence
• Powell Street Cable Car, Union Square
• Haas Lilienthal House, 2007 Franklin Street, Pacific Heights District
• Filbert Street Steps, Telegraph Hill District
• Castro Theatre, 429 Castro Street, Eureka Valley District
• Beach Chalet, 1000 Great Highway, Golden Gate Park-restaurant
• Dutch Windmill, JFK Drive near Great Highway, Golden Gate Park
• Twin Peaks Overlook, Twin Peaks
• 3900 block of 24th Street, Noe Valley District-as the Castro District
• Angler's Lodge, Golden Gate Park-as log cabin
• California Palace of the Legion of Honor, Lincoln Park, Outer Richmond District
• Fort Point National Historic Site, Marine Drive, Golden Gate National Recreation Area

Telefon
1977, Metro Goldwyn Mayer
A Russian agent is instructed to seek out and destroy a ring that oppose detente with the West.

Director: Don Siegel
Screenwriters: Walter Wager, Peter Hyams, Stirling Silliphant
Production Designer: Ted Haworth
Art Director: William F. O'Brien
Cinematographer: Michael Butler
Partial Cast: Charles Bronson, Lee Remick, Donald Pleasance, Tyne Daly, Alan Badel, Patrick Magee, Sheree North

• Embarcadero Center, The Embarcadero-walkways
• Hyatt Regency Hotel, 5 Embarcadero Center, The Embarcadero-lobby and garage

Tell Me a Riddle
1980, Godmother and Filmways
A dying woman, long a recluse, is reconciled with her family.

Director: Lee Grant
Screenwriters: Joyce Eliason, Alev Lytle
Author: Tillie Olsen (novella)
Production Designer: Patrizia von Brendenstein
Cinematographer: Fred Murphy
Partial Cast: Melvyn Douglas, Lila Kedrova, Brooke Adams, Dolores Dorn, Bob Elross, Jon Harris, Peter Coyote
Local Cast: Artist and puppeteer Ralph Chessé

• San Francisco International Airport
• Embarcadero Freeway, Embarcadero
• The Alexander, 230 Eddy Street, Tenderloin District-apartment building
• 2700 block of 24th Street, Mission District
• 654 Natoma Street, South of Market District-granddaughter's apartment
• Mini park, 24th Street near York Street, Mission District
• Cesar's Laundromat, 2750 24th Street, Mission District
• Jewish Community Center, 3200 California Street, Laurel Heights District-elder gathering
• Muni station, La Playa Street, Outer Sunset District
• Tunnel to Ocean Beach, near Judah Street and La Playa Street, Outer Sunset District
• Ocean Beach, Golden Gate National Recreation Area
• Mission Creek, Mission Bay District-deck
• Fort Barry, Marin Headlands, Golden Gate National Recreation Area -flashback scenes

PETER COYOTE

Multi-dimensional Marin County resid-ent Peter Coyote has appeared in several Bay-Area-filmed movies including *Purpose* (2002), *Patch Adams* (1998), *Sphere* (1998), *Jagged Edge* (1985), *Out* (1982), and *Die Laughing* (1980). He was a late blooming actor with his first part being in a non-speaking part in *Tell Me a Riddle*. He was born Rachmil Pinchus Ben Mosha Cohon on October 10, 1941 in Manhattan. His parents were Morris and Ruth (Fidler) Cohon. Cohon's attended Iowa's Grinnell College and in 1964 he graduated with a B.A. in English Literature, an interest he would continually pursue. Moving to the West Coast in 1974, he attended San Francisco State University earning a Master's Degree in creative writing. In 1976 he was appointed by Governor Jerry Brown to join the State Arts Council. He spent a short time with the San Francisco Actors' Workshop and then moved on to the radically political San Francisco Mime Troupe. For a while, he taught drama to young people in the Visitation Valley neighborhood, but in 1978 he reentered theater by joining the Magic Theater. His memoir of the Haight-Ashbury counterculture that he lived in was recorded in his book *Sleeping Where I Fall*, first published in 1998. His familiar dulcet voice can be heard narrating many PBS documentaries and other film projects.

Tenderloin
2009, Vanguard Cinema
A wounded Iraq War veteran is coaxed away from self-destructive behaviors by locals and his son.

Director: Michael Anderson
Screenwriter: Ned Miller
Cinematographer: Michael Anderson
Partial Cast: Kurt Yaeger, Jack Indiana, Tina Huang, Richard Conti, Celia de Blas, Stephan Smith Collins, Amanda Huelse

• Boyd Hotel-Tenderloin Housing Clinic, 41 Jones Street, Tenderloin District-apartment building
• Michael Bondi Metal Design, 2801 Giant Road, Richmond-as blacksmith shop
• Intersection of Golden Gate Avenue and Jones Street, Tenderloin District-parking lot

• Intersection of Dale Place and Golden Gate Avenue, Tenderloin District-purse snatching
• 200 block of Leavenworth Street, Tenderloin District-stroll with brother
• Intersection of McAllister Street and Jones Street, Tenderloin District
• Straight Forward Boxing Club, 30 Seventh Street, South of Market District
• Pier 30-32, The Embarcadero-kite flying
• Mission Thrift Store, 2102 Mission Street, Mission District
• Pink Diamonds Gentlemen's Club, 220 Jones Street, Tenderloin District-pole dancers
• Tenderloin National Forest Park, Cohen Place at Eddy Street, Tenderloin District

RICHARD CONTI

San Rafael based part-time actor Richard Michael Conti (not to be confused with actor Richard Conti, who starred in many film noir movies) is a native of New England. He was born in 1952 in Melrose, Massachusetts, and graduated from the University of New Hampshire in 1974 with a B.S. in Health and Physical Education. His first appearance in film was the year before in *My Brother Anastasia*. Later he was in the cast of several made-for-TV movies and then appeared twice in the popular series *Nash Bridges* during 1997–1998. He married Kathryn Keatsin 1989 and they have three children. In 2003 he appeared in the lead role of San Francisco City College's theater production of *The Memoirs of JFK*. He heads Conti Print Design in San Rafael, but despite this he has appeared in several Bay-Area-filmed productions including *Copycat* (1995), *The Rock* (1996), *Metro* (1997), *Stigmata* (1999), *The Californians* (2005), *Touching Home* (2008), and as George in Woody Allen's *Blue Jasmine* (2013).

Ten Thousand Bedrooms

1957, Metro Goldwyn Mayer
An American hotel mogul becomes smitten with a Italian woman when buying a hotel in Rome. To marry her, he has to get her three older sisters married off.

Director: Richard Thorpe
Screenwriters: László Vadnay, Art Cohn, William Ludwig, Leonard Spigelgass
Art Directors: Randall Duell, William A. Horning
Cinematographer: Robert J. Bronner
Partial Cast: Dean Martin, Anna Maria Alberghetti, Eva Bartok

• Mark Hopkins Hotel, 999 California Street, Nob Hill District

Terminal USA

1993, IndieFlix
A quirky, dysfunctional Japanese-American family live out their wierd existence smeared with gore.

Director: Jon Moritsugu
Screenwriter: Jon Moritsugu
Production Designer: Jennifer M. Gentile
Cinematographer: Todd Verow
Partial Cast: Sharon Moi, Ken Narasaki, Lenny Lang

• One Market Plaza, 1 Market Street, The Embarcadero-mall with rain fountain

Terminator II: Judgment Day

1991, Carolco
AKA: *T-2, T2-Terminator 2: Judgment Day*
An android returns from the future to save a boy and his mother from a murderous transformer robot.

Director: James Cameron
Screenwriters: James Cameron, William Wisher Jr.
Production Designer: Joseph Nemec III
Art Director: Joseph P. Lucky
Cinematographer: Adam Greenberg
Partial Cast: Arnold Schwarzenegger, Linda Hamilton, Edward Furlong, Robert Patrick

• Santa Clara County
• Office Building, 47131 Bayside Park, Fremont

Terror on Alcatraz

1986, Trans World Entertainment
AKA: *Nightmare on Alcatraz*
A former inmate returns to the scene of his prison escape to find a safe-deposit-box key, but his plans are interrupted.

Director: Philip Marcus
Screenwriter: Donald Lewis
Cinematographer: Greg von Berblinger
Partial Cast: Aldo Ray, Sandy Brooke, Veronica
Porche Ali, Bea Marcus, Lisa Ramirez

• Alcatraz Federal Prison, Alcatraz Island, Golden
Gate National Recreation Area

That Brennan Girl
1946, Republic Pictures
AKA: *Tough Girl*
A young mother neglects her baby for
the sake of a good time.

Director: Alfred Santell
Screenwriters: Doris Anderson, Adela Rogers St.
Johns
Art Director: James W. Sullivan
Cinematographer: Jack Marta
Partial Cast: James Dunn, Mona Freeman,
William Marshall, June Duprez

• San Francisco-Oakland Bay Bridge
• Saints Peter and Paul Church, 666 Filbert
Street, North Beach District
• Temple Emanu-El, 2 Lake Street, Inner
Richmond District
• Calvary Presbyterian Church, 2515 Fillmore
Street, Pacific Heights District
• Maiden Lane, Union Square District
• Sheridan and Bell, 120 Maiden Lane, Union
Square District-florist shop
• Intersection of Stanyan Street and Frederick
Street, Haight-Ashbury District
• 523 Frederick Street, Haight-Ashbury District-
residence
• Fisherman's Grotto, 9 Fisherman's Wharf
District
• Mark Hopkins Hotel, 999 California Street, Nob
Hill District-Top of the Mark Bar
• Carousel, Golden Gate Park
• Sharon Building, Golden Gate Park
• Donkey Course, Sharon Playground, Golden
Gate Park

They Call Me Mr. Tibbs!
1970, Metro Goldwyn Mayer and United Artists
A police lieutenant suspects a
crusading local minister of murder.

Director: Gordon Douglas
Screenwriters: Alan Trustman, James R. Webb
Art Director: Addison Hehr
Cinematographer: Gerald Perry Finnerman
Partial Cast: Sidney Poitier, Martin Landau,
Barbara McNair, Anthony Zerbe, Jeff Corey,
Juano Hernandez, Ed Asner

• 790 Stockton Street, Nob Hill District-apartment
building

• North Beach Playground, 651 Lombard Street,
North Beach District
• Golden Gate Bridge and toll booths
• 677 Rhode Island Street, Potrero Hill District-
Tibbs's residence
• Stockton Street Tunnel, Nob Hill District
• 838 Grant Avenue, Chinatown District
• Portsmouth Square, Chinatown District

They Came to Rob Las Vegas
1968, Warner Brothers
Criminals ambush an armored truck in
the desert.

Director: Antonio Isasi-Isasmendi
Screenwriters: Antonio Isasi-Isasmendi, Jo
Eissinger, Jorge Illa, Lluis Josep
Comerón
Author: André Lay (novel)
Art Directors: Antonio Cortés, Juan Alberto Soler
Cinematographer: Juan Gelpi
Partial Cast: Jack Palance, Lee J. Cobb, Elke
Sommer, Gary Lockwood, George Geret, Jean
Servais

• Aerial panorama of San Francisco
• San Francisco-Oakland Bay Bridge-night shoot
out scenes
• Hall of Justice, 850 Bryant Street, South of
Market District

"Hey, waitress, this
steak's tough."
"Well, you can't send it
back, you bit it."

They Drive By Night
1940, Warner Brothers
Two brothers struggle as truck drivers;
one comes to harm, while the other is
accused of his friend's murder.

Director: Raoul Walsh
Screenwriters: Jerry Wald, Richard Macaulay
Author: A. I. Bezzerides (novel)
Art Director: John Hughes
Cinematographer: Arthur Edeson
Partial Cast: George Raft, Humphrey Bogart, Ann
Sheridan, Ida Lupino, Alan Hale

• Produce District set with San Francisco-
Oakland Bay Bridge in background

They Knew What They Wanted
1940, RKO Radio Pictures

A waitress agrees to marry a vineyard owner in a long distance courtship but finds he sent a photograph of his handsome foreman.

Director: Garson Kanin
Screenwriter: Robert Ardrey
Author: Sidney Howard (play)
Art Director: Van Nest Polglase
Cinematographer: Harry Stardling Sr.
Partial Cast: Carole Lombard, Charles Laughton, William Gargan, Harry Carey, Frank Fay, Lee Tung Foo

• Waterfront
• Restaurant, Fisherman's Wharf District
• Vineyards, Napa County
• Eden Rock, Oakville-courtship location

LEE TUNG FOO

Lee Tung Foo, *aka* Lee Tong Foo and Frank Lee, was in born 1875 in Watsonville, the oldest son of parents of Chinese descent. The family who moved several times, but they finally settled in the San Joaquin Valley town of Ripon, where they started a laundry. After becoming a cook and servant in his early years, Foo went to Oakland to work for Zeno Mauvais, the owner of a music store and publishing firm. Encouraged by his employer, he was trained to sing by Margaret Blake Alverson of Oakland between 1897 and 1904. Alverson found him to have an indomitable will and determination to succeed. The pioneering Chinese-American vaudevillian made his stage debut in 1905 at the Empire Theater in Oakland. He captured his audiences with such novelty fare, for the time, as singing light opera, sometimes in German or Latin, wearing a tuxedo and then switching to a kilt costume for his famous Scott impersonations. Engagements in San Jose, Sacramento, and Fresno followed. He hit the international stage in 1908 when he appeared in Brussels and London. But by 1920 he had left the stage, knowing that vaudeville was on its way out. He married Alice (Pitch) and they moved to New York, where he became a restaurateur with two venues in Manhattan. Much later, he appeared in many minor film roles in a total of 68 movies, mostly in uncredited roles—not unusual in the industry's early days. His movie career started when he was 60, and most of his roles were as the stereotyped Chinese servant, as in *The Skull Murder Mystery* (1932). His Bay-Area-filmed credits include *Mr. Wong, Detective* (1938), *The Mystery of Mr. Wong* (1939), *Mr. Wong in Chinatown* (1939), *Barbary Coast Gent* (1944), and *The Show-Off* (1946). The final movie of his career was at age 87 when he appeared in the political thriller *The Manchurian Candidate* that was released in 1962. He died in 1966.

Thief of Hearts
1984, Paramount Pictures

A woman trapped in a boring marriage begins an affair with a handsome man who seems able to read her mind.

Director: Douglas Day Stewart
Screenwriter: Douglas Day Stewart
Art Director: Edward Richardson
Cinematographer: Andrew Laszlo
Partial Cast: Steven Bauer, Barbara Williams, John Getz, George Wendt, David Caruso, Christine Ebersole
Local Cast: TV anchor David McElhatton

• Golden Gate Bridge
• Mama's on Washington Square, 1701 Stockton Street, North Beach District
• The Embarcadero
• San Francisco-Oakland Bay Bridge
• San Francisco Bay-sailing
• Alta Plaza Park, Pacific Heights District-tennis court
• China Beach, Golden Gate National Recreation Area
• Alta Mira Hotel and Restaurant, 125 Buckley Avenue, Sausalito-restaurant deck
• Third Street Bridge, China Basin District
• Bethlehem Ship Yard, 900 Illinois Street, Potrero Hill District
• Robert C. Levy Tunnel, Broadway, Russian Hill District
• Telegraph Hill, Telegraph Hill District

Thieves' Highway
1949, 20th Century Fox
AKA: *Collision, Hard Bargain, The Thieves' Market*

A truck driver tracks down the racketeers who cheated and maimed his father.

Director: Jules Dassin
Screenwriter: A. I. Bezzerides
Author: A. I. Bezzerides *Thieves' Market* (novel)
Art Directors: Chester Gore, Lyle Wheeler
Cinematographer: Norbert Brodine
Partial Cast: Richard Conte, Valentina Cortesa, Lee J. Cobb, Jack Oakie

• San Francisco Produce Market, Washington Street, Produce District
• The Oregon Restaurant, 524 Front Street, The Embarcadero
• Hotel Colchester, 259 North Embarcadero, The Embarcadero
• Ferry Building, Herb Caen Way, The Embarcadero
• Gold Ridge Road, Sebastopol

Think Fast, Mr. Moto
1937, 20th Century Fox
Mr. Moto goes on a cruise to solve a case of gem smuggling.

Director: Norman Foster
Screenwriters: Norman Foster, Howard Ellis Smith, Wyllis Cooper, Charles Kenyon
Author: John P. Marquand (novel)
Art Director: Lewis H. Creber
Cinematographer: Harry Jackson
Partial Cast: Peter Lorre, Virginia Field, Thomas Beck

• Ferry Building, Herb Caen Way, Embarcadero District

The Third Day
1965, Warner Brothers
An amnesiac learns that he is a rich and unpopular tycoon facing major problems.

Director: Jack Smight
Screenwriters: Joseph Hayes, Robert Presnell Jr., Burton Wohl
Art Director: Edward Carrere
Cinematographer: Robert Surtees
Partial Cast: George Peppard, Elizabeth Ashley, Roddy McDowell, Sally Kellerman, Arte Johnson, Vincent Gardenia

• Intersection of State Highway Route 116 and State Highway Route 1, Jenner

Thirty Seconds Over Tokyo
1944, Metro Goldwyn Mayer

Planning of the first American attack on Japan after Pearl Harbor was bombed.

Director: Mervyn LeRoy
Screenwriter: Dalton Trumbo
Authors: Ted W. Lawson, Robert Considine (book)
Art Directors: Cedric Gibbons, Paul Groesse
Cinematographers: Harold Rosson, Robert Surtees
Partial Cast: Van Johnson, Robert Mitchum

• San Francisco-Oakland Bay Bridge-flight under
• Naval Air Station Alameda, Alameda Island

MERVYN LEROY

Director Mervyn LeRoy (1900–1987) grew up in San Francisco and eventually garnered the prestigious Irving G. Thalberg Life Achievement Award in 1976. LeRoy was born the only child of parents who lived a comfortable life at 62 Geary Street. But the Earthquake and Fire of 1906 wrecked the household; his father lost his prosperous import/export business. Son and father (mother had walked out) lived in the Presidio for six months after the conflagration. Possibly his appearance on the Alcazar stage at age six months in *The Squaw Man* influenced later leanings. He did some work at Essanay Studios in Niles in a Broncho Billy (Gilbert M.) Anderson film where he got to study Charlie Chaplin who was working there at the time. That experience led him to compete with some 1,000 other costumed applicants at Market Street's Pantages Theater in 1915. Leroy took first place in this competition for the best imitator of the comic Chaplin. Sid Grauman (of later Hollywood theater fame) was in the audience and offered the youngster a spot in his show that was about to open at the long-awaited Panama-Pacific International Exposition. He created a vaudeville act that played the Bay Area and beyond, and he eventually landed in Hollywood, where he contacted his cousin Jesse L. Lasky (of Famous Players-Lasky fame). In 1923 Lasky got LeRoy a job in the wardrobe department and later as a film tinter. Leroy was also a gag writer,

This Earth is Mine

1959, Universal Pictures
A California vineyard owner brings his granddaughter to the Napa Valley in the hope that she will consolidate his dynasty.

Director: Henry King
Screenwriter: Casey Robinson
Author: Alice Tisdale Hobart *The Cup and the Sword* (novel)
Art Directors: George W. Davis, Alexander Golitzen, Eric Oborn
Cinematographers: Winton C. Hoch, Russell Metty
Partial Cast: Rock Hudson, Jean Simmons, Dorothy McGuire, Kent Smith, Claude Rains, Anna Lee, Ken Scott

• Southern Pacific Railroad Depot, 1520 Railroad Avenue, St Helena
• Niebaum-Coppola Estate Winery, 1991 St. Helena Highway, State Highway Route 29, Rutherford
• Beaulieu Vineyards, 1960 St. Helena Highway, State Highway Route 29, Rutherford
• Charles Krug Winery, 2800 Main Street, State Highway Routes 29 and 128, St. Helena
• Beringer Vineyards, 2000 Main Street, State Highway Routes 29 and 128, St. Helena
• Cella, 7830-40 St. Helena Highway, State Highway Route 29, Oakville
• Paul Masson
• The Christian Brothers Winery, 2555 Main Street, St. Helena
• Louis M. Martini Winery, 254 South St. Helena Highway, Saint Helena
• Stag's Leap Wine Cellars, 6126 Silverado Trail, Napa
• Sucram Ranch

• Italian Swiss Colony, 26150 Asti Road, Cloverdale
• Sebastiani Vineyards and Winery, 389 Fourth Street East, Sonoma
• Schramsberg Vineyard, 1400 Schramsberg Road, Calistoga
• Mayacamas Vineyards, 1155 Lokoya Road, Napa

bought the estate in 1970. These last two acquisitions of the brand cheapened the estate's product and reputation. In 1975 film director and producer Francis Ford Coppola and wife Eleanor started a process that ultimately reunited the historic estate. They started by acquiring the parcel behind the winery including the main residence. Later, in 1995, they bought the balance of the original estate finally conjoining the historic acreage and buildings. Coppola and production designer Dean Tavoularis created several additions to the winery's courtyard landscape and inserted the cascading grand staircase of hand-carved wood inside the winery building's central entry turning the previously functional building into a public marketing venue.

This Gun for Hire
1942, Paramount Pictures

When a hired killer shoots a black-mailer and his female companion dead, he's is paid off in marked bills by his treasonous employer who is working with foreign spies.

Director: Frank Tuttle
Screenwriters: Albert Maltz, W. R. Burnett
Author: Graham Greene *A Gun for Sale* (novel)
Art Directors: Hans Dreier, Robert Usher
Cinematographer: John F. Seitz
Partial Cast: Alan Ladd, Veronica Lake, Robert Preston

• San Francisco-Oakland Bay Bridge
• Driving on San Francisco-Oakland Bay Bridge

This Space Between Us
1999, Atmosphere Entertainment

Two years after his wife's death, a man's once-promising filmmaking career is at a standstill, and he takes off with little more than a tape recording of his wife's last phone message and the will to re-discover himself.

Director: Mathew Leutwyler

Screenwriters: Matthew Leutwyler, Peter Rudy
Production Designer: Leonardo
Art Director: Nathalie Diericks
Cinematographer: David Scardina
Partial Cast: Jeremy Sisto, Poppy Montgomery, Clara Bellar, Alex Kingston, Garry Marshall
Local Cast: TV anchor Julie Haener

• Battery Spencer, Marin Headlands, Golden Gate National Recreation Area
• Golden Gate Bridge
• San Francisco-Oakland Bay Bridge
• The Cypress Club Restaurant, 500 Jackson Street, Jackson Square District
• Kilowatt Bar, 3160 16th Street, Mission District
• Elysium Bar and Restaurant, 2434 Mission Street, Mission District
• Paradise Lounge, 1501 Folsom Street, South of Market District
• Battery Marcus Miller, Presidio, Golden Gate National Recreation Area
• Yerba Buena Center for the Arts Theater, 700 Howard Street, South of Market District
• Panorama of San Francisco from Treasure Island
• Interstate Highway Route 280, John F. Foran Freeway, Potrero Hill District

Three Faces West
1940, Republic Pictures

German refugees flee Hitler to settle in the arid bleakness of the Dust Bowl.

Director: Bernard Vorhaus
Screenwriters: F. Hugh Herbert, Joseph Moncure March, Samuel Ornitz
Art Director: John Victor Mackay
Cinematographer: John Alton
Partial Cast: John Wayne, Sigrid Gurie, Charles Coburn

• Aerial shot of downtown San Francisco

The Three Stooges Go Around the World in a Daze
1963, Columbia

AKA: *Around the World in a Daze*
The great-grandson of Phileas Fogg takes a bet to duplicate his relative's trip.

Director: Norman Maurer
Screenwriters: Norman Maurer, Elwood Ullman
Author: Jules Verne *Around the World in 80 Days* (novel)
Art Director: Don Ament
Cinematographer: Irving Lippman
Partial Cast: Moe Howard, Larry Fine, Joe DeRita

• Golden Gate Bridge
• San Francisco-Oakland Bay Bridge

THX-1138
1971, Warner Brothers
A man tries to escape a repressive society in the 25th century.

Director: George Lucas
Screenwriters: George Lucas, Walter Murch
Art Director: Michael D. Haller
Cinematographers: Albert Kihn, David Myers
Partial Cast: Robert Duvall, Donald Pleasance, Maggie McOmie
Local Cast: Artist and puppeteer Ralph Chessé

• Robert C. Levy Tunnel, Broadway, Russian Hill District
• BART underground tubes
• Embarcadero Center
• Marin County Civic Center, 3501 Civic Center Drive, San Rafael
• Lawrence Hall of Science, One Centennial Drive, University of California Campus, Berkeley

MARIN CIVIC CENTER

Looking like some futuristic spaceship, architect Frank Lloyd Wright's design of leaping arches across the hills was an idea well before its time—a true reflection of its architect. The complex consists of an 80-foot diameter domed structure that acts as an axis point where two linear atrium-lit arms stretch outward. A sculptural 172-foot-high tower rises above the dome and acts as smokestack and radio tower. The Administration Building was completed in 1962 and the Hall of Justice Building followed in 1969, well after Wright's death in 1959 at age 92. A post office and auditorium reflect the same round design aesthetic but are freestanding structures. The county jail was added in 1994 by Taliesin Architects' (Wright's school) Aaron Green and is embedded into an adjacent hillside—with no impact to the original grouping. The landmark was also seen in the movie *Gattaca* (1997)—also, not surprisingly, placed in a future time.

Ticker
2001, Artisan Entertainment
AKA: *The Other Side of the Law*
A police detective takes on a terrorist gang who intend to set off a bomb.

Director: Albert Pyun
Screenwriter: Paul B. Margolis
Production Designer: Arnd Stockhausen
Cinematographer: Philip Alan Waters
Partial Cast: Tom Sizemore, Dennis Hopper, Steven Seagal, Jaime Pressly, Joe Spano

• Hall of Justice, 850 Bryant Street, South of Market District
• Buena Vista Café, 2765 Hyde Street, Ghirardelli Square
• Golden Gate Bridge
• Cable car at top of Crookedest Street in the World, 1000 block of Lombard Street, Russian Hill District
• Pier 3, Fort Mason Center, Golden Gate National Recreation Area
• San Francisco-Oakland Bay Bridge
• San Francisco City Hall, 1 Carlton B. Goodlett Place, Civic Center District
• Hyde Street Pier, San Francisco National Maritime Historical Park
• Ferry Building, Herb Caen Way, Embarcadero District

Ticket to Heaven
1981, Ronald Cohen Productions
A religious group coerces a wandering young man to join their fold.

Director: Ralph L. Thomas
Screenwriters: Anne Cameron, Josh Freed, Ralph L. Thomas
Production Designer: Susan Longmire
Art Director: Jill Scott
Cinematographer: Richard Leiterman
Partial Cast: Nick Mancuso, Saul Rubinek, Meg Foster, Kim Cantrell

• Golden Gate Bridge

Time After Time
1979, Warner Brothers
Notorious Jack the Ripper escapes via a time machine to modern times and is chased by author H. G. Wells.

Director: Nicholas Meyer
Screenwriters: Karl Alexander, Steve Hayes, Nicholas Meyer
Production Designer: Edward C. Carfagno
Cinematographer: Paul Lohmann
Partial Cast: Malcolm McDowell, Mary Steenburgen, David Warner, Charles Cioffi, Kent Williams

• California Academy of Sciences, 55 Music Concourse Drive, Golden Gate Park
• Union Street, Cow Hollow District
• Embarcadero Center-walkways
• San Francisco General Hospital, 1001 Potrero Avenue, Mission District
• Golden Gate Bridge

• Broadway, Telegraph Hill District
• Vaillancourt Fountain, Justin Herman Plaza, The Embarcadero
• Equinox Restaurant, Hyatt Regency Hotel, 5 Embarcadero Center, The Embarcadero
• 3601 Lyon Street, Marina District-as 2340 Francisco Street
• Palace of Fine Arts, 3601 Lyon Street, Marina District
• Muir Woods National Monument, Muir Woods Road, Golden Gate National Recreation Area

The Times of Harvey Milk

1984, Black Sand Productions
Documentary about the career and assassination of San Francisco's first elected openly gay supervisor.

Director: Robert Epstein
Screenwriters: Judith Coburn, Carter Wilson
Production Designer: Michael McNeil
Cinematographer: Frances Reid
Partial Cast: Harvey Fierstein, Harvey Milk, Dennis Richmond, Jeannine Yeomans, Sally Gearhart, John Briggs, Dianne Feinstein, George Moscone, Dan White

• San Francisco City Hall, 1 Carlton B. Goodlett Place, Civic Center District
• Market Street
• Intersection of Market Street and Castro Street, Eureka Valley District
• Castro Camera, 575 Castro Street, Castro District
• Intersection of Castro Street and 18th Street, Eureka Valley District
• Portola Beauty Salon, 2585a San Bruno Avenue, Portola District
• Duboce Park, Duboce Triangle District
• Hall of Justice, 850 Bryant Street, South of Market District

Titanic

1997, Paramount and 20th Century Fox
A third-class passenger meets a first class passenger on the maiden voyage of the purportedly unsinkable ship.

Director: James Cameron
Screenwriter: James Cameron
Production Designer: Peter Lamont
Art Director: Martin Lang
Cinematographer: Russell Carpenter
Partial Cast: Leonardo DiCaprio, Kate Winslet, Billy Zane, Kathy Bates, Frances Fisher, Gloria Stuart

• SS *Jeremiah O'Brien*, Pier 45, Fisherman's Wharf District-engine room scenes

SS JEREMIAH O'BRIEN

The last intact and operating World War II Liberty Ship of the thousands built, the *O'Brien* represents simplicity of design and functionality of purpose. The steam-driven ship (hence SS) was built in an astonishing 40 days in a South Portland, Maine boatyard and launched on June 19, 1943. Liberty ships were a crucial building block to winning the war. One of this ship's first missions was to carry troops, explosives and armored vehicles to Omaha Beach on France's Normandy coast just days after the major invasion of Normandy in 1944. Traveling the world later, she was designated as part of the reserve fleet. But in 1978 this ship was selected to be anointed a national monument and installed on the National Register as an historic object. Restoration efforts began the following year, and she sailed for the first time after 33 years. As a living history museum, the ship is staffed by volunteer caretakers who keep alive a reminder of our country's past.

Too Hot to Handle

1938, Metro Goldwyn Mayer
Two rival newsreel photographers join forces to find an aviatrix's missing brother who has disappeared in the Amazon jungle.

Director: Jack Conway
Screenwriters: Laurence Stallings, John Lee Mahin, Len Hammond
Art Director: Cedric Gibbons
Cinematographer: Harold Rosson
Partial Cast: Clark Gable, Myrna Loy, Walter Pidgeon

• China Clipper airboat, San Francisco Bay

Touching Home

2008, Winston Movie
Factual story about a father struggling to make amends with his twin sons as they pursue their dreams of professional baseball.

Directors: Logan Miller, Noah Miller
Screenwriters: Logan Miller, Noah Miller
Production Designer: Roy Rede
Art Director: Thomas Power
Cinematographer: Ricardo Jacques Gale
Partial Cast: Ed Harris, Logan Miller, Noah Miller, Clyde Winston, Brad Dourif, Lee Meriwether

• Old St. Mary's Church, Nicasio Valley Road, Nicasio-grave site
• San Francisco-Oakland Bay Bridge
• Nicasio Reservoir, Nicasio Valley Road, Nicasio
• Pt. Reyes-Petaluma Road, Pt. Reyes Station
• Nicasio Rock Quarry, Nicasio Valley Road, Nicasio
• Nicasio School House, 5555 Nicasio Valley Road, Nicasio
• Fairfax Theatre, 9 Broadway, Fairfax
• Samuel P. Taylor Park, Sir Francis Drake Boulevard, Lagunitas
• Bridge across Russian River, Monte Rio
• Country Club Bowl, 88 Vivian Street, San Rafael-bowling scenes

"For what it's worth, architect, this is one building that I figured wouldn't burn."

The Towering Inferno
1974, Twentieth Century Fox and Warner Bros
A fire puts a damper on a skyscraper's grand opening.

Director: John Guillerman
Screenwriter: Stirling Silliphant
Authors: Richard Martin Stern The Tower (novel); Thomas N. Scortia, Frank M. Robinson The Glass Inferno (novel)
Production Designer: William J. Creber
Art Director: Ward Preston
Cinematographer: Fred J. Koenekamp
Partial Cast: Steve McQueen, Paul Newman, William Holden, Faye Dunaway, Fred Astaire

• Golden Gate Bridge
• San Francisco City Hall, 1 Carlton B. Goodlett Place, Civic Center District
• Intersection of California Street and Kearny Street, Financial District
• Bank of America Building, 555 California Street, Financial District
• Hyatt Regency Hotel, 5 Embarcadero Center, The Embarcadero
• 2898 Vallejo Street, Pacific Heights District

FRANK M. ROBINSON

Frank Malcolm Robinson was born in Chicago, Illinois on August 9, 1926. As a teenager he became a collector of science fiction, which influenced him to become a writer. He worked as a copy boy for International News Service and later Ziff-Davis, a publisher of hobbyist magazines. The U.S. Navy drafted him in 1943 for World War II, and after the war ended he attended Beloit College in Wisconsin. He graduated in 1950 with a B.S. in physics. For the Korean War he again served in the Navy. When his tour ended he attended Northwestern University in Illinois and earned an M.S. in journalism in 1955. He worked for a number of magazines between 1956, topping of that segment of his life as a staff writer for Playboy from 1969 through 1973. By this time, he became able to become a freelance writer, and in 1968 his novel The Power was made into a movie with George Hamilton and Suzanne Pleshette. In this story, members of a special project team are being killed by telekinesis. Robinson moved to San Francisco in the 1970s and became a speechwriter for politician Harvey Milk who was assassinated along with Mayor Moscone. Robinson, who is openly gay, played himself in the movie Milk (2008).

The Towering Inferno is a merging of two very similar scripts by two studios. Both had purchased almost identical disaster-story properties: Fox had The Glass Inferno and Warner Brothers owned Richard Martin Stern's story The Tower. Fearing that such similar films might cancel out each other at the box office, the studios took producer Irwin Allen on his idea to combine the two scripts, split the costs, and share in the profits. Robinson then co-wrote the now famous screenplay with Thomas N. Scortia.

Train to Alcatraz
1948, Republic
A group of prisoners being transported by train to Alcatraz prison plot an escape.

Director: Philip Ford
Screenwriter: Gerald Geraghty
Art Director: Fred A. Ritter
Cinematographer: Reggie Lanning
Partial Cast: Don "Red" Barry, Janet Martin,
William Phipps

• Alcatraz Federal Prison, Alcatraz Island, Golden
Gate National Recreation Area

Treasure Island
1934, Metro Goldwyn Mayer
A boy treasure-hunts with pirates on
the high seas.

Director: Victor Fleming
Screenwriters: John Lee Mahin, John Howard
Lawson, Leonard Praskins
Author: Robert Louis Stevenson (novel)
Art Director: Cedric Gibbons
Cinematographers: Clyde De Vinna, Ray June,
Harold Rosson
Partial Cast: Wallace Berry, Jackie Cooper,
Lewis Stone, Lionel Barrymore

• Alaska Fisheries wharfs, Oakland

Treasure Island
1999, King Pictures
Set in the naval base of the same
name during World War II, two code
specialists each have a secret.

Director: Scott King
Screenwriter: Scott King
Production Designer: Nathan Marsak
Art Director: David Huffman
Cinematographers: Philip Glau, Scott King,
Jonathan Sanford
Partial Cast: Lance Baker, Nick Offerman, Jonah
Blechman

• Golden Gate International Exhibition, Treasure
Island-historic aerial footage
• San Francisco-Oakland Bay Bridge

Treasure of Monte Cristo
1949, Screen Guild
Productions
A descendant of Monte Cristo is
framed for murder in modern times.

Director: William A. Berke
Screenwriters: Aubrey Wisberg, Jack Pollexfen
Cinematographer: Benjamin H. Kline
Partial Cast: Glenn Largan, Adele Jorgens, Steve
Brodie

• Panoramic views of San Francisco from Twin
Peaks lookout
• Panoramic views of San Francisco from
Telegraph Hill
• Ferry Building, Herb Caen Way, Embarcadero
District
• Fisherman's Wharf District
• Intersection of Filbert Street Steps and
Sansome Street, Telegraph Hill District
• Cable car
• William H. Martin Residence, 2015 Franklin
Street, Pacific Heights District
• Old Hall of Justice, 750 Kearny Street, Financial
District-interior and exterior
• Renoir Hotel, 45 McAllister Street, Civic Center-
office interiors
• Marina Boulevard, Marina District
• Doyle Drive, east approach, Marina District
• Twin Peaks Boulevard, Twin Peaks District
• Fairmont Hotel, 950 Mason Street, Nob Hill
District-porte cochere

Tron
1982, Walt Disney
A computer-games designer gets his
revenge on an enemy by battling
things out in a computer-generated
world.

Director: Steven Lisberger
Screenwriters: Steven Lisberger, Bonnie MacBird
Production Designer: Dean Edward Mitzner
Art Director: John B. Mansbridge
Cinematographer: Bruce Logan
Partial Cast: Bruce Boxleiter, Jeff Bridges, David
Warner, Cindy Morgan, Barnard Hughes

• Lawrence Livermore National Laboratory,
National Magnetic Fusion Energy Center,
Livermore

True Believer
1989, Columbia
AKA: *Fighting Justice*
A tough idealistic lawyer is persuaded
to take on a client who may be
wrongfully imprisoned.

Director: Joseph Ruben
Screenwriter: Wesley Strick
Production Designer: Lawrence Miller
Art Director: Jim Pohl
Cinematographer: John Lindley
Partial Cast: James Woods, Robert Downey Jr.

• Oakland City Hall, One Frank H. Ogawa Plaza,
Oakland-city council chambers

True Crime
1999, Warner Brothers
AKA: *True Crimes*

An over-the-hill journalist tries to uncover evidence that can prove a death row inmate's innocence.

Director: Clint Eastwood
Screenwriters: Andrew Klavan, Larry Gross, Paul Brickman, Stephen Schiff
Production Designer: Henry Bumstead
Art Director: Jack G. Taylor Jr.
Cinematographer: Jack N. Green
Partial Cast: Clint Eastwood, Isaiah Washington, Lisa Gay Hamilton, James Woods
Local Cast: TV anchor Leslie Griffith, TV anchor Frank Somerville, Reverend Cecil Williams

• San Quentin State Prison, San Quentin
• Washoe House, 2840 Stony Point Road, Petaluma
• Oakland Tribune Building, 410 13th Street, Oakland
• Oakland Zoo, 9777 Golf Links Road, Oakland
• San Rafael Bridge
• Alameda County Courthouse, 1225 Fallon Street, Oakland
• Dunsmuir House and Gardens, 2980 Peralta Court, Oakland
• Intersection of 23rd Avenue and Park Street Bridge, Oakland
• Oakland City Center Plaza, Oakland

Tucker: The Man and His Dream

1988, Universal International and Lucasfilm

An industrial designer is put out of business after he creates a revolutionary new car design.

Director: Francis Ford Coppola
Screenwriters: Arnold Schulman, David Seidler
Production Designer: Dean Tavoularis
Art Director: Alex Tavoularis
Cinematographer: Vittorio Storaro
Partial Cast: Jeff Bridges, Joan Allen, Martin Landau, Frederic Forrest, Mako, Don Novello, Dean Stockwell, Lloyd Bridges (uncredited)

• Ridgecrest Boulevard, Mt. Tamalpais, Golden Gate National Recreation Area
• Rincon Center, 180 Steuart Street, South of Market District-lobby as restaurant
• Opera House and War Memorial, Civic Center-garden
• Oakland City Hall, One Frank H. Ogawa Plaza, Oakland-exterior and main lobby
• Hotel Oakland, 270 13th Street, Oakland-courtroom
• Paramount Theater, 2025 Broadway, Oakland-lobby
• Fox Theater, 1807 Telegraph Avenue, Oakland-launch venue
• Armstrong Residence, intersection of Charles Van Damme Way and Armstrong Drive, Sonoma-family home
• Hamilton Field, Hamilton Air Force Base,

Hangar Avenue, Novato-hangars
• Petaluma Speedway, 100 Fairgrounds Drive, Petaluma
• Ford Motor Company Assembly Plant, 1414 Harbour Way South, Richmond-assembly plant
• Alice Arts Center Theater, 1428 Alice Street, Oakland
• Telegraph Avenue, Oakland-parade of cars
• Contra Costa County Courthouse, 725 Court Street, Martinez-as Chicago courthouse
• 601 San Mateo Avenue, San Bruno-as malt shop

LLOYD BRIDGES

Lloyd Vernet Bridges Jr., appeared uncredited in *Tucker* as Senator Homer Ferguson, the despicable man responsible for shooting down Preston Tucker's dream car of the future. That Jeff Bridges, his son in real life, was playing the lead in this film was symbolic. Lloyd Bridges was born on January 15, 1913 in San Leandro to Lloyd Vernet Bridges Sr., who was in the hotel business, and Evelyn (Brown) Bridges. The family moved on several occasions, and Bridges graduated from Petaluma High School in 1931. He studied political science at UCLA and graduated from the University of California, Berkeley with a B.A. in 1936. Two years later he married Dorothy Simpson and they had three children. Bridges appeared in some 150 feature films over his career but became well known to television audiences with his starring role as diver Mike Nelson in the *Sea Hunt* series in 1958. He also appeared in the locally filmed movie *Out of the Past* (1947). Bridges died in 1998.

Tweek City

2005, Maverick Entertainment Group

A man's downward spiral into a life of drugs and life on the streets.

Director: Eric G. Johnson
Screenwriter: Eric G. Johnson
Production Designer: Don Day
Art Director: Guy Harrington
Cinematographer: Barry Stone
Partial Cast: Giuseppe Andrews, Keith Brunsmann, Eva Fisher

- Market Street
- Haight Street, Haight-Ashbury District
- Haight Street, Lower Haight-Ashbury District
- Auricular Records, 575 Haight Street, Lower Haight District
- Velvet Lounge, 443 Broadway, Telegraph Hill District
- Mission Street, Mission District
- 16th Street, Mission District
- Berkeley

Twisted
2004, Paramount Pictures
AKA: *Blackout* and *The Blackout Murders*
While a woman police officer is investigating a murder she finds herself at the center of an investigation when her former lovers start dying at a fast pace.

Director: Philip Kaufman
Screenwriter: Sarah Thorp
Production Designer: J. Dennis Washington
Art Director: Thomas T. Taylor
Cinematographer: Peter Deming
Partial Cast: Ashley Judd, Samuel L. Jackson, Andy Garcia, Jim Hechim, Richard T. Jones, Russell Wong, D. W. Moffett, Veronica Cartwright

- Golden Gate Bridge
- Tosca Cafe, 242 Columbus Avenue, Jackson Square District
- Palace of Fine Arts, 3601 Lyon Street, Marina District
- San Francisco City Hall, 1 Carlton B. Goodlett Place, Civic Center District-interior
- McCubby Cove, Pac Bell Park, South of Market district
- Fisherman's Wharf District-docks
- Crissy Field, Presidio, Golden Gate National Recreation Area-beach
- Pier 24/Hills Brothers Building, Embarcadero and Harrison Street, The Embarcadero
- San Francisco-Oakland Bay Bridge
- 3467 Pacific Avenue, Presidio Heights District-Ray's House
- The Saloon, 1232 Grant Avenue, Telegraph Hill District
- Vesuvio Cafe, 255 Columbus, Jackson Square District
- Six Flags Marine World, 1001 Fairgrounds Drive, Vallejo

Under Siege
1992, Warner Brothers
AKA: *Dreadnought*
A former SEAL is the only person who can stop a gang of terrorists when they seize control of the U.S. Navy battleship U.S.S. *Missouri*.

Director: Andrew Davis

Screenwriter: J. F. Lawton
Production Designer: Bill Kenney
Art Director: William Hiney
Cinematographer: Frank Tidy
Partial Cast: Steven Seagal, Damian Chapa, Troy Evans, David McKnight, Lee Hinton, Gary Busey

- Golden Gate Bridge

Under the Tuscan Sun
2003, Buena Vista
A just-divorced writer buys a French villa while on vacation hoping it will be the start of a new life.

Director: Audrey Wells
Screenwriter: Audrey Wells
Author: Frances Mayes *Under the Tuscan Sun: At Home in Italy* (book)
Production Designer: Stephen McCabe
Art Directors: Gianfranco Fumagalli, Gianni Giovagnoni
Cinematographer: Geoffrey Simpson
Partial Cast: Diane Lane, Raoul Bova, Sandra Oh, Lindsay Duncan

- Golden Gate Bridge
- 580 California Street Building, Financial District
- The Lucerne, 766 Sutter Street, Nob Hill District
- Mecca Restaurant, 2029 Market Street with vintage red Muni Pacific Electric car no. 1061
- San Francisco-Oakland Bay Bridge

The Unholy Wife
1957, Universal International
AKA: *The Lady and the Prowler*
A bored wife shoots a friend thinking it was her husband but is sentenced for the accidental death of her mother-in-law.

Director: John Farrow
Screenwriters: William Durkee, Jonathan Latimer
Art Directors: Franz Bachelin, Albert S. D'Agostino
Cinematographer: Lucien Ballard
Partial Cast: Diana Dors, Rod Steiger, Tom Tryon

- Beringer Vineyards, 200 Main Street, St. Helena-house exterior, interior and vineyards

RHINE HOUSE

The symbol of Beringer Vineyards is the ornate Victorian-style Rhine House; completed in 1884, it took two years to build at a cost of some $28,000. Beringer Vineyards was founded in 1876 by German-born Frederick Beringer (1840–1901), vint-

Unhook the Stars
1996, Miramax
An older woman suddenly has no one
to care for and learns that there is
more to life.

Director: Nick Cassavetes
Screenwriters: Helen Caldwell, Nick Cassavetes
Production Designer: Phedon Papamichael
Cinematographer: Phedon Papamichael
Partial Cast: Gena Rowlands, Marisa Tomei,
Gérard Depardieu, Jake Lloyd, Moira Kelly, David
Sherrill, David Thornton, Clint Howard

• San Francisco-Oakland Bay Bridge
• Chinatown District
• Caffe Greco, 423 Columbus Avenue, North
Beach District
• Palace of Fine Arts, 3601 Lyon Street, Marina
District
• Mikayla Restaurant, Casa Madrona Hotel, 801
Bridgeway, Sausalito

Until the End of the World
1991, Warner Brothers

In a future time, a woman tracks a
man across the planet.

Director: Wim Wenders
Screenwriters: Michael Almereyda, Peter Carey,
Solveig Dommartin, Wim Wenders
Production Designers: Sally Campbell, Thierry
Flamand
Art Directors: Steve Burns, Claudio Carrer, Ian
Gracie, Jan Schluback
Cinematographer: Robby Muller
Partial Cast: William Hurt, Solveig Dommartin,
Pietro Falcone, Jeanne Moreau, Max von Sydow

• Tosca Cafe, 242 Columbus Avenue, Jackson
Square District
• First Presbyterian Church, 2619 Broadway,
Oakland

Valley of the Heart's Delight
2006, Indican Pictures
A kidnapping ignites suspicion and
rage in 1933 San Jose, California.

Director: Tim Boxell
Screenwriter: Miles Murphy
Production Designer: Douglas Freeman
Cinematographer: Hiro Narita
Partial Cast: Gabriel Mann, Pete Postlethwaite,
Emily Harrison
Local Cast: Diva Val Diamond

• 2001 Broadway, Oakland
• Dunsmuir House and Gardens, 2980 Peralta
Court, Oakland
• Presidio, Golden Gate National Recreation Area
• Park Street Bridge, 29th Avenue, Oakland
• Fort Scott, Presidio, Golden Gate National
Recreation Area
• Camron-Stanford House, 1418 Lakeside Drive,
Oakland

"That was were you
made your mistake,
Judy. You shouldn't
keep souvenirs of a
killing. You shouldn't
have been that
sentimental."

Vertigo
1958, Paramount
AKA: *From Among the Dead*, *Illicit
Darkening*, *Listen Darkling*

A police detective with acrophobia falls for his quarry who has a very dark secret.

Director: Alfred Hitchcock
Screenwriters: Pierre Bioleau, Thomas Narejac, Alec Coppel, Samuel A. Taylor
Production Designer: Henry Bumstead
Art Directors: Hal Pereira, Henry Bumstead
Cinematographer: Robert Burks
Partial Cast: James Stewart, Kim Novak, Barbara Bel Geddes, Tom Helmore, Henry Jones, Ellen Kirby, Lee Patrick
Local Cast: Restaurateurs Roland Gotti, Victor Gotti

• Bethlehem Shipyard, 900 Illinois Street, Potrero Hill District
• Ernie's Restaurant, 847 Montgomery Street, Telegraph Hill District
• Brocklebank Apartments, 1000 Mason Street, Nob Hill District
• Claude Alley, Financial District-alley behind florist
• Podesta Baldocchi, 224 Grant Street, Financial District-florist
• Mission Dolores, 320 Dolores Street, Mission District
• California Palace of the Legion of Honor, Lincoln Park, Outer Richmond District
• Conly-Fortmann House, 1007 Gough Street, Western Addition District
• Presidio, Golden Gate National Recreation Area
• Fort Point National Historic Site, Marine Drive, Golden Gate National Recreation Area
• 900 Lombard Street, Russian Hill District-Scotty's residence
• Union Square, 333 Post Street
• Cypress Lawn Cemetery, Section 1, 1370 El Camino Real, Colma
• St. Joseph's Hospital, 355 Buena Vista East Avenue, Buena Vista Park District
• Empire Hotel, 940 Sutter Street, Nob Hill District
• Palace of Fine Arts, Marina District
• Ransohoffs, 259 Post Street, Union Square District-model for dress shop

CONLY-FORTMANN HOUSE

The four-story Renaissance Revival Victorian-style Conly-Fortmann House at the intersection of Eddy and Gough Streets played the part as the McKittrick Hotel perhaps because it was doomed to be demolished within the year after filming. It had survived the 1906 Earthquake and Fire, but became a victim of well-meaning mid-century urban redevelopment. Hitchcock probably selected the site because its paint was peeling from the neglected exterior. Consisting of 20 rooms, the building commenced water service in 1879. Sited on a double lot, the house was set back from the corner of Eddy and Gough providing a generously enclosed elevated lawn. The entry walk came across the lawn into what was virtually a double of the front entry's design on Gough Street. The elaborate interiors featured plasterwork, woodwork and wallcoverings suited to high Victorian taste. Much of the interior was intact until the building's demolition. Owner John Conly (1826–1883) and wife Emma (Heath) had three sons and two daughters. With schooling up to age 15 Conly arrived in California in August 1849 to participate in the Gold Rush and by 1856 was a State Senator. The same year, John Conly & Company opened as a banking establishment. Widowed in 1883, Mrs. Conly occupied the spacious residence until 1897, when the Fortmann family purchased the property and moved in. San Francisco native Henry Frederick Fortmann (1856–1946) was the president of Alaska Commercial Lines and was co-owner of the Pacific Brewery. Fortmann was active in many businesses and social organizations and occupied the house with his wife Julia (Schindler) and daughters Edna and Stella. The property is now the site of an athletic field for the adjacent Sacred Heart Cathedral Preparatory School.

A View to a Kill

1985, Metro Goldwyn Mayer and United Artists

AKA: *From a View to a Kill, Ian Fleming's View to a Kill*

Agent 007 James Bond fights a genetic superhuman bent on conquest of the world.

Director: John Glen
Screenwriters: Ian Fleming, Richard Maibaum, Michael G. Wilson
Production Designer: Peter Lamont
Art Director: John Fenner
Cinematographer: Alan Hume
Partial Cast: Roger Moore, Christopher Walken, Grace Jones, Tanya Roberts, Patrick Macnee, David Yip, Fiona Fullerton

- San Francisco City Hall, 1 Carlton B. Goodlett Place, Civic Center District-exterior and interior rotunda
- Fisherman's Wharf District
- Japantown, Western Addition District
- Embarcadero Freeway, The Embarcadero
- Third Street Bridge, South of Market District
- United States Custom House, 555 Battery Street, Financial District
- Transamerica Pyramid, 600 Montgomery Street, Financial District
- Millbrae
- Dunsmuir House and Gardens, 2980 Peralta Court, Oakland

Village of the Damned
1995, Universal
AKA: *John Carpenter's Village of the Damned*
Evil alien children use mind control over a small town's adults.

Director: John Carpenter
Screenwriters: David Himmelstein, Stirling Silliphant, Wolf Rilla, Ronald Kinnoch
Author: John Wyndham *The Midwich Cuckoos* (novel)
Production Designer: Roger Maus
Art Director: Christa Munro
Cinematographer: Gary Kibbe
Partial Cast: Christopher Reeve, Kirsty Alley, Linda Kozlowski, Michael Paré, Meridith Salenger, Mark Hamill

- Pt. Reyes National Seashore-with Roosevelt elk
- Drakes Beach, Pt. Reyes National Seashore
- Pt. Reyes Station-as town of Midwich
- Nicasio Schoolhouse, 5555 Nicasio Valley Road, Nicasio
- Druid's Hall, 4499 Nicasio Valley Road, Nicasio
- Dixon Marine Service Station, 12786 Sir Francis Drake Boulevard, Inverness-as Harolds
- Pt. Reyes National Seashore, Bear Valley Visitor Center, Bear Valley Road, Olema-red barn as birthing hospital

MARK HAMILL

Mark Richard Hamill was born in Oakland on September 25, 1951, the fourth of seven children. He grew up in a variety of locations in the United States and Japan, as his father was with the U.S. Navy. His mother was Virginia (Johnson) and father William Hamill, a captain. In San Diego he went to Hale Junior High School. He initially attended Nile C. Kinnick High School in Yokohama, Japan but with his father's transfer he finished at Annandale High School in Annandale, Virginia. He majored in drama at Los Angeles City College and made his acting debut on TV's *The Bill Cosby Show* in 1970. He married Marilou York in 1978, and they have three children. In recent decades he has mostly been mostly heard on TV in a variety of shows as well as in video games. He was catapulted to stardom as hero Luke Skywalker in George Luca's locally produced movies including *Star Wars* (1977), *Star Wars: Episode V-The Empire Strikes Back* (1980), and *Star Wars: Episode VI-Return of the Jedi* (1983).

The Vineyard
1989, New World Pictures
The magic in a mad doctor's anti-aging potion is beginning to wear off and he explores a way to revitalize its properties.

Directors: James Hong, William Rice
Screenwriters: James Hong, Douglas Kondo, James Marlowe, Harry Mok
Production Designer: Daniel Hime
Art Director: Jesse Cogal
Cinematographer: John Dirlam
Partial Cast: James Hong, Karen Witter, Michael Wong

- Fortino Winery, 4525 Hecker Pass Highway, Gilroy
- Guglielmo Winery, 1480 East Main Avenue, Morgan Hill
- Dunsmuir House and Gardens, 2960 Peralta Oaks Court, Oakland

The Virgin Machine
1988, First Run Features
A reporter goes to San Francisco to write about romance and has an affair with a stripper.

Director: Monika Truet
Screenwriter: Monika Truet
Cinematographer: Elfi Mikesch
Partial Cast: Ina Blum, Marcelo Uriona, Gad Klein
Local Cast: Clothier George Zimmer

- Seal Rocks, Pt. Lobos, Outer Richmond District
- Ocean Beach, Golden Gate National Recreation Area
- Market Street Cinema, 1077 Market Street
- 136 Taylor Street, Tenderloin District
- Billboard Café, 299 Ninth Street, South of Market District
- Pier 39, Fisherman's Wharf District
- El Rio Bar, 3158 Mission Street, Mission District

A Walk in the Clouds
1995, Twentieth Century Fox
AKA: *Caminando por las nubes, Un paseo por las nubes*
A couple pretend to be married in the post World War II era.

Director: Alfonso Arau
Screenwriters: Piero Tellini, Cesare Zavattini, Vittorio de Benedetti, Robert Mark Kamen, Mark Miller, Harry Weitzman
Production Designer: David Gropman
Art Director: Daniel Maltese
Cinematographer: Emmanuel Lubezki
Partial Cast: Keanu Reeves, Aitana Sanchez-Gijon, Giancarlo Giannini, Anthony Quinn

• San Francisco-Oakland Bay Bridge
• Golden Gate Bridge
• Mt. Veeder Winery, 1999 Mt. Veeder Road, Napa
• Mayacamus Vineyards, 1155 Lokoyo Road, St. Helena
• Beringer Vineyards, 2000 Main Street, St. Helena
• Duckhorn Vineyards, 3027 Silverado Trail, St. Helena
• Charles Krug Winery Redwood Cellar, 2800 Main Street, St. Helena
• The Haywood Vineyards, 18000 Gehricke Road, Sonoma

Warlock Moon
1973, Enchanted Filmarts
AKA: *Bloody Spa*
A college girl meets a boy and they take a trip to the country where they explore an abandoned spa.

Director: William Herbert
Screenwriter: William Herbert
Production Designers: Gage Cauchois, Rand Herbert, Douglas Saunders
Cinematographer: Larry Secrist
Partial Cast: Laurie Walters, Joe Spano, Edna MacAfee

• University of California Campus, Berkeley
• Arroyo del Valle Sanatorium, 5535 Arroyo Road, Livermore-as Soda Spring Spa

ARROYO DEL VALLE SANITORIUM

The spooky haunt of old crone Agnes Abercrombi was no artificial stage set but rather a real place that had served its purpose as a tuberculosis rehabilitation center. The facility opened in 1918 in the remote Alameda County town of Livermore that has a dry climate, which was thought to speed a patient's recovery from the dreaded disease, also known as consumption. The sanatorium's creation is credited to the work of Annie Florence Brown and Ethel Moore who were founding members of the Alameda County Tuberculosis Society. In 1924 the facility was enlarged for the specific treatment of children with TB and was known as Del Valle Farm. After serving some 10,000 patients the last patient left the sanatorium in 1960. The buildings sat vacant for many years and were eventually absorbed into the East Bay Regional Park District. In 1999 all the buildings were demolished to make way for new ones known as Camp Arroyo to house children with life-threatening illnesses and disabilities. Many of the former buildings' foundations remain as a reminder of the camp's past life.

The Wash
1988, Skouras Pictures
An older couple's painful separation and funny new romances.

Director: Michael Toshiyuki Uno
Screenwriter: Philip Kan Gotanda
Production Designer: David Wasco
Cinematographer: Walt Lloyd
Partial Cast: Mako, Nobu McCarthy, Sab Shimono, Patti Yasutake, Marion Yue

• Berkeley
• Oakland
• 5300 block of Geary Boulevard, Outer Richmond District
• Alexandria Theater, 5400 Geary Boulevard, Outer Richmond District
• Hank's Custom Rod and Reel, 205 East Jackson Street, San Jose

Water Under the Bridge
2003, Warner Brothers
AKA: *Save it for Later*
A boy finds his father wielding a weapon over the body of his best friend and in later years finds out the truth.

Director: Clark Brigham
Screenwriters: Clark Brigham,

Richard B. Taylor III
Production Designer: Chuck Voelter
Cinematographer: Barry Stone
Partial Cast: Scott Cooper, Gabrielle Anwar, Tommy Hinkley, Theresa Russell, Craig Sheffer, Charles Esten

• Panorama of waterfront and Ferry Building, The Embarcadero
• San Francisco-Oakland Bay Bridge
• CalTrain tracks under Interstate Highway Route 280, John F. Foran Freeway, Mission Bay District
• Panorama of Telegraph Hill
• Mission Hotel, 520 South Van Ness Avenue, Mission District
• Transamerica Pyramid from atop Telegraph Hill, Montgomery Street, Financial District
• 200 Sixth Street, South of Market District
• 473 Funston Avenue, Presidio-house
• Various murals, Mission District
• Abandoned Planet bookstore, 518 Valencia Street, Mission District
• 21st Street, Mission District
• Alcatraz Island, Golden Gate National Recreation Area
• RNM Restaurant, 598 Haight Street, Lower Haight Street District
• Lincoln Park Golf Course, Outer Richmond
• Grace Cathedral, 1100 California Street, Nob Hill District
• Ocean Beach, Golden Gate National Recreation Area

CLARK BRIGHAM

Creation of this indie film was the all-consuming work of Clark Brigham, whose first feature film is a love letter to San Francisco. The determined work paid off with its debut at the coveted San Francisco International Film Festival in 2003. Brigham's success was preceded by many unrecognized scripts. His training started with his attendance at the University of California, Santa Barbara where he studied English and film; he graduated in 1991. He made short films in his spare time and got some experience being an assistant on Rob Nilsson's Bay Area filmed *Chalk* in 1996. He ran a Mission-district nightclub that was shut down for unknown reasons and then decided to move his family to his wife's native England. While in England, he worked as a copywriter at an Internet advertising agency. After a year they returned to the U.S. and purchased a house in the remote Santa Cruz Mountain town of Bonny Doon. Back in the U.S. he again worked for a couple of ad agencies

but ultimately lost his position with the 2001 dot-com crash. Against all odds, he took a gamble with an idea for the film, *Water Under the Bridge*. A series of serendipitous events allowed him to develop the script and the low-seven-figure budget film got made with the fiscal help of an anonymous San Francisco investor. To date his only other known project has been a video short titled *Mosquito in the Room*, that was filmed in 2009.

The Weapons of Death
1982, Films International
A band of thugs kidnaps a girl and her half-brother gathers a team of expert fighters to get her back.

Director: Paul Kyriazi
Screenwriter: Paul Kyriazi
Partial Cast: Eric Lee, Bob Ramos, Ralph Catellanos

• Golden Gate Bridge
• Conzelman Road, Marin Headlands, Golden Gate National Recreation Area
• 800 block of Washington Street, Chinatown District
• Dragon Gateway to Chinatown, intersection of Grant Avenue and Bush Street, Chinatown District
• Spofford Street, Chinatown District
• East Bay Regional Park District

The Wedding Planner
2001, Columbia Pictures
AKA: *Wedding Planner*
A wedding planner falls in love with the groom of a couple who are clients.

Director: Adam Shankman
Screenwriters: Pamela Falk, Michael Ellis
Production Designer: Bob Ziembicki
Art Director: Gregory Bolton
Cinematographer: Julio Macat
Partial Cast: Matthew McConaughey, Jennifer Lopez, Kevin Pollak, Kathy Najimy

• Hyde Street Pier, San Francisco Maritime National Historic Park, Golden Gate National Recreation Area
• Transamerica Pyramid, 600 Montgomery Street, Financial District-from Hotaling Alley
• Aquatic Park, San Francisco Maritime National Historic Park, Golden Gate National Recreation Area
• Grace Cathedral, 1100 California Street, Nob Hill District
• Telegraph Hill District

- Lincoln Park Golf Course, Lincoln Park, Outer Richmond District
- Spreckels Temple of Music, Golden Gate Park
- California Palace of the Legion of Honor, Lincoln Park
- Japanese Tea Garden, 75 Hagiwara Tea Garden Way, Golden Gate Park
- San Francisco City Hall, 1 Carlton B. Goodlett Place, Civic Center
- Presidio, Golden Gate National Recreational Area
- Filoli Estate and Gardens, 86 Cañada Road, Woodside-gardens and tea house

The Well-Groomed Bride
1946, Paramount
A man and woman fight over the last known bottle of champagne in San Francisco.

Director: Sidney Lanfield
Screenwriters: Claude Binyon, Robert Russell
Art Directors: Hans Drier, A. Earl Hedrick
Cinematographer: John F. Seitz
Partial Cast: Olivia de Havilland, Ray Milland, Percy Kilbride

- Mark Hopkins Hotel, 999 California Street, Nob Hill District-Top of the Mark Bar
- Angel Island, Golden Gate National Recreation Area

What Dreams May Come
1998, PolyGram Filmed Entertainment
After dying in a car crash a widowed man searches the afterlife for his spouse and deceased children.

Director: Vincent Ward
Screenwriter: Ronald Bass
Author: Richard Matheson (novel)
Production Designer: Eugenio Zanetti
Art Directors: Jim Dultz, Tomas Voth, Christian Wintter
Cinematographer: Eduardo Serra
Partial Cast: Robin Williams, Annabella Sciorra, Cuba Gooding Jr., Max Von Sydow

- Museum of Modern Art, 151 Third Street, South of Market District
- Robert C. Levy Tunnel, Broadway, Russian Hill District
- San Francisco-Oakland Bay Bridge
- Mountain View Cemetery, 5000 Piedmont Avenue, Oakland
- St. Vincent's Church, School for Boys, 1 St. Vincent's Drive, San Rafael-church and colonnade
- Lake Merritt, Oakland
- Mare Island, Vallejo-USS Oriskany (CVA34)
- Filoli Estate and Gardens, 86 Cañada Road, Woodside-gardens and tea house

What's Up, Doc?
1972, Warner Brothers
Two researchers vie for a music research grant in San Francisco.

Director: Peter Bogdanovich
Screenwriters: Peter Bogdanovich, Buck Henry, Robert Benton
Production Designer: Polly Platt
Art Director: Herman Blumenthal
Cinematographer: László Kovács
Partial Cast: Barbra Streisand, Ryan O'Neil, Madeline Kahn, Kenneth Mars, Austin Pendleton, Mabel Albertson

- San Francisco Hilton, 333 O'Farrell Street, Union Square District-as Hotel Bristol
- Crookedest Street in the World, 1000 block of Lombard Street, Russian Hill District

• 23rd Street and Balboa, Richmond District-glass pane/car chase incident
• 2018 California Street, Pacific Heights District-as 888 Russian Hill, Professor Larabee's residence
• Chinatown
• Intersection of Van Ness Avenue and Clay Street
• South Terminal, San Francisco International Airport

THE CROOKEDEST STREET IN THE WORLD

Originally a straight, but steep street with a 27% grade, the 1000 block of Lombard Street, located between Hyde and Leavenworth Streets, is a favorite location of San Francisco visitors. On the one-way down direction, it boasts eight brick paved switchback turns that thrill drivers from all over the world. Claiming the moniker The Crookedest Street in the World, the current layout was created in 1922. The landscape of the in-between spaces is filled with hydrangea bushes fenced by neatly clipped hedges. The hydrangeas were a gift of local resident Peter Bercut in the 1950s and after his death the landscaping was named for him. (Another similar street, which is actually steeper, is the lesser-known portion of Vermont Street, between 20th and 22nd Streets on Potrero Hill, seen in *Magnum Force* (1973).

When a Man Loves a Woman

1994, Touchstone Pictures
AKA: *Significant Other*, *To Have and to Hold*
A family faces the potential ravages of alcoholism.

Director: Luis Mandoki
Screenwriters: Ronald Bass, Al Franken
Production Designer: Stuart Wurtzel
Art Director: Steve Saklad
Cinematographer: Lajos Koltai
Partial Cast: Andy Garcia, Meg Ryan, Ellen Bursten

• Buena Vista Cafe, 2765 Hyde Street, Ghirardelli Square
• Friedel Klussmann Memorial Cable Car

Turnaround, intersection of Hyde Street and Beach Street, Golden Gate National Recreation Area
• 1521 Masonic Avenue, Ashbury Heights District-house
• San Francisco-Oakland Bay Bridge
• San Francisco International Airport

Where Danger Lives

1950, RKO Radio Pictures
AKA: *White Rose for Julie*
A doctor falls in love with a patient who has murder on her mind.

Director: John Farrow
Screenwriters: Charles Bennett, Leo Rosten
Art Directors: Ralph Berger, Albert S. D'Agostino
Cinematographer: Nicholas Musuraca
Partial Cast: Robert Mitchum, Faith Domergue, Claude Rains, Maureen O'Sullivan

• Various views of San Francisco
• Market Street

Where Love Has Gone

1964, Paramount
A divorced couple's teen daughter stands trial for stabbing her mother's lover.

Director: Edward Dmytryk
Screenwriters: John Michael Hayes, Harold Robbins
Art Directors: Hal Pereiera, Walter H. Tyler
Cinematographer: Joseph MacDonald
Partial Cast: Susan Hayward, Bette Davis, Mike Connors, Joey Heatherton, Jane Greer, DeForest Kelley

• Golden Gate Bridge
• 10 Miller Place-Russian Hill District-residential skyscraper under construction
• San Francisco-Oakland Bay Bridge
• San Francisco International Airport
• 2700 Vallejo, Pacific Heights District
• Clipper Street, Noe Valley District
• Palace of Fine Arts, 3601 Lyon Street, Marina District
• 66 Calhoun Terrace, Telegraph Hill District

Where the Buffalo Roam

1980, Universal
The semi-autobiographical experiences of journalist Hunter S. Thompson.

Director: Art Linson
Screenwriter: John Kaye

Author: Hunter S. Thompson *The Banshee Screams for Buffalo Meat* and *Strange Rumblings in Aztlan* (stories)
Production Designer: Richard Tom Sawyer
Cinematographer: Tak Fujimoto
Partial Cast: Peter Boyle, Bill Murray

• Intersection of 18th Street and Pennsylvania Street, Potrero Hill District-crazy driving
• Intersection of De Haro Street and 18th Street, Potrero Hill District
• Intersection of 18th Street and Connecticut Street, Potrero Hill District-cop frisking
• Hills Brothers Coffee Plant Building, 2 Harrison Street, Embarcadero District-as Blast Magazine
• San Francisco City Hall, 1 Carlton B. Goodlett Place, Civic Center District-exterior

Who'll Stop the Rain
1978, United Artists
AKA: *Dog Soldiers*
A Vietnam War veteran smuggles drugs into the United States and involves his wife and friend.

Director: Karel Reisz
Screenwriters: Judith Roscoe, Robert Stone
Author: Robert Stone *Dog Soldiers* (novel)
Production Designer: Dale Hennesy
Cinematographer: Richard H. Kline
Partial Cast: Nick Nolte, Tuesday Weld, Michael Moriarty

• Cody's Books, 2454 Telegraph Avenue, Berkeley

Wildfire
1988, Universal
The lives of two orphans who are destined to be together.

Director: D. Zalman King
Screenwriters: Matthew Bright, D. Zalman King
Production Designer: Geoffrey Kirkland
Cinematographer: Bill Butler
Partial Cast: Steve Bauer, Linda Fiorentino, Will Patton

• Headlands Center for the Arts, 944 Simmonds Road, Marin Headlands, Golden Gate National Recreation Area-as orphanage
• Not-A-Bank, 26975 Shoreline Highway, State Highway Route 1, Tomales
• Gnoss Field Airport, 451 Airport Road, Novato
• Lakeville Highway, Petaluma
• Dixon Ranch, Petaluma
• Intersection of Second Street and Shoreline Highway, State Highway Route 1, Pt. Reyes Station-Circle Bar
• Wood Pontiac, Corby Avenue, Santa Rosa-car dealership
• St. Vincent's School for Boys, One St. Vincent Drive, San Rafael-as Mexico
• Bodega Bay

Wildflowers
1999, Monarch Home Video
A teenager who was raised in a commune accidently finds her long missing mother.

Director: Melissa Painter
Screenwriter: Melissa Painter
Production Designer: Andrea Soeiro
Art Director: Nathalie Diericks
Cinematographer: Paul Ryan
Partial Cast: Daryl Hannah, Clea DuVall, Eric Roberts, Tomas Arana, Richard Hillman

• Golden Gate Bridge
• City Lights Bookstore, 261 Columbus Street, Jackson Square District
• Caffe Trieste, 609 Vallejo Street, North Beach District
• Vesuvio Café, 255 Columbus Avenue, Jackson Square District
• North of intersection of Mesa Road and Purple Gate Road, Bolinas-as commune
• 3340 Folsom Street, Bernal Heights District
• El Paseo Restaurant, 17 Throckmorton Avenue, Mill Valley
• Muir Beach
• 28 South Forty Pier, Waldo Point Harbor, Sausalito-houseboat
• SS *Vallejo*, 36 Varda Landing, Sausalito-ferry
• The Fillmore, 1805 Geary Boulevard, Fillmore District-theater
• Ridgecrest Boulevard, Mt. Tamalpais Park, Golden Gate National Recreation Area

Wild in the Country
1961, Twentieth Century Fox
AKA: *Lonely Man*
A young man with problems discovers his ability to write when encouraged by a counselor.

Director: Philip Dunne
Screenwriters: J. R. Salamanea, Clifford Odets
Art Directors: E. Preston Ames, Jack Martin Smith
Cinematographer: William C. Mellor
Partial Cast: Elvis Presley, Hope Lange, Tuesday Weld, Millie Perkins, Gary Lockwood, Pat Buttram

• Ink House, 1575 St. Helena Highway, State Highways 29 and 128, St. Helena-counselor's house

The Wild Parrots of Telegraph Hill
2003, Shadow Distribution
Documentary about a homeless man who finds meaning when he befriends a flock of parrots.

Director: Judy Irving
Cinematographer: Judy Irving
Partial Cast: Mark Bittner, The Parrots

• Golden Gate Bridge
• Panorama of waterfront from Telegraph Hill
• Sidney G. Walton Square, Golden Gateway
• 243 Greenwich Street Steps, Telegraph Hill District
• Columbus Avenue, North Beach District
• Caffe Trieste, 609 Vallejo Street, Telegraph Hill District
• The Saloon Bar, 232 Grant Street, Telegraph Hill District
• City Lights Bookstore, 261 Columbus Avenue, Telegraph Hill District
• San Francisco Zoo, 1 Zoo Road, Parkside District
• Fort Mason Center, Golden Gate National Recreation Area
• Stow Lake, Golden Gate Park
• Coin Operated Wash-Dry, 347 Union Street, Telegraph Hill District
• San Francisco City Hall, 1 Carlton B. Goodlett Place, Civic Center District

The Witches of Eastwick
1987, Warner Brothers
Three bored, unmarried women in a picturesque East Coast village have their wishes granted, but at a great cost.

Director: George Miller
Screenwriter: Michael Cristofer
Author: John Updike (novel)
Production Designer: Polly Platt
Art Director: Mark W. Mansbridge
Cinematographer: Vilmos Zsigmond
Partial Cast: Jack Nicholson, Cher, Susan Sarandon, Michelle Pfeiffer, Veronica Cartwright

• Point Bonita, Marin Headlands, Golden Gate National Recreation Area

Witchtrap
1989, Highlight Video
AKA: *The Presence*
Parapsychologists try to make a haunted inn safe for guests.
Director: Kevin Tenney
Screenwriter: Kevin Tenney
Production Designer: Ken Aichele
Partial Cast: Linnea Quigley, James W. Quinn, J. P. Luebson

• Solano County Courthouse, 580 West Texas Street, Fairfield
• Stonedene Mansion, 293 Suisun Valley Road, Fairfield

The Woman on Pier 13
1949, RKO Radio Pictures
AKA: *I Married a Communist*
A shipping executive is blackmailed by Communists.

Director: Robert Stevenson
Screenwriters: Robert Hardy Andrews, George W. George, Charles Grayson, George F. Slavin
Art Directors: Albert S. D'Agostino, Walter E. Keller
Cinematographer: Nicholas Musuraca
Partial Cast: Robert Ryan, Laraine Day, John Agar, Janis Carter, Thomas Gomez

• Golden Gate Bridge
• San Francisco-Oakland Bay Bridge
• Pier 24, The Embarcadero-as Cornwall Shipping Company
• San Francisco waterfront
• Playland-at-the-Beach, 4800 Cabrillo Street, Outer Richmond District
• International Settlement Gateway, intersection of Pacific Avenue and Columbus Avenue, Jackson Square District

The Woman in Red
1984, Orion Pictures
A middle-aged married man fantasizes about infidelity.

Director: Gene Wilder
Screenwriters: Jean-Loup Dabadie, Yves Robert, Gene Wilder
Production Designer: David L. Snyder
Cinematographer: Fred Schuler
Partial Cast: Gene Wilder, Kelly Le Brock, Gilda Radner, Joseph Bologna, Judith Ivey, Charles Grodin

• Brocklebank Apartments, 1000 Mason Street, Nob Hill District
• 1360 Montgomery Street, Telegraph Hill District-apartment house
• Painted Ladies, 700 block of Steiner Street, Western Addition District
• New Union Grocery, 301 Union Street, Telegraph Hill District
• Le Club, 1250 Jones Street, Nob Hill District

Woman on the Run
1950, Universal International
AKA: *Man on the Run*
A man runs away after witnessing a murder and his wife is threatened by the killer.

Director: Norman Foster
Screenwriters: Alan Campbell, Norman Foster, Sylvia Tate
Art Director: Boris Levien
Cinematographer: Hal Mohr

Partial Cast: Ann Sheridan, Dennis O'Keefe, Robert Keith, Ross Elliott, Victor Sen Yung

• California Street Cable Car at intersection of California Street and Powell Street, Nob Hill District
• Union Square, 333 Post Street
• San Francisco City Hall, 1 Carlton B. Goodlett Place, Civic Center District
• Old St. Mary's Cathedral, 660 California Street, Chinatown District
• The Embarcadero
• Pioneer Park, Telegraph Hill District
• San Francisco-Oakland Bay Bridge
• Saints Peter and Paul Church, 666 Filbert Street, North Beach District
• Washington Square, North Beach District
• Intersection of Union Street and Montgomery Street, Telegraph Hill District
• Fisherman's Wharf District
• Old Hall of Justice, 750 Kearny Street, Financial District
• The Emporium, 835 Market Street, South of Market District
• Playland-at-the-Beach, 4800 Cabrillo Street, Outer Richmond District

VICTOR SEN YUNG

Sen Yung was born on October 18, 1915 in San Francisco to Chinese immigrants Gum Yung Sen and his first wife, who died in the 1919 flu epidemic. Yung attended the University of California at Berkeley where he majored in animal husbandry. He served in the U.S. Air Force during World War II and later led a prolific acting career in Bay Area film productions. The first was as "number two son" Jimmy Chan in *Charlie Chan at Treasure Island* (1939), followed closely by *Charlie Chan's Murder Cruise* (1940), and later by *Shadows Over Chinatown* (1946). These were but some of the 25 appearances Yung made in the popular stereotypical Charlie Chan series. Other locally shot movies he appeared in include *Chinatown at Midnight* (1949), *Key to the City* (1950), *Woman on the Run* (1950), *Blood Alley* (1955), *Flower Drum Song* (1961), and *Confessions of an Opium Eater* (1962). His last appearance in a locally-filmed production was in *The Killer Elite* (1975). An even longer assignment than the Chan series was his role as the cook known as Hop Sing in the popular *Bonanza* television series from 1959 through 1973. Sadly he died of accidental gas poisoning in his North Hollywood apartment on November 1, 1980. He is buried in Greenlawn Memorial Park in Colma.

Woman on Top
2000, 20th Century Fox

A chef becomes a TV sensation when she moves to San Francisco after her husband has been unfaithful. Soon her husband tries to win her back.

Director: Fina Torres
Screenwriter: Vera Blasi
Production Designer: Philippe Chiffre
Art Directors: Tracey Gallacher, Alexandre Meyer
Partial Cast: Penelope Cruz, Murilo Benicio, Harold Perrineau Jr., Mark Feuerstein

• Moscone Center North, 747 Howard Street, South of Market District-as airport
• Crookedest Street in the World, 1000 block of Lombard Street, Russian Hill District
• Fort Point National Historic Site, Marine Drive, Golden Gate National Recreation Area-as correctional institute
• Huntington Park, Nob Hill District
• Beresford Arms Hotel, 701 Post Street, Nob Hill District-as culinary school
• Powell Street cable car, Nob Hill District
• Metro Café, 311 Divisadero Street, Western Addition District
• Fort Mason Center, Building B, Golden Gate National Recreation Area-as TV station
• Palace of Fine Arts, 3601 Lyon Street, Marina District
• Intersection of Castro Street and Market Street, Eureka Valley District
• Crissy Field, Presidio, Golden Gate National Recreation Area
• Union Square, 333 Post Street

XXX: State of the Union
2005, Sony Pictures Entertainment

AKA: *XXX2: State of the Union*, *XXX Squared*, XXX^2, *XXX2*

A new agent in the XXX program is sent to Washington, DC to defuse a power struggle.

Director: Lee Tamahari
Screenwriters: Rich Wilkes, Simon Kinberg
Production Designer: Gavin Bocquet
Cinematographer: David Tattersall
Partial Cast: Ice Cube, Samuel L. Jackson, Willem Dafoe, Scott Speedman, Peter Strauss

• USS *Hornet* (CV-12), Naval Air Station Alameda, Alameda Island

X-Men: The Last Stand
2006, 20th Century Fox
AKA: *X-Men 3, X3*
When a cure is found to treat mutations, lines are drawn between the X-Men.

Director: Brett Ratner
Screenwriters: Simon Kinberg, Zak Penn
Production Designer: Ed Verreaux
Art Director: Chad S. Frey
Cinematographers: Philippe Rousselot, Dante Spinotti
Partial Cast: Patrick Stewart, Hugh Jackman, Ian McKellen, Halle Berry, Famke Janssen, Anna Paquin, Kelsey Grammer

• Golden Gate Bridge
• Alcatraz Island, Golden Gate National Recreation Area

Yamashita: The Tiger's Treasure
2001, MAQ Productions
A Filipino World War II veteran recalls the story of burying a treasure and how it was later found.

Director: Chito S. Roño
Screenwriter: Roy Iglesias
Art Directors: Margaret Cashion, Max Paglinawan, Fernan Santiago
Cinematographer: Neil Daza
Partial Cast: Armando Goyena, Danillo Barrios, Albert Martinez

• Golden Gate Bridge
• Crookedest Street in the World, 1000 block of Lombard Street, Russian Hill District
• Skyview Memorial Lawn, 200 Rollingwood Drive, Vallejo
• Viognier Restaurant, 222 East Fourth Street, San Mateo
• Marina Resort (Lake Berryessa), 5800 Knoxville Road, Napa

Yes, Giorgio
1982, Metro Goldwyn Mayer and United Artists
An international tenor falls for the woman throat specialist who cures his ailment.

Director: Franklin J. Schaffner
Screenwriters: Anne Piper, Norman Steinberg
Production Designer: William J. Creber
Cinematographer: Fred J. Koenekamp

Partial Cast: Luciano Pavarotti, Kathryn Harrold, Eddie Albert
Local Cast: Conductor Kurt Herbert Adler

• Golden Gate Bridge
• Sheraton Palace Hotel, Garden Court Restaurant, 2 New Montgomery Street, South of Market District
• Strawberry Hill Manor, 2260 Redington Road, Hillsborough-house and gardens

STRAWBERRY HILL MANOR

Sited in the tony town of Hillsborough, the stately two-story Italian-Renaissance style mansion now known as Strawberry Hill was once known as Villa Rose. Construction of this country residence on a 50-acre site was completed in 1912 for tycoon and social activist Joseph Donahoe Grant and wife Edith Maclay Grant. It was designed by architect Lewis P. Hobart. When the movie was filmed, the owners, Barrie and Ada Regan, were personal friends of star Pavarotti, and they were most likely instrumental in offering the elegant house and gardens for use in the film.

You Can't Beat the Law
1943, Monogram Pictures
A playboy is framed and sent to prison after his stolen car is found at a holdup.

Director: Phil Rosen
Screenwriters: Albert Beich, Charles R. Marion
Art Direction: David Milton
Cinematographer: Mack Stengler
Partial Cast: Edward Norris, Joan Woodbury, Jack La Rue

• San Quentin State Prison, San Quentin

Yours, Mine and Ours
1968, United Artists
Two widowers, both with several children, merge into one large family.

Director: Melville Shavelson
Screenwriters: Bob Carroll Jr., Madelyn Davis, Mort Lachman, Melville Shavelson
Author: Helen Eileen Beardsley *Who Gets the Drumsticks* (book)
Production Designer: Arthur Lonergan

Cinematographer: Charles F. Wheeler
Partial Cast: Henry Fonda, Lucille Ball, Van
Johnson, Tom Bosley, Morgan Brittany

• Golden Gate Bridge
• Senor Pico Restaurant, 900 Northpoint Street,
Wurster Building, Ghirardelli Square
• San Francisco Maritime National Historic Park,
Golden Gate National Recreation Area-bocce ball
court
• San Francisco Maritime National Historic Park,
Golden Gate National Recreation Area-fishing
pier
• Grant Avenue, Chinatown District
• Cable car
• San Francisco-Oakland Bay Bridge
• Fisherman's Wharf District
• Marin Headlands, Golden Gate National
Recreation Area
• Naval Air Station Alameda, Alameda Island-
runway
• Naval Air Station Alameda, Alameda Island-
aircraft carrier USS *Enterprise* (CVN 65)
• 555 West Essex Way, Naval Air Station
Alameda, Alameda Island-as Beardsley family
residence

USS ENTERPRISE

Nicknamed "The Big E" the massive aircraft carrier, a supercarrier of the Nimitz-class, was the world's first nuclear-powered naval vessel and the longest on the globe. It was built at the Newport News Shipbuilding and Dry Dock Company in Virginia, and the hull launched on September 24, 1960. The ship's statistics are staggering: she is 1,123 feet long, can carry 60-plus aircraft, serves up to 20,000 meals a day, has its own TV station and daily circulated newspaper. She was homeported at Naval Air Station Alameda from 1966 through 1989. She participated in every major conflict since she sailed and figured heavily in conflicts in the Middle and Far East by strategically displaying her power when tempers flared. Some highlights of her service include being a tracking station for America's first orbital spaceflight in 1962, and as part of the blockade during the Cuban Missile Crisis later that same year. In the fall of 2001, she was deployed to the North Arabian Sea as part of Operation Enduring Freedom in the aftermath of the September 11 attacks. The ship was inactivated on December 1, 2012 and is destined for the scrapyard—the end of a remarkable career.

Zodiac
2007, Warner Brothers and Paramount Pictures
The story of a murderer, based on actual events, who terrified the Bay Area with a string of brutal killings.

Director: David Fincher
Screenwriter: James Vanderbilt
Author: Robert Graysmith (book)
Production Designer: Donald Graham Burt
Art Direction: Keith Cunningham
Cinematographer: Harris Savides
Partial Cast: Jake Gyllenhaal, Mark Ruffalo,
Anthony Edwards, Robert Downey Jr., Brian Cox,
John Carroll Lynch

• Roosevelt School, 460 Arguello Avenue,
Richmond District
• Ferry Building, Herb Caen Way, Embarcadero
District
• San Francisco Chronicle Building, 901 Mission
Street, South of Market District
• Lake Berryessa, Napa
• ACT Geary Theater, 405 Geary Street, Union
Square District
• Intersection of Washington Street and Cherry
Street, Presidio Heights District
• 13th Street, South of Market District-underneath
Central Skyway Freeway
• Original Joe's, 144 Taylor Street, Tenderloin
District-restaurant
• North Point Theater, 295 Bay Street,
Fisherman's Wharf District
• 62 Varda Landing, Sausalito-houseboat
• Golden Gate Bridge
• Civic Center Plaza, Civic Center District-phone
booth
• Transbay Terminal, 425 Mission Street, South
of Market District-underpass
• Earl Warren State Office Building, 350
McAllister Street, Civic Center-exterior portico

THE END

APPENDIX A: Movies in Chronological Order

MOVIE	YEAR
Behind That Curtain	1929
The Cock-Eyed World	
The Beloved Bachelor	1931
The Maltese Falcon	
Never the Twain Shall Meet	
One Way Passage	1932
Ladies They Talk About	1933
Broadway Bill	1934
Fog Over Frisco	
Here Comes the Navy	
The Lemon Drop Kid	
Treasure Island	
Case of the Curious Bride	1935
Mutiny on the Bounty	
Stranded	
After the Thin Man	1936
Charlie Chan's Secret	
China Clipper	
Follow the Fleet	
Alcatraz Island	1937
Ever Since Eve	
The Go Getter	
The Last Gangster	
San Quentin	
Song of the City	
Think Fast, Mr. Moto	
Alexander's Ragtime Band	1938
Mr. Wong, Detective	
The Sisters	
Stablemates	
Too Hot to Handle	
Charlie Chan at Treasure Island	1939
Fisherman's Wharf	
Mr. Moto Takes a Vacation	
The Mystery of Mr. Wong	
Secret Service of the Air	
Smashing the Money Ring	
Cross Country Romance	1940
The Fatal Hour	
The House Across the Bay	
If I Had My Way	
Passport to Alcatraz	
Road to Singapore	
They Drive By Night	
They Knew What They Wanted	
Three Faces West	

Golden Gate Girl	1941
The Maltese Falcon	
Shadow of the Thin Man	
The Fleet's In	1942
Men of San Quentin	
Seven Miles from Alcatraz	
Stand by for Action	
This Gun for Hire	
Air Force	1943
Bombardier	
Destination Tokyo	
Happy Land	
Jack London	
Shadow of a Doubt	
You Can't Beat the Law	
The Fighting Sullivans	1944
Seven Days Ashore	
Thirty Seconds Over Tokyo	
Adventure	1945
Road to Alcatraz	
Shadow of a Woman	1946
The Show-Off	
That Brennan Girl	
The Well-Groomed Bride	
Born to Kill	1947
Dark Passage	
Devil Ship	
The Farmer's Daughter	
My Favorite Brunette	
Nora Prentiss	
Out of the Past	
All My Sons	1948
Every Girl Should Be Married	
I Remember Mama	
The Lady From Shanghai	
Million Dollar Weekend	
Race Street	
Raw Deal	
Train to Alcatraz	
All the King's Men	1949
Impact	
Malaya	
Red Light	
The Story of Molly X	
Thieves' Highway	
Treasure of Monte Cristo	
The Woman on Pier 13	
All About Eve	1950
Born to Be Bad	

D.O.A.	1950
Experiment Alcatraz	
Key to the City	
The Man Who Cheated Himself	
Riding High	
Shakedown	
Southside 1-1000	
Where Danger Lives	
Woman on the Run	
Close to My Heart	1951
Golden Girl	
The House on Telegraph Hill	
The Raging Tide	
Submarine Command	
My Six Convicts	1952
Scaramouche	
The Sniper	
Sudden Fear	
The Bigamist	1953
The Caddy	
No Escape	
The Caine Mutiny	1954
Crime Wave	
Cry Vengeance	
Duffy of San Quentin	
The High and the Mighty	
Blood Alley	1955
Cell 2455, Death Row	
Hell on Frisco Bay	
It Came from Beneath the Sea	
Many Rivers to Cross	
The Creature Walks Among Us	1956
Julie	
The Killing	
The Rack	
The Revolt of Mamie Stover	
Storm Center	
Crime of Passion	1957
Escape from San Quentin	
House of Numbers	
Kiss Them for Me	
The Midnight Story	
Pal Joey	
The Unholy Wife	
In Love and War	1958
I Want to Live	
The Lineup	
Vertigo	
Al Capone	1959

The Five Pennies	1959
Night of the Quarter Moon	
On the Beach	
This Earth is Mine	
The Facts of Life	1960
The Flower Thief	
Pollyanna	
Portrait in Black	
Flower Drum Song	1961
Man-Trap	
The Pleasure of His Company	
Susan Slade	
Swingin' Along	
Wild in the Country	
The Birdman of Alcatraz	1962
Days of Wine and Roses	
Experiment in Terror	
How the West Was Won	
The Birds	1963
It's a Mad, Mad, Mad, Mad World	
The Three Stooges Go Around the World in a Daze	
Good Neighbor Sam	1964
Man's Favorite Sport?	
Marnie	
Where Love Has Gone	
Dear Brigitte	1965
Doctor Goldfoot and the Bikini Machine	
In Harms Way	
Once a Thief	
The Third Day	
The Crazy-Quilt	1966
Mondo Topless	
The Gnome-Mobile	1967
The Graduate	
Guess Who's Coming to Dinner	
The Hippie Revolt	
Point Blank	
Funnyman	
The Boston Strangler	1968
Bullitt	
Finian's Rainbow	
Head	
Machine Gun McCain	
Petulia	
Psych-Out	
Revolution	
Skidoo	
They Came to Rob Las Vegas	
Yours, Mine, and Ours	

Colossus: The Forbin Project	1969
Daddy's Gone A-Hunting	
Eye of the Cat	
The Love Bug	
One on Top of the Other	
Take the Money and Run	
Fools	1970
Gimme Shelter	
The Kremlin Letter	
Little Fauss and Big Halsy	
The Strawberry Statement	
They Call Me Mr. Tibbs!	
The Andromeda Strain	1971
Dirty Harry	
Harold and Maude	
The Organization	
THX-1138	
Butterflies Are Free	1972
The Candidate	
The Godfather	
One is a Lonely Number	
Pete 'n Tillie	
Play It Again, Sam	
Slither	
What's Up, Doc?	
The All-American Boy	1973
American Graffiti	
Behind the Green Door	
Counselor at Crime	
Ground Zero	
The Laughing Policeman	
The Mack	
Magnum Force	
Profession: Adventurers	
The Second Coming of Suzanne	
Steelyard Blues	
Superdad	
The Conversation	1974
Escape to Witch Mountain	
Freebie and the Bean	
The Front Page	
Herbie Rides Again	
Lenny	
The Towering Inferno	
The Black Bird	1975
Funny Lady	
The Killer Elite	
Smile	
Burnt Offerings	1976

The Enforcer	1976
Family Plot	
Street People	
The Domino Principle	1977
Heroes	
Mr. Billion	
Nightmare in Blood	
The Pack	
Telefon	
Doctor Dracula	1978
Foul Play	
Gates of Heaven	
Heaven Can Wait	
High Anxiety	
Invasion of the Body Snatchers	
Lady of the House	
The Magic of Lassie	
The Manitou	
A Night Full of Rain	
Olly, Olly, Oxen Free	
Superman	
Who'll Stop the Rain	
...And Justice for All	1979
Escape From Alcatraz	
The Fog	
Hardcore	
More American Graffiti	
Phantasm	
The Promise	
Star Trek: The Motion Picture	
Swim Team	
Time After Time	
Can't Stop the Music	1980
Cardiac Arrest	
A Christmas Without Snow	
Die Laughing	
Heart Beat	
Inside Moves	
Little Miss Marker	
Nine to Five	
Serial	
Tell Me a Riddle	
Where the Buffalo Roam	
Charlie Chan and the Curse of the Dragon Queen	1981
Chu Chu and the Philly Flash	
An Eye for an Eye	
Raiders of the Lost Ark	
Shoot the Moon	
Ticket to Heaven	

Chan is Missing	1982
48 Hours	
Hammett	
Honkytonk Man	
Out	
Tron	
Yes, Giorgio	
The Black Stallion Returns	1983
Cujo	
The Right Stuff	
Signal Seven	
Sudden Impact	
Birdy	1984
Crackers	
Dim Sum: A Little Bit of Heart	
Electric Dreams	
Hard to Hold	
Impulse	
Indiana Jones and the Temple of Doom	
No Small Affair	
Thief of Hearts	
The Times of Harvey Milk	
The Woman in Red	
Creator	1985
Explorers	
Force of Darkness	
The Goonies	
Jagged Edge	
Maxie	
On the Edge	
Smooth Talk	
A View to a Kill	
Big Trouble in Little China	1986
Flight of the Navigator	
A Great Wall	
Howard the Duck	
The Men's Club	
Monster in the Closet	
Peggy Sue Got Married	
Quicksilver	
Salvador	
Sid and Nancy	
Star Trek IV: The Voyage Home	
Terror on Alcatraz	
Burglar	1987
Good Morning, Babylon	
Heat and Sunlight	
Innerspace	
Leonard Part VI	

P. K. and the Kid   1987
The Principal
Superman IV: The Quest for Peace
The Witches of Eastwick
Beaches   1988
Bird
The Dead Pool
Patty Hearst
The Presidio
Shoot to Kill
'68
Slaughterhouse Rock
Tucker: The Man and His Dream
The Virgin Machine
The Wash
Wildfire
The Abyss   1989
Black Rain
Casualties of War
Dead Pit
Eat a Bowl of Tea
Fat Man and Little Boy
Indiana Jones and the Last Crusade
Kinjite: Forbidden Subjects
Roger and Me
True Believer
The Vineyard
Witchtrap
Another 48 Hours   1990
Berkeley in the 60s
Die Hard II
Flashback
Flatliners
Pacific Heights
Predator 2
Pretty Woman
The Rookie
Sibling Rivalry
Class Action   1991
The Doctor
Dogfight
The Doors
Dying Young
Eve of Destruction
Shattered
Star Trek VI: The Undiscovered Country
Terminator II: Judgment Day
Until the End of the World
Basic Instinct   1992

Final Analysis	1992
Forever Young	
Kuffs	
Memoirs of an Invisible Man	
Nowhere to Run	
Out on a Limb	
Radio Flyer	
Raising Cain	
Sister Act	
Sneakers	
Stop or My Mom Will Shoot	
Under Siege	
And the Band Played On	1993
Being Human	
The Beverly Hillbillies	
Blood In, Blood Out	
Dragon: the Bruce Lee Story	
Fearless	
Heart and Souls	
Homeward Bound: The Incredible Journey	
Jack the Bear	
The Joy Luck Club	
Made in America	
Mrs. Doubtfire	
Poetic Justice	
Sister Act 2: Back in the Habit	
So I Married an Axe Murderer	
Tales of the City	
Angels in the Outfield	1994
Beverly Hills Cop III	
Clifford	
Forrest Gump	
Getting Even With Dad	
Golden Gate	
Interview with the Vampire: The Vampire Chronicles	
Junior	
Murder in the First	
Nina Takes a Lover	
When a Man Loves a Woman	
Born to Be Wild	1995
Copycat	
Dangerous Minds	
Jade	
Merlin's Shop of Mystical Wonders	
The Net	
Nine Months	
Outbreak	
Panther	
Village of the Damned	

A Walk in the Clouds	1995
Chalk	1996
Down Periscope	
The Fan	
Homeward Bound II: Lost in San Francisco	
Jack	
Larger Than Life	
Mother	
Phenomenon	
The Rock	
Scream	
Unhook the Stars	
Dream with the Fishes	1997
Farmer and Chase	
Fathers' Day	
Flubber	
The Game	
Gattaca	
George of the Jungle	
Home Alone 3	
I Know What You Did Last Summer	
Inventing the Abbotts	
Little City	
Lolita	
Mad City	
Metro	
The Rainmaker	
A Smile Like Yours	
Titanic	
City of Angels	1998
Desperate Measures	
Doctor Dolittle	
Dream for an Insomniac	
Homegrown	
How Stella Got Her Groove Back	
Hurlyburly	
More Tales of the City	
The Parent Trap	
Patch Adams	
Sphere	
What Dreams May Come	
Around the Fire	1999
The Bachelor	
Bicentennial Man	
Black Eyed Dog	
Crazy in Alabama	
Dumbarton Bridge	
Ed TV	
Eye of the Beholder	

The General's Daughter   1999
Gloria
Guinevere
The Insider
The Invisible Circus
Life
Mumford
The Other Sister
Seven Girlfriends
Stigmata
Suckerfish
This Space Between Us
Treasure Island
True Crime
Wildflowers
Bedazzled   2000
Boys and Girls
Down to You
Groove
High Fidelity
Just One Night
Mission
North Beach
Playing Mona Lisa
Sausalito
Woman on Top
All About You   2001
The Animal
Bandits
Bartleby
The Deep End
Dr. Dolittle 2
Ever Since the World Ended
Further Tales of the City
Haiku Tunnel
The Man Who Wasn't There
Never Die Twice
The Princess Diaries
Rollerball
Serendipity
The Sleepy Time Gal
Sweet November
Ticker
The Wedding Planner
Yamashita: The Tiger's Treasure
Cherish   2002
Enough
The First 20 Million Is Always the Hardest
40 Days and 40 Nights

Half Past Dead	2002
High Crimes	
Kung Phooey!	
Purpose	
The Sweetest Thing	
American Wedding	2003
Cheaper by the Dozen	
The Core	
Dopamine	
House of Sand and Fog	
Hulk	
Julie and Jack	
The Matrix Reloaded	
The Matrix Revolutions	
The Room	
Swing	
Under the Tuscan Sun	
Water Under the Bridge	
The Wild Parrots of Telegraph Hill	
American Yearbook	2004
The Assassination of Richard Nixon	
Dead & Breakfast	
50 First Dates	
Happily Even After	
Illusion	
Twisted	
Bee Season	2005
The Californians	
Just Like Heaven	
Memoirs of a Geisha	
Mistress of Spices	
Night of Henna	
Rent	
Rumor Has It...	
Tweek City	
XXX: State of the Union	
Colma: the Musical	2006
The Darwin Awards	
The Hamiltons	
Pursuit of Happyness	
San Franpsycho	
Valley of the Heart's Delight	
X-Men: The Last Stand	
August Rush	2007
Black August	
Blonde Ambition	
Curse of Alcatraz	
Georgia Rule	
Heartbreak Kid	

The Kite Runner	2007
Zodiac	
Birdemic: Shock and Terror	2008
Bottle Shock	
The Changeling	
Four Christmases	
Harrison Montgomery	
The Lost Coast	
Milk	
The Other End of the Line	
Touching Home	
Funny People	2009
La mission	
Land of the Lost	
Tenderloin	
Cats and Dogs: The Revenge of Kitty Galore	2010
Hereafter	
Howl	
My Name is Kahn	
Contagion	2011
Moneyball	
Rise of the Planet of the Apes	
About Cherry	2012
The Five-Year Engagement	
Good Deeds	
The Guilt Trip	
Hemingway and Gellhorn	
Knife Fight	
The Master	
On the Road	
Red Tails	
The Sessions	
Blue Jasmine	2013
Fruitvale Station	
The Internship	
Jobs	

APPENDIX B: Movies About the Bay Area but Not Shot There

The Adventures of Bullwhip Griffin

1967, Buena Vista
Two aristocrats and their butler head West during the California Gold Rush.

Director: James Neilson
Screenwriter: Lowell S. Hawley
Author: Albert Sidney Fleischman *By the Great Horn Spoon* (novel)
Art Directors: Carroll Clark, John B. Mansbridge
Cinematographer: Edward Colman
Partial Cast: Hermione Baddeley, Cecil Kellaway, Karl Malden, Roddy McDowell, Suzanne Pleshette

• San Francisco in period sets representative of post-Gold Rush era

The Adventures of Mark Twain

1944, Warner Brothers
The life of the foremost author of humor from a riverboat on the Mississippi to becoming an honorary fellow at Oxford.

Director: Irving Rapper
Screenwriters: Harold M. Sherman, Alan Le May, Harry Chandler
Art Director: John J. Hughes
Cinematographers: Sol Polito, Lawrence W. Butler, James Leicester, Edward Linden, Don Siegel
Partial Cast: Frederic March, Alexis Smith, Donald Crisp, Alan Hale, John Carradine, Percy Kilbride

• San Francisco

PERCY KILBRIDE

Character actor Percy W. Kilbride was born in 1888, the son of San Francisco machinist Owen Kilbride who lived in the South of Market District at 847 Howard Street. At age 12, Percy worked as a call boy in his hometown's Central Theater and later took up the stage with his first role in *A Tale of Two Cities*. His service in World War I curtailed his career, and after serving his country he acted in road and stock companies. Moving into movies in the 1930s, he was not noticed until much later. His notoriety began to peak when he created the country bumpkin role of Pa in the well-liked *The Egg and I* (1947) popularly thought to have been filmed in what was then the egg-producing capital of the U.S.A., Petaluma (but that is just lore). That role fostered the series of eight *Ma and Pa Kettle* movies that followed. Sadly, Kilbride did not profit from those roles and lived on Social Security during his retirement. He was a life-long bachelor and died in 1964 from injuries he sustained after being struck by a car during his daily stroll down Hollywood Boulevard. As a veteran, he was buried in San Bruno's Golden Gate National Cemetery. His other Bay Area movies include *The Well-Groomed Bride* (1946) and *Riding High* (1950).

April Showers

1948, Warner Brothers
Dad takes to drinking in a family vaudeville act.

Director: James V. Kern
Screenwriters: Joe Laurie Jr., Peter Milne
Cinematographer: Carl E. Guthrie
Partial Cast: Jack Carson, Ann Sothern, Robert Alda

• San Francisco

Around the World in 80 Days

2004, Disney Pictures
An inventor bets that he can circle the globe within 80 days.

Director: Frank Coraci
Screenwriters: David Titcher, David Benullo, David Goldstein
Author: Jules Verne *Le Tour du monde en quatre-vingts jours* (novel)
Production Designer: Perry Andelin Blake
Art Director: Robert Cowper
Cinematographer: Phil Meheux
Partial Cast: Jackie Chan, Steve Coogan, Cecile De France, Jim Broadbent

• A representation of Victorian San Francisco

Barbary Coast
1935, Samuel Goldwyn
AKA: *Port of Wickedness*
A ruthless club owner in the Barbary Coast saloon district transforms a lonely girl into a star attraction.

Director: Howard Hawks
Screenwriters: Ben Hecht, Charles MacArthur, Edward Chodorov, Stephen Longstreet
Art Director: Richard Day
Cinematographer: Ray June
Partial Cast: Miriam Hopkins, Edward G. Robinson, Joel McCrea, Walter Brennan, Brian Donlevy

• San Francisco in period sets

Barbary Coast Gent
1944, Metro Goldwyn Mayer
AKA: *Gold Town* and *The Honest Thief*
A bandit from the goldfields tries to go straight.

Director: Roy Del Ruth
Screenwriters: Grant Garett, William R. Lipman, Harry Ruskin
Art Directors: William Ferrari, Cedric Gibbons
Cinematographer: Charles Salerno
Partial Cast: Wallace Beery, Binnie Barnes, John Carradine, Chill Wills, Louise Beavers

• San Francisco

The Big House
1930, Metro Goldwyn Mayer
Rage, desperation and loyalty are daily situations in a prison institution with almost double the designed load of felons.

Directors: George W. Hill, Ward Wing
Screenwriters: Frances Marion, Joseph Farnham, Martin Flavin, Lennox Robinson
Art Director: Cedric Gibbons
Cinematographer: Harold Wenstrom
Partial Cast: Chester Morris, Lewis Stone, Leila Hyams, Wallace Beery, Robert Montgomery

• About San Quentin State Prison, San Quentin

Charlie Chan's Murder Cruise
1940, Fox

Charlie tries to discover the identity of a strangler who strikes multiple times on a cruise ship sailing the Pacific Ocean.

Director: Eugene Forde
Screenwriters: Robertson White, Lester Ziffren
Author: Earl Derr Biggers (story)
Art Directors: Richard Day, Chester Gore
Cinematographer: Virgil Miller
Partial Cast: Sidney Toler, Leo G. Carroll

• A representation of arriving in San Francisco from Hawaii

The Cheap Detective
1978, Columbia
AKA: *Neil Simon's The Cheap Detective*
A 1940s private eye gets involved with a complicated case.

Director: Robert Moore
Screenwriter: Neil Simon
Production Designer: Robert Luthardt
Art Director: Phil Bennett
Cinematographer: John A. Alonzo
Partial Cast: Peter Falk, Ann-Margret, Eileen Brennan, Sid Caesar, Stockard Channing, James Coco, Dom Deluise, Louise Fletcher, John Houseman, Madeline Kahn, Fernando Lamas, Marsha Mason, Phil Silvers

• About San Francisco

Confessions of an Opium Eater
1962, Allied Artists
AKA: *Evils of Chinatown*, *Souls For Sale*
An early 19th-century adventurer is involved with helping runaway slave girls and victims of a tong war.

Director: Albert Zugsmith
Screenwriter: Robert Hill
Author: Thomas De Quincey *Confessions of an English Opium Eater* (book)
Art Director: Eugène Lourié
Cinematographer: Joseph F. Biroc
Partial Cast: Vincent Price, Linda Ho, Richard Loo, June Kyoto Lu

• Period representation of San Francisco

Dark Intruder
1965, Universal
Police call in an occult expert to help solve a series of murders.

Director: Harvey Hart
Screenwriter: Barré Lyndon
Art Director: Loyd S. Papez
Cinematographer: John F. Warren
Partial Cast: Leslie Nielsen, Peter Mark Richman, Judi Meredith, Werner Klemperer

• San Francisco circa 1890

Drums of Tahiti
1954, Columbia
A smuggler buys a bride in San Francisco to help him run guns against the French colonial government.

Director: William Castle
Screenwriters: Robert E. Kent, Douglas Heyes
Art Director: Paul Palmentola
Cinematographer: Lester White
Partial Cast: Dennis O'Keefe, Patricia Medina, Francis L. Sullivan

• A representation of San Francisco circa 1877

Escape in the Fog
1945, Columbia
A nurse recovering from a nervous breakdown keeps having dreams of murder. When she meets the hospital's officer in charge of psychology, she is shocked by what she discovers.

Director: Budd Boetticher
Screenwriter: Aubrey Wisberg
Art Director: Jerome Thoms
Cinematographer: George Meehan
Partial Cast: Otto Kruger, Nina Foch, William Wright, Konstantin Shayne, Ivan Triesault, Ernie Adams

• San Francisco-Oakland Bay Bridge (This is probably a set piece, the bridge never had a sidewalk. Also the sections of the bridge seen in the movie are a replication of the Oakland cantilever section not the San Francisco suspension section that has a solid railing with no horizontal pipe railing.)

Fireman, Save My Child
1954, Universal International
Incompetent firemen accidentally catch a gang of crooks.

Director: Leslie Goodwins
Screenwriters: John Grant, Lee Loeb
Art Directors: Alexander Golitzen, Eric Orborn
Cinematographer: Clifford Stine

Partial Cast: Spike Jones, Hugh O'Brien

• About 1910 San Francisco

Flame of Barbary Coast
1945, Republic Studios
A cowboy becomes involved with a night club queen and their fortunes are resolved by the Earthquake and Fire of 1906.

Director: Joseph Kane
Screenwriter: Borden Chase, Prescott Chaplin
Art Director: Gano Chittenden
Cinematographer: Robert DeGrasse
Partial Cast: John Wayne, Ann Dvorak, Joseph Schildkraut, William Frawley, Virginia Grey, Russell Hicks, Jack Norton, Paul Fix, Marc Lawrence

• An impression of turn of the century San Francisco

A Free Soul
1931, Metro Goldwyn Mayer
A lawyer's daughter falls for his gangster client.

Director: Clarence Brown
Screenwriters: John Meehan, Becky Gardnier, Willard Mack
Author: Adella Rogers St. Johns (book)
Art Director: Cedric Gibbons
Cinematographer: William H. Daniels
Partial Cast: Norma Shearer, Leslie Howard, Lionel Barrymore, Clark Gable, James Gleason, Lucy Beaumont

• Skyline of San Francisco

Frisco Jenny
1933, Warner Brothers
AKA: Common Ground
A Barbary Coast madame is prosecuted for murder by her son.

Director: William A. Wellman
Screenwriters: Gerald Beaumont, Lillie Hayward, John Francis Larkin, Robert Lord, Wilson Mizner
Art Director: Robert M. Haas
Cinematographer: Sidney Hickox
Partial Cast: Ruth Chatterton, Donald Cook, Robert Warwick, Louis Calhern, Helen Jerome Eddy

• A representation of 1906 Golden Gate Park with refugee tents after the 1906 Earthquake and Fire

The Frisco Kid

1979, Warner Brothers
AKA: *No Knife*
A Polish rabbi travels to San Francisco and along the way befriends a bank robber.

Director: Robert Aldrich
Screenwriters: Michael Elias, Frank Shaw
Production Designer: Terrence Marsh
Cinematographer: Robert B. Hauser
Partial Cast: Gene Wilder, Harrison Ford

• A representation of 1850 San Francisco

Frisco Sal

1945, Universal Pictures
AKA: *Frisco Kate*
A singer arrives in a Barbary Coast saloon to find her brother's killer.

Director: George Waggner
Screenwriters: Gerald Geraghty, Curt Siodmak
Art Directors: Robert Clatsworthy, John B. Goodman
Cinematographer: Charles Van Enger
Partial Cast: Susanna Foster, Turnhan Bey, Alan Curtis, Andy Devine

• A representation of period San Francisco

Gentleman Jim

1942, Warner Brothers
An upstart in the unsanctioned back room sport of boxing beats out the top ranking boxer of them all.

Director: Raoul Walsh
Screenwriters: Vincent Laurence, Horace McCoy
Author: James J. Corbett *The Roar of the Crowd* (book)
Art Director: Ted Smith
Cinematographer: Sidney Hickox
Partial Cast: Errol Flynn, Alexis Smith, Jack Carson, Alan Hale, William Frawley

• About San Francisco

JAMES CORBETT

San Francisco native James Joseph Corbett was frail as a child but became a champion heavyweight boxer. Corbett was born in San Francisco on September 1, 1866, one of nine children of a livery stable owner on Hayes Street. Jim matured into a professional who trained and later became a trainer at the Olympic Club. His moniker, Gentleman Jim, came from his peers at the club because he dressed like a dandy and had friends that included bankers and the like. (He despised the moniker that memorializes him.) He once challenged and defeated the great boxer John L. Sullivan in a 21-round bout. In 1894 Corbett was in one of the first fights ever to be recorded on film, a match that took place in Nevada. He died on February 18, 1933.

HARRY CROCKER

The tall and good-looking Henry J. Crocker Jr. was born on July 2, 1893 to parents Henry Joseph and Mary (Ives) Crocker in San Francisco. The senior Crocker was a banker and sat on the boards of several companies. The family of eight resided in the Pacific Heights District at 2301 Laguna Street in a large stone-faced residence with a number of servants. Harry attended the prestigious Taft College preparatory school in Watertown, Connecticut followed by study at Yale University where he received his initial dramatic instruction. During World War I he trained at the Naval Aviation School in Boston, where he achieved the rank of ensign and then was given an assignment in France. He received further acting experience in Los Angeles starting in 1924. His first film appearance was the next year as a WW I doughboy in *The Big Parade* for MGM. He was the publicist for Charlie Chaplin's *The Gold Rush* (1925), a position he would occasionally dabble in for much of the rest of his life. In 1927 he appeared with actress Marion Davies in *Tillie the Toiler* that consequently brought him into the San Simeon circle of William Randolph Hearst. In *The Circus* (1928), he appeared as a tightrope walker. Charlie Chaplin hired Crocker again, this time as his assistant director for the production of *City Lights* (1931), but after a disagreement Crocker departed. His appearance in *Gentleman Jim* (1942) was uncredited (as most of his appearances were), where he played the part of his relative Charles Crocker. Later in his life he worked as a columnist for the Hearst newspapers. He reconciled with Chaplin and served as his business manager during the filming of *Limelight* (1952), in which he appeared as a music hall patron. He died on May 23,1958 in Beverly Hills.

Girl Rush
1944, RKO Radio Pictures
Two unsuccessful vaudeville entertainers search for gold during the California Gold Rush of 1849.

Director: Gordon Douglas
Screenwriter: Robert E. Kent
Authors: László Vadnay, Aldar Laszlo "Petticoat Fever" (story)
Art Directors: Albert S. D'Agostino, Walter E. Keller
Cinematographer: Nicholas Musuraca
Partial Cast: Wally Brown, Alan Carney, Frances Langford, Robert Mitchum

• San Francisco

Gold Is Where You Find It
1938, Warner Brothers
Gold Rush miners settle in California as farmers and a land war ensues.

Director: Michael Curtiz
Screenwriters: Warren Duff, Robert Buckner
Author: Clements Ripley (story)
Art Director: Ted Smith
Cinematographer: Sol Polito
Partial Cast: George Brent, Olivia de Havilland, Claude Rains, Margaret Lindsay, John Litel

• Period piece

The Great Ziegfeld
1936, Metro Goldwyn Mayer
The life of famed Broadway impresario Florenz Ziegfeld Jr.

Director: Robert Z. Leonard
Screenwriter: William Anthony McGuire
Art Directors: Cedric Gibbons, Eddie Imazu

Cinematographers: George J. Folsey, Karl Freund, Merritt B. Gerstad, Ray June, Oliver T. Marsh
Partial Cast: William Powell, Myrna Loy, Luise Rainer, Frank Morgan, Fanny Brice, Virginia Bruce, Reginald Owen, Ray Bolger

• A representation of San Francisco

Hello Frisco, Hello
1943, 20th Century Fox
AKA: *Hello, San Francisco, Hello*
An ambitious vaudevillian takes his quartet from a honky-tonk to the big time, while spurning the love of his troupe's star singer for a selfish heiress.

Director: H. Bruce Humberstone
Screenwriters: Robert Ellis, Helen Logan
Art Directors: James Basevi, Boris Leven
Cinematographers: Charles Clarke, Allen Davey
Partial Cast: Alice Faye, John Payne, Jack Oakie, June Havoc, Lynn Bari, Ward Bond

• A representation of Pacific Avenue, Barbary Coast District at the turn of 19th century

How to Be Very, Very Popular
1955, 20th Century Fox
Two girls who make a hasty escape hide out in a college fraternity house.

Director: Nunnaly Johnson
Screenwriters: Nunnaly Johnson, Howard Lindsay, Lyford Moore, Harlan Thompson
Author: Edward Hope (novel)
Art Directors: John DeCuir, Lyle R. Wheeler
Cinematographer: Milton R. Krasner
Partial Cast: Bette Grable, Sheree North, Robert Cummings

• Probably about San Francisco but not shot there

Inside Straight
1951, Metro Goldwyn Mayer
A ruthless businessman rises to the top through greed and corruption.

Director: Gerald Mayer
Screenwriter: Guy Trosper
Author: Guy Trosper
Art Director: Daniel B. Cathcart, Cedric Gibbons
Cinematographer: Ray June
Partial Cast: David Brian, Arlen Dahl, Barry Sullivan, Mercedes McCambridge, Paula Raymond, Claude Jarman Jr., Lon Chaney Jr., John Hoyt

• San Francisco

The Jazz Singer
1927, Warner Brothers
A youth defies his father in his dream to be a singer.

Director: Alan Crosland
Screenwriters: Samson Raphaelson, Alfred A. Cohn
Author: Samson Raphaelson "The Day of Atonement" (short story)
Cinematographer: Hal Mohr
Partial Cast: Al Jolson, May McAvoy, Warner Oland

• A representation of Coffee Dan's, O'Farrell Street at Powell Street, Union Square District

Land of the Lost
2009, Universal
A doctor is sucked into a space-time vortex with two others who experience dinosaurs and other fantastic creatures.

Director: Brad Silberling
Screenwriters: Chris Henchy, Dennis McNicholas
Authors: Sid Kroft, Marty Kroft (TV series)
Production Designer: Bo Welch
Art Directors: John Dexter, Maya Shimoguchi
Cinematographer: Dion Beebe
Partial Cast: Will Ferrell, Anna Friel, Danny McBride, Jorma Taccone, John Boylan, Matt Lauer

• A representation of the Golden Gate Bridge in a desert landscape

The Mad Martindales
1942, 20th Century Fox
An eccentric family is in dire financial straits and their plots to get out of debt.

Director: Alfred L. Werker
Screenwriter: Francis Edward Faragoh
Authors: Ludwig Hirschfeld, Wesley Towner, Edmund Wolf Not for Children (play)
Cinematographer: Lucien N. Andriot
Partial Cast: Jane Withers, Marjorie Weaver, Alan Mobray, Gig Young, George Reeves

• San Francisco circa 1900

Madonna of the Streets
1930, Columbia Pictures

A wealthy man fails to include his mistress in his will and she works undercover to get the money after his death.

Director: John S. Robertson
Screenwriter: Jo Swerling
Author: W. B. Maxwell "The Ragged Messenger" (story)
Cinematographer: Sol Polito
Partial Cast: Evelyn Brent, Robert Ames, Ivan Linow

• A representation of the Barbary Coast

Man from Frisco
1944, Republic Pictures
An engineer has revolutionary ideas about ship building techniques during World War II.

Director: Robert Florey
Screenwriters: Ethel Hill, Arnold Manoff
Authors: George Worthing Yates, George Carleton Brow (story)
Art Director: Russell Kimball
Cinematographer: Jack A. Marta
Partial Cast: Michael O'Shea, Anne Shirley, Gene Lockhart, Dan Duryea

• A representation of the Richmond shipyards

HENRY KAISER

The character in Man From Frisco, Matt Braddock, was based on the life of Henry J. Kaiser (1882–1967), a frontier entrepreneur, who was a household name during the 1940s. The genius, and dropout, worked on a grand scale—and in record time. His can do attitude played a vital role in the construction of Hoover, Bonneville, Grand Coulee, and Shasta Dams; and created the Kaiser-Permanente medical care program. As a visionary, Kaiser developed the North Bay's Richmond as a huge shipbuilding center after the government's launch of the Liberty Ship program in 1941. Built at an unprecedented rate using mass production prefab techniques, 747 vessels eventually slid down the ramps from Richmond until V-J Day in 1946. One technique he instituted was welding, not riveting the hull's steel plates, which took less time. He also built cargo planes for the war effort. Later he manufactured the "Henry J" Kaiser-Frazer automobile and created residential housing developments in California and Hawaii. He was also the founder of Kaiser Steel and Aluminum.

The Man Who Could Work Miracles
1936, United Artists
A man is given powers beyond his wildest imagination.

Director: Lothar Mendes
Screenwriters: H. G. Wells, Lajos Biro'
Author: H. G. Wells (short story)
Production Designer: Vincent Korda
Cinematographer: Harold Rosson
Partial Cast: Roland Young, Ralph Richardson, Edward Chapman, Ernest Thesiger, Joan Gardner, Joan Hickson, George Sanders

• A representation of San Francisco

The Man Who Wasn't There
2001, Good Machine International
A barber blackmails his wife's boss and lover for money to invest in dry cleaning, but his plan goes terribly sideways.

Directors: Joel Coen, Ethan Coen
Screenwriters: Joel Coen, Ethan Coen
Production Designer: Dennis Gassner
Art Director: Chris Gorak
Cinematographer: Roger Deakens
Partial Cast: Billy Bob Thornton, Frances McDormand

• A representation of Santa Rosa

Mr. Wong in Chinatown
1939, Monogram
A Chinese princess is murdered after seeking help from the authorities.

Director: William Nigh
Screenwriters: Hugh Wiley, Scott Darling
Cinematographer: Harvey Neumann
Partial Cast: Boris Karloff, Marjorie Reynolds, Grant Withers, Huntley Gordon, George Lynn, Lee Tung Foo

• Various opening scenes of San Francisco but not on location

Mother Wore Tights
1947, 20th Century Fox
A vaudeville team and their growing family.

Director: Walter Lang
Screenwriter: Lamar Trotti
Author: Miriam Young (book)
Art Directors: Richard Day, Joseph C. Wright
Cinematographer: Harry Jackson
Partial Cast: Betty Grable, Dan Daily, Mona Freeman, Connie Marshall

• A representation of the Ferry Building
• About Oakland

My Gal Sal
1942, 20th Century Fox
A songwriter romances a singer and finds success in the gay '90s New York City.

Director: Irving Cummings
Screenwriters: Seton I. Miller, Darrell Ware, Karl Tunberg
Author: Theodore Dreiser "Twelve Men" (story)
Art Directors: Richard Day, Joseph C. Wright
Cinematographer: Ernest Palmer
Partial Cast: Rita Hayworth, Victor Mature, John Sutton

• A representation of the San Francisco Opera House that stood on Mission Street near Third Street, South of Market District

Nob Hill
1945, 20th Century Fox
A saloon owner tries to get into society in the Gay '90s.

Director: Henry Hathaway
Screenwriters: Wanda Tuchock, Norman Reilly Raine
Author: Eleanore Griffin (story)
Art Directors: J. Russell Spencer, Lyle R. Wheeler
Cinematographer: Edward Cronjager
Partial Cast: George Raft, Joan Bennett, Vivian Blaine, Peggy Ann Garner, Alan Reed

• About San Francisco

Pacific Rim
2013, Warner Brothers

As a war between humankind and monstrous sea creatures is waged, humans find that a seemingly obsolete special weapon may win the war.

Director: Guillermo del Toro
Screenwriters: Travis Beacham, Guillermo del Toro
Production Designers: Andrew Neskoromny, Carol Spier
Art Directors: Elinor Rose Galbraith, Richard L. Johnson
Cinematographer: Guillermo Navarro
Partial Cast: Charlie Hunnam, Idris Elba, Rinko Kikuchi

• A representation of the Golden Gate Bridge

Paranormal Activity 3
2011, Paramount
In 1988 young sisters Katie and Kristi befriend an invisible entity who resides in their home.

Directors: Henry Joost, Ariel Schulman
Screenwriters: Christopher Landon, Oren Peli
Production Designer: Jennifer Spence
Art Director: David Wilson
Cinematographer: Magdalena Górka
Partial Cast: Lauren Bittner, Christopher Nicholas Smith, Chloe Csengery

• A representation of Santa Rosa during the 1980s.

Romeo Must Die
2000, Warner Brothers
A cop avenges his brother's killer and falls for the daughter of a businessman who is involved in a money-deal with his father.

Director: Andrzej Bartkowiak
Screenwriters: Eric Bernt, John Jarrell
Author: Mitchell Kapner (story)
Production Designer: Michael S. Bolton
Art Director: James Steuart
Cinematographer: Glen MacPherson
Partial Cast: Jet Li, Isaiah Washington, Aaliyah

• Set in Oakland

The Saint Strikes Back
1939, RKO Radio Pictures
AKA: *The Saint Strikes Twice*
Simon Templar, the Saint, travels to San Francisco to solve crime mysteries within the police department.

Director: John Farrow
Screenwriter: John Twist
Author: Leslie Charteris *Angels of Doom* (novel)
Art Director: Van Nest Polglase
Cinematographer: Frank Redman
Partial Cast: George Sanders, Wendy Barrie, Jonathan Hale

• About San Francisco

Salome, Where She Danced
1945, Universal Pictures
During the Austro-Prussian War a dancer is suspected of being a spy and flees to the United States.

Director: Charles Lamont
Screenwriter: Laurence Stalings
Author: Michael J. Phillips (story)
Art Directors: Alexander Golitzen, John B. Goodman
Cinematographer: W. Howard Greene, Hal Mohr
Partial Cast: Yvonne De Carlo, Rod Cameron, Walter Slezak, David Bruce, Albert Decker, Marjorie Rambeau, John Litel

• Period piece

MARJORIE RAMBEAU

Actress Marjorie Rambeau was born on July 15, 1889 in San Francisco. Her parents were Marcel and Lilian (Kindelgerger) Rambeau who separated when Marjorie was a child. Marjorie and her mother went to Alaska, where the youngster sang and played banjo in saloons and music halls. With her mother in tow, her stage debut was on the Sullivan and Considine vaudeville circuit as a child of 12 in 1901. The next year she was a leading woman in a stock company in Portland, Oregon. Thereafter she migrated to British Columbia and started her own theater company in Westminster as producer and leading lady. During the 1910s through the 1920s she was a prominent Broadway lead with her first appearance in *Eyes of Youth* in 1917. During the early and mid-teens she also became a star of San Francisco's Alcazar Theater stock company, but now at almost 40 years old in the late 1920s she went to Hollywood as a character actress in film. She was most often seen in parts as

San Francisco

1936, Metro Goldwyn Mayer
The loves and career problems of a Barbary Coast saloon owner in 1906.

Director: W. S. Van Dyke
Screenwriters: Robert Hopkins, Anita Loos
Art Director: Cedric Gibbons
Cinematographer: Oliver T. Marsh
Partial Cast: Clark Gable, Jeanette MacDonald, Spencer Tracy, Jack Holt, Jessie Ralph, Ted Healy, Shirley Ross

• Representations of San Francisco

The San Francisco Story

1952, Warner Brothers
A wanderer bound for China stops in San Francisco and gets involved with politics.

Director: Robert Parrish
Screenwriters: D. D. Beauchamp, Richard Summers, William Bowers
Production Designer: George Jenkins
Art Directors: Robert Clatworthy, Bernard Herzbrun
Cinematographer: John F. Seitz
Partial Cast: Joel McCrea, Yvonne De Carlo, Sidney Blackmer, Richard Erdman, Florence Bates

• About 1850s San Francisco

The Sea Wolf

1941, Warner Brothers
Survivors of a ferry crash are picked up by a psychopathic captain of a freighter.

Director: Michael Curtiz
Screenwriter: Robert Rossen
Author: Jack London *The Sea Wolf* (novel)
Art Director: Anton Grot
Cinematographer: Sol Polito
Partial Cast: Edward G. Robinson, Alexander Knox, Ida Lupino, John Garfield, Gene Lockhart, Barry Fitzgerald, Stanley Ridges, David Bruce, Howard Da Silva

• 1900 period with recreated Barbary Coast and wharf areas

Silver Queen

1942, United Artists
A chivalrous gambler rescues a girl from a villain.

Director: Lloyd Bacon
Screenwriters: Forrest Halsey, William Allen Johnson, Cecile Kromer, Bernard Schubert
Production Designer: Ralph Berger
Cinematographer: Russell Harlan
Partial Cast: George Brent, Pricilla Lane, Bruce Cabot, Lynne Overman

• Period San Francisco

The Son-Daughter

1932, Metro Goldwyn Mayer
Gang wars in Chinatown prevent true love from blossoming.

Directors: Clarence Brown, Robert Z. Leonard

Screenwriters: John F. Goodrich, Claudine West, Leon Gordon
Authors: George Scarborough, David Belasco (play)
Art Director: Cedric Gibbons
Cinematographer: Oliver T. Marsh
Partial Cast: Helen Hayes, Ramon Novarro, Lewis Stone, Warner Oland, Ralph Morgan, H. B. Warner, Louise Closser Hale

• About Chinatown, San Francisco

South of Market District, on Clara Street. He worked with Tom Mcguire, impresario of several California theaters, for a number of years. Being of short stature with a high voice, Belasco's work veered to the side of writer. More known for his work in the theater, Belasco crossed over to film and co-wrote *The Son-Daughter* screenplay, a piece he had written for the stage years before.

Song of the West
1930, Warner Brothers
An Army scout heads West to be part of the Gold Rush but has a secret in his past.

Director: Ray Enright
Screenwriters: Oscar Hammerstein II, Laurence Stallings, Harvey F. Thew
Cinematographer: Devereaux Jennings
Partial Cast: John Boles, Vivienne Segal, Joe E. Brown, Ann Sothern

• About San Francisco

The Time of Your Life
1948, United Artists
A saloon is host to a wide variety of characters.

Director: H. C. Potter
Screenwriters: William Saroyan, Nathaniel Curtis
Production Designer: Wiard Ihnen
Cinematographers: James Wong Howe, Joseph A. Valentine
Partial Cast: James Cagney, William Bendix, Ward Bond, Broderick Crawford

• Nick's Pacific Street Saloon, 7 Pacific Street, San Francisco-a set

WILLIAM SAROYAN

Novelist, playwright, short story writer, and lyricist Saroyan was born on August 31, 1908 in Fresno to Armenian immigrant parents who fled their home country; his preacher and fruit farmer father was named Armenak and mother Takoohi a housewife. William was the youngest of four children, and by 1910 the family had moved to San Francisco. His father died from perito-

nitis when William was just three, and he and his siblings were placed in foster care at the Methodist Fred Finch Orphanage in Oakland from 1911 to 1916. The family was able to reunite back in Fresno after the separation joined by his maternal grandmother. The young Saroyan sold newspapers and became a messenger with a postal-telegraph company to make money. He was expelled from school at age 15, never to return to formal education, although he once took a typing class, knowing that writing was to be the course of his life. At about age 19 he did a stint in New York, thinking he could make something of himself, but he returned to California six months later. He moved to San Francisco to live in a second-floor apartment at 348 Carl Street. While in the city he drew inspiration for his next story. His first writing success came with the publication of "The Daring Young Man on the Flying Trapeze," a short story that received an O. Henry Award in 1934. From this work, the author went on to generate more than 400 short stories, of which "My Name is Aram" is held to be the most notable. In 1939 Saroyan had developer Henry Doelger build a home at 1821 15th Avenue in Golden Gate Heights for his mother and sister. He stayed there ocassionally working in the lower level. His play *The Time of Your Life*, won the 1940 New York Drama Critics' Circle Award and the 1940 Pulitzer Prize for drama; it was later released as a movie in 1948. He went to Hollywood's MGM in 1941 to film his work *The Human Comedy*, which was released in 1943 with stars Mickey Rooney and Frank Morgan. Drafted into the army in 1942, he was discharged in 1945. In the meantime he and Carol Grace married in 1943, when she was 17, but they divorced in 1949. They remarried in 1951, but stayed together for only a year. They had two children from this union. From 1958 onward Saroyan mostly lived abroad in Paris but also maintained a home in Fresno. Known for his "original and irreverent stories, he celebrated the joy of living in spite of poverty, hunger and insecurity," according to Encyclopedia Britannica. Saroyan died on May 18, 1981 of cancer in the Veterans Hospital in his hometown of Fresno.

Trade Winds
1938, United Artists
A woman commits a murder and assumes a new identity, only to find that she is being followed by a detective.

Director: Tay Garnett
Screenwriters: Tay Garnett, Dorothy Parker, Alan Campbell, Frank R. Adams
Cinematographer: Rudolph Maté
Partial Cast: Fredric March, Joan Bennett, Ralph Bellamy, Ann Sothern

• A representation of San Francisco

20,000 Leagues Under the Sea
1954, Walt Disney
Victorian scientists at sea are wrecked and captured by a mysterious captain of a futuristic submarine.

Director: Richard Fleischer
Screenwriter: Earl Felton
Author: Jules Verne (novel)
Production Designer: Harper Goff
Art Directors: John Meehan, Harper Goff
Cinematographer: Franz Planer
Partial Cast: Kirk Douglas, James Masob, Paul Lukas, Peter Lorre, Robert J. Wilke, Carlton Young, Ted de Corsia

• A representation of a Victorian period San Francisco interior

Weeds
1987, Kingsgate Films
A San Quentin inmate, sentenced to life without parole, writes a play that catches the interest of a reporter.

Director: John D. Hancock
Screenwriters: Dorothy Tristan, John D. Hancock
Production Designer: Joseph T. Garrity
Art Director: Pat Tagliaferro
Cinematographer: Jan Weincke
Partial Cast: Nick Nolte, Rita Taggart, Ernie Hudson

• About San Quentin State Prison

Wells Fargo
1937, Paramount
A history of the growth of the Wells Fargo delivery service.

Director: Frank Lloyd
Screenwriter: Stuart N. Lake, Gerald Geraghty, Frederick J. Jackson, Paul Schofield
Art Directors: Hans Dreier, John B. Goodman
Cinematographer: Theodor Sparkuhl
Partial Cast: Joel McCrea, Bob Burns, Frances Dee, Lloyd Nolan, Robert Cummings

• A representation of period Portsmouth Square and the Lick House Hotel

The Wharf Angel
1934, Paramount
A prostitute falls for a sailor who has a murder in his past.

Director: William Cameron Menzies
Screenwriters: Stephen Morehouse Avery, Samuel Hoffenstein, Frank Partos, Frederick Schlick
Cinematographer: Victor Milner
Partial Cast: Victor McLaglen, Dorothy Dell, Preston Foster, Alison Skipworth

• A representation of the Barbary Coast

The World in His Arms
1952, Universal Pictures
AKA: *Rex Beach's the World in His Arms*
A sea captain woos a Russian countess.

Director: Raoul Walsh
Screenwriters: Rex Beach, Borden Chase, Horace McCoy
Art Directors: Alexander Golitzen, Bernard Herzbrun
Cinematographer: Russell Metty
Partial Cast: Gregory Peck, Ann Blyth, Anthony Quinn, John McIntire, Andrea King, Carl Esmond, Eugenie Leontovitch

• A period film with sets representing San Francisco

APPENDIX C: Movies Purported to Be Shot in or Are About the Bay Area

Alone in the T-Shirt Zone, 1986
Charlie Chan's Greatest Case, 1933
Chinatown Squad, 1935
Condemned Women, 1938
The County Chairman, 1935
Daughter of Shanghai, 1937
Dealing: or the Berkeley-to-Boston
Forty-Brick Lost-Bag Blues, 1972
The Docks of San Francisco, 1932
Escape from San Quentin, 1957
Flight Angels, 1940
Frisco Kid, 1935
Frisco Lil, 1942
Frisco Waterfront, 1935
The Go Getter, 1937
Go Naked in the World, 1961
The Great Hotel Murder, 1935
The Hatchet Man, 1932
Have You Heard of the San Francisco Mime Troupe?, 1968
Heat Lightning, 1934
Hell Bent for Frisco, 1931
Her First Mate, 1933
High Tension, 1936
I Love a Soldier, 1944
The Impatient Years, 1944
International Settlement, 1938
It's All Yours, 1937
King of Alcatraz, 1938

King of the Jungle, 1933
Life is Cheap...but toilet paper is expensive, 1990
Living on Tokyo Time, 1987
The Mad Doctor of Market Street, 1942
Mad Holiday, 1936
The Man Who Came Back, 1931
Massive Retaliation, 1984
Mr. Dynamite, 1935
Night Song, 1948
Night Waitress, 1936
Safety in Numbers, 1930
San Francisco Docks, 1940
Shadows Over Chinatown, 1946
Side Streets, 1934
Son of the Gods, 1930
Split, 1989
The Steel Cage, 1954
Stonewashed, 1999
The Storm, 1938
Ten Dollar Raise, 1935
They All Come Out, 1939
Thirteen Hours by Air, 1936
Up in Arms, 1944
Usher, 2004
Walk a Crooked Mile, 1948
Welcome Danger, 1929
Winged Victory, 1944

SELECT BIBLIOGRAPHY

Ashcroft, Lionel. *Movie Studios and Movie Theaters in Marin: A History Since 1898.* San Rafael: Marin County Historical Society, 1998.

Auiler, Dan. *Vertigo: The Making of a Hitchcock Classic.* New York: St. Martin's Press, 1998.

Bell, Goeffrey. *The Golden Gate and the Silver Screen: San Francisco in the History of the Cinema.* Cranbury, NJ: Associated University Presses, Inc., 1984.

Culhane, John. *Special Effects in the Movies: How They Do It.* New York: Ballantine Books, 1981.

Gordon, William A. *Shot on This Site: A Traveler's Guide to the Places and Locations Used to Film Famous Movies and Television Shows.* New York: Citadel Press, 1995.

Hansen, Gladys. *San Francisco Almanac: Everything You Wanted to Know About Everyone's Favorite City.* San Francisco: Chronicle Books, 1995.

Hanson, Patricia King (editor). *The American Film Institute Catalog of Motion Pictures Produced in the United States.* (Feature Films: 1931-1940 and 1961-1970). Berkeley: University of California Press, 1993.

Kraft, Jeff and Aaron Leventhal. *Footsteps in the Fog: Alfred Hitchcock's San Francisco.* Santa Monica: Santa Monica Press, 2002.

Le Baron, Gaye and Joann Mitchell. *Santa Rosa: A Twentieth Century Town.* Santa Rosa: Historia, Ltd., 1993.

Lieber, Robert. *Alcatraz: The Ultimate Movie Book.* San Francisco: Golden Gate National Parks Conservancy, 2006.

McGrew, Patrick. *Landmarks of San Francisco.* New York: H. N. Abrams, 1991.

McGloin, John B. (S.J.). *San Francisco: The Story of a City.* San Rafael: Presidio Press, 1978

Olmsted, Roger and T. W. Watkins. *Here Today: San Francisco's Architectural Heritage.* San Francisco: Chronicle Books, 1968.

Reeves, Tony. *The Worldwide Guide to Movie Locations.* Chicago: A. Cappella Books: 2001.

Sklar, Robert. *Movie-Made America: A Cultural History of American Movies.* New York: Vintage Books, 1994.

———. *Film: An International History of the Medium.* New York: H. N. Abrams, 1993.

Smith, Dave. *Disney A to Z: The Official Encyclopedia.* New York: Hyperion, 1996.

Spoto, Donald. *The Art of Alfred Hitchcock: Fifty Years of His Motion Pictures.* New York: Hopkinson and Blake, 1976.

Stanger, Frank M. *South From San Francisco: San Mateo County, CA, Its History and Heritage.* San Mateo: San Mateo County Historical Association, 1963.

Steinberg, Cobbett S. *Film Facts.* New York: Facts on File, 1980.

Thomson, David. *A Biographical Dictionary of Film.* New York: A. A. Knopf, 1994.

Van Buskirk, Jim and Will Shank. *Celluloid San Francisco: The Film Lover's Guide to Bay Area Movie Locations.* Chicago: Chicago Review Press, 2006.

Weinberg, Herman G. *The Complete Greed.* New York: E. P. Dutton & Co, Inc., 1973.

Woodbridge, Sally B. *California Architecture: Historic American Buildings Survey.* San Francisco: Chronicle Books, 1988.

———. *Architecture-San Francisco: The Guide.* San Francisco: American Institute of Architects: 101 Productions, 1982.

Woodbridge, Sally B. and John M. Woodbridge. *San Francisco Architecture: The Illustrated Guide to Over 1000 of the Best Buildings, Parks and Public Artworks in the Bay Area.* San Francisco: Chronicle Books, 1992.

ACKNOWLEDGEMENTS

Several generous friends contributed to make this publication a reality.

The editorial talents of the sage Donald Andreini transformed my thoughts in the prologue to be more concise than they ever started out to be.

Many thanks go to Lorri Ungaretti who was great-hearted to review the manuscript with her sharp editorial eye.

Several people contributed their knowledge in a variety of areas including Kathryn Ayres, Stewart Bloom, Lew Baer, Richard Brandi, John Freeman, Nancy Ellen Jones, Jon Jost, Mary Keil, Austin Kearny, Mark Kessler of the University of California at Davis, John Korty, Elaine Molinari, Dave Smith of Disney Studios, Gail Stempler, Jack Tillmany, and Greg Walsh of the Margaret Herrick Library.

My deepest thanks go to literary agent and muse Robert Shepard who took on this project and taught me about the process of publishing—but more importantly he tried to teach me about writing. Ultimately no mainstream publisher bought the project, so he bowed out. But I contribute part of my never giving up hope of bringing this work to fruition to his belief in the concept.

SOURCES

The basis for the filmography was two primary sources. Basic information started with the encyclopedic *The American Film Institute Catalog of Motion Pictures produced in the United States*. In concert were each county or city's film commission who coordinate filming in their region. In some cases the movie studios provided information. Other resources were the Internet Movie Database and the Northern California Movies websites that were invaluable to fill in gaps. Beyond that are the countless mentions in periodicals including the *San Francisco Chronicle*, *San Francisco Examiner*, *Santa Rosa Democrat*, *Sonoma-Index Tribune*, *Oakland Tribune*, *Marin Independent Journal*, *San Francisco Weekly*, *New York Times, New York Sun* and *Life Magazine*, which helped to flesh out the listings. The Academy of Motion Picture Arts and Sciences, Margaret Herrick Library and Pacific Film Archive at U.C. Berkeley were the research sources for many still and off-camera photographs. Many of the films were viewed and the locations recorded in a reverse engineering project—a game to figure out where the scene was located. This project was completed over a twenty-one-year period.

I hope that someday this publication can be fully realized as I originally envisioned it with accompanying illustrations such as stills, screen captures, posters and lobby cards. Until then this will have to do.

Published by Castor & Pollux P., San Francisco, CA

ABOUT THE AUTHOR

A native of Connecticut, Christopher considered a design career in the theater, but after an apprenticeship moved to interior design and began his career with The Architect's Collaborative (TAC) in Cambridge, Massachusetts founded by icon Walter Gropius. Later, he relocated to California and worked as a designer with a number of leading firms including Gensler and the office of Orlando Diaz-Azcuy. In addition to a prolific design career, Chris is a well-known expert on the history of Golden Gate Park. His other publications are *San Francisco's Golden Gate Park: A Thousand And Seventeen Acres of Stories,* which was published by WestWinds in 2001 and *Golden Gate Park: San Francisco's Urban Oasis in Vintage Postcards* published by Arcadia in 2003. More recently he has been a history researcher for a variety of cultural and architectural projects.